"DEMONSTRATES A DETAILED UNDERSTANDING OF INTELLIGENCE WORK."—*The Washington Post Book World*

"FASCINATING . . . should be sent to every congressman and senator in Washington."—*The Tribune* (San Diego)

In the past twenty years, the nation's most important secrets have been betrayed by spies selling out their country—not for ideology but for cash. Most of them don't get caught! Discover why America is losing the counter-espionage war . . . and what must be done to stop the big money business of treason.

"REFRESHING AND INFORMATIVE . . . reveal[s] the symptoms of decaying counter-intelligence."
—*The Friday Review of Defense Literature*

"REVELATORY . . . ABSORBING . . . a wealth of insights on the state of the counter-intelligence art in the U.S."
—*Kirkus Reviews*

"ENGROSSING . . . reveals the patchwork nature of the agencies that make up the U.S. counter-espionage effort and the astonishing failure of that effort."—*Publishers Weekly*

"DEEPLY DISQUIETING . . . raises disturbing questions that call for answers."—*John Barkham Reviews*

also by Thomas B. Allen and Norman Polmar

Rickover: Controversy and Genius

Ship of Gold (a novel)

by Thomas B. Allen

A Short Life (a novel)
The Last Inmate (a novel)
The Quest
Shadows in the Sea
War Games

by Norman Polmar

The American Submarine
Atomic Submarines
Death of the *Thresher*
Guide to the Soviet Navy (triennial)
The Ships and Aircraft of the U.S. Fleet (triennial)

Merchants of Treason

America's Secrets for Sale

Thomas B. Allen and Norman Polmar

A DELL BOOK

Published by
Dell Publishing
a division of
Bantam Doubleday Dell Publishing Group, Inc.
666 Fifth Avenue
New York, New York 10103

To Our Colleagues and Friends of the Naval & Maritime Correspondents
Circle

For information address: Delacorte Press, New York, New York.

The trademark Dell ® is registered in the U.S. Patent and Trademark
Office.

ISBN: 0-440-20261-2

Reprinted by arrangement with Delacorte Press

Printed in the United States of America

Published simultaneously in Canada

March 1989

10 9 8 7 6 5 4 3 2 1

KRI

Contents

Introduction

The Federal Bureau of Investigation, the Central Intelligence Agency, the National Security Agency, the United States Navy, Army, Air Force—spies had been found in all of them. Then came the unbelievable: A U.S. Marine guard, surrendering to the charms of a beautiful Russian KGB operative, had stolen secrets from the U.S. embassies in Moscow and Vienna.

At the headquarters of the Naval Investigative Service in the Washington suburb of Suitland, Maryland, a widespread inquiry began. When two other Marine guards were arrested for espionage, the investigation became extensive enough to warrant a code word. A Marine officer bitterly suggested "Opengate." He was overruled. The investigation was code-named "Bobsled," for a situation that was rapidly going downhill. But, among counter-espionage investigators, Opengate endured as a remembered code word for what the Marines and all the other trusted Americans had done.

The Marines of Bobsled, when this book went to press, were the latest espionage case—and the latest fiasco—to confront a makeshift U.S. counter-espionage apparatus that seems able to find spies only when they give themselves up or when a Soviet defector can point them out.

If the parade of spies has been incredible, the failure of U.S. counter-espionage has been astonishing. There has been no accounting for this failure because the officials who are charged with protecting our secrets themselves live in a world of secrets that defies penetration. Energy that could be devoted to finding spies is devoted to protecting the bureaucratic bunkers of U.S. counter-espionage.

"We have more people charged with espionage right now than ever before in our history," William H. Webster, Director of the Federal Bureau of Investigation, proudly announced in December 1984. He said this to assure the American public that the FBI was winning the back-alley war against Soviet spies. Five months later, former Navy Radioman John Walker was arrested for running a spy ring that had been operating for *at least* seventeen years. Before the year was over, U.S. counter-espionage officials had sixteen other spy cases on their hands. In the U.S. intelligence community, 1985 became known as the "Year of the Spy."

But 1986 was, in many respects, still worse, for that was the year when the damage assessment started. U.S. officials not directly connected with intelligence finally learned what the spies had sold to the Soviet Union—and at what cost to the United States. Shocked officials learned, among other things, that even the Director of the FBI had no idea how wide and deep was the enormity of the espionage directed against the United States:

■ An FBI agent, while carrying on a love affair with an attractive Russian woman recruited by the KGB, gives away the secrets of his work as an FBI counter-intelligence agent.

■ A disgruntled ex-CIA agent slips out of the United States *while under FBI surveillance* and defects to the Soviet Union. He takes with him what he had learned while being trained by the CIA to work *in Moscow* as a case officer for the CIA intelligence network in the Soviet Union.

■ A KGB officer, who had defected to the United States with a drumroll of CIA-directed publicity, walks away from his CIA handlers in Washington and walks to the Soviet Embassy. He later appears in Moscow, demonstrating, merely by being alive, that he had not been the defector the CIA thought he was. The extent of his deception—and the possible consequences—are still being debated in the U.S. intelligence community. But his "expert information" is cited at a spy trial and his "confidential information" led U.S. authorities to spies they did not know were there.

So we can credit the KGB for an assist in capturing two U.S. spies.

■ A Navy civilian employee, who had once lost his top-secret clearance because he was dealing with South African officials, gets the clearance back—and begins spying for Israel. He also supplies his wife with classified documents about China to help her in her public relations work. And he had openly boasted about his spying.

■ A former National Security Agency analyst, financing a midlife crisis he tries to ease with drugs and sex, sells the Soviets his NSA expertise: how the United States eavesdrops on Soviet Union political and military communications. His revelations about an eavesdropping technique—one of the nation's most tightly guarded secrets—are so sensitive that he almost successfully bargains himself out of arrest.

U.S. servicemen and employees of U.S. intelligence agencies have been selling out the United States *for decades.* They have been clerks, analysts, counter-espionage specialists, officers and enlisted men from the Army, Navy, Air Force—and now the Marines. They are known as walk-ins, because they launch their careers by simply walking into a Soviet Embassy or Consulate and offering secrets for sale. Some walk-ins worked for the CIA and the NSA. Others have been men assigned to missile units, warships, and military headquarters. One such walk-in was a lowly Army sergeant assigned as a driver to the Deputy Director of NSA, who left his briefcase with the sergeant to return to his office after visits to the Pentagon and the Central Intelligence Agency.

The Soviets once recruited spies from the ranks of ideologically motivated Americans like the Rosenbergs. Now Soviet intelligence services must depend on the walk-ins, the spies they recruit, and their own "illegals," Soviet agents who were provided with deep cover to permit them to enter the United States, often through Canada, and to take up what appeared to be normal American lives. Often their jobs, though not directly in sensitive areas, did place them in positions where they could meet Americans who had access to secrets and could be bought.

Several illegals have been detected, usually by chance and rarely by American counter-espionage. Although the United

States employs many spy-catchers, we catch *very few* spies through traditional counter-espionage and detective work.

Senator Malcolm Wallop, a former member of the Senate Intelligence Committee, wrote as the Year of the Spy was coming to an end:

> There are far too many in the intelligence community who either do not understand counter-intelligence or who, understanding its concepts, have climbed to the top of their career ladders by opposing it.

The modern world of espionage never was a James Bond world of professional, stereotyped spies and high-level defections. Spying has become profitable part-time work for faceless, unglamorous people who, in their routine jobs, have access to their nation's secrets.

The spy-for-pay era is driven as much by the client's need for data as by the mercenary spy's need for cash. Marketplace espionage has many variations—sailors on aircraft carriers stealing spare parts for Iran . . . Silicon Valley corporations smuggling computer chips to Moscow . . . trusted intelligence agents spying for allies or friendly governments . . . bankers taking on the KGB as a silent partner. These betrayers of the 1980s are not driven by ideology or even vengeance. They are peddlers in a market set up and operated by the Soviet Union.

In that market the KGB buys priceless information at bargain prices—in cash. The greed of American spies and traitors costs the United States dearly. Rear Admiral William O. Studeman, the Director of Naval Intelligence, in an official assessment of the Walker-ring damage, said that the espionage of Walker and his spies "was of the highest value to the intelligence services of the Soviet Union, with the potential, had conflict erupted between the two superpowers, to have powerful war-winning implications for the Soviet side."

Officials have been quick to point to damage, which can be cleaned up through extra appropriations for items ranging from new submarines to the addition of more personnel in the spy-catcher bureaucracy. These damage assessments are some pieces of the espionage puzzle that have been made public, along with the arrests and the trials and the "official" stories that serve the spy-catchers but hide the inadequacies of the U.S. spy-catching efforts. In this book we try to put the pieces together and fill in where the pieces are missing.

Thomas B. Allen
Norman Polmar

Washington, D.C.

1

A Tale of Two Ships

On the night of April 23, 1980, the U.S. nuclear-propelled aircraft carrier *Nimitz* steamed northward in the Arabian Sea, beyond sight of the Iranian coast. The aircraft carrier and her escorting cruisers and destroyers were in a state of EMCON, or emission control; no radars or radios were being operated to preclude the possibility that their electronic emissions would be intercepted by Soviet or Iranian listening posts.

The next morning eight Navy RH-53D Sea Stallion helicopters were brought up, one by one, to the flight deck by elevator. The Sea Stallions, normally painted dark blue for their Navy minesweeping role, now bore colors identical to those of helicopters flown by the Iranian Air Force. The complex, highly secret operation to rescue the fifty-three Americans held hostage in Teheran was under way.

Beginning at 7:30 a.m., the helicopters lifted from the deck of the *Nimitz* for their flight to a location in the Iranian desert code-named "Desert One." There the helicopters, flown by Marine and Navy pilots, would load on board U.S. Army counter-terrorist troops, known as the Delta Force, who had been flown to the advance base by C-130 Hercules transports. The helicopters would then lift the troops to another secret location near Teheran for the assault on the former U.S. Embassy where the hostages were held.

The *Nimitz* broke radio silence to establish scant communications with the mission forces and with command authorities at various locations, including Washington. There, through an extraordinarily secure communications link, a senior U.S. intelligence officer heard the coded signal transmitted as the last helicopter left the *Nimitz* flight deck. He closed his eyes and prayerfully whispered, "I hope they don't catch the whole gang of them."

He knew, as did only a few other U.S. intelligence officials, that for some time—perhaps ten years—the Soviets had been able to read American military codes. Thus one of the most tightly guarded secrets in the U.S. intelligence community was about American secrets: They were in constant peril because U.S. military communications were being deciphered by the Soviet Union.

Planning for some kind of rescue mission had begun soon after Iranians seized the embassy in Teheran in November 1979 and took sixty-three Americans hostage. The planning itself was so secret that only a few Carter Administration civilian officials knew it was going on, and those who did left the details to military officers. While the planning was in its preliminary stages little concern was given to potential problems with communications security. This was a tactical matter that eventually would be handled at that level.

Military communications were routinely encrypted through a system in which most communications and intelligence experts were confident. The system consisted of two elements: cryptographic machines and "keylists," the coded keys to those machines. The keylists were changed every twenty-four hours. For the Soviets to read American military traffic, they would need both access to the machines and delivery of keylists on a schedule as regular as the one that was followed for delivery of the keylists to U.S. ships and military installations and intelligence agencies. A large bureaucracy, operating out of the supersecret National Security Agency, handled the creation, publication, and distribution of the keylists. The cryptographic machines, designed by NSA mathematicians and engineers, had been manufactured under tight NSA restrictions. All materials involved in the system were monitored by a strict inventory and "accountability log" administered by the NSA.

Sometime in the early 1970s, however, the NSA became concerned about possible breaches in U.S. cryptography. Word was passed through the intelligence and communications community, with special emphasis on Navy communications: Your message traffic is not as secure as you may believe. Specialists learned on a need-to-know basis that the NSA had tightly guarded information about a compromise of encrypted U.S. message traffic. When Navy officials asked NSA about the source of this critical news, the traditionally aloof and independent NSA declined to be more specific. A bureaucratic impasse developed. The Navy would not begin making costly and disruptive changes in its communications operations unless NSA told more about the possible security break. And NSA would tell no more.

The nation's cryptographic system had long been considered spyproof because a would-be penetrator would need to get his hands on both a regular supply of keylists and a machine. According to the cryptographers' doctrine, even if an enemy managed to get a machine, possession would do him no good without the keys, or what the system's operators referred to as "keying materials."

There are several types of cryptographic machines. The KW-7, one of the machines used on board the *Nimitz,* is a plain gray box about the size of a teletype. The vital parts of the machine are encased in shielding material to prevent the emission of electronic signals. A message is typed into the KW-7 in plain English. The signals go through cryptographic circuits within the box and are encrypted according to a code preset for that day by the numbers on the key material. The message is sent as a stream of grouped numbers. At the receiving end the message enters another machine, where the message can be decrypted only if the machine has in it the key numbers for the day. Messages are entered on what looks like a standard teletype keyboard; incoming messages print out electronically through the teletype component of the machine.

The keylists have evolved in form through the years. The key—the daily set of numbers that actuates the machine—was once simply printed on what was called a keylist. The radioman operating the cryptographic machine would punch keys corresponding to those numbers and the machine would then align its logic to decode and receive the messages being received that day or to encode and transmit the day's outgoing messages.

Later, the "keylist" became the "key card," which resembled an early IBM computer card (and often was still referred to as the keylist). Using the card version, the radioman opened a compartment on the side of the encryption machine, pressed the card against an electronic sensor, and closed the compartment. The sensor translated the card's holes into signals that gave the machine the day's key numbers. The cards are still used, but some machines now also accept keys in the form of cassette tapes. The key numbers are electronically imprinted on an ingeniously designed spool of tape that cannot be rerolled back into its container.

Like the keylist and cards, the tape is merely a medium for what Navy radiomen call "filling" the machine with the day's key numbers. Some machines also demand the simultaneous use of a key card and a CRIB (for Card Reader Insert Board), which has a function similar to that of the key card. But whether the radioman uses lists, cards, or tapes, the system is the same: a machine, a key, and—what is sometimes overlooked in descriptions of the system—a radioman.

Although the method of filling the machine kept changing through the years from the time of its development in the 1960s, the machine itself remained essentially the same, because cryptographic engineers, unlike automotive designers, do not believe in frequent model changes. There was also the matter of cost. The Navy and other users of NSA machines resist anteing up their share of costs when the NSA recommends improvements. Cryptography is a costly orphan when Pentagon budget planners set up priorities. Appropriations for weapons and for personnel have lobbies, but cryptography dwells in a secret world where people keep quiet about accomplishments (and failures).

"We knew the KW-7 was vulnerable," a former high-ranking Navy communications officer told the authors in 1987. "We never heard that NSA said there was a [security] problem with the keylist, except for some being lost once. We heard that they had been lost in [aircraft] crashes. And thirty machines had been lost in Vietnam.* But having the machines was not enough. The Soviets did not have computers that could calculate fast enough to understand the algorithm." The algorithm is the mathematical logic that translates a message's number groups into electronic signals that can be read by the machine's teletype system.

The KW-7 was carrying top-secret message traffic through the period of this vulnerability. But, the officer continued, "a Navy directive put out by NSA said that we should drop the KW-7 to confidential by 1987. The KW-84 was to be the replacement. All the services said to NSA, 'Go pound sand! We know you won't be able to deliver the KW-84.' " So the KW-7 continued to carry the nation's most vital messages.

In an attempt to solve the problem, the Department of Defense secretly tried to launch the Cryptographic Utilization Program, inevitably called by its acronym, CUP. The idea was to "pass the cup" among the Pentagon's users of cryptography, asking each one to contribute a share of the conversion cost. The services balked; they all had other bills to pay. CUP was never filled.

More than money was involved. A change in machines is a drastic change. A machine may stay in service for twenty years or more. There are thousands of various models of code machines scattered around the world, and the system depends upon every one of them, no matter its age or type, being able to transmit to and receive from every other machine in the net.

So the KW-7, with its suspected, mysterious vulnerability, continued as a weak link in the Navy's communications chain. The Navy tried to cut back in communications, shifting when possible from radio transmissions to NAVGRAMs, the Navy version of special-delivery mail, for low-level routine messages. There was also an increase in the cautious use of theoretically secure phones.

Communications officers pressed NSA for information on the vulnerability threat. "Give me concrete examples of messages you think were compromised," an officer remembered asking. The NSA answer, he told the authors, was simply "That's not the way we do business." All that he—and a few knowledgeable peo-

---

* Another source told the authors that thirty-two U.S. code machines fell into North Vietnamese hands during and after the war.

ple like him—could do was hope for the best and rely on the system's complexity as its best defense.

"We did not think," the officer said, "that simultaneous translation was possible." The worst-case theory, he explained, was that the Soviets could record some messages for a given day and then, perhaps months later, through trial-and-error computer runs, read a very small amount of that day's traffic.

Much of the confidence in the system rested on the fact that a variety of keylists served the machines. Keylists differed by area and by armed service. As many as twenty keylists might be in use throughout the world during a single twenty-four-hour period. A ship in the Atlantic would not be using the same keylist as a comparable ship in the Pacific. But as warship deployments from one region to another increased in the 1970s, the Navy discovered that a carrier suddenly ordered from, say, the south Atlantic to the Arabian Sea would have cryptographic problems because of the multi-keylist practice. So, in the late 1970s, the Navy went to a single, worldwide keylist.

Now, more than ever before, the security of the system depended upon the trusted radiomen who operated it.

The radiomen have top-secret clearance and follow the stringent rules set up to guard the nation's encoded messages. The rules are the heart of the Classified Materials System, which was developed by the National Security Agency and administered by a string of code handlers, beginning with the couriers who carry keying materials, in tamperproof packages, from the NSA's huge, tightly guarded printing plant at NSA headquarters in Fort Meade, Maryland, to secure NSA depots around the world. From there they are carried by the Armed Forces Courier Service or couriers supplied by the machines' possessors: embassies, military bases, intelligence agency offices, Navy shore stations, or ships throughout the world. In the Navy the final destination for this complex delivery system is a Navy radioman designated the CMS —for Classified Materials System—custodian.

A CMS custodian has a separate vault where he stores the keying materials. A submarine usually carries in its CMS vault a five-month supply of keys; a surface ship usually goes to sea with a three-month supply. Each ship also has a supply of ROB (Reserve On Board) keylists. In the event of a major compromise of contemporary codes, ships are given the order to "switch to ROB."

The CMS custodian doles out the key materials, as they are needed, to "local holders," the radiomen responsible for loading the key into the machine. The daily key materials are logged in, logged out, and destroyed under the supervision of the custodian. There is an accountability log for keying materials, from the moment they leave Fort Meade through every moment of their short lives and destruction, which must be witnessed by two people, who sign their names in the accountability log. Each cryptographic item has a number and each use is assigned a number. Whoever uses the item, such as a key card, signs his (or, rarely, her) name alongside the number assigned to the use. The enumeration of each piece of key material begins with a "birth number" and ends with a "death number."

Destruction of the keying materials after use is particularly important. Used materials would be of great interest to an enemy cryptographer. If an enemy were to acquire or manufacture a machine that would take U.S. key material, and if that enemy were to get key material for a specific day, he could play back a radio message he had snatched from the air and recorded on that certain day—and then not only read the message but also get an understanding of the cryptographic system's logic.

U.S. communications are continually monitored by a worldwide Soviet signal-intelligence intercept system that is reputed to be even larger than the one operated by the NSA. U.S. Navy warships are kept under intense surveillance by Soviet satellites, aircraft, and intelligence-gathering ships. Crewmen on U.S. Navy ships are admonished even to be careful about what they put in the garbage lest a trailing Soviet ship scoop it up and find a cryptographic nugget in the swill. The Plan of the Day, read by division officers or division chiefs each day at muster, warns sailors to be careful of what they throw overboard—or "Russians will be reading your mail."

Custodians are supposed to be more security conscious than anyone else. They have top-secret or TS/SI clearance. (SI stands for Special Intelligence. The security-rating system begins with "confidential," which is used as a label on information that can do some damage to U.S. interests if it is disclosed. Disclosure of "secret" information can do major damage, and disclosure of "top-secret" information can do very grave damage to national security.)

As a radioman moves up the ranks he or she is subject to more and more scrutiny. Both the Federal Bureau of Investigation and NSA conduct separate security investigations of radiomen eligible to be CMS custodians. The commanding officer selects the custodian, who is almost invariably the ship's or station's senior chief radioman. The custodian is personally responsible for cryptographic equipment and cryptographic manuals.

The cryptographic machines' technical manuals, because they must circulate through so many hands, are given the designation confidential. In fact, the manuals contain extremely sensitive information, which, if it appeared in some forms *outside* the thick covers of the loose-leaf manuals, would be considered top secret. The pages include the electronic schematic drawings that show the inner logic of the machines.

Working only from such manuals, a team of NSA engineers and mathematicians have built U.S. cryptographic machines. More than once such a team has demonstrated this to show the potential value of the manuals to a prospective enemy—and to dramatize the need for a higher classification of the manuals. But the armed services, particularly the Navy, have successfully argued for the low security rating on the manuals for practical reasons having to do with the need for quick access by low-ranking repair personnel who might not have anything more than a confidential clearance.

The NSA-Navy debate over classification of the manuals underscored the inherent weakness of the system: It was most vulnerable to penetration at the bottom of the security ladder. A low-ranking radioman, with or without top-secret clearance, could obtain access to the machines and the keying materials and steal their secrets. Getting a machine or learning how it operated might be impossibly difficult. But if the Soviets had the machines, all the low-ranking radioman would have to do would be to copy the key materials *before* use. The accountability log would show a normal birth-to-death record and no one could detect the loss.

But even more dangerous would be a traitorous CMS custodian. And the ultimate nightmare would be a traitorous CMS custodian on board a carrier or with routine access to the communications traffic of a carrier, the preeminent Navy warship.

Architects of the key-machine cryptographic system assumed that routine personnel security procedures would screen potential traitors from the ranks of the enlisted men and women who operate the communications equipment for the armed forces. The protection of the nation's cryptographic system depends ultimately on the radiomen. They are members, as one intelligence officer has said, "of the elite fraternity of naval communications specialists."

The radiomen in the communications centers of aircraft carriers like the *Nimitz* process more than two thousand messages on a typical day. The center, which is so modulated that it is essentially duplicated in every major ship and station in the Navy, consists of a transmitter and receiver room, a cryptographic room, and a message center, which prints the decrypted messages for logging, reproduction, and distribution. About sixty to eighty radiomen are assigned to a single carrier. Each of three "watches" has about twenty men, most of them working in the message center. There are always one or two people in the cryptographic room, which is off limits to unauthorized personnel. The CMS custodian may enter the cryptographic room and all other communications spaces in the carrier at will. And often, because of the nature of his job, he will be in the room alone.

All incoming and outgoing messages, including Red Cross telegrams to crewmen and other unclassified communications, are encrypted. This is done so that an enemy eavesdropper, hearing nothing in the clear, cannot infer changes in a ship's plans by hearing a sudden shift to encryption of messages. "Even happy birthday from Grandma gets coded," a radioman said, "so you can keep the Russkies guessing." Top-secret messages are separately logged and must be accounted for on a "disclosure sheet," which is signed by everyone who handled the message.

Some Navy communications stations are primary transfer points for ultrahigh-frequency messages relayed from satellites. The Navy shifted from high-frequency (HF) to ultrahigh-frequency (UHF) satellite relays in the mid-1970s. High-frequency messages can be transmitted 2,000 to 3,000 miles and are subject to atmospheric interference. Ultrahigh-frequency signals are of a better quality than high-frequency signals, can be sent at higher speed, and, because of the satellite system, can be sent and received over a larger area.

But the extremely reliable ultrahigh-frequency signals are also extremely vulnerable, for UHF transmissions can be easily intercepted and can provide a line of bearing that gives away a transmitting ship's position. Hostile interceptors have to be virtually within a line of sight and thus can be thwarted by well-aimed transmissions from ship to satellite. But any ship within what is called the "footprint" of the satellite can pick up transmissions relayed from it. Soviet ships seek out those footprints and also snatch, when they can, all electronic signals—radar as well as radio—transmitted by U.S. carriers and other warships.

Some of the messages transmitted to ships are through the time-honored Fleet Broadcasts, which date to World War I. Fleet Broadcast messages are transmitted over fifteen separate hundred-word-a-minute channels controlled by computers. A ship will monitor a couple of channels at a time; there may be channels designated for carriers, or cruisers, or for weather information. A ship copies only those channels it is required to read. Fleet Broadcasts go out either on high frequency or through a satellite relay.

About 99 percent of all U.S. defense message traffic is encrypted. Because the human voice is so richly varied, engineers have had trouble encoding it. The voice eludes electronic attempts to define it, break it down at the speaker's end, and reassemble it at the listener's end. So a great deal of the nation's most important transmissions are sent by teletype, encoded at one end and decoded at the other through the cryptographic machine-and-keylist system. The importance of these messages ranges from "Flash" down through "Operational-Immediate" to "Priority" and "Routine."

During the *Nimitz's* 1980 hostage-rescue mission, the Operational-Immediate and Priority messages sent to the carrier from Washington and other command centers included communications about the types of ammunition on board (all U.S. carriers usually have nuclear weapons in special magazines, guarded by Marines); intelligence estimates of the changing situation in Iran; the number and types of U.S. missiles sold to Iran (and now of potential harm to the seller); the rules of engagement for the mission—and the rules for what to do if attacked by Iranian forces; information about the activities of foreign embassies in

Teheran; and the operational plans of Air Force planes that might have to be drawn into the mission.

The worried senior intelligence official in Washington on the morning of April 24, 1980, was concerned about the possibility that the Soviets were reading those messages, perhaps as they were being received. If his suspicions were right, all of the extremely sensitive traffic was in, or would soon be in, Soviet possession. He was one of a handful of U.S. intelligence experts who had begun fearing penetration of the machine-keylist cryptographic system since January 23, 1968, when North Korea captured the U.S. intelligence ship *Pueblo.*

The spy ship *Pueblo,* operated by the Navy for NSA, had been monitoring electronic emissions off the coast of North Korea. On board the *Pueblo* were both cryptographic machines and keylists. Not all of the cryptographic material had been destroyed when the *Pueblo* and her crew were captured. Questions about the security of the system immediately began circulating through the Navy and NSA bureaucracies: What if the Soviets could reconstruct the machines that were crippled before the *Pueblo* surrendered? What if they crack the logic of the keylist numbers? Should the United States begin a crash program to replace the whole system? Worried U.S. intelligence officials realized that none of the crewmen knew for certain if all of the code machines had been destroyed. But cryptographic specialists assured the worriers about the *Pueblo* that the machines—even if they were recovered intact—would be useless without the current keylists.

The internal debate, out of which would come the earliest KW-7 warnings, was muffled within the labyrinth of the intelligence community. There, secrecy within secrecy was produced by compartmentalization, which kept people segregated inside their own specialties. A discipline of silence particularly ruled the cryptographers—an intensely parochial subgroup within the intelligence community. Cryptographers had an almost religious faith in their machine-key system. Protect the keylists and keep changing them daily, they said, and there would be no chance of penetration by anyone who merely possessed a machine. As an NSA official with thirty-five years of experience put it, "Without the key you cannot exploit the cryptography." That, he said, "is the unquestioned belief of the cryptographic community."

The concern about the cryptographic system was also alleviated by a general feeling that technology was taking over espionage. Cold War spying had entered a new phase in the late 1950s with the introduction of advanced-technology intelligence collection, especially spy planes like the American U-2, the later SR-71, and the subsequent use of intelligence-gathering satellites. The United States—through its technology—seemed to have the lead over the Soviet Union in surveillance and intelligence gathering. NSA scientists and engineers were especially proud of the way the agency carried out its two major missions: the encryption of U.S. communications and the electronic eavesdropping and decrypting of foreign communications.

Eavesdropping was the mission of the *Pueblo* when she steamed out of Sasebo, Japan, at 6 a.m. on the cold, blustery morning of January 11, 1968. Heading northeast through the Tsushima Strait toward the Sea of Japan, she hugged the coast of Japan to avoid the Soviet ships reported on patrol in the strait that separates Japan and Korea. On board the 176-foot Navy ship were eighty-three men—six officers, seventy-three sailors, two enlisted Marines who were Korean linguists, and two civilian Navy oceanographers. The *Pueblo,* the latest in a series of "passive" U.S. Navy intelligence-collection ships, was sailing under a cover story: She was supposedly conducting oceanographic and other environmental research in the Sea of Japan.

The *Pueblo* was one of the pieces on the espionage chessboard where, since World War II, the United States and the Soviet Union have been playing an endless game of deception and counter-deception, spying and counter-spying. To understand the events at Desert One in 1980—and the American spy plague of the 1980s—it is necessary to go to sea and learn how the U.S. Navy got into the spy game.

Day by day, in the North Atlantic, the Mediterranean, the Caribbean, and the Indian Ocean, ships of the U.S. Navy steam in company with Soviet warships—at times only a cable's length —608 feet—away. The Central Front of Europe is the only other place in the world where U.S. and Soviet forces watch each other continuously, with guns loaded and missiles at the ready. But it is at sea, against the Soviets or a Third World nation, that the United States will probably face the next crisis. And it is the U.S.

Navy that has been both a major seeker of Soviet secrets and a prime target of Soviet intelligence.

Since the 1950s the Soviet Navy has spied on the U.S. Navy. The spying began with passive intelligence spy ships, often called "spy trawlers" because the first of them were disguised as fishing craft. Both the Soviet Union and the United States also employed what intelligence analysts called "overt intelligence-collection platforms": aircraft, surface warships, submarines, and, from the early 1960s, satellites with intelligence-gathering missions.

By the time the *Pueblo* went to sea, some Soviet ships were being built specifically for the purpose of collecting intelligence. The ships, designated AGIs by Western intelligence officers, were unarmed, carried uniformed naval crews, flew the naval ensign, and were readily identifiable by their array of electronic intercept antennas. These spy ships plied the seas in "innocent passage" under international law, usually dogging Western warships during exercises or just cruising offshore where they could monitor radio and radar emissions. Some were also fitted with sonar to monitor submarine activities. By the early 1960s the Soviet Navy had several of these spy ships in service.

Beginning in the late 1950s, the U.S. Department of Defense had also begun nautical spying, using merchant-type ships to conduct electronic surveillance on the high seas, i.e., twelve miles or more off the coast of target countries. Even though the ships were painted gray and had Navy markings, they were not supposed to be considered hostile. They were unarmed because the Department of State considered guns to be a provocation.

The first few of these American spy ships were converted from World War II-built merchantmen. The first ship placed in commission in July 1961 was the USS *Oxford,* designated AGTR-1.* "The ship," the Navy said, "has been primarily equipped to conduct research in the reception of electromagnetic propagations. By equipping the ship with the latest antenna sys-

---

* The U.S. Navy's fetish for abbreviations officially began in 1922 with a scheme for ship designations. The scheme survives to this time with Soviet ships being given the U.S. designation AGI for Auxiliary, General purpose (AG), Intelligence (I). The *Oxford*'s designation AGTR was listed as Auxiliary, General purpose, Technical Research (TR), and the *Pueblo* AGER, for Environmental Research (ER).

tems and measuring devices, the Navy will have a highly sophisticated and mobile station which can be sent to various parts of the world to take part in research and evaluation experiments. . . . Because of the immediate or potential military application of the equipment, most of the work on board will be classified. In addition to research electromagnetic reception, the *Oxford* will also be equipped to conduct hydrographic and oceanographic research operations."

Claims about oceanography aside, the *Oxford* was, pure and simple, a spy ship. A few months after her commissioning, the ship was cruising off the coast of Communist-controlled Cuba and Fidel Castro was vehemently objecting to her intrusion. Even now, decades later, details are few about what the *Oxford* and her sister ships accomplished by electronically spying on an island only seventy miles from the United States. However, a Pentagon spokesman did once tell the Congress, "Electronic intelligence acquired by surface ships led to the photographic intelligence from aircraft which gave us indisputable evidence of the installation of Soviet missiles in Cuba in 1962. If we had not gathered this intelligence in such a timely manner, the consequences of a more extensive installation in Cuba would have been a far more serious threat to the security of the United States."

The *Oxford* was followed into service by the *Georgetown, Jamestown, Belmont,* and *Liberty,* all converted merchant ships. In this period two slightly smaller merchant ships were also converted to spy ships and placed in service as the *Private Joseph E. Valdez* and *Sergeant Joseph Muller.* These last two ships were manned by civilian crews with Navy technicians on board; all others had Navy crews with intelligence specialists from the Navy, other services, and other agencies on board.

The ships were extremely successful in gathering radar and radio emissions that specialists translated into intelligence information about the Soviet Union, Third World nations—and some allied nations. The success led to a decision in 1965 to build still another fleet of intelligence-collection ships. Although the smaller ships would have less intelligence-gathering capability, there would be many of them. Some sources cite plans to put as many as thirty into service.

The AGERs, as they were designated, were specifically designed to collect signals intelligence as well as hydrographic information. Signals intelligence (SIGINT) consists of electronic intelligence (ELINT), which is information derived from noncommunications electromagnetic radiations, such as radar; and communications intelligence (COMINT), which is information derived by intercepting communications.

The *Banner,* originally built as a U.S. Army cargo ship, was acquired and converted to the AGER-1 in 1965. The similar *Pueblo* and *Palm Beach* followed in 1966–67. Each of these ships was about 176 feet long and initially was armed with a pair of .50-caliber machine guns and small arms. The decision to install the "fifties" was a compromise between those in the Navy and the Department of Defense who felt that some minimal defense armament was needed and those who sided with the State Department in the belief that the mounting of any guns would be provocative.

The *Banner,* sailing under orders code-named "Clickbeetle," tested "the effectiveness of a small ship acting singly, and primarily, as a naval surface surveillance and collection unit" by operating unescorted off mainland China. Although she was occasionally harassed by Chinese and Soviet fishing craft, her mission was evaluated as successful. During these early operations the U.S. Air Force maintained combat aircraft on alert status in the Far East and the U.S. Seventh Fleet had destroyers ready to assist her. But the *Banner,* which operated primarily off Soviet Far Eastern ports, never required help.

While the *Banner* and other U.S. spy ships were operating with the regularity and the tranquility of Mississippi riverboats, another spy ship encountered disaster. In the summer of 1967, as Israel and Egypt again prepared for a clash of arms, the USS *Liberty* in the eastern Mediterranean moved closer to the Sinai coast to monitor military communications of both Israel (a U.S. ally) and Egypt (a Soviet client). When the conflict erupted the *Liberty* was ordered to move away from the coast. But that high-priority message was somehow lost in the U.S. military communications system. On June 8, 1967, she was mistakenly attacked by Israeli aircraft and torpedo boats. Thirty-four Americans were killed and several more injured.

By January of 1968 the *Banner* had successfully completed

sixteen intelligence-collection missions; her sister ship, *Palm Beach*, was at work in the Atlantic; the third sister ship, the *Pueblo*, was ready to begin her first mission, code-named "Pinkroot I"; and planning was under way for operating twelve to fifteen AGERs in the Far East against China, North Korea, and the Soviet Union. The *Pueblo* was to spy on naval activity off North Korean ports, record samples of electronic signals off the North Korean coast, and keep under electronic surveillance any Soviet naval ships in the area.

The *Pueblo* was fitted with an extensive array of sophisticated communications, cryptographic and electronic interception equipment. In addition to the two .50-caliber machine guns, she was armed with ten submachine guns, seven .45-caliber pistols, and one .30-caliber carbine. Also on board for emergency use in destroying the ship's tons of electronic equipment and hundreds of pounds of classified documents were some fifty concussion grenades (which had been designed not to destroy documents but to be dropped in the water as a defense against hostile swimmers), a few fire axes, some sledgehammers, and two antiquated paper shredders, each of which would take fifteen minutes to destroy a stack of paper eight inches high.

When the *Pueblo* was ordered to sea no naval or Air Force combat units in the area were placed on alert because the Navy had declared that potential risk to the ship was "minimal." At 11:50 a.m. on January 23, 1968, the *Pueblo* was steaming 15.8 miles off the port of Wonsan when a North Korean S.O. 1 patrol ship was detected approaching. The *Pueblo* and her crew were doomed.

The North Korean S.O. 1 was soon joined by torpedo boats. At 1:27 p.m. the first shots were fired at the U.S. ship. At 2:32 p.m. the *Pueblo* was boarded in international waters by North Korean troops.

Beginning at 12:55 p.m., the *Pueblo* had radioed U.S. commanders in Japan that she was being threatened. But no meaningful action was taken by U.S. forces in Japan or South Korea—or by Commander Lloyd M. Bucher, commanding officer of the *Pueblo*. Although some of his officers had earlier expressed concern about the approach of the North Korean craft, Bucher did not order the destruction of the classified documents and equipment until after the S.O. 1 had begun firing at his ship with a 57-mm cannon.

The ship's twenty-eight intelligence specialists had neither the facilities nor the training necessary for anything but haphazard attempts at destroying the cryptographic equipment and keylist materials. At 2:05 the *Pueblo* radioed, "Destroying all keylists and as much elec equip [electronic equipment] as possible. . . ." At 2:18 mention was made of some cryptographic machines: "We have the KW-7 and some cards in the [KWR-]37 and [KG-]14 to smash. I think that [is] just about it." And, at 2:30, ". . . destruction of pub[lication]s have been ineffective. Suspect several will be compromised." Two minutes later, as North Korean soldiers climbed on board from one of the torpedo boats, the *Pueblo* stopped transmitting.

Of the several hundred classified documents in the ship, an unknown number had been destroyed, some of the intercept, communications, and cryptographic gear had been smashed. Many documents had not been destroyed. Some *Pueblo* sailors later recalled seeing one or two canvas mattress covers stuffed with secret documents still on board. Scores of classified documents littered the ship's passageways. Also surviving were some diagrams and manuals for repairing the gear. No one in the crew could later remember seeing those documents burned or thrown overboard.

The North Korean troops herded most of the Americans— none of whom had been armed—into spaces that the boarders could control. The engine-room personnel continued to run the ship's engines. The *Pueblo* would enter Wonsan under her own power. At 10:30 p.m. on January 23 (local time) the *Pueblo* was moored to a pier in Wonsan. The eighty-three Americans were quickly taken ashore—some wounded by the spurt of North Korean gunfire. One sailor was dying. (The survivors would be interrogated, beaten, and forced to write confessions before being released eleven months later.)

North Koreans searching the ship soon forced their way into the triple-locked "sod hut," which got its name from Special Operations Detachment, the top-secret naval intelligence group that worked for NSA. The compartment, built over the forward deck, housed the ship's secret intercept gear. A short time later these devices and the related manuals and other documents were in the hands of the North Koreans' allies, the Soviets.*

For Johnson Administration officials grappling with the Vietnam War and the crisis that followed the seizure of the *Pueblo,* the possible compromising of enciphering equipment got little notice. Code machines were low priority for an outraged President who was talking in private about the possible use of a nuclear weapon against North Korea. For the Navy, the excruciating humiliation over the loss of a ship far transcended the loss of battered cryptographic equipment and outdated keylists. And for NSA, there was a bureaucratic war to be won.

A congressional inquiry into the loss of the *Pueblo* declared that a message from NSA, warning that the ship was sailing into danger, "was *not* brought to the attention of any responsible authority. . . . The departmental agency responsible for risk evaluation of the *Pueblo* mission at the Washington level was the Defense Intelligence Agency. That agency never officially received a copy of the NSA warning message." A copy of the message "gratuitously" delivered to NSA was "buried in the files," while the copy sent to the Chief of Naval Operations "was lost in transmission in the Pentagon."

The congressional inquiry was highly critical of the way military officials handled the NSA message: "At best, it suggests an unfortunate coincidence of omission; at worst, it suggests the highest order of incompetence." But the most enduring incompetence was glossed over: The nation's vital secrets were at risk and nothing was being done about it then. Nothing would be done about it.

The focus on the lost NSA message overshadowed a grave concern of some intelligence officials. There were far too many classified documents on board the ship and there was neither a plan nor means for the swift destruction of these documents and the electronic intercept and cryptographic gear. Most of all, un-

* The North Koreans may have given much if not all of the crypto and other communications gear to the Soviets, but the *Pueblo* remains at the port of Wonsan. Foreign visitors are shown through this "national memorial," as one Chinese officer labeled the ship after he was given the tour. He reported that the ship was kept in good condition, although all communications equipment had been stripped away.

heeded intelligence officials were infuriated over the fact that no one at high government levels seemed to care that the Soviets now had sufficient communications and cryptographic equipment to read the most secret American communications—*if* they could obtain keylists.

In the next few years the Soviets also obtained secret communications gear from their Vietnamese allies. The hasty American withdrawal from South Vietnam placed considerable communications equipment in Soviet hands, as did several crashed American aircraft and the South Vietnamese command posts that fell into Communist hands. And, as one U.S. admiral who was serving as an adviser to the South Vietnamese Navy just before the country fell, told the authors, "What some of the Vietnamese officers had in their heads was more important [to the Communists] than the hardware. They had the education and skill to recreate equipment that they had studied or worked on, or even to build it from diagrams that we had given to them.

"Once the Communists had taken over," he added, "there was no loyalty to our side." He did not directly accuse South Vietnamese officers of disloyalty to the United States, but he did imply that, with their families and futures at stake, they would tell all they knew about U.S. cryptographic technology.

Eventually, as memory of the *Pueblo* began to fade and as the fall of South Vietnamese command posts became a faint memory, only a few responsible intelligence officials persisted in voicing worry about the compromise of U.S. cryptography. But the planning for a hostage rescue received such high national security priority that the fear of cryptographic penetration, so long ignored and so deeply held inside the U.S. intelligence community, was again aired.

Administration officials were told the fears: There was evidence that U.S. communications were not secure. Investigations at high levels had turned up only the probability of compromise, which traced back to early in 1968 and the *Pueblo*. Now, in the spring of 1980, some communications specialists in the U.S. armed services were under suspicion because experts were convinced that a compromise could have come only through the use of an agent, a mole in the lower ranks of the cryptography system.

While the suspicion concentrated on enlisted men, especially in the Navy, some of the NSA's own secrets were beginning to flow to the Soviets early in 1980. Ronald Pelton, a former NSA employee, called the Soviet Embassy in Washington on January 14. In a conversation routinely recorded by FBI wiretappers, he said, "I come from ———— I, I, I am in, with the United States Government." He was seen entering the embassy. But not for five years would the FBI be able to identify the man from the "Government" as Pelton.

As planning went forward for a rescue attempt, concern increased that military aspects of the operation would be discovered by the Soviets through the decrypting of U.S. military communications and then passed on to the Iranians. A virtual radio blackout was ordered. So secret was the concern, however, that all that could be handed down to lower military planning levels was the warning: Be extremely careful about communications before and during the rescue.

The result, said a semiofficial review of the rescue, was that "the imposed silence on radio transmission was an underlying cause of the mission's collapse." Delta Force had "achieved communications security, but at too high a price." The extraordinary radio-silence orders had puzzled and exasperated planners because they had not been given the tightly held knowledge that the U.S. cryptographic system was suspected of being compromised.

And that is at least why one intelligence official who heard the *Nimitz* "launch" signal could only hope that the mission would succeed. He suspected, by April 1980, that many, if not all, of the top-secret messages that had been flowing for days into the communications center on board the *Nimitz* could be read in Moscow. He and the others who shared the awful suspicion could cling to only one long-shot possibility: that the Soviets were not being supplied keying materials promptly—in "real time"—but long after the keylists had been used.

If that was what was happening, then Soviet AGIs, satellites, and other electronic monitoring systems would be recording all of the U.S. rescue-mission traffic (along with countless hours of useless administrative traffic) in anticipation of *later* possession of the keys for those days. They would then decode what they had recorded. If that was the way U.S. cryptography was being penetrated, then the Soviets would not have the ability to *act on* the rescue information. But Soviet analysts would be able to understand and interpret U.S. naval operations in a crisis and could advise Kremlin strategists about the best ways to counter future U.S. naval action. Political-military analysts would be able to infer information about how U.S. decision-making machinery works. "It's like playing poker and knowing what was in the guy's last hand," a U.S. communications officer later said.

As the *Nimitz* launched the rescue helicopters, she was receiving and sending messages with some of the same types of cryptographic machines that had been on board the *Pueblo* when she had been captured twelve years earlier. Incredibly, the machine-keylist cryptographic system of 1968 was still in use in 1980. Keylists still were the key to the code machines on board the *Nimitz* and the code machines on every U.S. warship, on every U.S. military base, and in every U.S. intelligence communications center in the world.

The precautions against cryptographic penetration had been considerable: virtual radio silence in the *Nimitz* much of the time, meager communication between units of the ill-fated rescue operation. But communications continued to be received by the carrier, the hub of information affecting the mission. Radio messages to the *Nimitz* included highly sensitive information that had been obtained by intelligence agents, at great risk, from friendly and unfriendly foreign embassies in Teheran. Such knowledge would provide extremely valuable secrets to Soviet military and diplomatic analysts. Yet, the messages had to be sent because, ultimately, the needs of the mission transcended the fears of betrayal.

Thus, the April 1980 rescue mission failed, in part—if not primarily—because of severe restrictions on communications due to the fears of Soviet intercepts. Under President Carter's direction, planning then escalated to a more ambitious, massive military assault on Iran for possible execution in October—on the eve of the presidential election. Preparations for this operation ended abruptly when U.S. intelligence indicated possible Soviet knowledge of the plans.

The Soviet ability to read highly sensitive U.S. military and diplomatic communications was a result of betrayal by Americans. The latest treachery had begun, exactly as a few intelligence officials had feared, probably in the month of the *Pueblo* capture, January 1968, when a U.S. Navy communications officer—a Navy radio specialist designated a Classified Materials System custodian—drove from the huge naval complex base at Norfolk, Virginia, to Washington, D.C., parked his car, and flagged down a taxi. He was dropped off near the corner of M and Sixteenth Streets Northwest. He walked along Sixteenth Street to the wrought-iron gate of the Soviet Embassy, four blocks north of the White House, passed through the unlocked gate, and rang the door buzzer for admittance.

He was greeted inside by the embassy security officer on duty, one of the KGB staff assigned to the job of maintaining the physical security of the embassy and keeping watch over the Soviet citizens who work in the embassy. He wore a sport coat and open shirt. Very politely he asked the visitor his business. The visitor said he wanted to speak to "somebody in security." He repeated his request to a receptionist. He was taken to an office and shown to a chair in front of a desk. Three KGB officers entered the room.

The visitor at first said his name was "James Harper."* But his interrogator asked for identification and the visitor handed him a military identification card that identified the bearer as Chief Warrant Officer John A. Walker, Jr., the communications watch officer at the Atlantic Fleet submarine command in Norfolk. He managed the message traffic for all U.S. submarines in the Atlantic, Arctic, and Mediterranean waters.

Walker said he had something important to sell. "I asked him if they were interested in paying for this material and how much I could expect for it," Walker later recounted. "They responded that it would depend on the quantity and quality of the material, that I should provide them with a list of what I had—access to a shopping list, so to speak." He took a single sheet of paper from his pocket and handed it to one of the KGB men. It was a keylist, "the most sensitive keylist there was."

The Soviets gave Walker between $1,000 and $2,000 ("I've long forgotten [the amount])" for the keylist. They then smuggled Walker out of the embassy. Taking him out through the back alley, "They put me in back of a car with an individual on each side of me in the back seat, and they gave me a large coat to wear

* By coincidence this was the real name of a spy arrested in 1983. Walker said he used a brother's first name, then "thought of Johnnie Walker scotch and I. W. Harper whiskey and put them together."

with the collar [up] and a hat pulled down over my face." They then drove around Washington for a while and dropped Walker off. They took back the hat and the coat. Walker drove back to Norfolk and reported for duty. He was due to go on watch at 11 p.m. "I was late getting back to work."

About a month later Walker met a Soviet intelligence officer at the Zayre department store in Alexandria, Virginia, a suburb of Washington. While they walked around the neighborhood near the store, the Soviet questioned Walker closely about the Navy's cryptographic systems and technical manuals. Walker was told he would be paid between $2,000 and $4,000 a month for high-quality information, such as a full month's supply of key cards.

Walker was also asked for cryptographic manuals, presumably for the reconstruction of the damaged machines the Soviets were getting from their allies who had captured the *Pueblo*. About six months after Walker's first meeting at the department store, the Soviets passed to him a fist-sized device called a rotor reader.

The Soviet device, apparently built with the aid of knowledge gained from the *Pueblo* and Walker's contributions, could crack the logic of the KL-47 cryptographic machine. The rotor, which Walker rolled along the outside of the machine, read the wiring pattern of the rotors within the KL-47. Each of the machine's eight rotors had thirty-six settings that aligned the internal cryptography with the numbers on the keylist inserted in the machine. Contact points on the rotor reader made connections between rotors' settings; these connections were then translated to make a wiring diagram of the KL-47. With the wiring diagram and the technical manuals that Walker supplied, the Soviets could build their own KL-47s and feed them the keylists that were steadily supplied by Walker.

Walker began a long betrayal, supplying secret documents and keylists from other machines, including the KW-7. He gave the Soviet Union the keys that unlocked the codes guarding the nation's secrets. The keys still were in Soviet hands in 1980, when the hostage rescue mission failed.

By the time John Walker was arrested for espionage in 1985, the Soviet Union had received and decoded more than one million messages that United States military and intelligence units had sent through the cryptographic system that had relied on invulnerable machines, constantly guarded keylists, and trusted CMS custodians, who included John Walker—and the radioman he later recruited for spying, Jerry Whitworth.

Walker and Whitworth, and men and women who came after them in a plague of espionage against the United States, were of a new breed working an old trade. The mark of the new spy is treachery for money rather than for ideology, a sellout rather than a creed. The merchandising of code material, Walker once said, is "the kind of thing that is discussed occasionally in cryptographic centers—the possible value of the material." He knew the value and he knew that the Soviets would buy. His estimate of the Soviets as buyers in the modern espionage bazaar could become the anthem for the spies of the 1980s: "I perceived them to be the principal buyer in that market."

2

Spy Change: From Passion to Pay

The elegant building that John Walker entered on a January day in 1968 was the citadel of Soviet espionage in the United States. The Soviet Embassy, a three-and-a-half-story structure of gray stone and brick, was built in 1910 under commission of the widow of George M. Pullman, the sleeping-car magnate. The town house was never occupied by Mrs. Pullman or the intended occupant, her son-in-law, a congressman who did not run for reelection in 1910. The house was sold in May 1913 to another capitalist, who six months later sold it to the Imperial Russian Government.

With its steep, mansard-style roof, urn-balustered balconies, and mock French eighteenth-century architecture, the embassy projects a look of genteel aloofness. Its sidewalk entrance is protected by a black iron fence eight feet, four inches high. Its transomed first-floor French doors are sealed with louvered metal shutters. The dark first-floor windows are barred by decorative wrought-iron grilles.

The embassy's flat rooftop bristles with a thicket of antennas. Some are for communication with Moscow. Others pull in American television. And some are for electronic eavesdropping. Microwave receivers, which can intercept satellite-carried telephone conversations, are pointed toward the State Department or Central Intelligence Agency headquarters across the Potomac

River and down the George Washington Parkway. An omnidirectional antenna monitors transmissions from the FBI, along with the radio messages received and transmitted by some government agencies and by Washington's many police forces, which include the Uniformed Secret Service, whose men and women guard the embassies, legations, ambassadorial residences, and other diplomatic buildings in Washington.

Of the 139 foreign embassies in Washington, no other gets more attention than the Soviet Embassy. The entrance to the building is under constant surveillance by FBI counter-espionage agents. The main watch post long was located in an office of the venerable National Geographic Society Building, obliquely across Sixteenth Street from the embassy. The observers later moved to the AFL-CIO's Philip Murray Building, directly across from the embassy, a position that provides a better vantage point for surveillance cameras.

Down through the years the embassy watchers have not been looking primarily for Americans about to launch careers as spies for the Soviet Union. U.S. counter-espionage agents, aware that the embassy was the KGB's busiest branch office, were more interested in keeping watch over Soviet diplomats and embassy workers who came and went on errands that could have included espionage. Photographs have been routinely taken of people who enter and leave (although, according to FBI sources, there is no recognizable photo of Walker's one and allegedly only visit).

The value of the photographs lay primarily in their use as identification snapshots that FBI agents use in counter-intelligence investigations. Typically, an FBI agent would show a grainy photograph of a man near the embassy's ornate front door to a loyal American with security clearances. Then the agent would inform the astonished American that the genial fellow with the accent was asking questions at the hotel bar because he was a KGB agent trolling for information.

The U.S. counter-espionage system of 1968 did not work well against spies like John Anthony Walker, Jr., for he was an agent very different from most of the men and women who had worked for the Soviet Union since the Bolshevik Revolution of November 1917. Virtually all previous spies for the Soviet Union had been either Russians who, under various covers, had moved to the West to commit espionage or Westerners who sympathized with the idea of international socialism, symbolized and nurtured by the Soviet Union, the world's first socialist state.

The gray building on Sixteenth Street was a tiny bit of Russian territory that changed from imperial to socialist in the revolution of 1917. When the Bolsheviks took power the last czarist ambassador to the United States went into opulent exile in Paris, along with much of the embassy's imperial furniture, and the building became a ghostly embassy-in-waiting. It did not house an ambassador again until 1934, several months after the United States recognized the Union of Soviet Socialist Republics. In the interval the Soviets were represented not by an official delegation but by Amtorg, a commercial trade organization that juggled the missions of lobbying for recognition, buying U.S. products needed by the Soviets, lining up business contacts—and spying.

Soviet espionage predated American recognition of the Soviet government. In the wake of the Russian Revolution and Civil War, numerous émigrés, fleeing the Bolsheviks, came to American shores. Among them were several informers, spies of the Cheka—Chrezivchainaia Komisiya (Extraordinary Commission for the Struggle Against Counter-revolutionaries and Saboteurs) —established by Lenin to combat counter-revolutionaries and to punish "spies, traitors, plotters, bandits, speculators, profiteers, counterfeiters, arsonists, hooligans, agitators, saboteurs, class enemies, and other parasites."

White Russian agents, including the indomitable Sidney Reilly* and, at times, U.S. law-enforcement agencies, sought out and arrested the Bolshevik agents. (Those caught by American agencies were usually deported; those detected by the White Russian agents were usually executed.)

Immediately after their arrival in Washington, Soviet diplomats launched an aggressive information-gathering campaign aimed at both industrial and military targets, carrying on a tradi-

---

* A pseudonym. The child of an adulterous love affair, he was born in South Russia, near Odessa, in 1874. He took his natural father's name and was known as Sigmund Rosenblum before dubbing himself Sidney Reilly, a superspy who infiltrated the German General Staff in World War I and led an attempt to overthrow the Bolsheviks in 1918. He disappeared in the Soviet Union in 1925.

tion of buying or stealing Western technology that dated back to the reign of Peter the Great, czar from 1682 to 1725. Peter employed Western artisans and engineers as well as army and naval officers in his efforts to modernize Russia. The czar himself traveled to Western Europe to personally examine scientific and technical innovations, and worked as a common worker in the English shipyard at Deptford to gain firsthand knowledge of shipbuilding.

With the establishment of diplomatic relations between Soviet Russia and the United States, a horde of Russians came to America to buy and to steal technology. Particular targets were American heavy industry and the automobile industry. Hundreds of American workers went back to the Soviet Union to help build the socialist state.

On the military side, the Soviet representatives were particularly interested in American tank and warship technologies. The Soviets had already copied tank designs of the American J. W. Christie, and Soviet Marshal Mikhail Tukhachevsky had proposed to Stalin that the Soviets offer Christie large sums of money to design tanks in the Soviet Union. Stalin had turned down the suggestion.

Since Peter's time, Russians had purchased warships as well as their designs in the West. The Russian battleship *Tsessarevitch* was launched in France in 1901, and the battleship *Retvizan*, launched in the United States in 1900, was built by the William Cramp Shipyard in Philadelphia. In the early 1900s the Russians purchased submarines from American underwater pioneers Simon Lake and John Holland.

In the 1930s the Soviets had gone to Italy for assistance in building a new generation of battleships, but the Italians were reluctant to provide much help beyond the preliminary design. On November 24, 1936, the Soviets asked the U.S. Government for permission to negotiate with American firms for heavy armor. Permission for the armor was given, and this effort was soon extended to battleship designs as well as the 16-inch guns and their ammunition. (At the time U.S. commercial firms were unable to produce such large guns; all American 16-inch guns were manufactured at the Washington Naval Gun Factory.)

On August 24, 1937, representatives of the Soviet Government came to see William F. Gibbs, one of the leading U.S. naval architects. According to Gibbs, "We were naturally not anxious to do that and, in accordance with our invariable practice when a foreign nation consults us about the design of a naval vessel, we brought the matter immediately to the attention of the proper authorities in the Navy Department, and later the Department of State, and we stated that we were not willing to do any work or have any relations with the Soviets unless the government of the United States could assure us that it was a desirable thing from their point of view that we carry on."

The Navy Department, Gibbs recalled, "assured us that they thought it a desirable thing. . . ." Representatives of Amtorg and the Soviet ambassador in Washington told Gibbs that they wanted an "exceptional" ship. Gibbs and his design team proposed a ship more than 1,000 feet long with a displacement of some 72,000 tons, carrying a main battery of twelve 16-inch guns. By comparison, in the same month that the Soviets approached Gibbs the U.S. Navy ordered two modern battleships—each only 729 feet long and displacing 42,000 tons, with nine 16-inch guns. Some of the Gibbs' design variants provided the superbattleship with a flight deck for operating about thirty-five aircraft! The Soviets also expressed considerable interest in carrier aviation, seeking plans for the carrier *Ranger,* as well as other data on naval aviation.

Most U.S. Navy officers were opposed to helping the Communist state. Admiral William H. Standley,* the Chief of Naval Operations, complained, "Russian attachés, military, naval, and commercial, picked up everything—copies of all technical and trade magazines and military and naval professional magazines, blueprints, and everything from nuts and bolts to washing machines, tractors, and combine harvesters." While some Soviet diplomats were openly picking up information, others were secretly setting up a North American spy ring. Two of the outposts would be the Soviet Embassy on Sixteenth Street and the redbrick, three-story building that was the Soviet Embassy in Ottawa, Canada.

* Standley retired from the Navy in 1936. In February 1942, President Roosevelt sent Standley to Moscow as the U.S. ambassador, a post he held until October 1943.

* * *

In the years between wars the Communist Party of the United States followed a similar double path. The Party functioned openly as a constitutionally protected political organization, while an underground Communist Party of dedicated Americans stole government secrets and plotted to infiltrate the government itself. These underground Party members worked for the new world of socialism, not for money. Some traveled to Moscow for training by officers of the GRU, or Glavnoye Razvedyvatelnoye Upravlenie, the Chief Intelligence Directorate, the Fourth Bureau of the Soviet General Staff. Some recruited agents among relatives and friends. Members of Party espionage cells in the United States often got specific assignments from Moscow: Photograph blueprints of submarines being built at the Electric Boat Company in Groton, Connecticut. Get plans for U.S. Army installations in the Panama Canal Zone. Steal industrial secrets about U.S. processes for producing synthetic rubber and high-octane gasoline.

Most of the overseas spying by the Soviets in this period was under the aegis of the GRU. The GRU looked outward for the Red Government as well as for the military; the other Soviet intelligence agencies primarily were to maintain the internal security of the state, beginning with the Cheka, established in 1917. But internal security often meant tracking down and kidnapping or executing émigrés and others who threatened the state from outside of Soviet borders. By 1922 the excesses of the Cheka led to the establishment of the GPU, another security organization known by the abbreviation of its name. In time the GPU was succeeded by the OGPU, then the NKVD, which survived as a strictly internal police organization when the NKGB was established in 1941. During World War II external as well as internal police and intelligence powers were again vested with the NKVD, but in 1946 the NKGB reappeared, soon changed to the MGB, and from 1960 to KGB, which survives today, as does the GRU. (See Chapter 4.)

On the eve of World War II the principal targets for Soviet espionage shifted from military and industrial secrets to state secrets. Sometime around 1936, Colonel Boris Bykov, head of Soviet military intelligence in the United States, asked members of the Party's Washington espionage cell to supply him with a steady supply of State Department documents. One of Bykov's spies in the State Department later told the FBI that Bykov especially requested information that would "enlighten" the Soviets about "the war which Germany and Japan were preparing against the Soviet Union."

Bykov's demand for state secrets and enlightenment played to the sympathies of Americans enthralled with the promise of a world united by socialism and its promised equality for all men and women. Such was the ideology of Whittaker Chambers, an editor at *Time* magazine, that he said he chose a momentous ideological moment—"two days after Hitler and Stalin signed their pact" in August 1939—to emerge from the underground of the Communist Party of the United States and tell authorities what he knew about Americans spying for the Soviet Union. The signing of the 1939 German-Soviet nonaggression pact had been an act of heresy for Chambers and for many other Americans who had espoused communism, believing it to be the ideological antithesis of Hitler's hated Nazism.

Chambers, in his 1948 testimony before the House Committee on Un-American Activities, described his attraction to communism in words that made it sound like the intellectual version of a religious conversion. He, like many other Americans who embraced communism in the 1930s, saw himself as choosing the only path that a peace-loving, globally minded American intellectual could take.

"I had joined the Communist Party in 1924," he said. "No one recruited me. I had become convinced that the society in which we live, western civilization, had reached a crisis, of which the First World War was the military expression, and that it was doomed to collapse or revert to barbarism. I did not understand the causes of the crisis or know what to do about it. But I felt that, as an intelligent man, I must do something. In the writings of Karl Marx I thought I had found the explanation of the historical and economic causes. In the writings of Lenin I thought I had found the answer to the question, what to do?"

What he did was serve in a Moscow-directed underground organization centered in Washington. "The purpose of this group at that time," he said, "was not primarily espionage. Its original purpose was the Communist infiltration of the American Government. But espionage was certainly one of its eventual objectives."

Loyal Soviet agents and spies were forced underground after the signing of the mutual nonaggression pact, which permitted Germany to attack Poland one week later, on September 1, 1939, plunging Europe into World War II. However, when Hitler ordered his panzer divisions and the Luftwaffe to strike the Soviet Union in June 1941, the Soviets became allies of Britain and the United States. The attitude of the American people became pro-Soviet almost overnight, easing considerably the work of Soviet spies and sympathizers.

During World War II the FBI devoted most of its resources to tracking down Nazi spies and saboteurs in the United States—and, by presidential directive, in Latin America. But the FBI's Soviet Espionage Squad, which worked out of the bureau's field office in New York City, did keep a quiet watch on Soviet spies in the United States. FBI agents trailed suspected spies working from the spy nest that was the Soviet Consulate in New York, sometimes ran loyal Americans as double agents, and began learning the ways of counter-espionage. Arrests of Soviet spies were rare because U.S. officials did not want to disturb a touchy wartime ally.

One of the few Soviets arrested in the 1940s was Gaik Badalovich Ovakimian, who had been running North American spies since the 1930s. Charged with being an unregistered agent of a foreign power (a technical charge that sounded diplomatically nicer than espionage), he was not put on trial. Instead, the U.S. Government made a deal, trading Ovakimian for several Americans being held in the Soviet Union. (Maxsim Maksimovitch Litvinov, the Soviet ambassador to the United States at the time, had himself been traded many years before. Arrested in England in 1918, he was swapped for Bruce Lockhart, a British agent being held in Moscow.)

The postwar years ushered in many of the dilemmas that would perplex U.S. counter-espionage actions for decades to come. FBI officials and agents began to learn that cloak-and-dagger operations were more complicated and more frustrating than the cops-and-robbers gambits that had marked the long tenure of J. Edgar Hoover and his senior associates. FBI agents assigned to counter-espionage found that they could not make arrests even after they had built what, for other crimes, would have been a good case. Trained in the Hoover style of good-guy-versus-bad-guy criminology, the counter-intelligence agents had to operate in a world of murky morals where men and women broke the law for ideological motives rather than for greed, where confessed criminals could make deals, where decisions on whether to make an arrest swung on questions of national security and international relationships rather than on justice.

In those early postwar years espionage and subversion became an American obsession. Headlines told of Senator McCarthy's charges of spies and subversives in the State Department, of Americans giving away the secrets of the atomic bomb, of Americans who were burrowing from within, planning and working for the day when, suddenly, the United States would be taken over by the Soviet Union. Spy-catching became a morality play in which the forces of good, personified by the FBI, waged war against the forces of evil, personified by disloyal Americans who spied for the Soviets. Like all morality plays, this one taught simple, lasting lessons: The danger is within. Americans who spy do so because they are in the thrall of an alien ideology. Hunt down the disloyal Americans.

Almost lost in the simplicity was the fact that the real danger was from without. The American spies were being managed by a highly professional secret police and military intelligence apparatus in the Soviet Union. Soviet intelligence officers had a mission to perform: Get the U.S. secrets that the Kremlin wanted. It did not matter what the motive of the spies might be.

U.S. counter-espionage strategy in the 1950s focused on the ideological American spies rather than on their spymasters. A handful of FBI agents, put together in the Soviet Espionage Squad, was no match for the worldwide Soviet espionage apparatus that was powerful enough in its own government to command all the lavish resources and skilled people it needed. There was no way the United States could counter the KGB by building a KGB of its own. In the open society of a democracy, nothing even approaching such a monstrosity would be tolerated. And so the uneven battle went on, a handful of agents against a colossus, agents of a democracy against agents of a totalitarian state, the traditions of justice against the traditions of the czars and Stalin.

After World War II the FBI's Soviet Espionage Squad plodded along, recording the recollections of defected Communists like Whittaker Chambers and gathering information that might never become public while mainstream, crime-fighting agents won fame and promotions by living up to Hoover's image of the "G-man." Real FBI agents didn't skulk around tracking spies— they stormed into the crooks' hideouts and appeared on front pages grimly smiling for newspaper photographers as they hand-cuffed Public Enemy No. 1.

For an ambitious FBI agent, counter-espionage was not the most promising career path. The Soviet Espionage Squad "was Siberia time," Robert J. Lamphere, a member of the Soviet Espionage Squad, later wrote: "The enemy just went on and on; when you got rid of one spy, another would take his place. How would you get satisfaction?"

In 1945, when Elizabeth Bentley went to the FBI and told of her work as a courier carrying secrets from the Washington Communist underground to Soviet contacts in New York City, her case was initially assigned to the Soviet Espionage Squad. But soon it became apparent that her accusations were serious enough for Hoover to pass the information on to the White House and the Attorney General. The Soviet Espionage Squad then lost Bentley to the FBI's Major Case Squad, based in Washington. "My colleagues were disgusted at this bureaucratic move," Lamphere recalled.

The Judith Coplon "major case" helped to educate the FBI about the complexity of Soviet espionage. The trailing, arrest, and prosecution of Coplon introduced issues that would appear again and again in the FBI's handling of espionage, from the 1940s to the 1980s: When and how should the government arrest the accused spy? How legal is wiretapping? Does a United Nations employee have diplomatic immunity? In a trial, how can the government introduce evidence whose disclosure will jeopardize sensitive national security matters?

Judith Coplon worked in the Foreign Agents Registration section of the Department of Justice and had access to FBI files. When the FBI first heard her name mentioned as a courier for the Soviet spy ring, Hoover wanted her simply fired as a security risk. Counter-espionage agents recommended that she be kept on and closely watched. The Director finally gave in, and she was placed under surveillance, which included wiretapping, another risky area for FBI agents.

In 1939 the Supreme Court, in *Nardone* v. *U.S.*, had ruled that wiretapping was almost invariably unconstitutional. Responding to the Supreme Court decision, President Roosevelt had told Attorney General Robert Jackson that he felt the Court had not intended its interpretation to extend to "grave matters involving the defense of the nation." Roosevelt "authorized and directed" Jackson to use "listening devices" to monitor "the conversations or other communications of persons suspected of subversive activities against the Government of the United States, including suspected spies." This directive became the legal foundation for wiretapping in Coplon's case and, handed down like the family Bible from one Attorney General to the other, it remained so in many other espionage cases that followed.

The Coplon case inspired another innovation for the FBI: the use of bait to catch a spy. At the suggestion of Lamphere, a fake secret memo was prepared, signed by Hoover, and passed under Coplon's unsuspecting eyes. She had it in her handbag, along with other FBI documents, when a platoon of agents arrested Coplon and her Soviet contact, Valentin Akekseevich Gubitchev, a United Nations employee, in New York City in March 1949. The Soviets unsuccessfully claimed diplomatic immunity for Gubitchev. He had entered the United States as a member of the Soviet delegation to the United Nations but had become an employee of the UN Secretariat. The job shift lost him his immunity.

At Coplon's trial for theft of government documents and attempted theft of national defense documents, the prosecution introduced as evidence "data slips" that made references to FBI cases. The defense demanded that the FBI produce the files to which the slips referred so that the jury could evaluate their importance. The FBI, fearing the disclosure of national security information, responded by producing only photostats of the title pages and excerpts from the reports. The judge later ordered that the files be introduced.

Coplon and Gubitchev were convicted. Gubitchev was deported, in a deal engineered by the State Department. Coplon's conviction was set aside by an appeals judge on two issues: records of the wiretap should have been shown to her defense attorney and her arrest should have been with a warrant. (Congress soon passed a law authorizing warrantless arrest in espionage cases.)

Not all of the Soviet spies in the United States were—or are —traitors. Some are Soviet intelligence officers, trained in the Soviet Union, serving their nation as members of the MGB or, since the 1960s, the KGB. The most famous of the Russians known to have spied on America was an extremely professional intelligence officer whose working name was Rudolf Abel. (His real name has remained a minor mystery.) Russian-born, Abel had studied engineering and had a working knowledge of chemistry and nuclear physics, and was fluent in English, German, Polish, and Yiddish as well as Russian. He was an accomplished painter and photographer, knew his way around electronics, and was a fairly good jeweler. With such a broad sweep of talent, he could have used any one of several covers. He chose photography.

During World War II, Abel had served in the Red Army on the German front as an intelligence officer, and is reported to have penetrated the Abwehr (German military intelligence). He illegally entered the United States, through Canada, in 1949 and by 1954 he was working in New York City. He used a photographic studio in Brooklyn as a front while directing Soviet intelligence operations in the New York area.

At about that time the FBI had under routine surveillance not only the Soviet Embassy in Washington but also the Soviet Consulates in New York and San Francisco, and the Soviet Mission to the United Nations. Soviet intelligence officers operating out of these places under diplomatic cover were considered "legals," because, as officially accredited diplomats, they had entered the United States legally. Abel was an "illegal," a deep-cover intelligence officer who ran American agents.

Like nearly every Soviet spy ever discovered in the United States, Abel was *not* detected by U.S. counter-espionage forces. One popular story, stoked by Hoover's publicists, was that a hollow nickel, turned over to police by a New York newsboy, led the FBI to Abel. The nickel, and the coded message within it, could have been tracked to Abel, *but the clue was ignored by the FBI.* In reality, one of Abel's underlings, an alcoholic Soviet intelligence officer, defected and directed the FBI to Abel. He was arrested in 1957, convicted of espionage, and imprisoned until 1962, when he was exchanged for captured American U-2 pilot Francis Gary Powers.

Another illegal of that era was a man known as Gordon Arnold Lonsdale, who was planted in the United States as a potential spy at the age of eleven. His biography was still being studied by U.S. counter-espionage agents in the 1980s as an exquisite example of Soviet patience and skill in the creation of professional spies. The man known as Lonsdale carried the name of a child who had been born in Canada and taken by his mother to Finland, where he died, possibly during the Finno-Soviet War of 1939–40. Soviet espionage operatives obtained Lonsdale's Canadian birth record and passport, and used the documents to manufacture an identity for Conon Trofimovich Molody, the Moscow-born son of a Soviet science writer.

When Conon was eleven his mother sent him to live in California with her sister, who posed as his mother. He thus learned English in the best possible way. After five years in California, he returned to the Soviet Union, where he received a commission in the Soviet Navy and was trained in espionage. A Soviet grain ship carried him to Vancouver, where, with the Lonsdale documents, he established a Canadian identity. He attributed his odd accent —American English tinged with Russian—to his days as a lumberjack far from civilization.

In 1955 he journeyed to England, where he spied out British defense secrets while maintaining a front life as an entrepreneur whose enterprises included renting jukeboxes and manufacturing bubble-gum machines. One of his targets was a Royal Navy underwater weapons facility. In 1961 a routine security investigation at the facility led to his arrest and the roundup of four members of his ring. Two of them, Helen and Peter Kroger, also had identities created by the KGB and its predecessors.

Convicted in London's Old Bailey court for conspiring to pass information "which might be directly or indirectly to an enemy," Molody-Lonsdale was sentenced to twenty-five years in prison. In 1964 he was exchanged for British agent Greville Wynne, the go-between for Oleg Penkovskiy, a GRU colonel-turned-Western spy who had been captured by the Soviets.

Both Abel and Lonsdale were Russian-born. They were citizens of the Soviet state, educated by the Soviet state, and defenders of that state. They spied on the West because the West was the enemy of the Soviet state. Quite different, but still ideological spies, were the traitors: those men and women born, raised, and educated in the West who believed that the Soviet state—or more probably the Soviet system—held better promise for the human race.

Considering the large number of American and Soviet agents that had been planted in the 1930s and 1940s, the FBI unearthed relatively few of both kinds of postwar Soviet spies. Some foreign-born Communists were deported; others defected and lived on in the United States as informers. The most publicized cases did not result in convictions for espionage.

Whittaker Chambers, for example, had named several Americans as Communist spies. His most notorious accusation was that Alger Hiss, a former State Department official, had been a spy during much of his career. Hiss had served as an aide to President Roosevelt at the Yalta Conference in 1945 and was secretary general of the San Francisco conference that led to the creation of the United Nations. In the long, dramatic, and convoluted duel between Chambers and Hiss, the accused spy was eventually convicted of perjury, but never of espionage.

The Coplon case had generated lurid headlines but she had not even been charged with espionage, and she was never retried after a court had overturned her original conviction. A few other Americans seeking state secrets were named, but the Washington "spy probes" of the 1950s were media events staged by Senator Joseph McCarthy rather than courtroom prosecutions that sent spies to jail.

Chambers, Bentley, and General Walter Krivitsky, a high-ranking Soviet espionage officer in Europe, gave U.S. counterespionage agents the names of many alleged Soviet spies in the United States and Great Britain. As the FBI was learning, however, it was a long way from an informer's accusation of espionage to a conviction in a court of law. Krivitsky, incidentally, ended his career in spy-novel fashion. On February 10, 1941, he was found, dying of a gunshot wound, in a cheap hotel near Union Station in Washington, D.C. Officially, his death was termed a suicide, but some investigators believed the Soviets had assassinated him.

The Soviet espionage campaign to garner U.S. diplomatic secrets paralleled an intensive, wide-ranging effort to get the most important military secret of its time: the atomic bomb. The Soviets set up a network that extended from the United States and

Canada to Great Britain and included not only Soviet operatives but also American, Canadian, and British citizens who had become ideologically committed to the Soviet Union.

Ironically, it was a Russian's ideological conversion that began the unraveling of the spy network. On September 5, 1945, less than a month after the atomic bomb had ended World War II, Igor Sergeievitch Gouzenko, a cipher clerk in the Soviet Embassy in Ottawa, walked out of the embassy with an armload of secret documents. After barely escaping capture by embassy security officers, Gouzenko and his pregnant wife made several dangerous and frustrating attempts to get the documents to Canadian officials.

Finally, shocked Canadian intelligence experts began to examine the documents, which showed that the Soviets had used Canada as a base for their campaign to get the secrets of the atomic bomb. Gouzenko's documents gave U.S., Canadian, and British investigators enough leads to begin the long and complex process of cracking the atomic bomb spy ring.

Two of the spies were scientists. Dr. Alan Nunn May, a lecturer on physics at the University of London, had worked on the U.S. atomic bomb during the war and had given samples of uranium to Soviet agents. He was arrested in March 1946, pleaded guilty to violating the Official Secrets Act, and was sentenced to ten years. Klaus Fuchs, head of the theoretical physics division of Great Britain's atomic energy establishment at Harwell, confessed in January 1950 that he had given to the Soviets technical information that had accelerated the building of their atomic bomb. The secrets he passed included details about the complex gaseous-diffusion method U.S. scientists had developed for separating uranium 235, the fissionable material for the bomb, from uranium 238. Knowledge of this process saved the Soviet Union from engaging in long and costly development efforts.

Like May, Fuchs was charged not with espionage but with violation of the Official Secrets Act. He was put on trial in Old Bailey. Because the secrets involved a weapon of mass destruction, the judge who sentenced Fuchs described his crime as "only thinly differentiated from high treason." He could not be tried for high treason, which called for the death sentence, because it applies only to spying for an enemy; the Soviet Union was an ally. Fuchs pleaded guilty and was sentenced to fourteen years, the maximum sentence. (When he was released from prison in 1959 he went to East Germany, where he became the deputy director of the Central Institute for Nuclear Physics.)

Fuchs, trying to explain his ability to spy for the Soviet Union, said, "I used my Marxist philosophy to establish in my mind two separate compartments. One compartment in which I allowed myself to make friendships, to have personal relations, to help people and to be in all personal ways the kind of man I wanted to be. . . . I could be free and easy and happy with other people without fear of disclosing myself because I knew that the other compartment would step in if I approached the danger point. . . . Looking back at it now the best way of expressing it seems to be to call it a controlled schizophrenia."

"The mind of Fuchs," said a British prosecutor, "may probably be unique and create a new precedent in the world of psychology." Half of Fuchs' mind, the prosecutor said, was "beyond the reach of reason and the impact of fact. The other half lived in a world of normal relationships and friendships with his colleagues and human loyalty. The dual personality had been consciously and deliberately produced. He broke his mind in two, describing it as controlled schizophrenia. He has produced in himself a classic example of the immortal duality in English literature, Jekyll and Hyde."

The Jekyll and Hyde image suggests an involuntary spy, an otherwise decent patriot who falls under the spell of espionage. The description reflected a belief, peculiar to the early postwar years, that people who spied from ideological motives were merely misdirected, living, as Fuchs had rationalized it, "a controlled schizophrenia." They simply had allowed their belief in a better world of the future to overtake their innate patriotism.

Perhaps the image could be applied to some of those who stole state documents to "enlighten" the Soviet Union about U.S. and British diplomatic plans. But when the secrets had to do with the atomic bomb, the spies were stealing from their nation's arsenal, arming another nation with weapons that could destroy the spies' own homeland. In the atomic age, as Dame Rebecca West wrote in *The New Meaning of Treason,* "The traitor can change the community into a desert haunted by fear."

The most infamous ideological spies were the British Cambridge quartet and the American Rosenbergs. The Cambridge quartet—Burgess, Maclean, Philby, and Blunt—were all educated at Cambridge University in the early 1930s, a time of disillusionment for British young men, a time when many British intellectuals questioned the reliability of the West's political and economic systems.

Guy (Francis de Moncy) Burgess, whose father was a commander in the Royal Navy and whose stepfather was an Army colonel, was brilliant, sophisticated, and openly homosexual. While a student at Cambridge he was recruited by Soviet intelligence. After graduating from Cambridge in 1935, he unsuccessfully tried for employment with the Conservative Party and *The Times* of London. He finally was able to become a broadcaster for the British Broadcasting Corporation. Around this time, he later claimed, he began receiving payment from British intelligence for small jobs he was asked to do.

In December 1938, Burgess was offered a staff job in a new British secret service department devoted to propaganda and subversion. During this period he had a large London flat, which was often visited by Anthony Blunt, a homosexual friend from Cambridge who worked for MI5, the British agency responsible for counter-espionage. In 1939, Burgess joined the war propaganda section of MI6, the British espionage service.

Near the end of World War II, Burgess began his most successful burrowing as a Soviet mole in the upper reaches of the British foreign-policy establishment. For about two years, beginning in 1944, he worked in the news department of the Foreign Office, a seemingly innocuous position that nevertheless gave him access to diplomatic information and to the Foreign Minister's office itself. By 1946 he was secretary and personal assistant to Hector McNeil, Minister of State in the Foreign Office, a cabinet rank.

More promotions in the Foreign Office followed for Burgess, but by 1948 his career seemed to be in jeopardy when his drinking, unsatisfactory job performance, and a habit of openly discussing classified information led to a severe reprimand. Despite this record, in August 1950 he was posted to the British Embassy in Washington, with the rank of First Secretary.

During his brief, drunken stay in Washington, Burgess lived with Kim Philby, his wife, Aileen, and their four children. Philby was a temporary First Secretary at the British Embassy from

October 1949 to June 1951. One night, at a party in Philby's home, Burgess got drunk, disgusted all the guests—most of whom were FBI and CIA officials—lewdly insulted a CIA official's wife, and set a Washington record for most insults made in a single night. Burgess' recall to London soon followed. As Dame Rebecca has noted, Great Britain "would have been spared a great deal of trouble if we had simply kept our cupboards locked and had removed from our public service officials who were habitually blind drunk."

In the early spring of 1951, about the time of the notorious party, the FBI and MI5 were seeking the identity of a Soviet agent who had penetrated the Foreign Office and had served time in the British Embassy in Washington. On May 25, 1951, shortly after his recall and in the midst of the investigation, Burgess fled England for the Soviet Union with Donald Maclean, the head of the Foreign Office's American Department. In July 1951, Philby was asked to resign from the Foreign Service.

Donald Maclean was the son of a Liberal cabinet minister (who spoke strongly against the Official Secrets Act when it was introduced in 1911). He also was a homosexual—known to some friends as "Lady Maclean." Recruited by Soviet intelligence soon after his graduation from Cambridge in 1933, he later entered the Foreign Office and was posted to Paris in 1938. Maclean subsequently served in London and, from 1944 to 1948, as First Secretary to the British Embassy in Washington. In 1947 he was appointed as Britain's Secretary on the Combined Policy Committee on Atomic Development, which was concerned with British-U.S. atomic energy matters.

In 1948 he was promoted to Counsellor and Head of Chancery of the embassy in Cairo. After several binges and drunken brawls, he was recalled to London in May 1950. But later that same year he was appointed head of a Foreign Office delegation to the United States. Again his drinking forced his recall, a return that was probably quickened by a warning from Kim Philby that investigators were closing in on him. Flight to the Soviet Union would be much easier from London than Washington, and he fled to Moscow with Guy Burgess.

Harold Adrian Russell Philby, often referred to as the "third man" in the Cambridge ring, was the son of noted Arabist St. John Philby. Kim Philby—his nickname recalled the Rudyard

Kipling character who worked in India for the British secret service—was also recruited by the Soviets while at Cambridge. He traveled in Europe, married a member of the Communist underground in Vienna in 1934, and, posing as a pro-Fascist, covered the Spanish Civil War for *The Times*. In Spain he made his first contacts with British intelligence and subsequently served in MI6, the Secret Intelligence Service, at times under Foreign Office cover.

In 1941 he was offered an executive post in MI6, working in Section V, the counter-espionage department of the Secret Intelligence Service, which often has been called the "heart of the secret world." Three years later he was appointed to run a new unit of MI6 that would work against the Soviet Union. He was posted to Istanbul in 1947 as SIS station chief and two years later he was sent to Washington, where he was given the task of representing the SIS in Washington and collaborating with the newly formed Central Intelligence Agency. For two years he had weekly luncheons with James Jesus Angleton, the CIA's counter-espionage expert, and spent much of his time picking up information about Anglo-American operations against the Soviet Union.

Although many counter-espionage agents on both sides of the Atlantic believed that Philby had tipped off Burgess and Maclean in 1951, he was merely asked to resign from the Foreign Office, which later used its influence to get Philby hired by the London *Observer* and *The Economist* as their Middle East correspondent. From the mid-1950s to 1962 he worked in Beirut as a journalist and, at times, as an agent for *both* the KGB and the SIS. In 1963 he vanished from Beirut. He soon appeared in Moscow, where he wrote a book about his espionage career and went to work full-time for the KGB.

Philby's biographers contend that Philby, like Fuchs, was a man with " 'two separate sides to his head.' On one side was an unmistakable son of the British Establishment: a slightly taciturn, obviously charming product of a good public school and a smart Cambridge college; industrious, clearheaded, and believed to be trustworthy to a remarkable degree." On the other side was a Soviet spy.

All three of these British double agents—Philby, Burgess, and Maclean—had access to secret American material, especially information about U.S. counter-espionage efforts, plans for atomic bomb production, and, during the Korean conflict of 1950–53, strategic planning. Undoubtedly all three passed this sensitive information on to their Soviet controllers, along with vast amounts of secret British material.

For years after the exposure of Philby, Burgess, and Maclean there were suspicions and rumors that "the fourth man" in the Cambridge spy ring was Anthony Blunt, a friend of the other three, a Fellow of Cambridge's Trinity College, and during World War II an officer in counter-espionage (MI5). Immediately after the war Blunt had undertaken a highly secret mission to Germany on behalf of King George. In 1945 he was made curator of the royal family's art collection. For his many services to the crown, Blunt was knighted in 1956. By then the rumors of his espionage for the Soviet were widely circulating.

But not until 1979, while he was art curator to Queen Elizabeth II, was Blunt directly accused. After being guaranteed full immunity, he confessed to having been a Soviet agent in counter-espionage and a talent scout for Soviet intelligence while teaching at Cambridge. Stripped of his honors, he retired from public life and chose to remain in Britain with his paintings and friends.

Blunt's Cambridge colleagues—as well as Abel, Lonsdale, and other spies before and since—were publicly and warmly welcomed to Moscow, with great shows of affection. For some there were honors, awards, and promotions; for others, quiet retirement. To spies still out in the cold, the ex-spies in Moscow could be held up as living proof that the Soviet Union would get them back if they were caught, even trading them for convicted Westerners like Francis Gary Powers and Greville Wynne.

British spies are of great concern to the American counter-espionage establishment because of the long Anglo-American tradition of exchanging intelligence and counter-intelligence information. Revelations about Soviet moles in recent years have even included well-documented accusations against Sir Roger Hollis, head of MI5 from 1956 to 1965.*

* Peter Wright, the former deputy director of MI5, claimed in his memoirs in 1986 that Sir Roger, a reputed homosexual, was the "fifth man" in the Cambridge ring. Hollis was said to have been recruited as a young man in China. In 1987 the British Government, in an unusual

The British equivalent of the National Security Agency, the Government Communications Headquarters (GCHQ), was penetrated in the early 1960s by a KGB-recruited agent, Geoffrey Arthur Prime. A translator of Soviet communications intercepted by the British, Prime had been recruited in Berlin while he was working there for the GCHQ. Prime later moved to England and in 1976 was assigned to the extremely secret J Division, which focused on the interception of the most sensitive Soviet communications, much of which was shared with U.S. intelligence. Prime's sexual depravity—his victims were little girls—first alerted authorities to him. The investigation, spurred by his wife's revelations to the government, took a new turn when espionage was added to pedophilia. Prime eventually confessed. In 1982 he was convicted of espionage and sentenced to three years for sex offenses and thirty-six years for spying.

After exposure, British spies were often portrayed by the Soviets as misunderstood architects of a better world. Similarly, one of the myths of the American ideological spies was this: They came from the ranks of Americans who, for motives ranging from guaranteeing world peace to assuring Soviet power, believed that the United States should not have a monopoly on the atomic bomb. In fact, the Americans who gave atomic secrets to the Soviets had been committed to communism long before the atomic bomb was built.

Harry Gold, an American who was a courier for Klaus Fuchs, had been recruited as a spy as early as 1935. Gold, a biochemist, admired the Soviet Union as a "progressive" nation but did not admire the morality of the Communist Party of the United States, which he never joined. He told the FBI that he gave loyalty to the Soviet Union because he believed there was no anti-Semitism there. This naive belief was apparently engendered by Soviet propaganda that played up Stalin's support of the formation of a Zionist state in Palestine (because, in his view, this would lessen British influence in the Middle East). American Jews who became enamored of the Soviet Union selectively be-

court case dealing with Wright's memoirs, conceded as true no less than twenty-three criminal conspiracies and twelve acts of treason charged by Wright. Included in the list was the accusation that Hollis, who died in 1973, was a Soviet spy during his career as a British spymaster.

lieved the cynical pro-Zionist propaganda line and just as selectively ignored the evidence of Stalin's vicious anti-Semitism, which was rooted in Czarist pogroms and still blooms in the Soviet Union of the 1980s.*

Gold began his spy career in industrial espionage, obtaining for his case officers secrets about Kodak's color-film manufacturing and information about closely guarded processes for the manufacture of certain paints and solvents. Foreshadowing Soviet technological theft in the 1980s, Gold stole manufacturers' files on turbine engines and the manufacture of synthetic rubber.

When, near the end of World War II, the Soviets began concentrating their espionage on the atomic bomb, Gold became part of that effort, acting as a middleman between Fuchs and a Soviet handler. In June 1945, Gold's case officer, a Soviet who operated out of the Soviet Consulate in New York, ordered Gold to make a dangerous, two-stop courier run. He was to go first to Santa Fe, New Mexico, to pick up sketches and notes from Fuchs, who was then working at the secret atomic bomb site near Los Alamos, New Mexico. Then Gold was told to travel to Albuquerque, where—in a rare payment for secrets—he was to give $500 to an American soldier assigned as a technician at Los Alamos. The soldier handed over to Gold sketches of the system used to "focus" high-explosive pressure waves that drove together packets of uranium and produced the chain reaction of nuclear fission—the explosion of the atomic bomb.

Fuchs' arrest led to the arrest of Gold, who identified the soldier at Albuquerque as David Greenglass. Greenglass and his wife, Ruth, both members of the Communist Party of the United States of America, implicated two other members, his sister, Ethel, and her husband, Julius Rosenberg. The children of Jewish immigrants from Russia, the Rosenbergs had been born and raised in New York City. Julius graduated from City College of New York as an electrical engineer. Ethel, who had a beautiful operatic voice, was a high school graduate.

* In the Russian Revolution and Civil War that followed, however, Russian Jews overwhelmingly sided with, and fought for, the Bolsheviks. During Lenin's tenure as head of the Bolshevik government from 1917 to 1922, he appointed many Jews to important positions, including that of Foreign Minister.

The Rosenbergs were faithful followers of the Party line, calling for U.S. neutrality at the beginning of World War II and U.S. assistance for the Soviets after Germany attacked the Soviet Union in June 1941. In 1940, Julius began work as a civilian for the U.S. Army Signal Corps, but in 1945 was fired because of his pro-Soviet views. Like some American Communists of the 1930s, he lived a double life of avowed Party member and underground agent. Rosenberg, the FBI established, was the leader of a cell of engineers who during and after the war worked in defense plants and on military bases.

A number of Americans spying for the Soviets slipped out of the country after the arrests of Fuchs and Gold. Among them were two New Yorkers, Morris and Lona Cohen, who had known Colonel Abel and presumably were part of his ring. (In 1961, when the British arrested Lonsdale, two of his confederates, Helen and Peter Kroger, had New Zealand passports. But their fingerprints, taken over their objections, showed them not to be the Commonwealth subjects who spoke so vaguely of their past. The prints revealed them as Morris and Lona Cohen. As part of the Lonsdale-Wynne spy swap, the Cohens went to Moscow. This is the only publicly known instance of the West trading to the Soviet Union U.S. citizens who were convicted spies.)

David Greenglass told the FBI that soon after he was assigned to the atomic laboratory at Los Alamos in 1944, Ethel and Julius persuaded him to spy for the Soviet Union. Greenglass had worked as a machinist in the group that assembled the bombs that were dropped on Hiroshima and Nagasaki. Both Julius and Ethel were arrested on espionage charges in the summer of 1950.

"The Atomic Bomb Spy Ring," as the headlines called it, had, in the words of the FBI's Hoover, committed the "crime of the century," and at their trial Judge Irving Kaufman told them, "I consider your crime worse than murder."

The Rosenbergs and Greenglass were tried, along with Morton Sobell, a former classmate of Julius who was accused of being a member of the spy ring. The Department of Justice, through Hoover, recommended that Julius Rosenberg be executed and that Ethel Rosenberg and Sobell each be sentenced to thirty years; a fifteen-year sentence was recommended for Greenglass.

Gold, tried separately, was given a thirty-year sentence. Kaufman sentenced Ethel and Julius to death and gave Sobell a thirty-year sentence—with a recommendation of no parole. He sentenced Greenglass to fifteen years. The Korean War had begun less than a month before Julius Rosenberg's arrest. Kaufman linked the Rosenberg espionage to the war, declaring that by helping the Soviets to get the atomic bomb much earlier than they would have on their own, they had set in motion the events leading to the war and "undoubtedly have altered the course of history to the disadvantage of our country."

After more than twenty separate appeals over more than two years, the Rosenbergs were executed in the electric chair in Sing Sing Prison in Ossining, New York, on June 19, 1953. Ethel was the first woman executed in the United States for a federal offense since Mary Surratt was hanged in 1865 for taking part in the plot to assassinate President Lincoln. Julius and Ethel Rosenberg were the only American traitors ever to be executed during peacetime.

Like the other espionage agents of that era, they were dedicated, ideological spies. They *believed* in their cause; they believed in the Soviet Union or, at least, in the potential of the Soviet system, and they believed that the end justified the means. Their dedication survived what some already knew about life in the Soviet Union—the gulags, the lies, murders, and purges of Joseph Stalin, who ruled the Soviet Union from 1922 until his death in March 1953.

Ideological spies were so dedicated that they accepted little if any money from the Soviet Union. This was typical of Blunt, Burgess, Maclean, and Philby, all of whom lived quite well from the pay they received from the British intelligence services and their positions in the British Government or press establishment. It could be said that His Majesty's Government was funding their activities for Soviet intelligence.

The Rosenbergs lived austerely in a three-room apartment, which they rented for $45.75 a month. Although the prosecution at one point had accused the Rosenbergs of receiving gold payments from Moscow, it is evident that they—like most other ideological spies—worked on the basis of belief and dedication, and not for payment.

Ideology as a motive for espionage began to fade after Stalin's death. Only the most devoted could doubt the stories leaking through the Iron Curtain: Stalin's despotic rule, his slaughter of political enemies. There no longer could be doubt after Nikita Khrushchev, speaking at the Twentieth Party Congress in 1956, denounced Stalin's bloody regime. (The United States soon got copies of the "secret speech," a coup for which both the CIA and the Mossad, the Israeli intelligence service, claim credit.)

No longer could idealists find ideology to inspire espionage. Rather, it would be the promise of money that would lure Americans to the gates of the Soviet embassies, men like U.S. Navy Warrant Officer John A. Walker, Jr.

Between the Khrushchev speech and the capture of the *Pueblo* in 1968, some Americans did sell out their country, usually for money. Those who did approach the Soviet Government —defense workers, federal employees, military men—usually tried to sell secrets the way petty thieves sell hot goods: quick, cheap, and anonymously. The Soviets also blackmailed secrets out of some of these back-alley spies. But these sellers of secrets were throwaways, one-shot spies who could not maintain a steady flow of useful information. Or the Soviets, for various reasons, simply lost interest.

Two of the few exceptions were Navy Yeoman First Class Nelson C. Drummond, the first American black ever convicted of espionage, and Sergeant Robert Lee Johnson, who in the 1950s and early 1960s provided the Soviets with Army missile information and nuclear warfare documents.

Drummond, a clerk at the U.S. Naval Headquarters in London, had top-secret and Cosmic (NATO) security clearances. A Soviet-hired "spotter agent," who could have been a British barmaid or a fellow serviceman, noted that Drummond, a chronic gambler, was constantly in financial straits and passed his name to Soviet intelligence. One night in 1957 he was invited into a pub by a stranger who, while picking up the tab, gave Drummond some money and asked for a favor: a Navy ID card so that his friends could use the Navy Exchange. From there the demands went higher until Drummond was supplying classified documents.

When Drummond was transferred to a job where he had no access to classified documents, his Soviet handler broke off contact, warning Drummond that he was under investigation. The

Office of Naval Intelligence was in fact conducting a secret inquiry about missing documents; several sailors, including Drummond, were under suspicion. Drummond later found out that the missing documents were not the ones that he had given his handlers. This meant that the Soviets not only had inside information about the probe but had also probably recruited at least one sailor besides Drummond. If so, he or they were never caught.

In 1958, Drummond was assigned to duty in the United States, where for the next four years he continued his espionage work by passing secrets he picked up during duty tours in Boston, Norfolk, and Newport, Rhode Island. His contacts were diplomats assigned to the Soviet Mission to the United Nations. FBI surveillance of the Soviets apparently led to the arrest of Drummond, who in 1963 was sentenced to life imprisonment.

Sergeant Johnson, the other successful long-term Soviet recruit, was disgruntled over his failure to advance in rank and decided to get even with the Army. "I did not want to have anything further to do with the Army or the American way of life. . . . I decided to seek asylum with the Soviets," he later told intelligence interrogators.

Johnson was living with an Austrian-born mistress by whom he had a son. Through his mistress he contacted Soviet intelligence officers in East Berlin. At a meeting in February 1953 two KGB officers convinced Johnson to stay in the Army and work as a spy for Soviet intelligence. He agreed, and shortly thereafter life in the Army suddenly improved for Sergeant Johnson. He received Army permission to marry his mistress and he was transferred out of his infantry unit to the Berlin Command's G-2 Section (intelligence) as a file clerk. The swift transfer could indicate that other undetected soldier-spies were working for Soviets at military headquarters.

Drummond and Johnson were targets in what a classified U.S. intelligence document has described as a little-known KGB campaign to recruit low-level military personnel. "The files of U.S. security services," the U.S. document says, "are replete with instances of both direct and indirect Soviet probing of American military personnel in every quarter of the world. . . . Regardless of location, the Soviet objective is the same—spotting and development of character weakness and personal vulnerabilities which will facilitate recruitment and subsequent control, preferably control which can be maintained over the long term and after the recruited agent is rotated back to duty in the United States."

Johnson, the document said, "is a prime example of a soldier who 'went sour,' sought to defect to the Soviets, and instead wound up serving them as a recruited agent in both Europe and the United States over a span of more than a decade. During the period he received, by his own estimate, approximately $25,000 and, from the Soviet standpoint, it was money well spent."

The Soviets supplied Johnson with a camera and, as the clerk in charge of classified files, he systematically photographed every paper that looked important. His wife carried the film to Johnson's Soviet handlers. She, like Johnson, had been given a short course in espionage tradecraft.

When an Army friend, Sergeant James Allen Mintkenbaugh, arrived in Berlin and began work in G-2, Johnson recruited him as a spy. Mintkenbaugh was a homosexual—"and this fact," says a government report on the case, "interested the KGB handlers since the homosexual frequently is shunned by society and made to feel like a social outcast. Such a personality may seek to retaliate against a society that has placed him in this unenviable position." The KGB assigned Mintkenbaugh to spot other American homosexuals.

Johnson, who did not think he had been providing much information to the Soviets, began losing interest in both of his careers. In 1956 he was discharged from the Army. But Mintkenbaugh—and $500 from the KGB—convinced him to go back to the Army. He also got a much more interesting job. He was transferred to the Armed Forces Courier Transfer Station at Orly Airport near Paris.

Courier centers are warehouses of secrets. To and from them are dispatched some of the most valuable secret documents the United States possesses. Keylists for code machines, prepared by the National Security Agency, are sent to courier centers for further distribution. War plans and contingency plans, bulky documents too long and sensitive to transmit by code machine, also travel through courier centers. The Orly center handled cryptographic materials and highly classified documents destined for NATO, the U.S. European Command, and the Sixth Fleet in the Mediterranean. Johnson had access to the vault where the secrets were kept between the time they arrived from Washington and the time couriers took them to their destinations.

The U.S. document on Soviet intelligence describes Johnson's work at the center:

> Beginning in May 1961, Johnson assessed and reported about courier service personnel to the Soviets (thereby providing them a number of recruitment prospects) and photographed and described the Courier Station itself. All of this was preliminary to the real Soviet objective—a surreptitious penetration of the Courier Station vault for access to classified pouch envelopes. To achieve this, Johnson volunteered for permanent weekend duty at the Station during which time he would be alone at night and with physical access to the exterior of the vault. By making use of wax impressions of the key used to open the padlock and by using a Soviet-supplied radioactive device to X-ray the combination lock and read the combination, Johnson gained unauthorized access to the vault itself in November 1962 and began to supply Soviet Intelligence with pouch envelopes. On each occasion he removed up to 15 envelopes classified up to Top Secret from the vault, left his post briefly and passed them under cover of darkness to his Soviet contact who waited a short distance away. The envelopes were returned to Johnson within a few hours, after the Soviets had opened them, photographed the contents, and then resealed them. KGB document specialists were sent to Paris from Moscow to process the valuable material supplied by Johnson, including the delicate job of opening and resealing the envelopes. In the late spring of 1963 the Soviets suspended the vault operation for security reasons but planned to resume and expand it when the nights grew longer later in the year.

The classified report's section on Johnson ends at this point, raising questions that are not answered: How did Johnson get Army assignments that were so convenient to the KGB? How successful were his recruitment tips about other potential spies? Did another Army traitor take up his KGB tasks in the vault when the long nights of autumn came to Orly?

Unlike Drummond, Johnson did not continue his espionage when he was reassigned to the United States. Fearing betrayal by his wife—a frequent fate of spies—Johnson deserted the Army and became a drifter.

Mintkenbaugh, meanwhile, was being trained in Moscow. His homosexual life-style no longer was considered valuable to the KGB. He was ordered to marry a Soviet woman recruited by the KGB. Mintkenbaugh, the brighter of these two Army spies, was sent to Canada to get documents for illegals who would be slipped into Canada, probably by putting them aboard Soviet merchant ships sent to carry wheat back to the Soviet Union. The documents included birth certificates of Canadians who had died soon after birth or in childhood. (Because of the way vital statistics records are usually kept, there is no correlation of births with deaths. So the birth certificate of a dead child can be used by a spy decades later.) Mintkenbaugh was also told to go to work as a real estate salesman in Washington so that he could get personal information on military people and government employees looking for homes.

In 1965, Johnson was caught in what has become a typical way: He gave himself up. He implicated Mintkenbaugh, who was quickly arrested. Johnson's wife independently confirmed that both she and her husband had committed espionage.

A government report on Johnson and Mintkenbaugh says that both men "confessed to the roles they played on behalf of the KGB and both indicated that their motives had been revenge, Johnson wanting to 'get back' at the Army and Mintkenbaugh feeling that he was one of God's mistakes who should have died as a baby."

In 1965, Johnson and Mintkenbaugh were each sentenced to twenty-five years in prison. On May 19, 1972, Johnson's twenty-two-year-old son, Robert Lee Johnson, Jr., went to the federal prison in Lewisburg, Pennsylvania, to visit his father, whom young Robert had not seen for many years. Born just before Johnson had begun spying for the Soviets, Robert had grown up to see both his father and mother dishonored by espionage. He had retrieved his name and his honor by service in the Army in Vietnam. Then he performed one more act to purge the memory. He ended his visit by plunging a knife into his father, killing him instantly.

Sergeant Johnson's legacy included an odd bit of diplomatic mischief. In 1962 he had passed along to the Soviets what were probably his most sensational products: *CINCEUR* [Commander in Chief Europe] *Operation Plan NR 100-6,* which detailed U.S. plans for war in Europe, and *Nuclear Weapons Requirements Handbook,* which included a list of European targets for tactical U.S. nuclear weapons.

In the early 1980s versions of these documents surfaced in Europe. The KGB, having used them militarily years before to analyze NATO strategy, then recycled them for propaganda purposes during antinuclear campaigns in Europe. The documents were authentic only up to a point. KGB disinformation specialists could not resist adding more Western European "targets" to the actual list.

As ideology declined as a motive for espionage, the U.S. Government's interest in counter-espionage also took a turn downward. Part of the reason was that espionage was no longer equated with American Communists. By their speeches, by their absolute support of the Soviet Union, and by their membership in the Communist Party, the relatively few, true-Red American Communists were easily identified. Although they sided with the "enemy," they were not spies.

The people who turned out to be the modern Soviet spies were seemingly ordinary Americans—often "loyal Americans," by their twisted standards—who happened to be in the espionage business. They were not the wild-eyed Communists of the past. They could not be easily identified. Anyone could be a modern traitor-spy: a Democrat, a Republican, a military officer or an enlisted man, a worker in a sensitive federal agency, an employee of a defense contractor.

But no longer were spies appearing in American courtrooms. Not that many were being caught, for the Justice Department did not give FBI counter-espionage work high priority. And not many who were caught were put on trial. Spy cases were hard to shape for prosecution, and careers were not made by devoting a great deal of effort to investigations that did not result in headline-making indictments and convictions. The U.S. Government conducted no espionage prosecutions between 1966 and 1975, chiefly for two reasons: a lack of enthusiasm by prosecutors and CIA warnings about the perils of putting spies on trial.

By the 1970s it was apparent that Soviet espionage in the

United States had been steadily intensifying during the nonprosecution era. Concerned counter-espionage officials saw the rise in espionage as part of the Soviet effort to obtain U.S. high technology, especially new computer developments and electronics. Although the change in intensity was noted, little heed was given to a more significant change: The KGB was running a different kind of American spy.

When, in December 1984, William H. Webster, Director of the Federal Bureau of Investigation, proudly announced, "We have more people charged with espionage right now than ever before in our history," even he did not know the extent of Soviet penetration. The statement implied that the FBI was on top of the espionage menace. Webster was proud, as proud as one of his predecessors, J. Edgar Hoover, would have been in announcing the cracking of a major case.

Within the next twelve months ten Americans were arrested for espionage, and 1985 became the Year of the Spy. The spies were John A. Walker, Jr., his son, Michael, his brother, Arthur, and John's Navy buddy, Radioman Jerry Whitworth. Also, Larry Wu-Tai Chin, a retired Central Intelligence Agency analyst, who had spied for the People's Republic of China for thirty years; Jonathan J. Pollard, who had gathered material for Israel while working as an intelligence analyst for the Naval Investigative Service; his wife, Anne, who helped him and used classified material for work she was proposing for China; Ronald W. Pelton, a former analyst at the National Security Agency, who sold the secrets in his head to the Soviets; Sharon M. Scrange, a CIA clerk in Ghana who gave her Ghanaian lover the names of CIA agents in Ghana; and Randy Miles Jeffries, a messenger who attempted to sell highly secret congressional hearing transcripts to the Soviets. An eleventh spy was *not* under arrest: Edward L. Howard, a fired CIA employee trained to work handling our spies in Moscow, had eluded FBI surveillance agents and would manage to reach Moscow as an American defector.

Webster's 1984 spies had included Thomas P. Cavanagh, a former Northrop engineer who sold plans for the Stealth bomber to FBI agents masquerading as Soviet agents; several foreign nationals working as spies in the United States; and former FBI counter-espionage agent Richard W. Miller, who passed secrets to his lover, a Russian émigrée working for the KGB.

William Webster was surprised by Miller and the rest of the spies and so were key officials in the Reagan Administration. President Reagan tried to handle the spy issue as a box score, noting that the United States caught thirteen spies between 1975 and 1980, while his administration had caught thirty-four between 1981 and December 1985. But, in a radio address at the end of the Year of the Spy, he reflected his administration's confusion and apprehension. "Some of you may be wondering if the large number of spy arrests in recent weeks means that we're looking harder or whether there are more spies to find," the President said. "Well, I think the answer to both questions is yes."

No knowledgeable American official should have been surprised about the spy plague, for its symptoms are conspicuous. There is the hemorrhage—and endless loss of secrets of inestimable value. There is the infirmity—the inability to track and find the spies. And there is the cancer—the trusted Americans who are volunteering to spy not because they hate their country but because they want to earn some extra pieces of silver.

3

A Parade of Walk-ins

John Walker was a walk-in, someone who came out of nowhere, a volunteer spy. His motive was greed, the modern motive. He talked about his work as if he were a businessman. He earned about $1 million—tax free—as a traitor and he never gave any indication that he was driven by any other motive than greed.

U.S. spies can earn considerable sums of money, and in espionage, as in many jobs, money seems to be the major motivation for working. Yet, psychological profiles of Walker and other modern spies show something beyond the visible motive of greed.

"They want money. No doubt of that," a security expert said in an interview with the authors. "But there is something more, something beyond wanting the money." A tough, plain-spoken former FBI agent, he seemed embarrassed to talk about how a psychiatrist had analyzed the motivation of modern spies. "He said it had to do with their father and was mixed up with transferring hatred of him to their father*land*. Now I don't buy all that, but . . ."

The psychiatrist, on retainer to U.S. intelligence agencies and cleared for top-secret information, has been allowed extraordinary access to highly confidential files on modern spies, and he has talked at length with some of them. His evaluations have circulated among security officials in government and the defense industry. He has not published his findings in open psychiatric literature, and he would not talk directly to the authors. But he allowed himself to be paraphrased by the ex-FBI agent, who is now the security chief for a major defense contractor.

The psychiatrist sees spy recruitment as a transaction that is far more complex than one person inducing another into a new occupation, which is what the word "recruitment" implies. We can see a hint of the complexity in sports recruitment, in which a scout or coach lures a promising athlete with, say, the promise of a sleek sports car. But the recruiter is also working on the athlete's vanity, and the athlete is responding to the flattering realization that someone has selected him for something special. The visible greed for the sports car is there, and so is the invisible factor of vanity. Sometimes an amateur will attempt to become a professional without recruitment. The prime motivation for the decision may be money, but vanity is also there.

Most Americans arrested for espionage in the 1980s were, in fact, not recruited. As walk-ins, they volunteered their services. Psychological portraits of the major spies show complex motivations, which often include dissatisfaction with the job.

"The defector personality parallels the espionage personality," the psychiatrist said through his ex-FBI agent medium. "In my opinion, there is a parallel between wanting to be a spy and then turning into a defector, in terms of motivation. Whenever the KGB—or the CIA or FBI—gets a person to commit espionage, that person becomes a traitor. He goes through a *self*-recruitment that allows him to commit espionage."

The psychiatrist made a distinction between an intelligence officer, who is trained to serve his or her country, and an agent, who, for whatever the reason, is a traitor. "But, at some point, the intelligence officer equals the agent. They are both not what they seem to be."

The walk-in spy baffles psychiatrists working in the intelligence community's spy-spotting program. The psychological research, based primarily on exhaustive interviews of captured American spies, is aimed at finding patterns of behavior and quirks of character that could be used to spot potential security risks. Investigators know that walk-ins, who are usually dedicated workers and outspokenly patriotic Americans, can easily slip through the process designed to award secret and top-secret security clearances.

There are no realistic standards for checking the backgrounds of applicants for these clearances. This is the conclusion of another industrial security specialist, Lawrence J. Howe, a former CIA official who now is vice president for security at a major defense research firm, Science Applications International Corporation. Howe says that the clearance process normally focuses on the question of whether an applicant "displays any of the character flaws of a known traitor," such as Burgess or Maclean. "The existing personnel security suitability standards concentrate on symptoms, such as substance abuse, homosexuality, or excessive indebtedness without, in my opinion, an adequate understanding of the breakdown of the human decision-making process.

"Why does one individual accept constraints and another take the risk of committing espionage? Conscience does not necessarily make cowards of us all. The profile of a traitor may not be significantly different from that of many sociopaths or felons. Loyalty to country has become so abstract that an act of treason is not necessarily different from any other serious crime."

Spies also usually have two other characteristics: They relish the secret world of intrigue and they enjoy the chance to show others up as fools. This motivation, interestingly, often makes it easy to turn agents into double agents for the agent sees no difference between serving one country or another. He simply wants to be a spy. A former CIA officer tells of an agency specialist in recruiting in Latin America. "He was so good that we used to say that if he and a candidate got on an elevator on the first floor, the candidate would be recruited by the fifth floor." The CIA recruiter primarily used blandishment, not blackmail, to sign up prospects.

Intelligence officers, whether working for the CIA or the KGB, are not spies. They are loyal employees of their governments. Agents spying on their own country are traitors, and traitors know no loyalty except to themselves.

The typical spy enjoys deception and may have a personality bordering on, or well into, the psychotic. A Washington psychiatrist with a practice that includes CIA officials said she had learned enough of the secret world to see John Walker as someone who does not resemble the kind of people who hire spies.

In a discussion about Walker she said, "I think you might be

startled to see how neatly John Walker fits the classic description
of the antisocial personality. It is also referred to as the sociopath
or psychopath." She then produced a textbook list of words used
to describe a sociopath. Some of the actual words had been used
by counter-espionage specialists to describe Walker:

Incapable of loyalty to individuals or groups. Grossly selfish,
narcissistic, egocentric. Callous, manipulative, and contemptuous
of others. Impulsive—with little long-term planning. Unable to
feel guilt, remorse, or shame. Unable to learn from experience
and punishment. Low frustration tolerance. Tends to blame others for his behavior. Superficially charming. Untruthful. Insin-
cere. Shows poor judgment and has little insight. Incapable of
love at any deep level. Feels little anxiety or conflicts (*acts* rather
than feels). Has shallow interpersonal relations throughout his
life. Rarely commits suicide (has no sense of his own responsibility). Dramatic, exhibitionistic behavior. Often plays the impostor.
Often involved in criminal acts.

"Individual therapy," she said, "is almost impossible with
this type of patient. He sees nothing wrong with the way he is. He
blames others, and so has little to report about himself. He cannot form the necessary alliance with the therapist. When put into
a therapy group with other types of patients, the antisocial personality often manipulates and disrupts."

She had one more observation: "Walker will probably do
very well in prison. He'll manipulate others and he'll get along.
To the antisocial personality, one place is about the same as any
other place."

Because a walk-in like Walker has no loyalty, he leaves no
trail of ideological activities that would raise loyalty questions.
The walk-in does not spend years or months studying Lenin before conversion to espionage. A typical walk-in becomes a traitor
by choosing one day to cross an embassy threshold, walking out
of the world that keeps secrets and into the world that buys them.
And the secrets often are devastatingly important to the United
States.

Walk-ins who "volunteer information for sale," says a report
by the Senate Select Committee on Intelligence, are "the most
dangerous agents of all," accounting for "the greatest losses of
the most highly classified information." From the 1960s to the

1980s major Soviet intelligence successes have not been earned by
the clandestine efforts of the GRU and KGB but by walk-ins.

The walk-ins have included civilians and uniformed men
from the Army, Navy, Marine Corps, Air Force, and major defense contractors. Other walk-ins have worked for the CIA, the
National Security Agency, and the FBI. One of those highly dangerous walk-ins the Senate committee mentioned was an Army
sergeant with a menial job. He was assigned as a driver to Major
General Garrison B. Cloverdale, the assistant director and chief
of staff of NSA. After top-secret meetings with officials in Washington, Cloverdale often left his briefcase with the sergeant and
told him to return it to his office.

The driver, Sergeant Jack F. Dunlap, photographed what he
found in the general's briefcase and passed the film to a Soviet
intelligence officer whom the sergeant called "the bookkeeper."
He stole and copied an unknown number of classified documents.

Dunlap lived high on his spy money. He bought a cabin
cruiser, a Jaguar, and drove a late-model Cadillac to his job at
NSA. He never was under suspicion because he was, after all, a
wounded, decorated combat veteran of Korea, and a married
man with five children. No one seemed to wonder about his obvious wealth.

Because he was a soldier, he had not been required to take a
polygraph test when the Army assigned him to NSA. But, when
he made application to leave the Army while remaining at the
agency, he was hooked up to a polygraph machine. The tests,
which showed that he had engaged in some "petty thievery" and
"immoral conduct," triggered a deeper investigation. Dunlap was
assigned to a job in an office where he had no access to classified
documents. He knew that his spying days were numbered.

Shortly after the investigation began, Dunlap tried to kill
himself with sleeping pills. A little while afterward he drove to an
isolated spot, put a hose from the exhaust pipe into the partially
open window of his car and started the engine. His body was
found the next day.

Dunlap was buried, with full military honors, at Arlington
National Cemetery on July 25, 1963. The following month his
widow turned over to FBI agents a stack of classified papers she
had found while going through his belongings. The extent of his

espionage was never revealed and "the bookkeeper" was never identified.

On the day that investigators found Dunlap's body, Victor Norris Hamilton, an NSA Arabic-speaking specialist on the Near East, coincidentally turned up as a defector in Moscow. The Soviet newspaper *Izvestia* reported that Hamilton had asked for political asylum. He charged NSA with intercepting and decoding messages between Arab countries and their UN missions.

The United States announced on the same day that Hamilton had been discharged in 1959 from NSA for psychiatric reasons. Other sources said that although Hamilton did show signs of mental illness, NSA nevertheless kept him on the payroll because of his language skills.

Dunlap and Hamilton were the third and fourth known NSA traitors of the 1960s. Two NSA cryptographic specialists, William Martin and Bernon Mitchell, appeared at a Moscow press conference on September 6, 1960. They had slipped into Mexico and boarded a Soviet ship. Both homosexuals, they apparently volunteered to sell secrets to the KGB without having been blackmailed. (Blackmailing was a common practice at a time when homosexuality was far less tolerated than it would be two decades later.)

Martin and Mitchell did both diplomatic and military damage. They said that NSA, then little known to the public, had broken the codes of diplomatic message traffic of more than half the nations that encode their diplomatic message traffic. They said they had defected after three years at NSA because they did not approve of U.S. intelligence-gathering methods. The NSA defectors could give the Soviets a good idea of what kind of Soviet communications the United States were pulling from the ether and the seabed and successfully decrypting. It is unlikely that between them these traitors could have provided much information to the Soviets on U.S. communications and cryptography.

The Soviet ability to read encrypted U.S. communications between, to, or from military facilities and embassies would be of immense value in peace as well as in war. The contents of military and diplomatic communications are the nation's most secret materials. In World War II, Great Britain's most important weapon against German submarines and Luftwaffe bombers was a machine called Enigma—a copy of the German cryptographic device that created seemingly uncrackable codes. Enigma, based on original work done by Polish and French intelligence before those countries fell to the Germans, gave the Anglo-American armies and navies incredible insights into axis activities. In some instances the knowledge of German and Japanese communications led to clear-cut Allied victories. The decisive naval Battle of Midway in the Pacific and the Battle of the Atlantic, the campaign against the German U-boats, were won largely through Allied code-breaking efforts. Many other battles—on land, at sea, and in the air—were won because the Allies knew about enemy intentions, their order of battle, and even their logistics problems.

U.S. military communications are believed to have remained uncompromised through the postwar years. The first sustained penetration of secret U.S. communications channels coincided with the beginning of the 1960s walk-in parade when U.S. Army Warrant Officer Joseph G. Helmich, Jr., a code specialist at SACEUR headquarters in Paris, decided to sell some secrets.

Helmich, a lavish spender who lived beyond his means, was continually in debt. So many of his checks bounced at military clubs that one day in early 1962 his commanding officer warned him that if he did not clear up at least $500 worth of them he would be court-martialed. The officer gave Helmich a deadline for making good on the checks.

Helmich unsuccessfully tried to get a bank loan. Then, a day before the court-martial deadline, he walked into the Soviet Embassy in Paris and offered American and NATO communications secrets for cash. He sold the Soviets a maintenance manual, technical information, rotors, keylists for the KL-7 crypto system, the top-secret code machine in wide use by U.S. and allied military services and embassies. He also had knowledge of the operation of the KW-26, another code machine. As a warrant officer in the SACEUR communications center, Helmich had extensive access to U.S.-NATO diplomatic and military communications.

In 1964, Helmich was questioned about his lavish spending, but the investigation was dropped. Transferred to Fort Bragg, North Carolina, where he continued as a cryptographic custodian, Helmich kept up his work for the KGB, traveling to France and Mexico City to meet with his Soviet case officers. The FBI later estimated that he had earned about $131,000 in his three-year espionage career, which ended abruptly in 1966.

The FBI, which apparently did not learn about the loss until 1980, began questioning Helmich in August of that year. Helmich said at first that he had gotten some money from the Soviets but that he had not given them any classified information, although he did admit to having been paid $20,000 for what he did give them. In early 1981, Helmich was seen in Canada with known Soviet agents. Questioned again, he began talking. He was soon charged with espionage—for which there is no statute of limitations. Tried and convicted, he was sentenced to life imprisonment.

Walk-ins come from across the full spectrum of organizations that possess national security secrets—the armed services, federal agencies, and the defense industry. In an analysis of what caused several Americans to become spies in the late 1970s and early 1980s, the FBI saw money as the root of motivation for Helmich and four others who sold national security secrets to the Soviets:

William Holden Bell. An employee of the Hughes Aircraft Corporation, Bell sold secrets of several projects to a representative of the Polish intelligence service that worked closely with the KGB. He was more a go-along than a walk-in, for he was carefully recruited and led into espionage by a neighbor who turned out to be a Polish intelligence officer. Bell received about $110,000 in cash and gold coins worth about $60,000.

James Durward Harper, Jr. Using contacts among defense contractors in the swath of high-technology California known as Silicon Valley, Harper also sold information on missiles to the Polish intelligence service. Harper's "sole motivation for committing espionage was financial," the FBI analysis says. "Harper had no political agenda, and was most unsophisticated in the art of spying." He was paid at least $255,000.

David Henry Barnett. A former CIA intelligence officer, he sold the Soviets the names of CIA officers and Indonesian agents recruited by the CIA. "Barnett," says the analysis, "admitted he had sought out the Soviets and was recruited by them. . . ." He was paid $92,000.

Thomas P. Cavanagh. An engineer at the Northrop Corporation, he tried to sell secrets about the Stealth bomber to Soviet agents. He promised to deliver secrets for ten years for payment of $25,000 a month. But he made the promise to FBI undercover agents and was arrested for espionage.

Ronald W. Pelton, a former communications specialist at the NSA, was another traitor seduced by cash. He sold the secrets of U.S. communications interception techniques to the Soviets. He earned an estimated $35,000 during his five years as a spy.

John Walker and Pelton literally were walk-ins; both went through the front door of the Soviet Embassy in Washington. Three other spies detected in 1984 and 1985 also were walk-ins. *Edward L. Howard,* a former CIA employee, offered his services to the Soviets and then defected to the Soviet Union just as he was to be arrested by the FBI, which had him under surveillance. *Richard W. Miller,* the first FBI agent ever convicted of espionage, walked into the arms of a beautiful Soviet émigrée who worked for the KGB. *Randy Jeffries,* a Capitol Hill messenger, saw an opportunity to sell what he was supposed to destroy—classified congressional transcripts. He hoped to make a business of delivering material to the Soviets.

Also during the 1980s, unknown to the general public—or even to many ranking Pentagon officials—many walk-ins wore U.S. military uniforms. And, unlike civilians, these "military march-ins" often receive scant if any punishment for attempting or actually committing espionage.

A notorious case broke in December 1980 when Second Lieutenant Christopher M. Cooke, an Air Force officer assigned to a nuclear missile silo, walked into the Soviet Embassy and offered information about U.S. strategic missiles. Cooke was no master spy. He made a telephone call *from* the embassy to inquire about his car, and was detected by an amazed FBI agent on routine wiretap-monitoring duties.

The FBI, following procedures worked out between the Pentagon and the Department of Justice, alerted the Air Force to Cooke's apparent plans to become a spy. The Air Force Office of Special Investigations began questioning Cooke and, in the course of the interrogations, promised him a deal if he confessed. He thereupon confessed, expecting that he would escape serious punishment by admitting his plan to commit espionage.

When Cooke's case reached higher authority, however, an Air Force general denounced the deal—"Cooke is a traitor of the first magnitude and treason is the crime"—and ordered a general court-martial. Cooke claimed a foul, and the case was passed up to the U.S. Court of Military Appeals, which ordered charges dropped because of prosecutional misconduct. Cooke went free. Later he legally changed his name so he would not have to bear the embarrassment of being known as the man who once offered to be a spy for the Soviet Union.

The Soviets have not had to recruit Americans in uniform. U.S. servicemen have made contact—or appear to have planned to—on their own. In each of the following cases a U.S. serviceman has attempted to sell military secrets. Some were caught while attempting to make the sale to the Soviets or to Eastern Bloc nationals; others were apparently still hoarding secrets in anticipation of such a move.

■ In September 1977, Marine Corporal Joel Yager, stationed at the Marine Corps Air Station in Iwakuni, Japan, attempted to sell a secret document and three confidential ones to "a foreign national," who turned out to be employed by the Naval Investigative Service. Yager was not court-martialed.

■ A crewman on board the strategic missile submarine *James K. Polk*, Seaman Michael R. Murphy, called the Soviet Mission to the United Nations in June 1981 and offered to make what was later officially described as "a deal that would be beneficial to both the Soviets and himself." Murphy, who had a secret clearance, was honorably discharged from the Navy.

■ In June 1982, Intelligence Specialist Second Class Brian P. Horton, who was stationed at the highly sensitive Fleet Intelligence Center in Norfolk, Virginia, contacted the Soviets. When Horton wanted to reach the Soviets he did not try their embassy on Sixteenth Street in Washington but contacted the relatively unknown Soviet Military Office on Belmont Road, just off Massachusetts Avenue in northwest Washington. Horton, who had a top-secret security clearance, was convicted at a general court-martial on five counts of failure to report contact with a "hostile country national" and on one count of solicitation to commit espionage. His six-year sentence was later reduced to three.

■ Marine Private First Class Brian E. Slavens, a guard at a weapons center in Adak, Alaska, attempted to sell classified information to the Soviets, actually entering the embassy in Washington. He pleaded guilty to attempted espionage and received a two-year sentence.

■ The same month that Slavens visited the embassy, August 1982, Seaman Apprentice Ernest C. Pugh went from the Defense Language School in Monterey, California, to the Soviet Consulate in San Francisco and said he wanted to defect. The Soviets declined the offer, and the U.S. Navy no longer wanted him. He was given a "convenience-of-the-government" discharge.

■ In December 1982, David A. Hediger, a yeoman striker* on a submarine tender, also called the Soviet Military Office on Belmont Road. No action was taken against him, apparently because he had no access to classified material.

■ Aviation Anti-Submarine Warfare Operator Second Class Robert W. Ellis also contacted the Soviet Consulate in San Francisco and offered to sell documents from the naval air complex at Moffett Field. At the time, February 1983, he was with a patrol squadron based at Moffett. Apparently the FBI learned of his contact with the Soviets and set him up to sell an FBI agent classified documents. He was sentenced to three years confinement. (When Thomas Cavanagh was similarly duped by the FBI, he was sentenced to life imprisonment; see Chapter 12.)

■ Hospitalman Third Class Jeffery L. Pickering, in June 1983, sent a secret document to the Soviet Embassy. He was sentenced to five years confinement.

■ In the same month Marine Private First Class Alan D. Coberly, while AWOL from the First Marine Division in the Far East, went into the Soviet Embassy in Manila. He was sentenced to eighteen months.

■ A month later, in July 1983, also in the Philippines, a seaman striking for the intelligence specialist rating, Hans P. Wold, was picked up by a Navy shore patrol for being absent. He was found to be carrying undeveloped film of top-secret, compartmented information, apparently from his ship, the carrier *Ranger*. He received a sentence of four years.

■ And a month later another seaman striking for intelligence specialist, John R. Maynard, was taken into custody for being absent from duty. He was on the staff of the Commander in Chief

---

* U.S. Navy designation for non-rated sailors assigned to an on-the-job training program for a specific specialty.

of the Pacific Fleet. Investigators found in his locker fifty-one top-secret documents. He was sentenced to three years—far less than one month per top-secret document stolen.

■ Michael R. Moore, a Marine lance corporal, in February 1984 was apprehended for being AWOL. He had papers indicating his intention to defect to the Soviet Union through the embassy in Manila. He was given a "convenience-of-the-government" discharge.

■ When Operations Specialist First Class Bruce L. Kearn disappeared from the landing ship *Tuscaloosa* in March 1984, a search of his living space revealed a briefcase that contained 147 secret microfiche, seven confidential cryptographic publications, several other files, and a mass of child pornographic material. His sentence was one and a half years of confinement.

■ In April 1984, Marine Corporal Robert E. Cordrey contacted Soviet and Czech officials offering them information about U.S. nuclear, biological, and chemical warfare projects. Cordrey, an instructor at the Nuclear, Biological and Chemical Defense School at Camp Lejeune, North Carolina, had a secret clearance. He was convicted in August 1984 of eighteen counts of attempting to contact foreign representatives for the purpose of selling secrets. "The charges were not contested," says a government report, "and the case was not disclosed to the public until January 1985 due to the extremely sensitive nature of the investigation." Cordrey was sentenced to twelve years at hard labor. But his sentence was reduced to two years.

■ A radioman striker, Michael T. Tobias, on the landing ship *Peoria,* conspired to extort money from the U.S. Government by claiming he planned to sell key cards to an unnamed country. He took the cards, which he was supposed to destroy, off the ship and was later seen by government surveillance agents near the Soviet Consulate in San Francisco. He was arrested after attempting to make a deal with the Secret Service. Officials said that he had planned to leave the country. Tried in federal court rather than by court martial—this was after the 1985 arrests of the Walkers—Tobias was found guilty of four counts of conspiracy and three counts of theft of government property. He was sentenced to twenty years.

■ Airman First Class Bruce Ott, at Beale Air Force Base in California, was arrested in January 1986 when he attempted to sell papers on the SR-71 spy plane to two FBI agents posing as Soviet intelligence officers. Ott, who had hoped to be paid $160,000 for the documents, was sentenced to twenty-five years in prison by a court-martial.

■ In October of that year former Air Force Staff Sergeant Allen J. Davies contacted the Soviet Consulate in San Francisco offering information on U.S. reconnaissance projects, including electronic and infrared technologies—"out of revenge against the Air Force," according to a government affidavit. Davies had been "involuntarily separated" from the Air Force in 1984 for "poor job performance."

The fate of accused civilian spies is determined by the Department of Justice, whose major decisions about espionage are usually revealed in public courtrooms. Accused spies in uniform, however, may be handled in secret ways through proceedings that may never come to the attention of senior Department of Defense officials. This is because, by tradition, court martial decisions in the armed services are made at the level of the accused's commanding officer. And espionage had often been viewed as simply another crime to be settled by court martial.

H. Lawrence Garrett III, then General Counsel to the Department of Defense, touched on the issue when, in an apologia of military justice, he stated that, rather than an adjunct of civilian justice, "military justice is intended to provide for the fair adjudication and disposition of serious offenses affecting good order and discipline *within the military community*" [emphasis added].

Garrett thus reflected the view that military espionage, like military theft, belongs to the military. Although the effects of espionage surely reverberate far beyond the military community, the services have usually confined their interest to what problems the crime causes in the military unit involved, not to its impact on national security.

Theoretically, the Department of Justice has precedence over the Department of Defense in determining whether a serviceman (such as John Walker's son, Seaman Michael Walker) is brought to trial in a federal courtroom or left to the disposition of military justice. In practice, the Department of Defense has been allowed to handle most seemingly small-scale espionage cases involving servicemen.

The authors, wishing to know more details on these cases—especially the prison time actually served—requested further information from Garrett. His office passed the inquiry along to the Office of Naval Intelligence, apparently because the Navy had suffered the most from traitors in uniform.

In ONI, a veteran intelligence officer said, "What you are looking for, a data base on the disposition of espionage cases, simply does not exist." The officer said that he believed Garrett had handed down the list to the Navy for a second reason—because, of all the services, only the Navy has an office dedicated to national security matters. The other services have various ways of handling internal espionage cases. But there is no Pentagon or Justice Department system for coordinating the cases so that one service can compare how another is handling servicemen spies.

The Navy, long a special KGB target, has the largest number of cases and handles the largest number of inquiries about them. "Starting with the Walker case," the ONI officer said, "we have been asked for information from everybody and his cousin —not quite up to the President. We weren't able to get information we thought we had."

No verbatim records, for example, exist for some of the courts martial. Nor are there records showing where convicted sailors did their time. "We would like to track some of these people, find out what happened to them after sentencing. We haven't been able to because the information that does exist is not easily collated," the officer said. "Histories do not exist. You've seen what Butts had. He was just giving you an idea of what *we*—the Navy—knows *now*."

The officer was referring to testimony of Rear Admiral John Butts, then Director of Naval Intelligence, who was asked by Congress in the wake of the Walker case, to reveal the extent of espionage in the Navy. Neither the Army nor the Air Force could supply such information. (The list that begins on page 417 of this book was assembled by the authors from numerous official sources, including the Butts testimony.)

Butts' startling revelations about Navy and Marine spy cases led Secretary of the Navy John Lehman in 1986 to initiate a change in the manner in which the Navy handled national security cases.

After a year of effort, in January 1987 he published an AL-

NAV—a message addressed to the entire Navy and Marine Corps —directing that cases involving national security be handled at much higher levels than previously. Lehman, outraged about plea bargains and light sentences, ordered a tightening of courts-martial procedures. The ALNAV specifically required the Naval Investigative Service "to notify the Judge Advocate General [of the Navy] of national security investigations to ensure notification to SecNav [Secretary of the Navy] and other competent authority" to limit the disposition of such cases and provide guidance to the commanders involved.

Lehman told the authors, "We were letting too many of these men who stole our secrets get away."

Concerned about the theft of secrets, he ordered a cutback in the 860,000 security clearances held by Navy and Marine Corps personnel and civilian employees. Soon Navy publicists proudly announced that the equivalent of 197,000 clearances had been withdrawn and 146,200 had been downgraded. Although these numbers are open to interpretation and question, Lehman forced the Navy, more than the other services, to think security. But the tide was against him, as "the system" demanded that everything possible be classified.

Even as John Lehman was revising the Navy's policy for handling espionage cases and reorganizing naval counter-intelligence, another spy scandal would break that initially seemed destined to rival the Walker-Whitworth story. The new case, involving Marine security guards in Moscow, Leningrad, and Vienna, would again highlight poor U.S. security measures and incompetent counter-intelligence techniques.

This case began when Marine Sergeant Clayton J. Lonetree, at the U.S. Embassy in Moscow, who had been confined to quarters for forty-five days for drinking and lesser infractions, went out on the town after his confinement. By what he thought to be chance, he met, at a Moscow metro stop, Violetta Alexdrovna Sauna, a beautiful, brown-haired, gray-eyed translator at the embassy. Violetta had not given him much attention until that night, when he especially needed a friend to talk to.

Lonetree had taken the only path available for entry into the Marines' security guard program: He had volunteered, giving as his reason a desire to travel and gain "a career-enhancing billet." In August 1984 he began a six-week course at the Marine guard school in Quantico, Virginia, and, along with all the other graduates, was given a top-secret clearance. He could speak a little Russian and German.

Lonetree's first assignment was Moscow. There was little to learn on the job because all guards, whether on station in Moscow or London, had the same duties, as set down in the manual: protecting and safeguarding personnel and classified material in the embassy; conducting security inspections; and reporting violations through the chain of command that went from the Marine sergeant to the civilian security officer (a State Department employee) and up to the ambassador.

Moscow rules were a little different. Marines had to sign a nonfraternization agreement and promise to report all contacts with Soviets. In letters home Lonetree said he had become a minor celebrity, "surrounded" by Muscovites who gawked at him because they had never seen an American Indian. But for all the attention, he was often lonely and morose. He drank more than he should, and, according to a Marine officer familiar with Lonetree's record, he was "a loner and a loser."

Violetta changed all that. After meeting her at the metro stop he saw her now and then at the embassy, but only for an exchange of hellos. Then, in October, they met again, this time on a metro train. "Violetta said she was going home but continued to talk with me after missing her train stop," Lonetree later said. "We got off together at a later stop and began a long walk together, talking about various subjects, including American movies, books, food, likes and dislikes." They walked and talked for about two hours.

Their next opportunity to spend time together came on November 10 at the Marine Ball—an embassy tradition. Annually, the ball blatantly eclipses the nonfraternization agreement, for the Marines get a chance to dance with Soviet women employed at the embassy. To the twenty-odd Marines on the guard force, the agreement made no sense. They flirted openly with the women and, as young Marines inevitably would, they told stories of sexual conquests that sometimes were consummated in the notorious Marine barracks known as the Marine House.

At the ball Lonetree and Violetta danced and talked, but they had to postpone any dates because he had an important out-of-town assignment. Despite his poor disciplinary record, Lonetree had been selected as one of the guards drawn from various European embassies and dispatched to Geneva to augment the security force for the November 1985 summit meeting of President Reagan and Soviet leader Mikhail Gorbachev. Marine sources, maintaining that Lonetree had been selected through a lottery, deny that Lonetree had been selected because someone decided that an Indian on the presidential guard force would be a good image for propaganda purposes.

When Lonetree returned to Moscow his romance with Violetta deepened. He met her family, looked through her photo album, and, in January, they began making love in the small apartment she shared with her sister and mother. By then he had extended his tour of duty in the hardship post of Moscow and she had lost her job.

"We both agreed that it was not safe for us to be seen together in public or near her house," Lonetree recounted. "I would utilize counter-surveillance techniques in leaving the embassy and going to Violetta's house. These techniques included changing modes of transportation, vary[ing] my routes, back-tracking, and wearing different coats and changing them. I used the counter-surveillance to avoid being followed by the KGB."

Late in January, Violetta introduced Lonetree to her "Uncle Sasha," whose real name was Aleksiy Yefimov, an agent of the KGB, according to U.S. intelligence sources. Lonetree met several times with Uncle Sasha, who asked the Marine if he would like to be a friend of the Soviet Union. "At that time," according to Lonetree, "he began asking me a series of questions which were written on a list he held on his lap. He said the list had been prepared by a friend of his who is a general in the KGB and also a member of the Central Committee."

Now it was Uncle Sasha's turn to show Lonetree some photos, not of family members but of Marines and other people who worked at the U.S. Embassy. There were also some snapshots of men and women. Lonetree rearranged the photos to show Uncle Sasha who was married to whom. Lonetree also described in detail the layout of the ambassador's office. What else Lonetree told Uncle Sasha—and what he did for him and Violetta—may never be known because of the events that followed.

On March 9, 1986, the day before Lonetree's departure for the Marine guard force at the U.S. Embassy in Vienna, Uncle

Sasha gave Lonetree a piece of paper and dictated a statement, which the Marine remembered as this: "I am a friend of the Soviet Union. I will always be a friend of the Soviet Union, and will continue to be their friend." Lonetree signed his name to the paper and Uncle Sasha retained it. At this or another meeting with Uncle Sasha, Lonetree was asked to place a bug in the ambassador's office. He later said that he had refused, but that he did provide "plans," which authorities have not described.

Uncle Sasha—or, to use his name, Yefimov—said he wanted to continue to see Lonetree in Vienna. When the Marine agreed to meet him, Yefimov gave him what U.S. counter-intelligence officers call the "Vienna Procedure," a highly detailed set of instructions for setting up face-to-face meetings between Soviet spy handlers and their agents. Reflecting on that last Moscow meeting, Lonetree somehow managed to believe that "the KGB did not have me yet." He was wrong.

Soon after Lonetree reported for duty in Vienna, he was startled by a call from Yefimov—direct to the phone at the embassy's main guard post, where at that moment Lonetree happened to be on duty. Vienna is a city where the KGB is especially efficient.

Yefimov, stepping up the pressure on Lonetree, asked for photographs of U.S. workers in the embassy and other classified information. The Marine provided the information, and the KGB officer responded with the equivalent of about $1,000 in Austrian currency. Later, Lonetree handed over a floor plan of the embassy, a phone directory, and the names of the Austrian cleaning women, along with the rooms each woman was responsible for. He received $1,500 in U.S. cash then, and later an Austrian currency payment equivalent to $1,000. Lonetree bought Violetta a dress and Yefimov a silk tie.

Yefimov questioned Lonetree about a political officer at the embassy, wanted to know whether any Marines were homosexual or had alcohol problems, and asked Lonetree what he knew about the ambassador's secretary. "Sasha wanted me to ask her out," Lonetree recalled, "but I really never had plans to do this." He did not give the names of any "queers, dopers, or drunks" but, oddly, he did name a Marine who had once been an alcoholic but had become a born-again Christian.

Alone one night on guard duty, Lonetree slipped top secret

documents out of the embassy and hid them in a drain pipe on the roof of the Vienna Marine House. He also stole the contents of a burn bag—about 120 documents that included information on America's position on negotiations for a Mutual Balances Forces Reduction agreement with the Soviet Union.

After missing two meetings with an increasingly worried Yefimov, Lonetree showed up on December 12, 1986, at a rendezvous in a restaurant, where Yefimov introduced Lonetree to "George," the KGB officer who was replacing "Uncle Sasha." George, who was stationed in Vienna and spoke good English, immediatetly began questioning Lonetree about the layout of the ambassador's office and the routines of the embassy cleaning staff. There was also talk about getting Lonetree back to Moscow and his beloved Violetta, perhaps with the aid of a Soviet diplomatic passport. "I was never told why they wanted me in the Soviet Union," Lonetree later said. "However, I felt that it was probably for training and not to defect." George told Lonetree the two of them would meet on December 27 to plan the Moscow trip. Lonetree could see that tough, demanding George was no Uncle Sasha. (U.S. intelligence identified George as a KGB officer who goes by the name Yuriy Lysov.) "I realized in light of the Walker case, I was in trouble," Lonetree said. On Sunday, December 14, two days after his introduction to George, Lonetree went to an embassy Christmas party. He looked around the room for the one person who might understand, the CIA station chief in Vienna.

U.S. intelligence officials tightly hold information about what happened next. But some sources say that a high-ranking CIA officer listened to Lonetree and instinctively moved to make Lonetree a double agent to get more information on the KGB presence in that city so favored by the KGB. To the CIA, information about the KGB in Vienna had to be more important than working up an espionage case against a Marine guard. Presumably, the CIA wanted Lonetree to meet Lysov on December 27 and see what developed. There also may have been interest in letting Lonetree sneak back into Moscow.

But interagency warfare soon broke out. Relations between the United States and the Soviet Union were extremely chilly at the time. In the wake of the Daniloff-Zakharov swap, the United States had laid off many Soviet nationals working for the embassy and consulate, including Violetta.* Then the Soviet Government had angrily withdrawn all of the rest of its citizens. The State Department did not want any unnecessary trouble, and neither did the U.S. Embassy, where diplomats were doing chores once done by Soviets. The diplomats were augmented by Marines who were given extra duty in what became known as the "charforce."

The Department of Defense, stung by a swarm of servicemen spies, had its own position: There would be no turning of Lonetree. His fate belonged in the hands of the Pentagon, not the CIA. According to a Memorandum of Understanding, known as the MOU, jurisdiction belonged to the Naval Investigative Service—although the Justice Department, if it wished, could claim precedence in an espionage case. The dispute was finally settled at a high government level: Turn Lonetree over to NIS agents for questioning.

On Christmas Eve 1986, two NIS agents took Lonetree to a room in the Hotel Strudlhof in Vienna. They told him he was accused of unlawful solicitation, acquisition, possession, and disclosure of sensitive and classified information. He was also charged with failing to report contacts with "representatives of a hostile country." A little after 7 p.m. he signed a statement acknowledging and waiving his rights. "I have decided," the statement said, "that I do not desire to remain silent, consult with a retained or appointed lawyer, or have a lawyer present at this time."

Questioning continued for days, ending finally on December 29 at the Hilton Hotel in London. Lonetree told his story, from the chance meeting at the metro station in Moscow to the arranged meeting with Uncle Sasha and George in Vienna. The NIS detained Lonetree and immediately launched a widespread investigation of Marine guards who were, and who had been, stationed in Moscow, Leningrad, and Vienna.

In March 1987, more than two months after formal espionage charges were made against Lonetree, the NIS arrested twenty-one-year-old Corporal Arnold Bracy on suspicion of espionage. His Moscow tour had overlapped Lonetree's. Now came

---

* She got a job in the Irish Embassy. Lonetree called her there, from a Marine House phone in Vienna, at least four times without arousing suspicion.

incredible charges that the two Marines had frequently allowed KGB agents into the embassy at night, giving the Soviets access to secret documents and cryptographic equipment.

In the panic that followed, embassy officials, fearing that the KGB had bugged communications rooms, cut back messages to and from Washington. The entire Marine guard force in Moscow was replaced. Secretary of Defense Weinberger said that the United States had suffered "a very great loss." Congressional critics clamored for the razing of the unfinished and unoccupied building that was to be the new U.S. Embassy, which was said to be riddled with electronic listening devices.

A third Marine, Staff Sergeant Robert S. Stufflebeam, deputy leader of the Moscow guard unit, was charged with failing to report fraternizing with Soviet women. Out of the past came still another accusation: A former Marine, John J. Weirick, was arrested on suspicion of espionage while he had been a guard at the U.S. Consulate in Leningrad from November 1981 to November 1983.

Three major investigations competed with each other. The State Department was looking into how and why State administered the Marines but had nothing to do with selecting them. The Pentagon was examining how Marine guards were selected and trained. NIS was expanding its criminal investigation, sending some seventy agents out to interview hundreds of former Marine guards.

By June the NIS investigation was in shambles. The NIS and the Marines asked for help from the Department of Justice, which declined to give any. Weirick was released from the brig, a free civilian who, it turned out, could not be court-martialed because of a statute of limitations peculiar to the Universal Code of Military Justice; the set of laws under which Weirick, a civilian, was arrested. The Marines had to drop all charges against Bracy, who had recanted a confession that he said he had given under duress. The Marines also dismissed charges that Lonetree had allowed KGB agents to wander through the embassy.

The NIS was back to what Lonetree had originally told them about Uncle Sasha and Violetta and George. Lonetree was court martialed, and in August 1987 an eight-officer jury convicted him of thirteen counts of espionage, conspiracy, and failure to report contacts with Soviet citizens. He was also specifically convicted of revealing to the Soviets the names of CIA agents. Lonetree was given a thirty-year sentence.

By the time Stufflebeam faced a court martial the following month, the case against him had dwindled to charges of having sex with Soviet women. He finally was accused only of drinking in off-limits Moscow bars. For this trivial offense he was demoted in rank from staff sergeant to sergeant. Thus did the great Marine spy scandal end.

U.S. intelligence officials still insisted that a serious breach of security had occurred in the embassy early in 1986. But the NIS investigation had uncovered only the Lonetree incident. There seemed no way to prove the most shocking claims, which even Secretary Weinberger had apparently believed: that KGB agents had wandered at large in the U.S. Embassy.

Yet, it was all possible. No one would think twice about seeing a Marine escorting a Russian around the embassy, even at night. After all, that's what Marines and Russians were for—to do the chores: for the Russian, perhaps repairing a broken light switch; for the Marine, making sure that was all the Russian was doing. You can't be too careful.

Much could be learned from the incident—especially lessons about interagency rivalry in espionage cases and about the use of NIS agents in major cases. But, given the history of counter-espionage in the United States, little will probably be learned. The KGB seems to be ahead in the espionage war, mostly because the KGB *does* learn lessons.

Valuable as the walk-in is to Soviet spymasters, they would, given the choice, prefer a made-in-Russia spy over an American walk-in. Their next choice is recruitment. And, just as U.S. enlisted men were prime targets for recruitment in the 1960s, they still are in the 1980s. This was spectacularly demonstrated in 1987 with revelations about attempts to recruit members of the elite Marine guards at the U.S. Embassy in Moscow.

U.S. counter-espionage officials, as so often happens when a spy case breaks, professed shock and surprise about the Moscow Marine affair. The officials should not have been surprised, for in a classified report analyzing KGB techniques, Marine guards are specifically singled out as likely candidates for recruitment.

Sometimes, however, recruitment backfires. Professional as

they are, Soviet intelligence officers sometimes pick the wrong U.S. serviceman to recruit.

Hungarian-born Otto Attila Gilbert arrived in the United States in 1957 in the wave of Hungarians fleeing the Soviet occupation of their homeland and became a naturalized citizen in 1964. He may have entered the United States as a trained illegal or he may have been recruited after he arrived. How many times he was called to duty has not been disclosed by U.S. investigators. But it is known that sometime in the late 1970s he was drawn into an attempt to recruit a U.S. Army officer. The operation was run by the Hungarian Intelligence Service, which, like the Polish Intelligence Service, coordinates its activities with the KGB in the United States.

The plot began in December 1977 when Army Warrant Officer Janos Szmolka, like Gilbert a Hungarian-born naturalized U.S. citizen, made a trip to Budapest to visit his mother. Szmolka at that time was stationed in the Army's Criminal Investigation Detachment at Mainz, West Germany.

Szmolka was in his mother's home when a family friend took him aside and told him that a "representative of the government" wanted to talk to him privately. Szmolka apprehensively agreed to meet the representative at a restaurant. The man introduced himself as Lajos Perlaki and said he was a Hungarian intelligence officer. In an unusually blunt recruitment speech, Perlaki said that Hungary wanted Szmolka to spy in exchange for "favorable treatment" of Szmolka's mother and married sister, his closest blood kin.

Army security regulations called for Szmolka to report the recruitment attempt. He had to weigh the regulations against fears that the promise of favorable treatment implied unfavorable treatment if he did not cooperate. He knew from briefings that what had happened to him had happened numerous times to soldiers with relatives in Eastern Bloc countries. How many of them had reported such blackmail threats no one knew.

In January 1978, Szmolka returned to Hungary. While he was visiting his sister in Budapest he was passed a letter telling him how to contact Perlaki in a restaurant. Perlaki promised Szmolka "tens of thousands of dollars" for spying and then gave him a list of seemingly innocuous documents he was to collect for the Hungarians: a copy of the publicly available Uniform Code of

Military Justice, training manuals that contained information about the use of polygraphs, procedures for military police investigation, and a copy of the standard operating procedures for Szmolka's criminal investigation detachment. Perlaki was using a traditional technique to test the apprentice agent by getting him to deliver unimportant information whose disclosure could do no apparent harm to his country.

Six months later Szmolka and his wife drove to Budapest, picked up his mother, and headed back to West Germany. At the Hungarian-Austrian border, guards ordered Szmolka to pull out of the line of vehicles waiting to cross. He was sent forward to the border and waved on to Austria. Just before he entered Austria his car was ordered to stop at a hut in the checkpoint's no-man's-land, and a smiling Perlaki appeared to tell him that all his future crossings would be as easy as this one.

Soon after Szmolka's mother flew home from the visit—the first that she had ever been allowed—he began getting phone calls and letters from Hungarian intelligence officials. But he said he was unable to go into Hungary soon again because he feared that the Army would become suspicious.

The Hungarians eased the pressure on him, waiting until December 1979 before insisting on a meeting, not in Budapest but in Vienna, the Soviets' favorite spy city. At the meeting Szmolka met Perlaki and Vince Konc, who acted as if he was Perlaki's superior. The two intelligence officers berated Szmolka for his failure to appear in Hungary or supply the material requested. Szmolka then did hand over some documents, and said he had some complaining to do.

He had not seen any improvement in the treatment of his mother, he said. She could barely get by on her government pension. Don't worry, they told him. She soon would be getting additional money that would come from Hungarian intelligence coffers but would appear to come from him. Perlaki and Konc, alternating protests of friendship with harangues about the need for information, began questioning Szmolka intensely about his knowledge of NATO war plans. They told him they needed data on the deployment of new Pershing missiles to Western Europe, the location of storage sites of nuclear weapons, and details about cryptographic communications. They promised him a minimum of $20,000 if he could get them an Army cryptographic machine.

Szmolka was stunned. He tried to explain that he had no access to such top-secret information. They pressed him, telling him to use his investigator's credentials to get into restricted areas. They also told him to look for financially strapped soldiers or civilians who could get this information.

When Szmolka said that he would soon be reassigned to the United States and would have even less chance of getting information to them, they gave him what spies call accommodation addresses in Hungary, instructions for using a code, and the equivalent of about $650 in Austrian and West German currency. They assured him that if he had something to hand over to them, arrangements could be made for delivery in the United States.

Szmolka soon learned that his mother was indeed getting a monthly supplement to her pension checks. He had no further chance to visit her, however, because he was about to leave for his next duty assignment—Fort Gordon, near Augusta, Georgia.

The U.S. Army Signal Corps, whose responsibilities include maintaining White House communications, maintains a cryptographic school at Fort Gordon. The Hungarians, and certainly their Soviet colleagues, were especially intrigued about what Szmolka could send them from Fort Gordon. But Szmolka, although still a criminal investigator, had little chance to obtain information that would be of great interest to his handlers. He continued to report regularly through letters to Budapest addresses. The letters contained little of importance. Chief Warrant Officer Szmolka seemed to be a reluctant spy.

Finally, in March 1981, Szmolka again flew to Vienna, where Perlaki and Konc enthusiastically greeted him. They took him in an embassy car to one of Vienna's finest restaurants and began a round of wining and dining. One night, at a restaurant on the outskirts of Vienna, the two Hungarians got so drunk that Szmolka had to drive the car and deposit them at the embassy. A sobered Perlaki paid Szmolka $3,000 for sixteen rolls of undeveloped film of what the U.S. officer had to admit were unclassified documents.

Perlaki, losing his mood of good fellowship, demanded that Szmolka's future deliveries consist of documents stamped secret. Perlaki specified that he wanted the Army documents concerning the movement of nuclear weapons and manuals from the Signal Corps cryptographic school. When Szmolka had the documents he was to write to a mail drop in a Paris suburb and say that he had obtained "1964 Kennedy half-dollars," the code for documents.

The days of meetings ended with Perlaki giving Szmolka another $3,000 in expense money and final instructions on how the transfer of documents should be handled. If Szmolka succeeded in getting the material demanded, he was to ask, in his coded letters to Paris, for the help of a Hungarian agent in the United States. The rendezvous would be either in Augusta or Atlanta.

Szmolka returned to Fort Gordon, signaling his safe arrival with a postcard of the Augusta National Golf Club's thirteenth green and the message, "I enjoyed the vacation and seeing old friends. My return was uneventful and was able to make all of my connecting flights. Thanks for your hospitality and hoping to see you in the future. Timothy."

For nearly a year Szmolka corresponded through the Paris address, telling of limited success in getting some of the information requested. Then, early in 1982, he wrote to say that he had obtained some highly classified information and needed a face-to-face transfer. On March 27, Szmolka got a letter telling him that an agent would meet him in Augusta on April 17, take the material, and pay him an undisclosed sum of money.

Late on the night of April 15, Szmolka's home telephone rang. A man's voice gave the code word identifying him as the agent. He told Szmolka to meet him at noon near the lofty Confederate monument in downtown Augusta. He would have a camera on a multicolored camera strap hanging from his right shoulder and would be carrying a copy of the *Augusta Herald*. Szmolka said he would be driving his van to the rendezvous.

Shortly before noon Otto Attila Gilbert of Forest Hills, New York, walked up to Szmolka and asked, "Where's the Peachtree Plaza Hotel? I am from out of town." Gilbert then accompanied Szmolka to his van. Inside, Szmolka handed classified documents to Gilbert, who paid Szmolka $4,000. The two men stepped out of the van and into a circle of FBI agents.

The agents snapped handcuffs on Gilbert and shook hands with Szmolka, who had been working as an undercover agent passing "authorized material" all along. He and his van were wired with microphones that recorded Gilbert's incriminating words. Faced with the chance of life imprisonment, Gilbert entered into a plea bargain by pleading guilty to conspiring to receive and transmit classified military documents. Three other counts of espionage were dropped. He was sentenced to fifteen years. The Army report on the case does not mention what happened to Szmolka's mother after her son surfaced as a U.S. double agent. Many official espionage stories conclude without neat endings.

The people who accept the walk-ins and the people who recruit the dropouts are members of the largest and in some ways the most professional intelligence organizations in the world—the KGB and GRU. These organizations date back seventy years—a life span almost twice as long as the CIA's. They have a record of success and of failure. But an assessment of the American betrayers, from the Rosenbergs to Lonetree, shows that Soviet spymasters have been extremely impressive at their job. "They are damn good," says a veteran FBI counter-intelligence agent.

4

The Spymasters

America's betrayers—the walk-ins and the come-alongs—are spies who are directed and paid by two Moscow spymasters: General Viktor Chebrikov, head of the KGB and a full member of the ruling Politburo, and, far junior to Chebrikov in political ranking, General of the Army Petr Ivashutin, the chief of Soviet military intelligence, the GRU. Both men are veteran intelligence officers, and the organizations that they direct are the largest, and in many respects the most capable, intelligence organizations in existence.

The KGB or, more formally, Komitet Gosudarstvennoy Bezopasnosti (Committee for State Security), has been the name since 1954 for the Soviet agency responsible for state security. "The basic function of the KGB may be expressed in one guiding phrase: not to allow the collapse of the Soviet Union from inside," according to one Soviet defector. The KGB's mission is portrayed in its symbolic crest: the sword and shield of the Motherland.

KGB agents are generally depicted by the Western media as being large, bullnecked, strong, and stupid. Some still are. Soviet defector Arkady Shevchenko, who had been Under Secretary General of the United Nations, described one KGB operative in New York as "muscular, and blond, he looked like the incarnation of a Gestapo stereotype," who liked to talk about the skyscrapers in Manhattan. "All those shining towers," he said, "they look so strong, so tall, but they're just a house of cards. A few explosions in the right places and *do svidaniya* [good-bye]."

Murder, kidnapping, and intimidation have been the tools of the trade for Soviet security-intelligence organs, from the Cheka to the KGB. But there are several recent examples of KGB and, especially, GRU operatives acting in a sophisticated and innovative manner. A senior U.S. Air Force officer, approached by a Soviet Air Force officer in a Washington-area bar, was asked by U.S. authorities to maintain the contact. Two months later, at a few minutes after seven on a dark and rainy morning, the U.S. officer was caught in northern Virginia traffic on Telegraph Road, driving to his office in the Pentagon.

Suddenly the American officer was distracted from his frustration by a knock on his car window—it was Vladimir Ismaylov, the Soviet colonel making a most unusual, and virtually unobservable, contact with a U.S. officer. Obviously the Russian had done his homework, and done it well.

On another occasion a U.S. government employee was contacted by a Soviet intelligence operative. After some discussions, the contact was allowed to drop. But two or three years later, after the American had moved, been divorced, and changed his car, the same Russian met him in a drugstore to renew the contact.

More devious and concealed operations have also occurred. Donald Ultan, a thirty-year-old, Brooklyn-born employee of the American Embassy in Vienna, was a target for Soviet intelligence because he was a code clerk—the highest priority for KGB and GRU efforts. The complex and somewhat bizarre plan had a Soviet agent who was a naturalized citizen of a Western country invite a close friend of Ultan for a drink.

Thus was arranged a "chance" meeting in a cafe with a semiretired Belgian businessman who was, of course, a KGB officer. This, in turn, was maneuvered into a meeting with Ultan. The KGB officer never appeared to be particularly interested in Ultan, but instead scheduled more encounters with Ultan's friend. There followed many hours of friendly meetings in cafes and coffeehouses, chess playing, and an occasional outing. Ultan, Jewish and fluent in French, began a pleasant association with the

Belgian, who claimed to be Jewish (with relatives in Israel) and who also spoke French.

Only after five months did the KGB agent ask Ultan to provide code information for money. After a brief delay, Ultan went to the embassy security officer and revealed the KGB contact. The Soviet effort against Ultan was sophisticated and, in the words of a U.S. intelligence report on the incident, "well-planned."

Ultan and other Americans involved with codes—such as Navy radio specialists John Walker and Jerry Whitworth—are the top targets of Soviet espionage. According to the U.S. Government's classified manual *Soviet Intelligence Operations Against Americans and U.S. Installations,* "It is this broad category of code clerks, secretaries, Marine guards, etc., which the Soviets regard as particularly vulnerable since (in the words of one KGB directive) 'they do not belong to the privileged class and are worse off financially.'" The last point is critical: Most of the Americans who have betrayed America to the Soviets have done so for money.

The Soviets continually try to introduce "class wars" into their spy recruiting. This was evident in the KGB's attempt to recruit a black Marine and the Marine who was a full-blooded American Indian as major targets among the guards at the U.S. Embassy in Moscow in 1985–86. However, one Marine officer who served in the embassy during this period (without direct responsibility for the guards) was quick to point out that the Soviet efforts to turn embassy staff as well as guards into spies "is a blanket operation."

"These [American] people are in Moscow for a short time, two years," he told the authors. "The Soviets go after them all; certainly some appear more vulnerable to their attempts than others, but almost everyone at the embassy—especially the junior people and enlisted Marine guards—are the subject of KGB attention."

The classified manual on KGB interest in Marine guards is amazingly prophetic. It accurately notes the potential personality weakness of typical young Marines and, in describing what damage a recruited Marine can do, the report reads like a scenario for events that some investigators say actually happened:

U.S. Marine enlisted men, assigned as guards at diplomatic installations abroad, are especially interesting targets to Soviet Intelligence because of their frequent access to safe combinations, their presence (sometimes alone) in embassies while on night duty and their obvious capability—in the event of recruitment—to emplace microphone and transmitter listening devices.

Although handpicked for their protective duty assignments abroad and given special training and security indoctrination, Marine guard personnel are, for the most part, young and unmarried and often "on the town" in their off-duty hours. They are inevitably exposed to temptations which the Soviets can put in their paths. They are approachable by local nationals who are recruited agents of Soviet Intelligence and often by Soviets themselves. There have been repeated approaches of both types in every part of the world and also attempts at recruitment.

The manual describes an Austrian agent of the KGB who "was told to cultivate persons of two categories within the embassy—local citizens working as switchboard operators and Marine guard personnel." Soviet intelligence officers had first conceived of this "cultivation" soon after Marine guards were assigned to embassy duty in 1949. The traditionalist KGB was still issuing the same orders in Vienna in 1986, when the KGB approached Lonetree who had already been recruited in Moscow.

Another KGB gambit in Vienna involved a volleyball team of Marine guards. A Soviet team challenged the Marines to a game. That one was played at the Marine compound. The next one was scheduled on Soviet territory. This, says the manual, was "an unprecedented gesture which clearly was intended to give the Vienna KGB American-operations specialists a chance to cultivate Marines socially and open the way for possible further contact, assessment and development.

"To make it a festive occasion," the manual continues, "virtually the entire Soviet colony turned out in force, complete with wives and children, and the game was preceded by a film showing and followed by drinks and other refreshments." KGB officers circulated among the Marines, "sizing up potential prospects."

Later the officers appeared at a bowling alley frequented by the Marines and said they would like to learn how to bowl.

The manual gives three other accounts of similar KGB moves aimed at Marines:

In Cyprus a few years ago, Marine personnel frequented a local bar whose owner was subsequently determined to be a member of the illegal Cypriot Communist Party and a spotter for Soviet Intelligence. He is known to have introduced a number of Marines to Soviet Intelligence officers stationed in Cyprus, one of them a GRU officer, Nikolay Ivanovich Ranov, who spoke fluent English and posed successfully as a European businessman at the time introductions were made. Ranov, in fact, had official cover as local representative of the Soviet airline, Aeroflot. The Cyprus Government expelled him for espionage in March 1967. A disarmingly simple Soviet attempt to open a relationship with an embassy Marine guard took place in Copenhagen. A KGB officer, Aleksandr Ivanovich Roganov, came to the American Embassy with a group of Soviet visa applicants, a routine visit in his official cover as vice-consul. While waiting in the reception room, Roganov engaged the Marine guard on duty in casual conversation during which he elicited his name, rank, address and telephone number. Two days later he telephoned the Marine at the guard residence and invited him to a public performance to be held a few days later. The Marine properly reported the invitation, was told not to accept it, and subsequently told Roganov not to bother him again.

In Djakarta, Indonesia, in 1962, KGB officer Aleksandr Aleksandrovich Losev made repeated efforts to cultivate—and in one instance tried to recruit—Marine guard personnel. It was his practice to walk in on Marines at the bar of a local hotel, buy their drinks, and follow them back to the Marine quarters for more socializing. He offered to take one guard on a weekend outing and provide him with female companionship. The climax came when he stopped another Marine on the streets of Djakarta and, after a long conversation, attempted to recruit him on the basis of large payments to provide information available to him as chief of the guard force, including identification of American intelligence personnel in Indonesia.

The persistent Soviet attempts to recruit Marines is well known to U.S. counter-espionage officials charged with training and monitoring the 1,300 Marine guards assigned to 140 diplomatic posts throughout the world. The officials, indeed, would have been required to read the manual excerpted here as well as updated versions of similar Soviet recruitment ploys. But, if the Moscow Marine events of 1986–87 are compared with what *should* have been known about KGB exploits, one must conclude that, besides not reading the manuals on the KGB, they also have not read their Hegel: "What experience and history teach is this —that people and governments never have learned anything from history, or acted on principles deduced from it."

The Soviets have been quick to understand that today the primary motivation for Americans to spy is cash. And there are increasing reports of "pleasant" KGB officers. (GRU officers have always appeared more affable than KGB operatives.) Author John Barron, in his *Breaking the Ring,* described how Vitaly Yurchenko, while the KGB security officer for the Soviet Embassy in Washington from 1975 to 1980, met regularly with FBI agents, whom he got to know in the course of their mutual business: protecting the Soviet Embassy. According to Barron, who is often an unofficial spokesman for the FBI, Yurchenko and his FBI colleagues met at Danker's on E Street in northwest Washington, near the National and Warner theaters as well as FBI headquarters, which has the "congenial, sometimes roisterous atmosphere of a neighborhood pub." Barron wrote:

> Many of the patrons are judges, Justice Department lawyers, and FBI, IRS, Secret Service, and Customs agents who convene after-work to trade jokes and professional gossip.
> Yurchenko loved to drink Scotch with them and be accepted into their company. . . . On a wintry evening as he and an [FBI] agent stood at the far end of the bar, [Justice Department official John] Martin stepped in out of the snow. The agent called, "John, come meet a friend." Introducing Martin, he said, "John's the man who puts your spies in jail."
> In a tone of mock confidence, Yurchenko responded, "Always he is trying to fan the flames of Cold War and spy mania.

He knows we have no spies." All three laughed, Yurchenko the loudest.

As the old recruiting posters used to say, "This Is the Enemy!" Regardless of the tactics of their operatives, the recent success of the KGB and GRU demonstrate that they are effective in taking advantage of those who would betray the United States and other Western nations.

The origins of an all-powerful KGB can be found in the Okhrana, the domestic police-spy apparatus of czarist Russia. Czarist police intelligence operatives can be traced back even beyond the era of Peter the Great, who as czar from 1672 to 1725 is considered to have been the founder of "modern" Russia. The term *Okhrana,* which dates from about 1881, was used to identify the political police—specialists trained to investigate political crimes (in some cases crimes set up by Okhrana agents to provoke arrests) by the infiltration of the numerous subversive groups in Russia. Foreign intelligence collection was virtually nil, as evidenced in part by the catastrophic Russian military failures in the 1904–1905 war with Japan and in World War I.

For thirty-six years the Okhrana was active, feared—but relatively ineffective when "enemies of the state" harassed and then overthrew the Romanav dynasty. On December 20, 1917, a few weeks after the Bolsheviks took control of Russia, Lenin directed the establishment of the Cheka. To head this police-intelligence force, Lenin chose Feliks Edmundovich Dzerzhinsky (1877–1926), who, because of his Polish nobility origins, was called "The Knight of the Proletariat." Dzerzhinsky, a political agitator, had been imprisoned by the czarist regime. He participated in the Bolshevik Revolution in 1917 as commandant of the Bolshevik headquarters, and was personally responsible for safeguarding Lenin and other party leaders. He was considered Lenin's "closest personal friend."

The actions of the Cheka were brutal and virtually unchallenged. In his purported memoirs ace spy Sidney Reilly, a virulent anti-Bolshevik agent and organizer of counter-revolutionary activities in Russia, wrote:

The Tcheka raids were conducted with a degree of callousness and brutality which to a civilized mind is inconceivable. On one occasion, when the inhabitants of one apartment failed to remove the chain from the door through the extremity of terror, a Red soldier threw a bomb [grenade] through the opening. In another place they had no response to their knocking. The victim this time was an old lady, confined to her bed through a stroke, which had resulted from the murder of her husband before her eyes during the massacres of the previous year. Nobody else was in the flat and one of the Red soldiers, impatient at the delay, threw a grenade at the door. The bomb exploded, killing or wounding five soldiers. The soldiers returned that night and butchered the old lady in her bed as a "reprisal" for the damage.

Soldiers, workers, tram drivers, pensioners—anyone was a potential victim for the Cheka. Murder, arrest, torture, and disappearance were commonplace. Even a wife who left her flat to go shopping might never return, caught up in a Cheka sweep of an area that took in anyone without proper papers or seen speaking with or even standing with someone who was suspect.

The excesses of the Cheka, which was in large part comprised of revolutionary sailors and soldiers, led to its being renamed GPU—the General Political Administration—in February 1922. It was changed again, in 1923, to OGPU, for Unified State Political Administration. By 1925, under Dzerzhinsky's leadership, the Cheka and its successors are believed to have executed over 250,000 enemies of the Bolshevik leadership and their families. It was estimated that by that time another 1,300,000 prisoners were in Russia's approximately 6,000 jails. In addition, hundreds of thousands of other Russians were being exiled to the first Soviet prison communities in remote areas, the start of the Gulag Archipelago—the constellation of prison-concentration camps for political and criminal prisoners that sweeps across a desolate Soviet landscape.

Dzerzhinsky's passion for protecting the Revolution—and searching out and destroying counter-revolutionaries—led to the first significant overseas intelligence efforts of the Russians. First czarist officials and White officers were sought out in Europe and even in the United States. They were watched, reported on, and sometimes executed.

This first Soviet spymaster is reported to have died of a stroke during an argument with Stalin on July 20, 1926. Conclusive evidence is lacking, but rumors persisted that the stroke suffered by the forty-eight-year-old Dzerzhinsky was induced by something more violent than Stalin's arguments. (The street on which the infamous Lubyanka Prison was located, the site of Cheka headquarters, was renamed for Dzerzhinsky, and Nikita Khrushchev ordered a statue of that supreme Chekist erected outside of the prison.)

The renaming of the Cheka to GPU was the start of a series of name changes of the state security apparatus: from 1923, OGPU; from 1934, NKVD; then splitting in 1941 to "state" security NKGB and internal security NKVD; combined again that same year under the NKVD, separated again in 1943, but with names changed in 1946 to MGB (state) and MVD (internal); merging briefly in 1953, when Stalin died, under the MVD; separated again in 1954 as the KGB (state) and MVD (internal); combined in 1960 as the KGB, only to be separated to its present state in 1966, with KGB for state security and MOOP and (from 1968) MVD for internal security.

Regardless of name, from Cheka to KGB, the purpose of the organ has been the same—to protect the Kremlin leaders from all enemies, foreign and domestic. To efficiently undertake such security, the KGB requires intelligence of all types—political, economic, and military.

The men chosen by Stalin to direct the organ were all *his* men. They had very different personalities and characteristics, but all shared in one trait: ruthlessness.

Dzerzhinsky's immediate successor was his deputy, V. R. Menzhinsky, like his late chief a Pole and an aristocrat. Menzhinsky served as head of the state police-intelligence organ for eight years. He fell victim to a heart attack on May 10, 1934. (Menzhinsky was known to have had a heart condition and was under the care of top Kremlin physicians.)

The tradition of the post passing to the deputy was continued with the appointment of Genrikh G. Yagoda. A pharmacist by profession, he may have contributed to the death of Lenin, who had suffered from a series of heart attacks before his death.

On December 1, 1934, Sergey Kirov, a founder of the Bolshevik Revolution, was assassinated—by a former Chekist. This was the opening shot of the series of massive purges initiated by Stalin. Yagoda, as head of the NKVD, was in charge of the investigation of Kirov's assassination and initiated the flood of arrests that followed.

Stalin, however, needed someone more ruthless than Yagoda, and in September 1936 he appointed Nikolay Yezhov, a man of an impoverished background and a former political commissar in the Red Army, to the top Chekist position. Yezhov continued the purges with increased fervor. Under his direction, in June 1937, the purges extended from the political leaders of the country, especially the surviving old Bolshevik leaders, to the military. During the next couple of years three of the five Marshals of the Soviet Union were arrested, tried, and executed (charged either with helping "enemies" or other counter-revolutionary activities). Scores of senior Army officers, the commanders of the Baltic, Black Sea, and Northern fleets, and the Amur River Flotilla, and tens of thousands of lesser officers were arrested and executed.

In his detailed history, *The Great Terror,* British historian Robert Conquest recounts how the Army political commissars—those charged with the political control of the Army—also fell victim to the NKVD: "By rank, all seventeen Army Commissars went, with twenty-five of twenty-eight Corps Commissars. At the Brigade Commissar level, two survived out of thirty-six." In many instances wives and sisters were arrested and deported to "internal exile," although few were intentionally killed.

Among the victims of the purges during the brief period that Yezhov ran the NKVD were 3,000 of the senior NKVD officials of Yagoda's regime. They were denounced as former czarist police spies, thieves, and embezzlers and then executed.

Needing a still stronger policeman, spy, and now executioner, in December 1938, Stalin appointed the most notorious head of the state security organ—Laventi Pavlovich Beria. A longtime Chekist, Beria had been a close associate of Stalin, head of the secret police in the dictator's native Georgia, and a methodical policeman and intelligence collector. Soon after his appointment Beria was made a candidate (nonvoting) member of the ruling Politburo, the first chief of the secret police to join that body. (At the time there were ten full voting members, including Stalin and the newly appointed Nikita Khrushchev.)

Beria was infamous in the Soviet Union, as a policeman and as a lecher. He regularly picked up young girls on the street and took them to his office, where he forced them to perform sodomy and then raped them. The threat of arrest of their families was usually a sufficient threat for them to suffer in silence, although some are reported to have committed suicide in shame. One of his victims, a young girl who had voluntarily come to Beria's office to plead for her arrested brother, was held for several days and raped repeatedly. Beria then decided to "keep her" by marrying her. The change in his marital status did not end his perversions with young girls and with women employed by the NKVD, sometimes in his own home as well as in his office.

This was the start of a new era in Soviet intelligence collection. Beria was the acme of policemen, at least in the Stalinist sense. Of particular significance, he increased surveillance in foreign countries of the few remaining old Bolsheviks, among them Leon Trotsky, who had been Stalin's rival to succeed Lenin. Despite strong security measures, Beria's people succeeded in "executing" Trotsky in Mexico in August 1940.

Many thousands more fell to the pistols of Beria's executioners as Stalin's purges continued until the Soviet Union and Germany went to war in June 1941. Beria's predecessor, Yezhov—who had at one point intended to arrest Beria—was himself arrested on Beria's orders, taken to a psychiatric institute, and a short time later reportedly was found hanging from a window bar. The survivors of the Yagoda-era NKVD leadership as well as many of the Yezhov period were also executed by Beria's NKVD executioners.

With the outbreak of war, Beria became one of Stalin's most important lieutenants. Internally, the secret police had increased responsibilities—to protect the Kremlin leadership and to ensure the loyalty of the armies fighting the Germans. The latter role included the establishment of NKVD fighting formations.

Beria also became involved with foreign intelligence. Soviet diplomatic delegations to Britain, Canada, and the United States were assigned NKVD operatives to seek out military information that could be of value to the Kremlin. In addition, a Soviet purchasing commission was established in the United States to speed the transfer of arms to the Soviet Union. With more than one thousand employees, the commission became a collection point for secrets.

Beria thus became an international spymaster. The most important secrets that his agents—overt and covert—collected were those dealing with the atomic bomb, research for which was already under way in the Soviet Union, as it was in several European countries and the United States. In the United States his agents collected military, scientific, and political intelligence.

During the war the NKVD was responsible for internal security of the Soviet Union, as well as ensuring the loyalty of the Army. Under Beria's direction a new counter-espionage organization was formed—Smersh, the name an abbreviation of the Russian words *Smert Shpionam,* meaning "death to spies." Originally part of the NKVD, Smersh in 1943 was given all counter-intelligence and security responsibilities for the armed forces.

Smersh meant terror to all military men who even thought for a moment of defection or not giving their utmost for the motherland. Among the NKVD officials who served in Smersh and went on to senior positions in Soviet intelligence was Ivan Serov. An intelligence officer, he survived the purges of the GRU and transferred to the NKVD. He was deputy chief of Smersh in 1941, a deputy to Beria in 1943–45, the deputy chief of Smersh in Soviet-occupied Germany in 1945.

Serov distinguished himself in the pursuit and liquidation of the anti-Soviet inhabitants of Estonia, Latvia, and Lithuania in 1940 and again in 1944–47. He is reported to have been personally involved in the mass murder of the Polish officers in Katyn Forest.*

* In April 1943, German troops discovered the mass graves of Polish officers in Katyn Forest, west of the Soviet city of Smolensk. After the division of Poland by Nazi Germany and the Soviet Union in 1939, several thousand Polish officers and noncommissioned officers had been interned in Soviet prison camps. The Germans occupying Soviet territory subsequently found the mass graves of 4,000 Poles in Katyn Forest and indications that there were perhaps 6,000 more bodies buried in the area.

The Soviets denied responsibility for the mass murders, blaming them on the Germans. Witnesses on the scene of the discovery—including several Americans—and a subsequent U.S. government inquiry concluded that the Soviets were unquestionably responsible for the massacre.

After the war Beria's star continued to rise. Stalin put him in charge of atomic bomb development, along with the administration of the state security and intelligence organs. Closer and closer to Stalin, Beria envisioned himself as Stalin's successor. On the night of March 1, 1953, Beria apparently walked the short distance from his own villa to Stalin's dacha at Kuntsevo. Beria met alone with the dictator in Stalin's study. A short time later Stalin was found lying on the floor of the room, having suffered a stroke. Stalin regained consciousness only briefly and was unable to speak. He died late on March 2.

Racing back to his headquarters in Lubyanka Prison, Beria set in motion plans to take over the government. Realizing his own unpopularity, he named Georgi Malenkov, a weak colleague, as premier, and assigned others to a collective leadership, with himself as a vice-chairman of the Council of Ministers. He, of course, retained control of the NKVD. (Among his first acts were the closing of Stalin's dacha and the transporting of all of the late dictator's belongings to warehouses; purges were begun of the physicians who had examined the dictator's remains.)

But Beria survived only until June 26, when he went to the Kremlin for a meeting of the leadership. The events of that tumultuous day are still difficult to determine. In a joint plot of the collective leadership and the military, Beria may have been arrested or shot to death at that time, possibly by Marshal Georgi Zhukov, the Soviet Union's leading military hero. Some reports cite a trial as late as December 1953 with Beria being shot immediately afterward, or sometime between the June and December dates. Regardless, the most powerful man in the Soviet Union at that moment and the first Chekist to achieve full membership in the ruling circle was dead by the end of 1953.

General Serov, deputy chief of the GRU, was one of the conspirators against Beria. After the fall of Beria, Serov became chairman of the KGB. Together with Ambassador Yuri Andropov, he seized the leaders of the Hungarian Revolution of 1956 by deceit and took part in their torture and execution, earning the nickname "the hangman of Hungary." In December 1958, Serov became chief of the GRU. As an ex-KGB and ex-Smersh officer,

---

(The Soviets did not include the Katyn Forest murders among their charges against Nazi war criminals at Nuremberg after the war.)

he had many enemies in the GRU. Under his leadership, corruption in the GRU attained unbelievable proportions. The years when Serov was chief of the GRU were also the most unproductive in its history. It was the only period when GRU officers voluntarily made contact with Western services and gave them much more valuable information than they took from them. Serov was demoted and stripped of his decorations in 1962 because of the defection of Colonel Oleg Penkovskiy to Western intelligence. Serov disappeared from view in 1963.

Serov's immediate successors were essentially faceless men—policemen and spymasters, some highly successful. Aleksandr Shelepin and later Vladimir Semichastny tried to "improve the image" of the KGB. But it was under Yuri Andropov that the KGB made its major strides in both image and effectiveness as an intelligence organization. Andropov became chairman of the KGB in 1967, and gained full membership in the ruling Politburo in 1973.

Andropov brought a new level of discipline, decision, and intelligence to the security organ. Foreign intelligence collection became more sophisticated and, although like the West, the Soviets were increasingly using high-tech methods of intelligence collection, the use of "on-the-ground" spies and agents was reinforced. In May of 1982, Andropov moved from his post as chairman of the KGB and returned to the powerful Party Secretariat, a move that placed him in the front ranks of candidates to succeed the ailing Leonid Brezhnev, General Secretary of the Communist Party and de facto ruler of the Soviet Union.

When Brezhnev died in late 1982, Andropov succeeded him. The Western press labeled the new Soviet leader a "relatively open-minded man." A strange description for a longtime Chekist. At age sixty-eight he was described by *The Washington Post* "as an urbane man who can speak English." Hungarian officials, the report continued, "recall Andropov's stay in Budapest as Soviet ambassador during the military intervention by Moscow in 1956 and the suppression of the uprising. Despite his role in preparing for Moscow's invasion, he is remembered as a diplomat who took the trouble to learn Hungarian and understand the country's distinctive culture." Then, based on his plans and recommendations, Soviet tanks savagely invaded Hungary.

Andropov's tenure as head of the Soviet Union would be

KGB ORGANIZATION

KGB

DIRECTORATES

- FIRST CHIEF DIRECTORATE (FOREIGN)
- SECOND CHIEF DIRECTORATE (INTERNAL)
- THIRD DIRECTORATE (ARMED FORCES)
- FIFTH CHIEF DIRECTORATE (DISSIDENTS)
- SEVENTH DIRECTORATE (SURVEILLANCE)
- EIGHTH CHIEF DIRECTORATE (COMMUNICATIONS)
- NINTH CHIEF DIRECTORATE (GUARDS)
- CHIEF BORDER GUARDS DIRECTORATE

DEPARTMENTS

- OPERATIONAL RECORDS
- REGISTRY AND ARCHIVES
- SPECIAL INVESTIGATIONS
- STATE COMMUNICATIONS
- PHYSICAL SECURITY
- FINANCE
- TECHNICAL OPERATIONS DIRECTORATE
- ADMINISTRATION DIRECTORATE
- PERSONNEL DIRECTORATE

THE KGB AND EQUIVALENT U.S. INSTITUTIONS

KGB COMPONENT	FUNCTIONS	U.S. COUNTERPARTS
First Directorate	HUMINT, active measures, counter-intelligence, analysis	CIA Directorate of Operations, Directorate of Intelligence; FBI
Second Directorate	domestic counter-intelligence, counter-subversion, industrial security	FBI; Department of Energy Safeguards and Security; Defense Industrial Security Agency
Third Directorate	counter-intelligence and counter-subversion in armed forces	Defense Investigative Service; Naval Investigative Command; USAF Office of Special Investigations; Army Criminal Investigations Division
Fifth Directorate	embassy security and internal security	Executive Protection Service; Secret Service; FBI
Seventh Directorate	surveillance equipment	FBI; Defense Advanced Projects Agency;
Eighth Directorate	signals intelligence, communications security	National Security Agency; Army, Navy, Air Force
Ninth Directorate	leadership protection; protection of sensitive installations	Executive Protection Service; Secret Service; Marine Corps embassy guards
Border Guards Directorate	protection of frontiers, prevention of smuggling	Border Patrol; Coast Guard; Customs Service

Adapted from Jeffrey T. Richelson, *Sword and Shield* (Cambridge, Mass.: Ballinger Publishing Co., 1986), p. 33.

brief. He became General Secretary in November 1982. Three months later Andropov's diabetic kidneys ceased to function and he was placed on an artificial kidney machine. His last public appearance was in August 1983, nearly six months before his death on February 9, 1984.

The rise of a KGB chairman to the highest Soviet position was, in the long perspective, unexpected. But then so was the arrangement after Beria's fall, when Khrushchev and then Brezhnev ruled the Soviet Union, with the armed forces and the KGB —the two most powerful institutions in the Soviet Union—kept in close balance. But, while Beria had sought to rule the Soviet Union through intimidation and murder, Andropov had achieved the top position through intelligence, cunning, and hard work.

Andropov had been succeeded as head of the KGB by Vitaly Fedorchuk, who served only briefly before being appointed Minister of Internal Affairs (when Andropov replaced Brezhnev). He has been followed as chairman of the KGB by Andropov's former deputy in that post, Viktor Chebrikov.

Selected for full membership on the ruling Politburo in 1985, Chebrikov directs a KGB headquarters and field operation comprised of more than 100,000 professionals—larger than all Western intelligence services combined. In addition, the KGB has a combat force of an estimated 200,000 to 250,000 heavily armed and well-trained border troops; possibly as many as 50,000 additional signal troops charged with providing reliable and rapid communications for the Soviet leadership; 12,000 maritime border troops that protect the sea frontiers of the U.S.S.R., operating some 200 ships and craft, from 3,900-ton frigates to armed icebreakers and patrol boats; and the elite Guards Directorate, which provides protection for Kremlin leaders.

Sharing the responsibility for espionage with the KGB and its predecessors has been the GRU or the Chief Intelligence Directorate of the General Staff—Soviet military intelligence, also referred to as the Fourth Bureau of the Soviet General Staff. An Army intelligence service was established in June 1918 as the intelligence department of the Eastern Front, the command organization for five Red armies and the Volga flotilla. Only twenty-five days later the Cheka savagely executed the Front intelligence staff, as well as most of the other staff sections and the Front commander, M. A. Muravev, who was attempting to betray the Bolsheviks and join his troops with a Czech legion. (Some reports indicate that Muravev may have committed suicide when he realized his demise was approaching.)

Soon after, Trotsky, the head of the Army, demanded of Lenin that he allow an independent Army intelligence branch or turn over command of the military to Dzerzhinsky and the Cheka. Lenin accordingly ordered Dzerzhinsky to allow the Army to have its own intelligence arm, although it was not until October 21, 1918, that Lenin signed the decree to establish the top-level intelligence department—originally the Registrational Directorate of the Field Staff, the highest command structure at the time. This directorate evolved into the GRU. The first chief of the directorate was Simon Ivanovich Aralov, an official of the Cheka!

From that time the head of the GRU is believed to have always been a former general or other senior official of the Cheka and its successors. Today the head of the GRU is Petr Ivashutin, a former deputy chairman of the KGB who has headed military intelligence since about 1963. He was appointed after the discovery that GRU Colonel Penkovskiy was a Western spy. Ivashutin was in Smersh during the war; afterward he became head of the KGB's Third Directorate (armed forces) and then a deputy chairman of the KGB.

The GRU, which has always been concerned primarily with intelligence collection against foreign military activities, established operatives in the 1920s and 1930s in several European countries. Although initially a narrow, nonpolitical organ in comparison with the Cheka and its successors, the GRU also suffered greatly from Stalin-initiated purges. The first purge of the GRU was in November 1920, when hundreds of intelligence officers were shot because, according to Lenin, they had given incorrect evaluations of the situation in Poland.

The second purge of the GRU was in 1937. The acting head of the GRU, M. S. Uritski, was arrested and shot, as were other GRU officers. NKVD agents went to other countries where they murdered GRU illegals as well as intelligence officers of the GRU *and* NKVD who had refused to return to the Soviet Union. A rebuilding of the GRU began, but another wave of arrests and executions started in the summer of 1938. GRU chief Yan Berzin was executed on July 29, 1938; his successor, Nikolai Ezhov, was also arrested and shot. John Erickson, the doyen of watchers of the Soviet military, observed, "With the purge of the senior officers went a purge of their staffs; in the technical and specialist branches [including GRU], the eliminations reached right back into the design centers and the training staffs."

In 1941 the GRU was divided into the strategic and operational intelligence services. During the war the strategic network agents were able to successfully penetrate the German General Staff through Switzerland (Operation Dora) and to steal U.S. atomic secrets by way of Canada (Operation Zaria).

After the war, in 1947, Stalin chose to remove the intelligence functions from both the Army and the NKVD. A new intelligence organization, the Committee of Information, was formed under the leadership of V. M. Molotov (later Foreign Minister) and, subsequently, Victor Abakumov. Two years later Abakumov was executed and the Committee of Information was abolished, with the GRU reestablished as the military intelligence branch of the General Staff.

The GRU appears to be a fairly straightforward military intelligence organization. Like the KGB, it has personnel serving overseas under diplomatic cover in Soviet embassies, the United Nations, the Aeroflot Soviet national airline, and other overseas activities. All Soviet naval and military attachés are GRU officers or at least have undergone GRU training—just as U.S. naval and military attachés are intelligence specialists or have had some intelligence training before going overseas.

In addition to "human intelligence" (HUMINT in military jargon), the GRU, like the KGB, maintains a worldwide "signals intelligence" (SIGINT) collection network that intercepts foreign radio, radar, television, and other electronic transmissions. This network includes ground stations (with massive overseas SIGINT complexes in Cuba and Vietnam), aircraft, surface ships, submarines, and satellites.

There is some duplication of GRU and KGB efforts, but such duplication is not necessarily considered bad from the Soviet viewpoint. Redundant intelligence collection efforts are found throughout the Soviet armed forces, where efficiency and cost-effectiveness are not a consideration when it comes to obtaining information that can help the survival of the state. (Internal security is not duplicated; that is strictly the domain of the KGB.)

The GRU is rarely mentioned in the Western press; generally the KGB—and its predecessors—are given credit for Soviet espionage achievements. However, the GRU successes included the spy ring highlighted by the Whittaker Chambers-Alger Hiss case in the United States; the Richard Sorge case in Japan; Rudolph Roessler and his Lucy ring in Germany during World War II; atomic bomb spies Klaus Fuchs and Alan Nunn May; Colonel Sig Wennerstrom in Sweden; former CIA employee William Kampiles; and numerous others who spied for the Soviet Union.

There are two areas of overlapping responsibility between the KGB and GRU—internal *military security* and the *Spetsnaz* forces. The Third Directorate of the KGB is responsible for counter-intelligence within the armed forces, with agents assigned to all branches of the military. These modern Chekists generally wear standard military uniforms, but are readily known as KGB officers and report only through the KGB chain of command. Covert KGB officers are also assigned to all the military services.

Within units and on board naval ships the KGB officers recruit men to report directly to them. One KGB defector, a former captain assigned to a motorized rifle regiment in East Germany, said he was told that "when recruiting informers, you must not only convince them but also compel them to work for us. The KGB has enough power for that." Without KGB approval no officer in the Soviet armed forces can be promoted or sent to a military academy (senior school); enlisted men who do not pass KGB scrutiny can be dismissed from the military—with a bad mark on the record that follows them into civilian life.

The Spetsnaz forces are somewhat similar to the U.S. special operations forces, e.g., the Army's Green Berets and the elite Delta Force, and the Navy's SEAL teams. The Soviet Spetsnaz troops are controlled by the GRU in wartime and for training exercises. However, they are assigned to KGB control for special operations, such as the initial military operations in Czechoslovakia during the 1968 occupation of that country by Soviet forces.

Both the KGB and GRU maintain two categories of intelligence officers in the United States—legal and illegal.

A "legal" is a KGB or GRU officer who has diplomatic

GRU ORGANIZATION

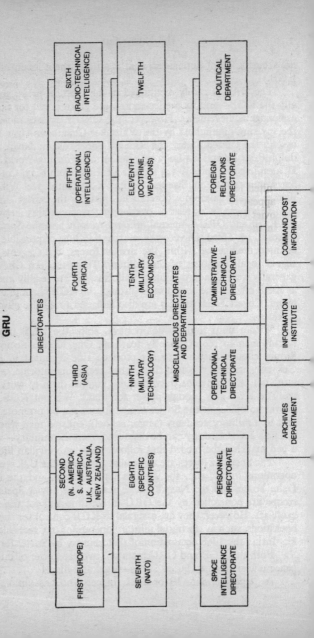

GRU

DIRECTORATES

FIRST (EUROPE)	SECOND (N. AMERICA, S. AMERICA, U.K., AUSTRALIA, NEW ZEALAND)	THIRD (ASIA)	FOURTH (AFRICA)	FIFTH (OPERATIONAL INTELLIGENCE)	SIXTH (RADIO-TECHNICAL INTELLIGENCE)

SEVENTH (NATO)	EIGHTH (SPECIFIC COUNTRIES)	NINTH (MILITARY TECHNOLOGY)	TENTH (MILITARY ECONOMICS)	ELEVENTH (DOCTRINE, WEAPONS)	TWELFTH

MISCELLANEOUS DIRECTORATES
AND DEPARTMENTS

SPACE INTELLIGENCE DIRECTORATE	PERSONNEL DIRECTORATE	OPERATIONAL-TECHNICAL DIRECTORATE	ADMINISTRATIVE-TECHNICAL DIRECTORATE	FOREIGN RELATIONS DIRECTORATE	POLITICAL DEPARTMENT

ARCHIVES DEPARTMENT	INFORMATION INSTITUTE	COMMAND POST INFORMATION

cover and, in the event of exposure, diplomatic immunity. Although his designated diplomatic position may be, say, second secretary or naval attaché, he works in the embassy or a consulate—the "legal residency"—as an intelligence officer. His duties include the gathering and analyzing of information from open sources and the recruiting and running of agents.

An "illegal" intelligence officer is planted in the country. Some illegals live and work publicly as Soviets, perhaps as correspondents for Tass, the Soviet news service, or as employees of the United Nations Secretariat. Others are planted so deep that they appear to be ordinary Americans with no connection with the Soviet Union.

In the early 1960s, when the KGB and the GRU began to have trouble finding ideologically motivated Americans who would spy for the Soviet Union, the two Soviet intelligence services had to turn increasingly to using their own people as illegals and to doing risky business with walk-ins.

Nondiplomatic illegals usually set up innocuous enterprises that give them cover and some freedom of movement. The KGB provides them with an elaborate, verifiable synthetic life (a "legend" in spy talk). They rarely attempt to find jobs that require security background checks. They live in places where they can observe defense activities or where they can meet Americans who work in sensitive posts. Colonel Abel was a classic example of a well-concealed illegal, as were his confederates, the Cohen-Krogers, who appeared in both the Lonsdale and Rosenberg cases. (They operated a rare-books business out of their bungalow in Ruislip, England, close to the headquarters of the U.S. Third Air Force.)

In 1968 another KGB colonel-to-be entered the United States. A Czech, he studied in East Germany under KGB tutelage and was given a legend and the name "Rudolph Herrmann" (the name of a real German who had died in the Soviet Union during World War II). Herrmann was sent, as an emigrant from West Germany, first to Canada. He was accompanied by his wife, a German, who was also trained by the KGB.

After several years as an up-and-coming intelligence officer in Canada, where his two sons were born, Herrmann and his wife obtained a U.S. visa and moved to Hartsdale, New York, a suburb of New York City. The home they bought there was selected according to KGB specifications: no nearby high-tension wires (which would interfere with radio reception), out of view from other houses, on high ground, and clear of any obstructions to the east, from where the KGB Moscow Center's radio transmissions would come.

Herrmann, who by then had advanced to colonel, did not seek out classified information. As the resident illegal, he would take over the agents run by the resident legal, operating under diplomatic cover, in the event that the Soviet diplomatic mission to the United States was disabled because of a breaking of diplomatic relations or war. Herrmann, who, unlike the legals, could travel freely, also found sites in various places in the United States for "drops," the hiding places that intelligence officers and agents use for the exchange of messages, money, and pilfered material.

"He was given an assignment to assume an identity and just be available for specific assignments," an FBI agent familiar with Herrmann said in an interview. "He was told to do such things as take a picture of that house or get to casually know this man. He never knew what he was doing in terms of the full picture."

Herrmann free-lanced, with great success, as a photographer and filmmaker. He instructed his older son, Peter, in spy tradecraft and enlisted him in the KGB, which put Peter on a path that would lead from Georgetown University to a law school and perhaps ultimately to a sensitive government post or high elective office, all under KGB direction.

Peter was a junior at Georgetown in 1977, when the FBI turned him and his parents into double agents. After two years, fearing that the KGB was catching on, the FBI gave the defector family another identity—a new legend appliquéd on the old—and moved everyone to a new location, where they now really do live as ordinary Americans.

The use of Czech, East German, Polish, and other foreign citizens to penetrate intelligence targets is a regular practice of the KGB (and to a lesser extent the GRU). Indeed, all of the Warsaw Pact intelligence services—political and military—have continuous and intensive liaison to (but not necessarily from) the Soviet intelligence services. In addition, the Soviets periodically benefit from other allies and clients, as when the North Koreans captured the U.S. intelligence ship *Pueblo* in January 1968.

Reports persist that the KGB planned and organized the taking of the American ship. *The New KGB* stated, "Andropov [head of the KGB] and his deputy Viktor Chebrikov became convinced that the *Pueblo* could be induced to respond to certain stimuli and gently drawn into a trap. In anticipation of such an event personnel from the Eighth Chief Directorate [of the KGB] were dispatched to the Far East to be on hand when and if the trap snapped shut."

Although there are indications that the Soviets knew of the *Pueblo*'s schedule before she departed Sasebo, Japan, on January 11, 1968, for her first—and final—intelligence collection mission off the North Korean coast, a review of the official and unofficial records of the events that followed make it appear highly unlikely that the hapless *Pueblo* was caught in a KGB-directed trap. Rather, American timidity and, at times, stupidity and North Korean aggressiveness led to the taking of the ship. The fact that no Russians were present at any of the many interrogations of the crew, along with several other factors, make it even more doubtful that KGB agents were active participants.

Soon after the *Pueblo* docked in Wonsan, North Koreans were swarming through the ship. Within a day or two so were Russians, who had flown into Wonsan. They minutely examined the mass of crypto gear and publications that had not been destroyed and removed large amounts of material from the ship. There was probably some fear of a U.S. bombing attack to destroy the ship and the sensitive material on board, in the same manner that the wreckage of the first U.S. Navy A-6 Intruder attack bomber that crashed in Vietnam had been deliberately bombed to protect its secrets.

The KGB—and to a lesser extent the GRU—also operates through international organizations. The United Nations headquarters, in New York, and its subordinate agencies are staffed with large numbers of Russians, many of whom are intelligence operatives. A 1985 report of the U.S. Senate Select Committee on Intelligence said eight hundred Soviet citizens were assigned in the United States. The FBI uses larger numbers—between 1,200 and 1,400.

In addition, the Senate report continued, the Soviets have influence over the two hundred Eastern Bloc employees at the UN. According to the Senate report, "Approximately one-fourth of the Soviets in the UN Secretariat are intelligence officers and many more are co-opted by the KGB or GRU. All Soviets in the Secretariat must respond to KGB requests for assistance." Not said was that every Soviet being assigned to the United Nations is vetted by the KGB before his or her travel to the West is approved.

According to former UN official Arkady Shevchenko, who defected to the West,

it was easy to distinguish KGB professionals from diplomats and others. The first giveaway was money. The KGB had it and spent it much more generously than real diplomats. A Foreign Ministry employee would need to hoard the dollar portion of his salary for as much as a year or more before he could afford to buy a used American car. KGB agents had the cash to get one as soon as they arrived in New York. They also had money to entertain lavishly. A mid-level Mission or Secretariat staffer who is regularly seen treating non-Soviets to round after round of drinks is almost certainly using KGB funds. And if the generous host or hostess is well dressed, there can be little doubt. Only the KGB pays its people well enough for them to afford the best in Western clothing.

These KGB activities are, of course, partially subsidized by the United States, which pays for most of the UN operation. The Soviet Government receives some $20 million per year in salary kickbacks from Soviet employees at the United Nations.

The KGB and GRU actively use UN positions for access to Americans to support intelligence collection. For example, Anatoliy Andreyev, an intelligence officer working as a UN librarian in 1973, met a civilian employee of the U.S. Department of Defense at a librarians' conference. For a year the two exchanged unclassified documents of "mutual" interest. Then Andreyev offered to help the American financially in exchange for specific classified documents. After a protest to the United Nations, the Soviet quietly left the United States.

The United Nations assignments permit Soviets to travel to areas of the United States (and in other countries) where Soviet citizens would normally not be allowed. But perhaps most dangerous from the West's viewpoint, senior Soviet officials in the

United Nations have access to the personnel files of all UN employees, permitting them to identify potential collaborators and blackmail victims.

Along with New York and its large Soviet mission to the United Nations, the largest overseas KGB operations are located in Bonn, Cologne, London, Tokyo, and Vienna. (Paris was one of the largest KGB stations until a mass expulsion in 1983 and a smaller spy expulsion in 1987.)

Washington, D.C., oddly enough, was not on this list that was compiled by the U.S. Department of Defense. The nation's capital is, of course, a principal center of Soviet espionage activities—HUMINT and SIGINT. The Soviets have a staff of KGB officers at the embassy on Sixteenth Street (a short walk from the White House) and the new embassy compound on Tunlaw Road in northwest Washington. The military attachés in Washington, most if not all of whom are GRU officers, work in the Soviet Military Office on Belmont Road, at Massachusetts Avenue, an exclusive residential and embassy area.

The targets of the KGB and GRU officers stationed in Washington are primarily the U.S. military establishment and the Congress. All Soviets are restricted to a twenty-five-mile circle, measured out from the Ellipse, a park between the Washington Monument and the White House. Within the twenty-five-mile area there are some locations that are off limits to the Soviets, especially the several military complexes in the area. But a principal target is "the open Hill," the expression used by Senator John Warner to describe to the authors the large number of Soviet agents who are reported to be walking through the Capitol and the adjacent House and Senate office buildings. "It's a price we have to pay for our freedom," he added.

In the hallways and committee rooms on Capitol Hill the Soviets—quite legally—listen to conversations and pick up innumerable documents, including hearings (inevitably censored) of the defense, intelligence, and economic committees. Other places where Soviet agents are often seen include the numerous bars and restaurants frequented by U.S. military and government officials and contractors from defense industry who are visiting Washington.

To imagine what an astute KGB officer could do on Capitol Hill, start with what can be so easily collected in closed-door, classified congressional hearing rooms on the Hill by someone with limited access and no security clearance. He was Randy Miles Jeffries, a twenty-six-year-old messenger for a company that transcribed congressional hearings and other proceedings. His employer, the Acme Reporting Company, had told him to destroy transcripts marked secret—even though he was not cleared to handle classified documents. Instead of destroying the documents, he hid them and called the Soviet Military Office.

(Coincidentally, just before the theft, the Defense Investigative Service had inspected Acme and approved the firm's security procedures. After Jeffries' arrest prosecutors revealed that he had been convicted of possession of heroin in 1983. He had worked as a low-level employee of the FBI from 1978 to 1980.)

With the inevitable FBI eavesdroppers listening in, Jeffries identified himself to the Soviet on the phone as "Dano" and said he had three documents—"Very, uh, classified top-secret documents"—for sale. Jeffries took a cab to the military office and showed sample title pages of the documents. He offered the entire set of documents for $5,000.

An FBI agent posing as a Soviet intelligence officer named "Vladimir" called Jeffries and said he was "ready to do business." The agent set up a meeting in a motel room, where Jeffries told of twice passing samples to the Soviets. If that was true, the FBI had not detected either of the meetings. Jeffries handed over the documents, which included transcripts of House Armed Services Subcommittee hearings on such subjects as military communications equipment, including a proposed airplane-to-submarine link; research into "blue-green lasers" for communications with submerged submarines; information about the nuclear arsenals of the United States and the Soviet Union; and details about the way U.S. radar could track Soviet cruise missiles.

The documents were never recovered. Jeffries said that a friend had destroyed them, supposedly before the FBI made the arrest. In a plea bargain the Department of Justice dropped a charge of delivering classified material to the Soviet Union in exchange for Jeffries' guilty plea to supplying national security documents to an unauthorized person. He was sentenced to three to nine years in prison.

Rivaling Capitol Hill as a fountain of intelligence for the KGB is Embassy Row. Soviets are eager for invitations to the uncountable embassy parties in Washington, where a U.S. official from the State Department, or a general, or an admiral from another NATO country can be overheard discussing a project or schedule with someone from another allied nation.

At a party at the Chinese Embassy an assistant Soviet naval attaché came up to a defense analyst, whom he had met once or twice before. (The meetings included a visit by the analyst to a Soviet destroyer during a port visit. The attaché had been the navigator.) The officer, after a brief word of greeting, immediately asked this question: "Do the U.S. Navy's rapid-deployment ships have an amphibious assault capability as well?" The analyst, taken aback, gulped some of the wine in his glass and answered, cautiously, "No . . ." Secretary of the Navy John Lehman walked by and, recognizing the analyst, exchanged greetings. The analyst introduced the beaming Soviet officer to Lehman and then slipped over to another conversation a few feet away.

Parties have their moments. Signals intelligence is gathered continuously. Sophisticated electronic intercept gear at the Soviet Embassy enables the KGB Residency to listen in on telephone and radio conversations throughout the Washington area. The FBI estimates that the Soviets have forty specialists in Washington to operate the SIGINT equipment (although that number is assumed to have been reduced as a result of the 1986 expulsions by the Reagan Administration).

San Francisco, which has a Soviet Consulate, is also a sub-center for KGB and GRU operations. The KGB Residency at the consulate has for its principal target the technology-rich Silicon Valley just south of the city, and the several U.S. military installations in the area, including the large naval carrier base and communications center at nearby Alameda (where Jerry Whitworth spied), as well as the Naval Air Station Moffett Field, with its several squadrons of antisubmarine aircraft and the NASA research facility.

Beyond the Soviet intelligence agents—legal and illegal—who are more or less permanently assigned in the United States, there are regular Soviet sports, educational, trade, and scientific delegations visiting the United States. All of these are believed to include KGB agents whose primary purpose is to watch the members of the group while they are outside of the Soviet Union.

However, the KGB agents assigned to certain trade and scientific groups are certainly seeking intelligence while in the United States.

The careers of KGB intelligence officers and FBI counter-intelligence agents often parallel each other. FBI agents tell of trailing KGB legals for years and then, one day, spotting a familiar face—the son of the KGB officer. (No daughter has been reported.) "Soviet spies are part of an oligarchy," the FBI agent said. "People outside the oligarchy aren't trusted. After twenty or thirty years, we get to know the next generation—sons, relatives, exchange students on the way up."

Espionage is an old, conservative occupation, handed down through the generations by spies who come in from the cold to teach tradecraft at espionage schools on both sides of the Iron Curtain. Techniques do not change that much from decade to decade. David W. Szady, a veteran FBI counter-espionage agent who worked on several Year of the Spy cases, philosophized about why the classical ways are the best and the most reliable.

"Dead drops here, face-to-face meets overseas. They are classical because they work," he said. "Radio is often a problem because of the chances of detection and the need to maintain the equipment, which is often miniaturized and delicate. In my experience, the classic ways work. No worrying about radios. The Vienna Procedure: brush contacts in the street, face-to-face meetings in the park, training in a safe house overseas. There are only three basic needs of an espionage operation: a way for the agent to get ahold of someone in an emergency, a way for the intelligence officer to get information from the agent, and a way to pay him."

Intelligence officers and agents on one side get to know counter-intelligence agents on the other side, and all the experienced players know the rules and the moves of the game. An FBI agent and his wife went on a picnic one day near the Delaware Water Gap. While he was looking around for a place to put down the blanket and hamper, he saw a member of the Soviet UN Mission walking in the woods. The agent knew instantly that the Soviet was servicing a drop. "We flooded the area next day," an agent recalled, "and we saw someone else come along and pick up a pipelike object."

The agent did not finish the story. Agents who cautiously

tell espionage stories usually leave out the ending if there is no arrest and prosecution. Often, when a Soviet legal is photographed committing an act of espionage, word is passed through diplomatic channels and the diplomat-spy is quietly sent home. The U.S. counter-espionage community is usually satisfied with that ending. The Soviet's photograph quickly circulates through the community and is passed to intelligence agencies in friendly countries. The Soviet's years of training now are wasted, for he can never effectively spy as a legal in any of those countries in the photo-sharing network.

An undisclosed number of illegals in America have been detected, often by chance and rarely by American counter-espionage. One spy spotter was the proverbial little old lady. This one, who lived in Michigan's Upper Peninsula, became suspicious when she heard about a stranger looking for a copy of his birth certificate. She had lived in the town long enough to know that the name on the birth certificate he sought was that of a resident who had died in childhood. Believing that the man seeking the birth certificate was a spy, she took her suspicions to the nearest federal authority figure—the local Marine Corps recruiter, who called an FBI field office.

An agent involved in the case takes up the story: "It was assigned to a young agent who took it seriously and started following up on the tip. He managed to convince his superiors that the old lady had probably discovered a KGB technique. We found the guy in a cabin and asked him what he was up to. Things were different then. We questioned him without any formalities.

"We began checking. We requested from Social Security the names of all people in their thirties and forties asking for Social Security numbers, figuring that after getting a fake birth certificate the next move would be to apply for a Social Security card. We thought it would be rare for someone that age not to have a number. Through this check we found about six or seven illegals, all around the New York, New Jersey area."

As in the case of the spy at the picnic, the agent did not say what happened to either the original illegal or the others. Many illegals, like Herrmann, have been discovered and turned into double agents—"doubled"—rather than prosecuted. The illegal is flushed from cover quietly and confronted with a choice: arrest or an immediate shift of allegiance from the KGB to the FBI. Illegals, given the choice, rarely pick arrest, for the chances of conviction and jail are high and the chances of parole are low; the only hope is for a spy swap sometime in the future.

Other illegals may be immigrants from Cuba, Hungary, Poland, Czechoslovakia, and other Eastern Bloc countries who enter the United States as political refugees or in other acceptably legal ways. The immigrants may even enter under their true identities. But they are illegals at heart, for though they go through legal immigration procedures, they are "sleepers"—agents sent to the United States to live normal lives and await orders. They are under control by case officers of their own national intelligence agencies reporting to the KGB. They may not become active agents for years.

The effectiveness of the KGB and GRU as intelligence collection agencies is impressive. The hundreds of KGB and GRU operatives themselves glean massive amounts of information—secret and open—for their spymasters in Moscow. In recent years, though, it has been the well-recruited, well-managed American traitors who have justified the spymasters' massive budgets. Compared to the inestimable worth of the secrets that the Americans betrayed, they received low wages. But for those who sold out their country, the tax-free riches often seemed to be of magical immensity.

And for Jerry Whitworth, lavishly spending his wages of betrayal, the old adage had a new twist: A spy and his money are eventually parted.

5
"A Model Image . . ."

In the early evening of Friday, September 30, 1983, a silver Rolls-Royce pulled away from the glittering entrance of the Hyatt Regency in downtown Oakland, California, and headed toward the Bay Bridge to cross San Francisco Harbor. The tall, slim man in the backseat took a bottle from a cooler, opened it with a pleasing pop, and poured champagne for himself and the blond-haired woman at his side. They clicked glasses and toasted a new chapter in their lives. Then, for the second time that year, they settled back in the plush comfort of a hired Rolls-Royce.

The Rolls crossed the bridge, slipped through the dusky waterfront streets to downtown San Francisco, and pulled up before La Bourgogne, one of the city's most elegant restaurants. The chauffeur, an employee of a car-hiring firm called Rent-a-Rolls, recalls that when the woman got out of the car she turned to him, gave him a $20 bill, and said, "Go out and get something to eat." He drove off to a humbler restaurant.

Jerry Whitworth and his wife, Brenda, went inside and were shown to a banquette whose leather seats were tufted in gold. They contemplated menus that offered fresh Maine lobster as well as Dover sole flown in from France. There is no record of what they ordered that evening. They often paid their bills in cash.

When Jerry and Brenda finished dinner, the silver Rolls returned, picked them up, and, while they sipped brandy, whisked them back to the Hyatt Regency. There, in a suite that Whitworth had rented for the night, friends gathered to celebrate Jerry's retirement from the U.S. Navy. One of the friends was John A. Walker, a Navy radioman who had retired seven years before. Jerry picked up the bill for Walker's $108-a-night room. The Rolls, the party, and his own four-day stay at the new Hyatt cost Whitworth another $869.98. With incidentals, the weekend bash had cost the retiring chief well over $1,000.

Usually, the chauffeur said, his passengers were wealthy tourists who wanted to see the sights of San Francisco. Never before had he been hired to give first-class Rent-a-Rolls treatment to a sailor, and in Oakland at that.

If San Francisco was a tourist town, Oakland was a sailors' town. The sprawling Naval Air Station in nearby Alameda was home port to the aircraft carriers *Enterprise,* with about 5,500 men on board, and *Coral Sea,* with some 4,500 men. The station was also the home port of the combat supply ship *Niagara Falls* and three oceangoing oilers. These ships, along with an ancient repair ship at the Naval Supply Center in the port of Oakland, were manned by another 5,600 sailors. Several thousand more sailors, officers, and civilians worked ashore at the air station and supply center.

The Oakland area's large Navy community, like Navy communities everywhere, was divided along several lines. The married made friends with the married. Singles prowled bars with singles. Aviators felt most comfortable with other aviators. Above all, officers lived separate lives from the enlisted men and women. And within each of these rank-conscious divisions there were many subdivisions, mainly determined by the number of gold stripes on an officer's sleeve or the number of inverted chevrons on an enlisted sleeve. Just as captains clustered with captains, yeomen had yeoman pals, and radiomen became friends with other radiomen. Navy chiefs, who had attained the highest enlisted rating in their specialty, tended to maintain their own tight circle, occasionally admitting a first-class fellow specialist on the threshold of becoming a chief.

Senior Chief Radioman Jerry Whitworth had about as many friends, especially among senior radiomen, as any other typical Navy chief would be expected to have. But he had far more money than chiefs were supposed to have. If any of his friends wondered about all that money, they kept their questions to themselves. Chiefs on ships and ashore could make their own rules. Many had their own way to make money. Everyone in the Navy knew it, but few acknowledged it publicly. Some chiefs assigned to duties in the galley and the commissary could make a little money stealing food or a little more money taking kickbacks from suppliers. The chiefs in personnel could make money selling transfers. The chiefs in the pharmacy could make money selling drugs. But what could chiefs in the radio shack sell?

There were a few people, high in the Navy, who knew what chiefs in the radio shack and the CMS custodians could sell. There were also a few people who knew that one way to find out who was selling was to find out who was spending. For a long while that obvious move was not made.

Jerry Whitworth's 1983 spending spree had begun in February, when his ship, the aircraft carrier *Enterprise,* entered port at Subic Bay in the Philippines. For most of the crew Subic Bay was a chance to go on liberty in a sex-for-sale port where pleasures of many kinds could be bought by a sailor with not many dollars in his pocket. But for Whitworth, the ship's chief radioman, the Subic visit was a chance for a quick trip back home to California. He took leave and flew from Manila on February 9. The next day (still February 9 because he had gained a day crossing the international date line) he went to a safe-deposit box, withdrew a wad of cash, mostly in $50 bills, walked into the True Recordings store in Oakland, and bought a Sony Walkman and transformer for $363.04 in cash. That same day he bought a $2,000 security system for his home in San Leandro, just down the bay from Alameda.

Whitworth also found time that day to make payments on his three loans from the credit-union office at the Alameda Naval Air Station. He paid, in cash, $1,000 on one loan and $500 on each of the other two. The chief who paid in cash was well known to the workers in the credit-union office. He had opened an account there in 1978 with $200 in cash. The next year he got a loan for $4,168.50 toward the purchase of a 1979 Mazda RX7. In 1980 he got a loan for $6,075 on a Dodge B-200 "house car," a converted van with carpeting, paneling, plush seats, and small bay windows. The Dodge cost $11,310.50. The next year he traded in the Mazda for a 1981 Toyota Celica Supra Coupe, whose $16,675 cost he financed through a $5,000 credit-union loan, the allowance on the Mazda, and $2,000 in cash. Unlike most sailors, Whitworth did not pay off his loans through allotments from his Navy paycheck or a personal check drawn on the family's joint checking account. Whitworth always paid cash.

On February 14, Whitworth went into the Mitsui Manufacturers Bank in San Jose, about fifty miles south of San Francisco, counted out forty $50 bills, and purchased a $2,000 cashier's check. He then used the check to open an account at the investment banking firm of Kidder, Peabody & Company. He listed his employer as the U.S. Navy and the nature of his business as "national defense."

Two days later he bought an IBM computer, along with a variety of software and accessories, for $6,531.59. During his leave he spent more than $17,700 in cash, either directly with currency or by first converting the cash into theoretically untraceable cashier's checks and then using them to open bank accounts, contribute to investment accounts, or make purchases. On his return to the Philippines on February 20 he slept not in his bunk aboard the *Enterprise* but in the Hyatt Manila at a cost of $167.96. It was a most unusual leave for a Navy radioman, even a chief.

Whitworth kept up his spending even while the *Enterprise* was at sea. On March 11, from somewhere in the Pacific, he sent Brenda a cable: HI, DARLING. . . . I'D LIKE YOU TO BUY 10 (TEN) KRUGERRANDS ASAP. USE CASH. . . . DISCRETION PLEASE. Brenda purchased the Krugerrands at a San Francisco money exchange for $4,380—in cash.

In mid-April, a few days before the *Enterprise* was due to return to Alameda, the Rent-a-Rolls office telephoned the air station's security office, reported that a rented Rolls would need permission to drive through the gate to meet a sailor coming home on the *Enterprise*. The security office asked for the license number of the car and the name of the chauffeur.

Thus cleared for the base, the Rolls, with Brenda Reis Whitworth as the sole passenger, went through the gate as part of the long line of lesser cars filled with wives, children, sweethearts, and friends welcoming home the *Enterprise*'s crew. The carrier hove into sight on time, and the welcomers cheered, but the carrier ran aground and the welcomers had to wait ten more hours. That sent the cost of the Rolls up to $470, plus a $40 tip to the chauffeur.

When a member of a Navy ship's company goes ashore, he follows an old and honored ritual. Whitworth, leaving the *Enterprise,* approached the gangway, shifted an attaché case to his left hand, saluted the officer of the deck, and said, "I request permission to leave the ship, sir." The officer of the deck saluted and granted permission. Whitworth, completing the ritual, turned aft and saluted his nation's flag. Still clutching the attaché case, he then walked down the gangway and headed for the Rolls. When Jerry Whitworth went ashore he almost always carried an attaché case.

The Whitworths' two-Rolls year ended with a three-night stay over Christmas in the $183-a-day Deluxe King Room of the Stanford Court on Nob Hill, one of San Francisco's finest hotels. That bill totaled $726.69. By the last day of 1983 the Whitworths had spent more than $130,000. That year the U.S. Navy paid Chief Whitworth a little over $23,000. Brenda, a University of California graduate student, was not employed.

For years lavish spending had been a way of life for Jerry Whitworth and Brenda Reis (she sometimes preferred to use her maiden name). He carried his cash in a money clip. Once, noticing it was missing after a flight, he wrote a thank-you note to the airline because an attendant had found and returned the clip, with his $800 still intact.

He had discovered the good life just after he met Brenda, and he lavishly shared it with her. There were the $500 box seats at the San Francisco Opera, the $3,000 worth of original oil paintings bought for cash in a single day, the $1,500 Salvador Dali prints, the top-of-the-line VCR for $1,218.90 in cash, the $1,124.86 for Brenda's personal development and image development classes at the John Robert Powers Modeling School. There was the proper kind of parrot for a wealthy mod sailor—a noisy red cockatoo that cost $954. And there was the $800 worth of naughty underwear, bought for Brenda at Victoria's Secret Lingerie Store. Between them, by 1985, they had opened forty-two checking and savings accounts, forty-four credit-card accounts, and a constantly changing series of safe-deposit boxes.

Their romance had begun one day in 1973, when Whitworth was assigned to escort a group of high school students touring the Naval Training Center in San Diego. Drawn from several states, they had earned the tour as part of a program for winners of a science contest. Whitworth found himself giving a great deal of attention to a bright and pretty blond girl named Brenda. She was sixteen and he was a divorced, thirty-three-year-old instructor at the radioman's school. "Jerry made a big impression on me," Brenda Reis later said. She went back to her family's farm in Kintayre, North Dakota, and she and the tall, slim sailor began writing to each other.

Brenda had been discovered by a soul mate, for Jerry Whitworth knew what it meant to rise each day to the endless cycle of life on a farm. He had been brought up by an uncle and aunt who grew soybeans on a small spread in Muldrow, an Oklahoma town with one traffic light, about 1,500 people, and not much to offer young men who did not like farming. In 1956, just turned seventeen, Whitworth did what countless farm boys have done. He joined the Navy.

He made a lasting friendship with another recruit, Roger Olson, who lived in California. In one of those conversations in which new buddies tell each other all about their lives, Whitworth said that he was nine years old the last time he had seen his father. Olson's family lived not far from where Whitworth thought his father lived. One time he and Olson went to California, visited Roger's family, and then went on a search for Whitworth's father. They found him, sleeping off a drunk, in the back room of the Blue Moon Cafe in the little town of Mendota. He had two days' growth of beard and was lying on a bed. All Olson remembered was that Johnny Whitworth sat up and said, "Hi, Jerry."

At the end of his first Navy enlistment, Whitworth returned to Oklahoma and went to a junior college for a while. Soon he was talking again to a Navy recruiter, who told Whitworth that on his next enlistment he would be eligible for technical training. Whitworth asked for gunner's mate school. He got his third choice—radioman's school. This put him on a career path designed to keep people in the Navy for twenty years by providing them with the incentive of pay and promotion and the security of a pension and retirement at an early age.

For many who took the Navy career path—"lifers," young recruits called them—there were few detours from first enlistment to retirement. But for Whitworth, through the 1960s and into the 1970s, the end of every enlistment inspired doubt and hesitation. Instead of automatically reenlisting, he would take all the leave time he had accumulated, detour into civilian life, and then, at the last moment, sign up again, just in time to keep intact the service record that assured him a pension.

On duty, Whitworth was always the conscientious sailor. His performance records are studded with accolades, especially about his personal appearance: "He presents a model image . . . uniform always immaculate. His hair is always neatly trimmed and shoes highly polished." In June 1969, when President Nixon met with South Vietnam's President Nguyen Van Thieu at Midway to plan U.S. troop withdrawals from Vietnam, Radioman First Class Jerry Whitworth, aboard the USS *Arlington,* helped to handle the communications of the White House press covering the event.

The communications relay ship, *Arlington,* had been converted in 1963–65 from a light aircraft carrier to a floating radio ship. Before the proliferation of satellite communications, the *Arlington* and a sister ship, *Annapolis,* served as floating radio stations to relay messages to local commanders from the Pacific command headquarters at Pearl Harbor and the nation's military and political leadership in Washington. At Midway the relay was to the White House staff. For a future spy the *Arlington* was an invaluable training ground. The ship was laden with the Navy's latest communications and crypto gear and manned by communications specialists who would unquestionably share their professional secrets with a bright young radioman like Jerry Whitworth.

Later, when he worked as a radioman aboard the aircraft carrier *Constellation,* he told his division officer that he had become so interested in world events that he hoped to leave the Navy, complete college, and become a teacher of economics. Instead, he got a divorce and, after the usual spell of doubt, he reenlisted.

When Whitworth met Brenda he was nearing one of those

intersections on the career path. He reached it in the summer of 1974, and he took the usual detour. He and Roger Olson spent two months cruising in Roger's twenty-foot sailboat from San Diego down to Baja California and talked about sailing around the world.

This time, Whitworth said, he would really quit the Navy. He signed up for flying lessons at Lindbergh Field, the main airport in San Diego, and started planning to make a living as a pilot. In his vision of his latest career plan, he would fly out to sea, spot swordfish, and radio their location to charter fishing boats, whose captains would pay a fee for the service. It was at the airport one day in the early fall of 1974 that he got the vision of another life. The vision was conjured up by his friend John Walker.

Walker, like Whitworth, had enlisted in the Navy as a teenager, running away from one life to find another in the Navy. But when Walker left Scranton, Pennsylvania, he had run away from trouble, not boredom. Arrested for breaking into a store, the eighteen-year-old was saved from a jail sentence by the plea of his older brother, Arthur, who convinced a judge that the Navy, in which Arthur had already found a home, would save John from a life of crime. The judge took Arthur's advice and allowed John to enlist in the Navy.

John Walker, who had not completed high school, went from boot training to radio school in Norfolk. He took the career path to radioman,* passing through a series of radio schools and then joining the fleet, where he served both on surface ships and submarines. Cleared for top secret and given "special," or code word, clearance, he was also trained in cryptography, a trusted handler of highly classified messages. On two of his ships and at two shore stations he had been the CMS custodian.

Besides the usual oath of allegiance all men and women take when they enter the armed forces of the United States, radiomen are given another oath. They "solemnly swear and declare upon my honor" that they will not reveal the secrets entrusted to them. They also promise to notify the Naval Investigative Service or the

---

* Radioman, like all other Navy rates that have the suffix *man,* applies to both men and women. The Navy considers *man* part of the name of the rate, not an indication of the sailor's sex.

FBI "should an unauthorized individual attempt to solicit" classified information from them. When they leave the service they sign debriefing documents in which they swear that they have no classified information and that they will never transmit any classified information to any unauthorized person.

Whitworth, Walker, and other radiomen, especially aboard ship, belong to an elite, a group that has the first word on everything. Shipmates say of radiomen, "They deliver the mail": the ship's missions and ports of call, weather forecasts, promotions and transfers, personal messages to crewmen from families ashore. Radiomen possessed secrets ranging from gossip to national security. Secrets were a kind of commodity, and the keeping of secrets was not so much a sacred trust as a privileged job.

At one time, the cryptographic part of the job had been entrusted only to officers. But, as cryptography, like communications, became more and more a technical matter, the Navy shifted the responsibility for secrets-keeping from officers to enlisted men and women. Navy Captain David L. Ricketts, who has commanded one of the Navy's five master communications stations and headed the satellite communications division of the Naval Telecommunications Command, conceded that the system has not always worked. "Many officers and many enlisted people have had careers ruined because they were found to be handling the material improperly," he said. Radiomen could indeed get into trouble by not following the rules. But, because they belonged to an elite group, they usually were able to close ranks to outsiders, including officers.

Secrecy also means power, and chief radiomen had a great deal of power through knowledge—"the fount of all wisdom," as one of them put it. "The most successful admirals," he added, "will tell you the reason they are admirals today is because a chief trained them." Of some 800,000 men and women in the U.S. Navy, there are only 3,200 chief radiomen, and they are carefully distributed throughout the Navy's many ships and shore stations.

Now and then a Navy radioman would be in a bar near a base and someone—perhaps another radioman, perhaps a retired one—would say that he had heard about "somebody" who would pay some money for a few yards of what radiomen called "yellow," the sheets of yellow paper that spun off the "monitor roll," a continuous printout of teletype traffic containing complete messages and garbled messages, information on ship movements, happy birthday greetings to crew members from families ashore, instructions about the taking on of fuel and supplies, transmissions about the innumerable details of shipkeeping. All of the yellow was classified, but many radiomen scoffed at the classification, since so much of the yellow was boring and innocuous.

Radiomen told each other tales of offers for yellow and joshed each other about sudden sources of income. Some of John Walker's buddies on the Polaris submarine *Simon Bolivar,* for instance, wondered where their radioman had gotten the money in 1966 to open the Bamboo Snack Bar in Ladson, South Carolina, near the Navy base in Charleston.*

There is reason to believe that sometime in the 1960s, Walker began dabbling in espionage, passing off to middlemen bits of yellow. As Walker later told the story, the tottering finances of the bar inspired him to try this tepid form of espionage. Most authorities believe that his story of the visit to the Soviet Embassy in 1968 is true, and officially that year is given as the start of his espionage career. But the authors have been told by authoritative sources that the dabbling in espionage took place earlier and that the visit to the embassy marked Walker's *formal* acceptance of life as a Soviet spy in the U.S. Navy.

By 1968, Walker had reached the rank of warrant officer, which took him out of the enlisted ranks but not quite up to the level of a commissioned officer. A Navy warrant officer is not a commissioned rank. Rather, a "warrant" indicates proficiency in some specialty; a commission bestows true officer's status. Even a lowly ensign, as a commissioned officer, outranks a Navy warrant officer with twenty years of service. At heart, Walker was still the consummate Navy chief: the man who knew the ropes, the man who knew how to make things work, the man to see for favors.

On the table of organization, he was a vital specialist in communications. At the time that he walked into the Soviet Embassy in 1968, he was serving as watch officer for the Atlantic Fleet submarine force. The force was one of the Atlantic Fleet's four "type commands" (the others being air, surface, and Ma-

---

* The bar later became a Veterans of Foreign Wars post, with Walker as landlord.

rines). Type commands of the Atlantic and Pacific fleets were administrative rather than operational. They were responsible for personnel assignment, ship training, maintenance, providing proper equipment, munitions, and other support. But in both fleets the submarine forces were also operational commands—they actually directed submarine activities.

Thus a watch and communications message center officer had access to the entire fleet's operational plans, communications, and probably even detailed data on intelligence and enemy forces. Walker could tell his Soviet spymasters how much the U.S. Navy knew about them. He probably could also tell them the operating areas for all U.S. submarines and details of changes in their missions after they deployed. He could provide other invaluable data for Soviet military planners and analysts. One of the keylists he regularly supplied, for example, was so secret that only he, as message center officer, could handle it.

Walker's next duty assignment, in September 1969, took him across the country from Norfolk to San Diego, where he became for a short while the director of the Navy's basic radioman school and then director of the practical application laboratory, a place that gave students realistic training with communications equipment. The lab, Walker later regretfully remarked, "wasn't the best duty station for spying." He was making only about two drops a year, and his spy pay was down from his standard—"No one should expect less than $4,000 a month if producing good yellow"—to about $2,000 a month.

While he worked on the submarine force staff he had passed to the Soviets a steady supply of operations cryptographic information. The radio school could not provide Walker with operational cryptographic messages or even a few feet of good yellow. He did the best he could, passing "naval correspondence that would come across my desk, portions of operations orders, some intelligence information."

Walker's staff of about fifteen instructors included Jerry Whitworth, whom Walker soon cultivated. Their friendship puzzled Michael O'Connor, a fellow radioman, who would one day describe Whitworth as "a squared-away individual" and Walker as "arrogant, noisy, inconsistent," a "ding-dong, an asshole." Walker, O'Connor said, "liked to have all the toys of the rich. He liked to have things around him that would indicate he was well-to-do."

Walker flashed his wealth, taking young enlisted women to dinner in expensive San Diego restaurants, boasting about his vaguely described investments, playing the captain-host of parties aboard his sailboat, *Dirty Old Man*. Whitworth, who had learned to enjoy sailing on his cruise with Roger Olson, was a frequent passenger on the *Dirty Old Man*.

Walker, married since 1957 and the father of three daughters and a son, in San Diego began living in bachelor quarters while his wife found a family home after the transcontinental trip. Walker and Whitworth spent a great deal of time socializing. Although Walker was only two years older than Whitworth, Walker acted the part of the older, wiser man giving counsel to a young associate, who, as usual, was wondering what he was going to do with his life. On cruises aboard the *Dirty Old Man*, Walker often steered the conversation around to Whitworth's ethical attitudes. Whitworth fancied himself an intellectual. He said he was an atheist, a devotee of the anarchist author Ayn Rand, and a libertarian who believed in absolute individual freedom.

Walker knew that his own next assignment would probably be on a ship, and that duty held some promise for an improvement in the secrets he would deliver. But "I couldn't imagine how I was going to try to make drops in the Washington, D.C., area twice a year while I was on a ship that could be deploying for six months or more." Besides, in 1975 he would have completed his twenty years and could retire. He needed a partner who had access to highly sensitive information.

By mid-1971, near the end of his assignment at the school, Walker had sized up Whitworth as a good candidate for recruitment. "I realized I couldn't go on with this forever," Walker later said. "My wife was an extremely unstable alcoholic. It became obvious that she was telling her relatives literally what I was doing. I felt that I would have to get out of the Navy at a minimum time, twenty years."

Walker began to plan a future for himself. He would have an agent aboard a ship who would gather material for him. Walker could then pick it up at ports anywhere in the world and deliver it to Soviet contacts in Washington or elsewhere. According to

Walker, he made these plans without informing his KGB handlers.

In conversations with Whitworth ashore and aboard the *Dirty Old Man,* Walker was exploring Whitworth's attitude toward espionage—"subtly," as Walker described the process. "Just questions that would try to probe his possible larceny in his heart." One day Whitworth casually remarked that although he had been divorced for several years, he had not notified the Navy of the change in his marital status and, as a result, he continued to draw a small basic housing allowance that was given only to married sailors. Walker had found the larceny in Whitworth's heart.

The popular movie *Easy Rider* gave Walker a metaphor for taking the larceny out of Whitworth's heart and putting it to work stealing secrets. The long-haired, anti-Establishment motorcycle riders in the movie would seem to be the opposite of the two career sailors, especially Whitworth, so frequently commended for his correct haircut, spotless uniforms, and highly polished shoes.

But Walker said he saw a similarity between his free-spending life-style and the carefree ways of the hippies in *Easy Rider.* The two sailors talked about the movie, about the hippies deciding to take a chance to make one big drug deal. When Walker asked Whitworth whether he had ever thought about taking a chance to make a big killing—as the hippies had in the movie— Whitworth admitted he had. From then on it was a matter of waiting for the right moment of translation from theory to reality.

When Walker got his orders to the combat supply ship *Niagara Falls,* he temporarily postponed his plan. On the *Niagara,* as chief radioman and CMS custodian, he could once again steal cryptographic material and operational messages for the Soviets. His deliveries would dramatically improve and he would be able to get back up to his accustomed $4,000-a-month spy pay.

During Walker's three years on board the *Niagara Falls,* the ship twice spent long periods in the western Pacific, once for fourteen months and once for ten months. But he managed to make about two drops in the Washington area each year. He provided the Soviets with nearly 100 percent of the cryptographic material from the ship's battery of code machines. Using a Minox camera the Soviets had given him, he shot a photograph of each day's keylists. Later he would strictly follow the rules for destroying them, and the birth-to-death record would show that the keylists had lived an uneventful life from the time the National Security Agency issued them until their duly reported destruction aboard ship.

Walker estimated that every three months he went through six to eight rolls of film, each of which contained thirty-six exposures. He had no trouble getting the film off the ship. He simply tossed the rolls into his attaché case and waited for the day when the ship returned to her home port. He would then take leave, fly to Washington, and, following extremely detailed instructions, make a drop.

By the time he reported aboard the *Niagara Falls*, Walker had every reason to be confident in his spycraft. He had gotten his first lesson about drops in February 1968, a month after he had walked into the Soviet Embassy, when he had met his Soviet handler at Zayre's department store in a suburb of Washington. The Soviet intelligence officer, a legal from the Soviet Embassy subject to the twenty-five-mile travel restrictions on Soviet diplomats, could not take the chance of breaking the rules by traveling to Norfolk.

The Soviet had scolded Walker for leaving his first shipment of keylists in a National Airport locker because the lockers were frequently checked by security officers looking for bombs. The Soviet introduced Walker to the procedure for a dead drop, which the Soviets formally called "an exchange": secrets for money. Walker was told he would be paid in cash, mostly in $50 and $20 bills. The Soviets disliked other denominations because, they believed, the Treasury Department kept close watch on $100 bills and higher currency.

Over the years the exchanges had varied little: Walker drives for several miles along a route, usually in suburban Maryland outside of Washington. When he is certain he is not being followed, he drops a signal bottle (later, as soda bottles became less popular, he drops a 7-Up can). A Soviet intelligence officer drops a similar bottle or can at a different location. In theory, officer and spy would be seeing each other's signal almost at the same time and dropping their packages at the same time at different locations.

The packages of crypto material and other information that Walker left were carefully wrapped and then placed in a plastic trash bag, the kind that inundate the nation's countryside. Trash was packed in with the spy material, but it was "clean trash"— bottles and cans that were carefully washed out, scraps of paper, empty Q-tip and other small discarded boxes. Dirty trash would have smells that could attract animals that might carry off the trash bag to their lair.

The Soviet would drop a package containing Walker's money, instructions about the next scheduled drop, and sometimes tips on spying. Once Walker was told to read *The French Connection,* a true account of the New York Police Department's breakup of a drug ring, to get a good description of surveillance techniques.

The package Walker deposited contained classified material, usually in the form of photographs that Walker had made with the palm-sized Minox camera, "the standard spy size," as he once described it. The Soviets provided the camera and usually the film, along with very specific instructions: Use black and white film (Plus-X Pan, ASA 125). Set the camera at $1/100$ of a second, hold it eighteen inches from the document, illuminate the document by placing within a foot of the document a lamp containing a 75- or 100-watt bulb.

Walker planned that Whitworth would take over the photographing of keylists and other secret communications materials while Walker would continue to be the drop man. In his conversations with Whitworth, Walker had gone to the threshold of recruiting Whitworth, but had not directly admitted that, for them, the *Easy Rider* score was to be espionage.

Walker, a now-and-then kind of husband and father, had moved his family to Union City, down the bay from Oakland, the *Niagara Falls'* home port. Once, while Walker was at sea, Whitworth went from San Diego to Union City, stayed at the Walker home, and went sailing with Walker's wife, Barbara. When they were at sea he began asking questions.

Barbara had known of Walker's spying for years, probably from the beginning. At least twice she went on drops with him. One time the money he picked up in his package was so tightly rolled, she had to iron the bills flat before they could spend them.

When she and Whitworth talked, in the sailboat and later in

the Walkers' family room, Whitworth wanted to know what Walker had been hinting at in his questioning back in San Diego. "I told Jerry," Barbara recalled, "that John was recruiting him to spy. He said he hesitated because John bragged too much, and he didn't trust him. I said something to the same effect, that he couldn't be trusted." Barbara, who once had an affair with John Walker's brother, Arthur, said that her times alone with Whitworth had been platonic. Whitworth, however, once said he would never think of trusting Walker alone with Brenda.

The word *trust* came naturally to radiomen, for their duty depended upon a special kind of trust, one that did not necessarily involve faith. The rules for destroying cryptographic material, for instance, stated that the destruction had to be done by two people—one radioman to do the destroying and one to watch the other. *I trust you. You trust me.* At this point in his career Walker especially needed someone he could trust in that special way. Time was running out on his one-man espionage enterprise.

In 1974, Walker would be leaving the *Niagara Falls* and Whitworth would be leaving the radio school for a new at-sea assignment. Walker felt that the time had come to, as Walker put it, make the sales pitch: A steady supply of good crypto meant a steady supply of cash.

One day in September 1974, Walker turned up in San Diego and arranged to meet Whitworth in Boom Trenchard's Flare Path restaurant and bar at Lindbergh Field. By then Whitworth had his pilot's license and was still planning to end his Navy career and begin his spot-the-swordfish scheme.

"We went to a secluded portion of the bar, at a table," Walker remembers, "and I told him I was interested in using him in an illegal activity, and that even discussing it was illegal. If he wanted me to talk about it, we would. If he didn't wish to speak about it, we would not. And that would be the end of it. He said he was interested in hearing the proposal.

"I wanted a declaration from him whether he was interested or not, and I pointed out it was even illegal to be talking about it. He was excited and was interested in hearing what I had to say. I made him swear a blood oath that . . . if he didn't want to cooperate, he would not turn me in. And he said for me to continue.

"I told him I'd been involved in selling classified material for a number of years, and it was profitable, and I would build him into the—into the sale. He responded affirmatively, that he would be interested.

"Well, he was most curious as to who the buyers were. I told him it was—that I wasn't sure. I was working with people that I had met, possibly could have been organized crime, Mafia, but that the buyers were allied countries, such as Israel, or private defense organizations, such as *Jane's Fighting Ships* [an unofficial British annual publication that describes, in photographs and words, the ships of the world's navies]. The word *Soviets* was not used.

"We discussed the money. I told him he could expect to make $2,000 a month, roughly, for standard message traffic, and that . . . he could expect to make more for cryptographic." Walker predicted that Whitworth would make more money from traffic from the KW-7, a code machine usually devoted to important secret messages, than from the code machine known as KY-8. To get the most income, Walker advised, "just go for the highest classification and most sensitive categories." They agreed on a fifty-fifty split.

"I explained that it was my plan to get out of the military at the end of twenty years. That doing espionage was very difficult, due to ships' deployments." He told Whitworth that "we needed one person keeping contact with the buyer and the other person obtaining the material on a ship or station, and that my job would be to run between him, wherever he was in the world, and wherever the drop point was."

There was nothing to fear, Walker said. He had been operating for years and had not had any problems. A two-man ring would not be that much more difficult to operate safely. Whitworth said he was worried about Walker's wife, but Walker assured him that Barbara "should not be a problem, as long as she was adequately compensated and paid." Whitworth insisted that his name never be given to Walker's contacts. Walker agreed, but with the material in his next Washington drop he enclosed a note identifying Whitworth by name.

The Soviets were shocked to learn of the recruiting of Whitworth. They told Walker, through a note with his next drop, that the KGB did its own recruiting and did not allow agents to do so on their own. Walker shrugged off the complaint; he felt there was nothing they could do about it. The KGB's concern about Whitworth faded a short while later when Walker's handlers started to see what his unauthorized recruit was sending them.

On October 10, 1974, Whitworth made up his mind. He reenlisted in the Navy and enlisted as a spy for Walker. All was working according to plan. Walker's three-year tour of duty on the *Niagara Falls* ended about this time, and Walker returned to Norfolk, where he was assigned first to the staff of the amphibious force and then to the staff of the service force commander. Walker retired from the Navy in July 1976, but, thanks to Whitworth, he continued being a spy.

Early in 1975, as Whitworth was about to learn a new phase of Navy communications, he and Walker met at Walker's home in Norfolk. "Well, we finalized the agreement to work in espionage," as Walker put it, and he sealed their partnership with a payment of $4,000 to Whitworth. Shortly after the meeting Whitworth reported for duty at the Army Communications School in Fort Monmouth, New Jersey, where he would take a short course in satellite communications technology and procedures. Whitworth's graduation present to Walker was a classified manual entitled *Tactical Satellite Communications System AN/WSC-5*, which Walker copied and passed on to the Soviets, who at that time were far behind the United States in satellite communications.

The course at Fort Monmouth was in preparation for Whitworth's next assignment. He had volunteered to be the petty officer in charge of satellite communications at the Naval Communications Station in the Navy's most desolate duty station—"the Rock." That was the Navy name for Diego Garcia, a tiny atoll in the Chagos Archipelago, in the Indian Ocean, south of the Maldive Islands.

The island, though a U.S. Navy facility, was still technically part of the British Indian Trust Territory. The dot in the middle of the Indian Ocean was far more important than its size and isolation implied. The Navy wanted it as a communications and intelligence center in an area that had lacked a Western presence since the withdrawal of British forces years before. The Navy was also building an airfield and a deep-water anchorage there for the replenishment of surface ships and submarines.

Walker soon got word that his partner was at work. In a handwritten "Hi, Johnny" letter dated June 28, 1975, Whitworth wrote, "I've finally made my first dive. It was real good. My future dives don't look very diverse. We will have to wait and see. . . ." Scuba diving was one of the recreational pastimes available on the barren atoll. Because Whitworth really had an interest in scuba diving, Walker and Whitworth had decided that references to diving would be their personal code for Whitworth's espionage.

Whitworth left the Rock early in 1976 and, on a long, leisurely leave that followed, visited his childhood home in Oklahoma, spent some time in the Virgin Islands, saw Walker in Norfolk, and stopped by North Dakota to see his young pen pal Brenda Reis. In May, just before he sailed from San Diego in the aircraft carrier *Constellation,* he and Brenda were married. He kept the marriage a secret, probably because his Navy pay records still carried him as married to his first wife.

Whitworth's new assignment would greatly improve the material Walker delivered to the Soviets. As the carrier's Classified Materials System custodian, Whitworth had access to all cryptographic materials and, if he wished, virtually every word received and transmitted by the aircraft carrier.

The carrier's first cruise was a short one. The *Constellation* returned to her home port of San Diego on August 6. Eleven days later Walker went to his safe-deposit box in Norfolk, took out some cash, and flew to California. On the weekend of August 19 he had dinner in San Diego with Jerry, Brenda, Roger Olson, and a Navy enlisted woman who had been a frequent guest aboard the *Dirty Old Man* in the old days.

Olson despised Walker. "That John Walker would sell out his own mother," Olson told Whitworth.

"You don't know Johnny," Whitworth replied. "If you got to know Johnny, you'd like him." Whitworth particularly liked Walker that month because sometime before Walker returned to Norfolk he gave Whitworth $8,000 in cash. Whitworth had passed Walker his first sample from the *Constellation*—between 70 and 80 percent of all the cryptographic material that had flowed to and from the ship while Whitworth was on board. On September 7 the carrier sailed for a long Pacific cruise, a "deployment" in Navy parlance.

A meeting pattern developed. Walker would usually travel to San Diego when the *Constellation* returned to port, although sometimes Whitworth, who liked to travel, would fly to Norfolk, as he did in April 1977. In that typical meeting Whitworth went to Walker's home, handed over the classified material, and received $12,000. The amount of money reflected a delay in payment rather than the value of the material handed over. "The money lagged," according to Walker. The Soviets took time to examine and validate the material before payment. "It was not a COD operation." Sometimes payments were made a year or more after delivery.

By 1977, Walker, divorced from Barbara, had begun a cover career as a private investigator in the Norfolk area and looked forward to years paced by a profitable rhythm—a meeting with Whitworth and then a dead drop near Washington to leave secrets and pick up money. Soon after Walker made the drop of the April 1977 film delivery, however, he was contacted and told that the next shipment would not be a drop. Whitworth, who, as a radioman, knew the ship's schedule well in advance, had told Walker that the *Constellation* would pay a port visit to Hong Kong in August. The Soviets instructed Walker to go to Hong Kong, pick up the delivery, and fly to Casablanca, Morocco, where he would meet an intelligence officer.

Face-to-face meetings of agent and handler are always risky. But, to the KGB, tightening control on Walker was worth the risk. Here was an agent who had recruited another agent on his own, who had not spoken directly to a control officer since the face-to-face meeting near Zayre's department store in 1968, and who, with his free-living ways, seemed more vulnerable to detection as a civilian than he had been as a sailor. He needed to be reined in.

Whitworth, as a leading chief, had no trouble arranging for leave in Hong Kong from August 10 to August 17. Like other crewmen, he was able to make hotel reservations through Navy communications. He chose the Holiday Inn.

Whitworth met Walker in the hotel and handed him a box of Q-tips. Under the top layer of Q-tips were cartridges of Minox film. The film was undeveloped. Whitworth told Walker what he had photographed and Walker made a roll-by-roll list of the purchased secrets. By then the secrets were all routine: keylists for code machines, messages between the aircraft carrier and shore stations, messages to and from other ships in the carrier battle group, operations orders, operational plans, details of battle-group problems, and supply shortages.

Walker, who had arrived in Hong Kong on August 10, left twenty-four hours later. He flew via Bangkok and Cairo to Casablanca, where he met Patsy Marsee, a girlfriend from Norfolk. At night, using hand-printed instructions he had received at his last dead drop, Walker took a cab to a designated spot in the port city, walked a prescribed route for several blocks, and met his Soviet contact. From now on Walker would be meeting Soviet intelligence officers more often.

Back in Norfolk, Walker got out his planning calendar for January 1978 and wrote *F/F-1* on the date January 21 and *FF* on January 27 and 28. The Soviet in Casablanca had given him the schedule for the next face-to-face meeting: January 21 in Vienna. (The other days were alternative meeting dates set up in case the scheduled meeting was missed by either party.)

Walker met Whitworth again on November 28, 1977, in San Diego, where Walker paid Whitworth $6,000 for three months' worth of secrets from the *Constellation* and headed back to Norfolk. Walker kept the Whitworth film rolls until January 19, when he flew to Europe. Following the elaborate directions of what he called the "Vienna Procedure," he went to a specified car-rental firm, rented a car, and drove it around the city, tracing streets on a map. He parked exactly where he was told to park, got out of the car, and began walking along a corkscrew route that spiraled him through some twenty turns. He had to time his pace so that when he reached the rendezvous point his contact would be approaching from the opposite direction.

"As soon as we made visual contact, I would pass the material to the agent," Walker recalled, lapsing into the stiff, formal language of his "exchange" instructions. "He would disappear with that for fifteen minutes or so and then come back for the verbal discussion," which would include some talk about Communist ideology. The contact, "struggling to remember the nomenclature and the names of the equipment," would ask Walker to try to get certain information or to discontinue some line of secrets in which the Soviets had lost interest.

At the end of the meeting the Soviet would give Walker, in

writing, the procedures for the next face-to-face meeting. Walker would have eleven such meetings in Vienna. On one trip Walker left Norfolk early enough to take his mother to Italy. On the way back, to ease getting his cash payment through U.S. customs, Walker put the bills in a money belt and strapped it to his mother. The smiling customs man waved the plump old lady through.

Walker was told to destroy his copies of the Vienna Procedure. He kept them, just as he kept his records for trips made through Mr. Happy Travel Service, just as he kept the receipts for the hotels in Vienna and other cities on his espionage rounds, or, as Walker sometimes called it, using the Soviet word for spying, "cooperation." He also kept his business planning calendars. There he noted his face-to-face meetings with *F-F* scrawled on the appropriate dates. As a spy, Walker was stupidly arrogant, showing the characteristic "poor judgment and little insight" of the sociopath. But stupid as he may have been, for a long while no one caught him.

Whitworth's tour of duty on the *Constellation* ended in July 1978. His next ship would be one that had given Walker one of his most successful runs, the *Niagara Falls.* Because the ship was berthed in Alameda, Whitworth and his wife had to move to the San Francisco Bay Area. Early in July, Brenda closed the safe-deposit box at the Bank of America in El Cajon, near San Diego, and shortly after opened one in a bank in San Leandro, the Whitworths' new residence. During the month of the move to San Leandro, Whitworth and his wife spent more than $8,700 in cash and made down payments on a variety of articles, from a new Volkswagen to several original oil paintings, the kind that are sold as "investments in art."

When Whitworth reported aboard the *Niagara Falls* the commanding officer wanted to make him assistant CMS custodian, at least until he got to know the ship. But Whitworth convinced the captain to appoint him custodian right away. That had been Walker's job aboard the ship, and Whitworth got from his friend firsthand instructions on just how to enter the vault containing cryptographic materials, open the inner safe in complete privacy, and photograph keylists. Whitworth had better opportunity for espionage aboard the small *Niagara Falls* than aboard the *Constellation.* The supply ship had the same type of cryptographic equipment that the aircraft carrier used and tuned into most of the same radio circuits. And on the *Niagara Falls* Whitworth had unrestricted access to all cryptographic equipment and materials—just as Walker had had.

The *Niagara,* an auxiliary ship, was rarely considered an important ship for the sending and receiving of high-priority fleet communications. She was a lowly supply ship that sailed the Pacific carrying supplies—beans and bullets—to warships. But the *Niagara* and her sister ships, as well as the combat oilers, had to have access to the highest level of communications in order to make their vital rendezvous with the warships. For a spy the *Niagara Falls* was a perfect roost. One of the odd coincidences of the Walker-Whitworth espionage saga is that each man had a tour of duty aboard this spymaster's dream.

Whitworth made a fine impression on his division officer, who commended his new radioman for his "immaculate and impeccable appearance," as well as for his professional and volunteer activities. Whitworth acted as a drug and alcohol counselor —and, incidentally, getting to know who in the crew was potentially susceptible to blackmail. Using his experience with the still relatively new satellite communications system, Whitworth got permission to examine all related equipment in his ship—and, at every opportunity, in other ships. He appeared so conscientious about wanting to compare communications equipment that officers on other ships welcomed him aboard so he could learn all he wanted to learn.

Whitworth was such a good radioman—despite other duties, he "maintained the Classified Materials System account in error-free condition"—that he was recommended for advancement to senior chief petty officer and, if he wished, passage into a program that would lead to a commission. "He would well serve on an embassy staff, a joint or combined staff," a personnel report on him said, "and his wife is that kind of Navy wife who would be an asset in any of these assignments."

Whitworth made a similar good impression on the officers of the KGB, which gave him a raise from $2,000 a month to $4,000. Walker called his protégé's production "at least good, if not excellent" and claimed credit for getting Whitworth the raise. But Whitworth believed the quality of the material he was now supplying was worth even more. Walker agreed.

In an inspired pitch at his next face-to-face, he pointed out that the Soviets were getting far more for the paltry money paid to him and Whitworth than they were getting for the huge sums of money spent on various ineffective guerrilla groups around the world. The handler, according to Walker, said he "would take my arguments to his boss and see what could be resolved."

Whitworth's phenomenal deliveries came to an end in August 1979 when he was transferred from the *Niagara Falls* to the naval communications center at the Naval Air Station in Alameda. But Walker was not dismayed, for he had great hope for even better crypto from Alameda, which, like Walker's erstwhile post in Norfolk, processed not merely messages for a single ship but messages for an entire oceanic command structure. Alameda was one of the Navy's fifty-six telecommunications centers, which handled satellite-carried ship-to-shore and ship-to-ship communications, including messages to and from all ships and aircraft operating out of Alameda. By Navy doctrine such centers were in operation in time of peace just as they would be in war.

Walker's hopes plummeted, however, when, at a meeting in Norfolk on August 13, Whitworth, while collecting a $12,000 payment, said that he had decided to retire from the Navy. Once again Whitworth had come to an intersection on his career path and once again he was walking to the edge of retirement. He made out papers requesting retirement—technically a request for transfer to the fleet reserve—effective September 30, 1980.

Using the usual slow-motion form of communication between him and the Soviets, Walker passed this disturbing information along in a note contained in the package he deposited at a dead drop near Washington in September 1979. On the weekend of January 18, 1980, he met with Whitworth, got a shipment of cryptographic material, and tried to convince Whitworth to stay on.

Walker warned Whitworth that he faced a drastic change in his well-being if he quit spying. "He had a fairly rich life-style," according to Walker. "Expensive cars, clothing, and an almost hobby of gourmet dining." Walker told Whitworth that, with a "nonworking student wife" and only Navy retirement pay to live on, he would have to give up his luxuries.

Walker had read Whitworth as well in 1980 as he had when he first recruited him in 1974. Whitworth had indeed become a big spender—sometimes splurging as much as $15,000 in a month. Once, years ago, he had told a friend he needed no more belongings than what he could pack into his Volkswagen. By the 1980s another friend said, "Jerry tended to prefer a decadent lifestyle." She recalled one of the small ways he showed off his wealth. "He would replenish my liquor cabinet. He would often comment that I needed to upgrade what I had in there. So he liked to buy Courvoisier or Chivas or Dry Sack or better wines than I had there." Jerry told her that he, the farm kid from a town with one stoplight, had learned to savor a better life by emulating the life-style of a good friend he admired. The friend's name was John A. Walker, who, Jerry said, sometimes made use of his initials to create the nickname Jaws.

A week after meeting with Whitworth, Walker went to Vienna, passed along the latest Whitworth shipment, got a reaction from his handler to the news about Whitworth's looming retirement, and was told to make his next Washington drop on May 18, a Sunday. (The KGB usually scheduled drops on weekends because the Soviets had noticed that FBI surveillance of embassy legals slackened on Saturdays and Sundays.)

Next to the date May 18 on his 1980 planning calendar Walker wrote a large *1* and *$*—signifying that at the drop that day he had picked up $200,000, of which half—$1 for $100,000— was due him. He called Whitworth the next day and guardedly told him that he was about to get $100,000, a payment covering his services over the previous year and into the future.

The $100,000 was essentially a reenlistment bonus from the KGB. Whitworth had withdrawn his retirement request on April 7, after getting Walker's life-style lecture. He notified the Navy that he had changed his mind. He said he wanted to remain on active duty.

Whitworth had more than $100,000 to celebrate. The KGB was even going to pay for a new van. "Jerry was unable to photograph cryptographic material in his office in Alameda," Walker later explained. "And we discussed various ways in which we might solve the problem. I suggested it might be possible to remove that material from the office overnight or during lunch, and he felt that that would be too long a period of time. And too dangerous.

"So I suggested going to a vehicle in the parking lot, which would be quick. And we decided that if he had a van, he would photograph the material in the van, right next to the building, rather quickly. So, with that plan in mind, [at] the next meeting with the Soviets, I told them that Mr. Whitworth needed a van to continue his work. They responded affirmatively.

"And there was another side deal. The [Soviets] had just started at that point, or previous to that, where they were going to offer $10,000 bonuses to Mr. Whitworth if he could produce 100 percent complete chain of cryptographic [keylists] on each delivery, where no days would be missing, and certainly no months. Jerry had almost accomplished that at that point. And they viewed the van as both a bonus and an operating expense."

Whitworth had purchased the van in anticipation of the KGB bonus. So when Walker, accompanied by Pat Marsee, arrived at San Francisco Airport for the $100,000 meeting in June, Jerry and Brenda met them and surprised them by taking them to the van and sitting them on a couch at a table. Candles were lit, glasses were filled, cheese and crackers were passed around. They drove to the Whitworths' San Leandro home in style, sipping champagne and watching the view speed past the van's darkened bubble windows.

In November the two spies met again for a more routine kind of meeting. Whitworth passed his material to Walker, who shortly after delivered it to his handler in Vienna. The crisis of Whitworth's retirement had passed. The cryptographic material continued to flow from the Navy communications center in Alameda to the Soviets via Walker, and the cash flowed back. At a meeting in July 1981, Walker passed Whitworth $50,000—a total of $40,000 for ten months' work plus $10,000 for the van.

Up to now Walker had scrupulously documented his meetings with Whitworth, his dead drops around Washington, and each face-to-face rendezvous with Soviet contacts overseas. The pattern begins to change after December 1981, coincidentally when Whitworth's "excellent delivery" of cryptographic material from Alameda abruptly ends.

The cutoff came when the Navy moved Whitworth from Alameda, putting him on what the Navy calls temporary additional duty at the Naval Communications Station at Stockton, in central California, about seventy miles east of San Francisco. Although Stockton had more code machines than Alameda had, Whitworth, because his assignment involved administrative duties, had no contact with cryptography during his three months at Stockton.

From this point on Walker is less precise about the documentation of his espionage business. The pattern of meetings—with Whitworth, with the Soviets—also changes. And Walker, becoming suspicious about Whitworth, steps up his search for another supplier.

As traffic manager at Alameda, Whitworth had been able to put his hands on a copy of every message sent or received—and photograph it. He could earn his $10,000 KGB bonus for "100 percent complete chain of cryptographic." In Stockton, assigned to administrative work, Whitworth lost easy access to cryptographic material. Walker was beginning to panic and the KGB was beginning to get anxious.

By January 1982, Walker had not seen Whitworth for nearly six months. They had a quick meeting late in January—Walker arrived on Friday and returned to Norfolk on Monday, with a scant supply of material. Although the meeting with Whitworth was brief, Walker still had time for some other urgent business. He called his daughter Laura, who lived near San Leandro, and told her he had to talk to her.

She sensed what the topic would be. About three years before, while she was an enlisted woman in the Army, she had taken leave from Fort Polk, Louisiana, and had visited her father in Norfolk. Like her mother, two sisters, and kid brother, she knew her father was a spy. He took her to Knickerbocker's Restaurant, a treat for a married daughter who was broke and trying to cope with a husband who had drug problems.

Over dinner "we started talking about how I could earn more money while I was in the Army by—he didn't explain how at first. And then he began to ask me what exactly I did, what kinds of equipment I worked with, and if it were possible for me to advance from just a training mode." She said later that he had not directly asked her to spy.

When she told him she could not stay in the Army because she was pregnant with his first grandchild, "he suggested that that could easily be eliminated by abortion, that that didn't have to be a problem. I said I wouldn't do it."

Now, three years later, out of the Army, struggling with a tottering marriage, a husband still on drugs, and a son almost two, she put her son in her old car, prayed that it would start, and drove to Whitworth's home in San Leandro, where she picked up her father. They drove for a few blocks. Then he motioned for her to stop at a store, where he bought a camera so he could take pictures of his grandson, Christopher.

"To avoid audio detection" by the FBI—a fear that now began to haunt him—Walker said they had to talk outdoors. He directed her to a park in San Leandro. He told her she could return to the Army and spy for him at Whitworth's current rate, $4,000 a month. There was a problem—Christopher—but that could be solved. Walker suggested that if she did return to the Army, she might have to give up custody because the Army probably would not allow the reenlistment of a young mother.

"Her situation was the pits, as usual," Walker recalled later. "Her husband may not have been working. I'm not sure if she was. Her cars were barely running, and they didn't seem to have any plan [on] how they were going to enjoy the mainstream of American life and get jobs."

There was a way to get into the mainstream, he said, making his pitch: "The network that had safely been operating for years, a godfather operation offered to a child, in which she could make some money and get out of the pits. I continued talking to Laura about the possibilities of getting into espionage for profit, and, at that time, she agreed to do so."

He told her not to worry about what to do with Christopher. He would take the child and find some way to raise him in Norfolk. Or, and this seemed more likely, he would talk her mother, who by now was living in Maine, into taking him. As Walker recalled the walk in the park with Laura and Christopher, "She said that she would do it. She had some things to get together first." He said he paid her a retainer but could not recall how much.

As Laura recalled the conversation, "He said he would hire a nanny, and I could go into the Army, and I could spy for him. He said that anything was valuable. And he mentioned journals, manuals, repair manuals. But the most desirable was codes, any kinds of codes I could get my hands on. No matter how old. They were still valuable."

A few weeks later she returned to San Leandro and had dinner with Whitworth, whom she had known for several years. Bank records show that he wrote out a check to her for $600. She has described this as a loan that she did not pay back. Now Laura, for a while, leaves the spy saga. She will return later.

On February 13, less than two weeks after the short, busy visit to San Leandro, Walker had a face-to-face meeting in Vienna. Now, suddenly, nothing is going right. His Soviet handler criticizes him for the "diminished quality" of the information he is now supplying. There is also the problem of Arthur, another recruiting effort that has infuriated the KGB.

Back in Scranton, many years before, it had been Arthur who had convinced the judge to give his younger brother a break and let him join the Navy. Arthur had retired from the Navy, as a lieutenant commander, in 1973. At some time in 1980—after the scare over Whitworth's retirement—John had asked Arthur for help again. This time Arthur provided his brother with some documents Arthur had seen while working for a defense contractor, VSE (Value Systems Engineering), in Virginia. The KGB dismissed the material from Arthur as, according to John, "very low-level junk." Worse still was the reaction to John Walker's revelation that he had attempted to recruit Laura. The methodical KGB appeared to be losing faith in John Walker and his dangerously haphazard way of doing business.

In March, Whitworth was transferred back to Alameda. Walker hoped for the 100 percent good crypto to start up again. But Whitworth's duties had changed, and he no longer had easy access to cryptographic material. They met—curiously, Walker made no record of the meeting—and tried to figure a way for Whitworth to improve his access. Walker had to make a drop on Sunday, June 13, and he did not have much to drop. His next face-to-face in Vienna would not be until January 15—a long time for the KGB to evaluate the faltering Walker, a long time for him to figure a way to improve his deliveries.

In the past Walker usually had given Whitworth his share of the cash soon after the drop. But this time Walker did not appear in San Leandro with the money—$60,000—until September 28. By then Walker knew that Whitworth would again be leaving Alameda and its treasure trove of crypto. But this time he was headed not for the crypto Siberia of Stockton but to sea. Now they had a better chance at getting secrets that would please the Soviets. To regain access to keylists, Whitworth had requested sea duty. The Navy had complied and ordered him to the aircraft carrier *Enterprise,* which was berthed at Alameda.

The aircraft carrier was at sea in October 1982 when Whitworth's orders came through. The Navy flew him out to the ship. This is not an unusual event. Planes carrying mail and high-priority supplies shuttle frequently between carriers and shore, and often enlisted men and officers are squeezed in with the cargo. Before he left Whitworth went to a camera store where he had left his old Minox for repairs, found it was not ready, and bought a new one. He also ordered, and got before his departure, twenty rolls of film. Around this time Whitworth once more began the paperwork for ending his naval career. He submitted notice of his intention to retire in October 1983. He did not tell Walker about the retirement plans.

Now began Whitworth's year of living luxuriously, a year of rented Rolls-Royces, champagne, travel, and cash, cash, cash. Walker was not around when Brenda triumphantly rode the Rolls through the gates to meet the returning *Enterprise* in April 1983. Not until June did Walker fly to California to pick up the first delivery of whatever Whitworth had managed to get from his time on board the carrier. The news was not good. As senior chief radioman, Whitworth explained, he had an administrative job that had kept him away from the day-to-day stream of cryptographic material.

Walker's routine at such meetings involved what he called a debriefing of Whitworth to learn what was on the film, which was always passed to Walker, and then to the Soviets, undeveloped. After hearing what Whitworth was delivering, Walker later said, he knew that the "cryptographic was somewhat of a disappointment" and "sketchy at best." When Walker questioned Whitworth about this he said he had something extra. He had managed to photograph "a year's worth" of messages because he had been able to track back through message traffic dated from months before his arrival. But messages, particularly old messages, were not as valuable to the Soviets as cryptographic material, and Whitworth knew it.

Walker, somewhat annoyed, took one of the envelopes that had contained Whitworth's delivery and jotted down what he later said was Whitworth's description of what he had photographed and delivered in the Minox film rolls: ALL MSGS S ONE TS INTEL OPERATIONAL OPLANS FLTEX WESTPAC IO LOI CHALLENGE VN TERR WATERS INTRUSION USSR TERR BY F14s SHOT ABOUT ONE-THIRD ON HAND. Then Walker drew a line on the envelope and wrote, PRD OCTOBER '85 PROMOTION CAUSING PROBLEMS. CMS PROSPECT. POOR UNTIL SEPTEMBER. FAIR AFTER. BETTER AFTER OCTOBER WHEN ACOMM TRANSFERRED TECH MAN IMPOSSIBLE UNLESS ALT NEXT WESTPAC: MAY '84

The first set of jottings gives a rare insight into just what the Soviet Union was getting from Whitworth. The jottings are translated here from Navy sources and, when quotation marks are used, from Walker's own definitions:

ALL MSGS S: all secret messages received by and transmitted by the *Enterprise* from about June 1982 to June 1983.

ONE TS: one top-secret message.

INTEL: messages pertaining to intelligence.

OPERATIONAL: messages pertaining to the operations of the carrier and her battle group.

OPLANS: A battle group goes to sea under directed operational plans. Oplan messages that are received while the group is at sea modify the original plan and contain such information as new changes in rules of engagement for dealing with hostile forces.

FLTEX: A reference to a fleet exercise, an elaborate, multiship war game that may last for a month. In September 1982, in the northern Pacific, an exercise involving the *Enterprise* and the aircraft carrier *Midway* took two battle groups to within striking distance of Soviet defenses on the Kamchatka Peninsula.

WESTPAC IO: Western Pacific, Indian Ocean.

LOI: letters of instruction are sent by the commander of forces, in this case the Commander in Chief of the Pacific Fleet, to the battle group. A letter of instruction outlines specific responses to situations that have developed since the drawing up of operational plans.

CHALLENGE VN TERR WATERS: Very sensitive instructions were given the *Enterprise*'s battle group about the way to conduct operations off Vietnam. One of the documents Whitworth handed over showed that the *Enterprise* "had penetrated the territorial waters of Vietnam . . . and, as a result of that, [received] a challenge from the North Vietnamese."

INTRUSION USSR TERR BY F14s: "There were also messages in the envelope [on which Walker jotted] that described an intrusion or penetration of Soviet territory by F-14 fighter jets from the USS *Enterprise.*"

SHOT ABOUT ONE-THIRD ON HAND: For this delivery, Whitworth photographed ("shot") or Xeroxed, one third of the messages he had managed to see. The rest of the messages "were still on the ship, and it was too dangerous to remove them." When Walker asked him how many documents and messages Whitworth had seen, he used his hands to represent a stack of messages nearly a foot high.

To Walker, *next westpac: may '84* was significant because deployment of the *Enterprise* to the western Pacific "dramatically increases the amount of cryptographic on board, especially when it transits between two ocean areas. The ship would bring the Eastern [Pacific/Third Fleet] cryptographic as well as the Western Pacific [Seventh Fleet] cryptographic." (The worldwide single keylist system had not yet gone into effect.)

The other jottings reflected Walker's concerns about Whitworth's dual career as sailor and spy. His PRD—"projected rotation date" from the *Enterprise* to a new duty station—would come in October 1985. The other notes—beginning with *promotion causing problems*—referred to an ironic fact: "He had been promoted to senior chief [radioman], and he was literally being promoted out of having access to cryptographic. . . . The only way he could get access is to become CMS custodian or the alternate." *tech man impossible unless alt* meant that Whitworth —and the Soviets—would not be able to get technical manuals for cryptographic gear unless Whitworth became the alternative CMS custodian.

Whitworth had a poor chance of becoming alternative CMS custodian *until september. fair after. better after october,* when the assistant communications officer (*acomm*) was transferred. When that happened "Mr. Whitworth would apply for that job, thus getting into the cryptographic vault." Walker obviously did not know that, in October, Whitworth intended to be a civilian.

Walker translated his back-of-the-envelope jottings to a note composed on his home computer and enclosed a printout with the film that he left at a drop near Washington a week after his meeting with Whitworth. He usually added the note so that the Washington KGB contact would have an idea about what was on the undeveloped film, which would be forwarded to Moscow from the Soviet Embassy via the safe and sure diplomatic pouch. Because of the slow, cautious method of communication with his handlers, Walker knew that not until his next face-to-face in Vienna would he get a KGB appraisal of Whitworth's latest disappointing delivery.

Walker no longer could afford to be cautious. He asked Whitworth to come to Norfolk as soon as possible and bring with him the *Enterprise* messages that he had not photographed. Late in July, Whitworth told the chief radioman in charge of the message center that on the following weekend he was going to fly to Norfolk and back. He had to make the quick trip, he said, to see Walker. The radioman would remember the conversation. Whitworth at this time seemed to be alternating between acting like a spy who wanted to get caught and acting like a spy who wanted to stop spying.

It was little more than a month after Walker's drop when Whitworth arrived in Norfolk—empty-handed. He said he had inadvertently packed his latest batch of secrets with his personal belongings, which movers had taken off the ship and put in storage, preparatory to Whitworth's move to his new residence, a rented mobile home in Davis, about sixty miles inland from Alameda. Brenda, Whitworth said, was taking courses at the University of California at Davis in a program that was to lead to her getting a doctorate in nutrition.

Walker could certainly see that Whitworth again was showing the familiar signs: He was getting "wishy-washy" about staying in the Navy. Now, though, there was something new. Whitworth also had been showing signs of fear. From the *Enterprise* he had sent Walker a newspaper clipping about federal efforts to track down spies. And he asked Walker to especially find out how U.S. Army Warrant Officer Joseph G. Helmich, Jr., had been caught. Helmich, like Whitworth a code specialist and lavish spender, had been tried, convicted, and sentenced to life imprisonment in 1981.

Walker said he would ask his handlers. He later told Whit-

worth that Helmich had tried to quit being a spy but had
changed his mind. Helmich had been given a signal procedure for
recontact, Walker said, but he had refused it because he had
wanted a clean break from espionage. "So he did something
overt, tried to approach an embassy or something, and that's how
he actually got caught in trying to make that contact with the
Soviets." (The information parallels the official U.S. account
given in Chapter 3.)

Walker had more on his mind than a need to calm down
Whitworth. To have something to show for the next Vienna Procedure in February 1984, Walker needed the rest of that one-foot
stack of messages from the *Enterprise*. But Whitworth said he
had to wait for his own move from ship to shore and the transfer
of the package of secrets from the storage facility in Alameda to
Davis.

The move of the goods to Davis made Whitworth's retirement obvious. He now had to admit that he was leaving the
Navy. Walker knew he was in trouble. He had had what he called
"minor suspicions" about Whitworth dating back to his stint in
Stockton, when the cryptographic material had dried up. The
suspicions later grew when the first batch of material from the
Enterprise included the sketchy supply of crypto and photographs of only some of the promised messages.

On January 28, 1984, Walker met Whitworth in Davis, expecting to pick up photographs of the remaining messages. But
Whitworth said he had not yet gotten around to photographing
them. As Walker told what happened next, he angrily took Whitworth off to a motel, away from Brenda's eyes, and together they
photographed the stack of messages, using Whitworth's Minox.
Walker left immediately, after having spent only twelve hours
with Whitworth. There had been little camaraderie between the
two old friends who had been colleagues in betrayal and now
were wary conspirators worrying about mutual betrayal. Neither
of the old friends knew that one betrayer was already plotting to
lead U.S. authorities to the other.

A week later Walker was in Vienna, where he learned that
none of the earlier *Enterprise* photographs of cryptographic material had come out. Although the documents had been photographed with a brand-new Minox and freshly dated film, *all* of
the frames in *all* the rolls of film were fogged. All of the film was

useless. The list that Walker had written down and given the Soviets—that tantalizing list, with its *all msgs S one TS intel operational*—was only a list. None of the material Walker and Whitworth had promised had appeared in the ruined photographs. For some time Walker had believed that something was going wrong. Now Walker's KGB handler told him that the Soviets believed something was going wrong. Very wrong.

6
The Spy Hunters

The KGB had reason to worry. The long-running Whitworth-Walker operation seemed to be heading toward a climax. Subtle changes in patterns signaled that some U.S. agency might have awakened to the compromise of Navy cryptography. Whitworth, the spendthrift spy, was simultaneously inviting suspicion and wavering about continuing. Walker, a once solitary agent turned independent broker of secrets, was making outrageous claims about recruiting successors to Whitworth. But none of his potential spies possessed what had made Whitworth such a prize: access to a continuous stream of U.S. cryptography. Walker was rapidly becoming less and less valuable to the KGB.

Department Sixteen, which ran the KGB's most sensitive operations, had given Whitworth and Walker extraordinary protection. Their operations had been tightly compartmentalized, with knowledge restricted to the fewest possible officers. Sometimes an officer from Department Sixteen would be dispatched from Moscow to the Soviet Embassy in Washington solely to service the Walker drop. He would then immediately return to Moscow, his stay so short that he would be unregistered by FBI surveillance agents who focused their watch on permanent KGB operatives.

By 1983 the Whitworth-Walker operation had competition for such KGB resources. The KGB and GRU had so many espionage operations under way in the United States that strains were beginning to show. Once Walker had been the star spy. Then came Whitworth. Now there were other good producers, each a supplier of a different brand of secret.

Ronald Pelton, an analyst for the National Security Agency —ever a prime KGB target—had walked into the Soviet Embassy in Washington in 1980 and had talked to Vitaly Yurchenko, a skilled KGB officer with special knowledge about the involvement of the U.S. Navy in intelligence-gathering work. By 1983, Pelton had made two pilgrimages to Vienna and interrogators were sweeping his brain clean. James Harper, an electronics engineer, had been supplying information about ballistic missiles since 1979 and had also made his pilgrimages to Vienna. And the chief KGB resident at the Soviet Consulate in San Francisco was reporting a brazen attempt to dangle a beautiful Russian émigrée at the FBI in hopes of compromising an FBI counter-intelligence agent. These are the Soviet spies who would be exposed. There undoubtedly were more, including moles who are still in place.

Viewed in espionage's hall of mirrors, the Soviets' espionage riches reflected the severe poverty of U.S. counter-intelligence. As one of the FBI's spy hunters later remarked, "The walk-in traffic was getting out of hand" around the Soviet Embassy and the Soviet Military Office in Washington. FBI surveillance teams suspect that espionage was on the minds of several Americans who had been observed boldly walking into the embassy. FBI telephone tappers monitored a number of phone calls to the embassy and Soviet military facilities from Americans, particularly servicemen, who said they had secrets to sell.

To the Soviets this was a bonanza for which to allocate additional resources. Doctrine once had said that American spies had to be recruited. This new breed consisted of volunteers, an unexpected phenomenon that the KGB cautiously exploited. To American counter-intelligence the phenomenon was much more complex. The American walk-ins came from every sector of the national security community. There were greedy enlisted men— usually with financial debts that were out of hand—offering to peddle Army, Navy, and Air Force secrets. There were civilian federal employees like Pelton who could bring the Soviets secrets from federal agencies engaged in clandestine activities so confidential that they were unknown even to all but the most senior-ranking U.S. defense officials. And there were civilians like Harper who worked in the military-industrial complex, a domain that was a "gray," unknown territory to U.S. counter-espionage.

The KGB was a monolithic, centrally directed, smoothly operated organization. U.S. counter-espionage was a patchwork of agencies that often worked at cross-purposes. The KGB never had to duel with shrewd defense attorneys in a court of law. U.S. counter-espionage worked under the stern gaze of American justice. In the Soviet Union there was no Congress that controlled budgets and sicced watchdogs on intelligence agencies. In the Soviet Union the KGB answered to none but the Kremlin. In the United States the Federal Bureau of Investigation might catch a spy—and then learn that the fate of the spy would be determined not in a courtroom but in a conference room where, time after time, the Central Intelligence Agency would convince the Department of Justice not to prosecute.

The walk-ins exemplified the problem. The FBI, the nation's officially designated counter-espionage agency, knew that an unprecedented number of Americans were selling or trying to sell secrets to the Soviets. But the FBI could not cover all the holes out of which the walk-ins scurried. By long tradition the FBI kept its eye on the Soviet Embassy, the Soviet United Nations Mission, and the consulates, offices, residences, and other facilities where Soviet legals, protected by diplomatic immunity, lived and worked. Surveillance of every American suspected of spying was physically impossible. Full-time surveillance of a single suspect could tie up the time of as many as thirty agents.

Despite decades of work against Soviet and Soviet Bloc espionage efforts in the United States, the FBI in the 1980s still lacked the experience and the skills equal to the task. Trained primarily to war against professional criminals rather than amateur traitors, the FBI represented the best the nation had to offer. But the bureau was still a casualty of history, an agency designed to catch 1930s gangsters that was given the additional responsibility of counter-espionage in World War II.

All U.S. spy and counter-spy organizations are outgrowths of ad hoc organizations and efforts developed mainly under wartime pressure. The modern beginnings, in fact, can be traced to World War I, when U.S. espionage activity, aimed against Imperial Germany's spies and saboteurs, was spread among intelligence groups in the State Department, the Army, the Navy, and the Justice Department. The legal basis for their work was the Espionage Act of 1917, which made giving aid to a U.S. enemy unlawful. In 1918 the act was amended to prohibit speech or writing "intended to incite resistance to the United States or promote the cause of its enemies." This act, much amended, has remained the nation's basic espionage law. Its view of espionage as an ideological menace has also persisted.

Soon after the war, reacting to public panic toward "Red" threats of revolution extending from Russia to America, the Justice Department became the focal point for actions against suspected subversives and spies. The department's Bureau of Investigation became the principal U.S. weapon against spies, though the bureau drew upon expert help, primarily from the Office of Naval Intelligence (ONI). The bureau, which became the Federal Bureau of Investigation in 1935, worked closely with ONI in the 1930s in the conviction of two U.S. Navy spies, one a former yeoman and the other a cashiered officer. Both had been spying for Japan. The ONI also uncovered several other Japanese efforts that involved Americans. By the eve of World War II the spy threat, mostly from Japan, had reached serious proportions, and tracking down and catching spies became a major activity of Army and Navy intelligence branches, plus the FBI.

These groups were especially successful against several Japanese attempts to get intelligence about the U.S. Fleet and its bases. Japanese efforts to garner information about U.S. naval capabilities in the Pacific were observed as early as 1912, when the new battleship *Arkansas* arrived at Panama, carrying President Taft for an inspection of the Canal Zone. According to one naval officer who was on the scene, "There were unobtrusive but alert Japanese waiters in the Tivoli Hotel, a few barbers in the newly opened shops, dentists scattered over the town, and of course fishing vessels manned by Japanese crews. Superimposed on these scattered activities was the beehive of the Japanese Consulate, working virtually day and night protecting, as they said, the interests of Japan . . . We suspected that some of them were spies, but the general attitude was: 'So what!' "

In time the military intelligence services and the FBI did become concerned as Japanese aggression in the Far East tended to threaten the U.S.-controlled Philippines and Guam. In April 1940 the U.S. Fleet was ordered to use Pearl Harbor as its base. Japanese intelligence interests immediately shifted to the Hawaiian Islands. The large Japanese-American communities in Hawaii and southern California made it easy for Japanese agents to meld into the population. Although there are no known instances of espionage by any Americans of Japanese descent, some Americans, including the two ex-Navy men, did sell and attempt to sell secrets to the Japanese. There appeared to be no ideology involved. They did it for cash.

With the outbreak of World War II in Europe in September 1939, the FBI concentrated on suspected German spies and saboteurs. And, with Stalin having signed the nonaggression pact with Hitler that permitted the Germans to invade Poland and thus ignite another world war, suspected Communists took on a new importance for the FBI. The FBI got better but its counterespionage skills couldn't even be compared to the wartime effectiveness of its British cousin, MI5, the Security Service. Indeed, FBI Director J. Edgar Hoover was continually at odds with MI5. Hoover refused to work with William Stephenson—code name "Intrepid"—who was sent to the United States by Churchill to help coordinate U.S. and British intelligence activities.

In a classic example of Hoover's noncooperation policy, MI5 operatives in Bermuda revealed to the FBI the secret of the German microdot photography—the reduction of a photographic page to the size of a dot—that could be hidden under a postage stamp or hidden on the back of a tie. Several spies were revealed by subsequent FBI interception of microdot messages.

Subsequently, Dusko Popov, a voluntary double agent really working for the British (under the code name "Tricycle"), came to the then-neutral United States in August 1941 to form a bogus spy ring for the Germans. He gave the FBI its first examples of the German microdot process as well as a list of questions that German intelligence officers wanted answered about the United States. Many of the questions pertained to the U.S. base at Pearl Harbor. The FBI ignored the possible significance of the German interest in Pearl Harbor. The FBI completely alienated Popov and he had to return to England, where he continued to work for the British. Hoover claimed credit for discovering the microdot scheme through the FBI's having "captured" a German spy (namely, Popov) in his article "The Enemy's Masterpiece of Espionage" in the April 1946 issue of *Reader's Digest*. Some Anglo-American authorities have cited Popov as Britain's most successful double agent. But Hoover dismissed Popov as a "Balkan playboy" because of his tastes in food, wine, and women.

During the war the FBI's counter-espionage jurisdiction was extended beyond U.S. borders to all of North and South America. While in theory this should not have caused friction with the military forces operating overseas, Hoover did have problems with the military services, especially the OSS—the Office of Strategic Services. Established in 1941 by William Donovan, a personal friend of President Roosevelt, the OSS was a military organization that reported directly to the Joint Chiefs of Staff. The OSS was to carry out intelligence, sabotage, and other missions behind enemy lines. But Hoover's insatiable appetite for knowledge and information often transcended the OSS's need for closely held military information.

The FBI and military intelligence services failed miserably during the war to detect and capture the new generation of betrayers—not the German spies and saboteurs (several landed by submarines) and sympathizers, but the Soviet sympathizers who were willing to steal America's secrets—primarily atomic bomb secrets—and pass them to the Kremlin.

After the war the business of catching spies continued to be, by presidential directive, totally in the hands of the FBI. The OSS was abolished immediately after the war. But the establishment of the Central Intelligence Agency in 1947 and the National Security Agency (NSA) in 1952 meant that there were two other national intelligence agencies, which, directly and indirectly, through their intelligence collection activities, now had a role in detecting foreign espionage activities. Neither agency had powers of arrest or other "police" powers—those were reserved for the FBI and, within the military services, for their internal security personnel.

By law the head of the CIA was designated as the Director of Central Intelligence, with a charter to coordinate all U.S. intelligence activities. The FBI, however, continued to be the lead espionage agency, operating with complete independence. Until his death in 1972, J. Edgar Hoover kept his FBI off limits to any influence, even presidential influence.

The FBI concentrated its resources on what Hoover viewed as the protection of national security. This view was ratified in 1947 when a presidential directive gave the FBI the responsibility for investigating the loyalty of federal employees and applicants for federal employment. In 1948 the Department of Justice moved against the Communist Party of the United States under the Smith Act, which prohibited advocating the violent overthrow of the government. The FBI got the mission of arresting and developing cases against 145 Communist Party leaders. Many of the 109 convictions came from trials at which FBI informants, planted in the Party, appeared as star government witnesses.

These cases, along with the Reds-in-government issue of the McCarthy era, set the tone of FBI counter-espionage work: spies were ideologues; infiltration of subversive organizations was a sound tactic; the opposition was the Communist Party of the United States, not the KGB. Tactics became more sophisticated in the 1960s and 1970s, but the ideological heritage lingered even as the major motivation for American spies became greed rather than a desire to help bring about a Soviet America.

The FBI under Hoover never developed a professional interest in the subtleties of counter-espionage. As an example of FBI attitudes in the 1950s, British intelligence official Peter Wright, in his book *Spycatcher*, tells of a courtesy visit to what he thought was his U.S. counterpart. Wright, then MI5's first scientist, met with Dick Millen, the FBI officer who, though a lawyer rather than a scientist, was the director of technical research for the FBI. Wright was taken to the firing range in the basement of the FBI headquarters and given a lesson on pistol-firing techniques. "Millen proudly informed me that even 'the old man himself,' Hoover, regularly practiced his prowess." Wright was also taken to a course in "advanced gunslinging" taught by an old American Indian who shot over his shoulder "at a Ping-Pong ball perched on top of a water fountain."

Two additional major intelligence players were established in the 1960s: the Defense Intelligence Agency (DIA) and the Defense Investigative Service (DIS). DIA's missions included coordination of various military intelligence activities; performance of much of the analysis previously done by the individual armed services; and the handling of other intelligence work that was not getting done. DIS was to watch over the security apparatus in the defense industry by investigating employees seeking security clearances and by administering the complex regulations that governed the handling of classified material by people working in the defense industry.

Today a welter of intelligence and counter-intelligence organizations—plus intelligence groups within the Army, Navy, and Air Force—are engaged, with various degrees of skill and success, in catching spies. Some authorities say even the mission cannot be defined by the players carrying out the mission. One expert has suggested that "counter-espionage" no longer describes the art or science of catching spies. He calls such spy-catching *defensive* counter-espionage as opposed to the *offensive* variety, which includes the penetration and disruption of hostile intelligence services.

The question of how to conduct defensive counter-espionage often flares into bureaucratic turf battles and has inspired a long line of presidential and National Security Council directives that attempt to correlate the surveillance, apprehension, and prosecution of spies. The Reagan Administration set up the Senior Interagency Group-Intelligence (SIG-I) to, among other responsibilities, "develop standards and doctrine for the counterintelligence activities of the United States; resolve interagency differences concerning the implementation of counterintelligence policy; and develop and monitor guidelines, consistent with applicable law and Executive Orders, for the maintenance of central counterintelligence records."

The Director of Central Intelligence is the chairman of SIG-I. Other members include the President's national security adviser, the Deputy Secretary of State, the Deputy Secretary of Defense, and the Chairman of the Joint Chiefs of Staff. The FBI, which is supposed to be the nation's lead counter-espionage agency, is represented one bureaucratic layer down the ruling-level SIG-I, in one of the "interagency groups," the Interagency Group for Counterintelligence, whose chairman is the Director of the FBI. Down there, the FBI is not at a policy level. Under pressure from the bureau, a senior FBI agent was assigned to the National Security Council staff as a day-to-day adviser on matters of counter-espionage, which, in the realpolitik of Washington in the 1980s became, in effect, counter-espionage about terrorism much more than against Soviet espionage.

By training and tradition, the FBI is a reactive agency, a police organization that goes to the scene of the crime, looks for clues, and then sets off to find the criminal. Espionage is not that kind of crime and counter-espionage is not that kind of police work. As a senior FBI counter-espionage official told the authors, "Espionage is a unique crime. There is no victim. Even in a white-collar crime you have a victim. And there may not even be any evidence [in espionage]. It may be just two people, one giving information and the other taking it."

But to the traditionalists in the FBI, an FBI counter-espionage agent is just another cop and espionage is just another street crime. Often a case is *handled* like a typical crime: An agent is tipped off by an informer. Or the crook—in this instance a KGB officer—makes a mistake. The FBI moves in and performs the specialties for which it is rightfully renowned: the gathering of evidence, the arrest, the preparation of a case for trial.

FBI counter-espionage has also learned to exploit Soviet recruiting techniques, but what is usually required is KGB error (recruiting a patriotic American) and luck (a patriotic American who could act the part of a spy while being run by the FBI). In the 1980s, for example, the FBI used a civilian employee who worked for the Navy as a counter-espionage agent. From about 1981 to 1983, William Tanner, employed at the Naval Electronics Systems Engineering Center in Charleston, South Carolina, acted as a Soviet agent while reporting to the FBI. Based on Tanner's evidence, his contact, Alfred Zehe, an East German exchange professor, was arrested in Boston, convicted of espionage, and later exchanged in a spy swap between the United States and East Germany.

The FBI can give federal prosecutors fine cases, but the bureau cannot give the United States protection from the spies who are stealing and selling America's secrets. Like military physicians on a battlefield, FBI counter-espionage agents in the 1980s had to practice triage—allocating resources by priority. Little time could be given to tracking down the anonymous walk-ins and the telephone call-ins who were keeping KGB intelligence officers so busy. Rather, the FBI's counter-espionage efforts were allocated primarily to keeping track of KGB officers working under cover as Soviet diplomats.

Desperate to stanch the flow of walk-ins, the FBI decided to expend some resources on a trick against the Soviets. On April 16, 1983, Lieutenant Colonel Yevgeny Barmyantsev left the Soviet Military Office in Washington and drove to a secluded road in rural Maryland, at the edge of his permitted travel zone, a radius of twenty-five miles from the Soviet Embassy. As Barmyantsev picked up a plastic garbage bag, FBI agents popped up from the bushes around the drop site and arrested him for spying. The Soviet officer reacted by tossing the bag in the air and urinating in his jeans.

Barmyantsev, a military attaché, had been caught in a scam that the FBI called "a controlled walk-in." John Stine, chief of security for a Washington defense research firm, had volunteered to act as the walk-in. Imitating a genuine seller of secrets, he had won over the military officers, who, as relatively low-ranking GRU operatives, would almost certainly not know about the KGB's Whitworth-Walker case. Stine had offered to sell secrets about ballistic missiles to the Soviets, and Soviet intelligence officers warily encouraged him. After five months the Soviets had finally arranged a dead drop, following classic, tradecraft techniques. Although this was a GRU operation, there was a KGB signature in the decision to set up the drop on a Saturday, under the KGB doctrine that there was less FBI surveillance on weekends.

Barmyantsev was swiftly declared PNG—Persona Non Grata—by the U.S. Government and recalled to the Soviet Union. The FBI said it had set the trap to make the Soviets nervous about dealing with future walk-ins.

But the arrest of Barmyantsev and an obvious intensifying of FBI surveillance of suspected Soviet intelligence officers did not dissuade the KGB from adhering to its own schedule. John Walker made one of his routine garbage-bag drops nine weeks later (on a Sunday) near where Barmyantsev had found Stine's bag. The wooded, desolate Maryland area had been so often used by Soviet case officers that agents in the FBI's Washington field office called it "drop-site country."

If Walker wondered about how close he came to sharing Barmyantsev's fate, he did not reveal his fears to Whitworth, who had enough fears of his own. Walker assumed a tough-guy stance toward his vacillating friend, warning him that getting himself out of espionage was risky and that a false move could get both of them killed. Then, shifting toward his good-guy side, Walker attempted to convince Whitworth to get a government job that would keep him in the cryptography field.

At his Vienna meeting with his KGB handlers in February 1984, Walker could no longer conceal the fact that Whitworth had ended his Navy career. "My contact was very concerned and didn't seem to trust Whitworth entirely," Walker said of the tense Vienna meeting. His Soviet contact was not impressed by Walker's claim that he now had his son Michael and brother Arthur collecting for him and that he was working on his daughter Laura as well as his half-brother Gary, an unrated Navy enlisted man whose lowly job, keeping helicopters clean, did not give him access to any secrets. Both Gary and Laura later said that they had turned down John Walker's offer. But, describing them to his Soviet contact, Walker made them sound at least like spies-in-training. Walker's testimonial added to the Soviets' distrust and dismay. "They were not happy that I had again recruited without their permission," Walker added.

The Soviet intelligence officer, worried more than ever before about being overheard by sophisticated surveillance equipment, told Walker that, rather than refer to members and would-be members of his so-called ring by name, they should be referred to by code letters. As they walked along Vienna's frigid streets, Walker, his feet warmed by electric socks, took a three-by-five card from his pocket and, despite the cold, began scribbling on the card.

Before the meeting he had already written *17 March Saint Pa, 22 April Easter, 28 May Mem Day,* a note to himself that the Soviets should not schedule a drop or face-to-face meeting on those days. Now he began writing down the letters that the KGB case officer assigned: *Gary F, Jer D, Art K, Mike S.* (Walker has also mentioned an *A,* but claimed that the letter also referred to Whitworth and that "I never did memorize the initials for the players," anyway.) There is also a mysterious *R.* More about this in Chapter 9.)

The Soviet case officer may have been stunned to see his walking companion assiduously taking notes, but the Soviet was more concerned about Whitworth. Sensing the looming loss of the KGB's best source of American military communications, the officer began closely questioning Walker about Whitworth. Walker assured him that Whitworth planned to try to get a civilian job that would continue to give him a chance to steal cryptographic material and intercept messages.

Walker stressed that he had recruited a new potential treasure in his son Michael. The KGB officer would be certain to view this news with alarm. The KGB did its own recruiting. Father-to-son recruitment was not unknown in the elite, highly disciplined KGB. But John Walker acted more like a talent scout than a wary recruiter. And Michael Lance Walker did not seem like high-grade talent. A poor academic record in high school and a general lack of interest had turned him away from college. He had taken his father's advice and joined the Navy because, his father had hinted, there was money to be made in the Navy.

But Michael had little chance for the promotions that would make him a valuable spy. Unlike the days when John Walker went from courtroom to boot camp, the Navy of the 1980s was no longer satisfied with the second-rate. Recruiters were not accepting petty criminals passed along by small-town judges. Taking advantage of high underemployment rates in the civilian world, the Navy was demanding and getting the best grade of recruit ever to sign up in peacetime. And, in a Navy more and more dependent upon high technology, advancement went to young men and women who knew how to study, how to take tests, how to get ahead. In the modern Navy his father now knew only from a distance, Michael would have stiff competition if he tried to qualify for radio and cryptography school.

Besides, unlike John Walker or Uncle Arthur, Michael had not entered the Navy as a career sailor. Michael planned, from the beginning, to be a sailor spy. Michael knew, from his Navy role model, that spying now was supposed to run in the family.

As Michael remembered his first acquaintance with family espionage, his drunken mother "came up to my room—it was about midnight—dragged me downstairs into the living room, started screaming and yelling at me" and, in the midst of the diatribe, shouted, " 'Your father is a spy!' " Michael, then about thirteen years old, had told her he did not believe her.

Sometime later, when he was in high school, he and his dad would often go to a neighborhood bar together. Michael could see that his father was wealthy. He owned a couple of boats, an airplane, and was a lavish spender, especially around young women. After a few drinks John Walker would say that someday he would tell Mike about how he made his money. Michael had suspicions, but, he claimed later, he did not then know that his father was a spy.

Michael joined the Navy in December 1982, when he was twenty. His first assignment after boot camp was as a yeoman striker—a plain seaman striking for advancement in a specialty— aboard the aircraft carrier *America*. When he came back from his maiden cruise, in July 1983, he took leave and went ashore to visit his father, with whom Michael had been living when he enlisted. They went to Dad's den one night and Michael began talking to Dad about his job aboard the *America*.

"At first I made reference that I was handling classified information. I was giving my Dad a rundown of the job I had, and he was interested," Michael later recalled, speaking as if he were telling a family story.

"Then, a few weeks later, he approached me and said, 'Well, I can pay you if you deliver classified information to me from your work space. . . . You want to make the money, there's a lot of it out there to be made.' " He told Michael that he could make " 'anywhere from a thousand dollars a week to five thousand dollars a month.' "

In October 1983, Michael, by then engaged to be married, was living on the base of the Oceana Air Station in Virginia Beach. One night as he went on liberty he stuck a classified document under his uniform shirt and took his first stolen secret home to Dad. "Well, he was pleased," Michael recalled. "He was happy that I actually had the guts to do it. He didn't say a whole lot. He thumbed through the document, and he said this was good, and that's about it." Later, they went up to John's second-floor workroom, where John showed his son how to use a Minox camera. They also talked about the fact that Michael's mother knew his father was a spy. Walker told his son, "She is a problem and can put us away." It was a warning that would haunt them both.

On January 31, 1984, Michael was transferred to the nuclear-propelled aircraft carrier *Nimitz*. He reported first to the ship's Special Services department, which supervises recreational activities aboard ship and arranges for liberty trips ashore. In September, Michael shifted to work, again as a yeoman striker, in the operations office of the *Nimitz.*

The carrier left drydock, where it had been undergoing repairs and updating, and went on a series of shakedown cruises and returned to Norfolk. Right from the beginning on his new job Michael stole documents and, when the ship docked, went ashore to deliver them to his father.

So, in Vienna, John Walker passed along more than Michael's name. He also could point out that Michael had supplied secrets for the previous drop and expected payment. The Soviet contact agreed and gave John Walker the dates for the next Washington-area drop and the next Vienna face-to-face. Walker jotted down *meet '85 Vin* with a date eleven months away: Saturday, January 19, 1985. (There were, as usual, two fallback dates: Sunday, January 20, and Saturday, January 26.)

On the plane flying back from Vienna, Walker transferred the notes from the three-by-five card to what he grandly called his "Private Detective's Notebook." In this spiral-bound book he put the letters-for-names code, along with notes about what the Soviets specifically did and did not want. He was told, for example, not to attempt to intelligence information or cryptographic materials from certain systems. He was not given a reason for the restrictions.

He also wrote some rough notes: *3 k per month equals 36,000, 4 equals 48,000. . . . spent over 60 K to build up. . . . D wife may make 100 K. . . . producing good yellow.* As Walker later explained the notes, they were reminders of arguments he was working on to convince the Soviets that Whitworth and Walker needed more money for that good yellow. He planned to ask for $1 million a year. Whitworth, according to Walker's translation of the notes, could not, as a civilian, be expected to engage in the risky business of espionage for a mere $6,000 a month.

Walker had a peculiar pride about his espionage work. "No member of the organization or prospective members has any of the classic problems that plague so many in this business," he once wrote to the Soviets in his best executive manner. "We have no drug problems, alcoholic problems, homosexuality. All are psychologically well-adjusted and mature. And the organization could launder funds." (Barbara, though, claimed that Walker had told her Whitworth was bisexual and used drugs. And Michael did not have a clean record. When he had been given his Navy physical examination, he had been told to go home, stop smoking marijuana, and come back in a month. He did this, and passed the physical. He had no record of drug abuse in the Navy.)

In Vienna, Walker had been told that the next drop would be only a few weeks away, on April 15, 1984. U.S. counter-espionage officials can only speculate on why the Soviets set a Washington-area drop so soon after the Vienna face-to-face. But it now is known that Department Sixteen officers would make a surprising decision about the tightly controlled Whitworth-Walker case. They would reveal details to Vitaly Yurchenko, the KGB officer who had been on duty in the Soviet Embassy in Washington in 1980 when Ronald Pelton, the NSA analyst, had walked in. Department Sixteen had questions to ask about the tottering enterprise that Walker called "my organization."

Just before Walker's scheduled April 15 drop, Whitworth had crossed the country by train—a method of travel he enjoyed —to deliver a set of fresh photographs of the *Enterprise* documents. He told Walker that the film represented another attempt to photograph that portion of message traffic that had wound up as fogged film in his previous attempt. Walker, leaving Whitworth behind in Norfolk, put the new film in the package for the Soviets and went off, alone, to make the routine drop near Washington. But the situation was far from routine.

There was, for instance, Michael's indiscretion. Walker had told Michael, the eager new spy, to keep up the deliveries but not to expect any payment until after the drop. Anxious for the money, Michael violated one of his dad's cardinal rules by calling John Walker on April 14 and asking, "Is there money coming tomorrow?" John Walker angrily slammed down the phone.

On Monday, April 16, John called a chastened Michael and asked him to come by the house. He went into the kitchen and sat down. John disappeared for a moment into his den and then came out with a stack of $20 bills. They counted them together. One thousand dollars. "Be careful with your money," John Walker told his son. "Don't blow it." Then John went back to the den and came out with a scroll of computer paper. He put another piece of paper over the computer readout, to hide part of it from Michael, and showed him something that applied just to him.

Michael saw his code letter, *S*, for the first time and read the note, which, his father hinted, had come from his Soviet contact. The note said of *S*: "Photographs were good. This man receives $1,000." Another part of the letter, as Michael called it, said of another agent, "The photographs were bad. This man receives no money."

John turned to Michael and, Michael recalled, "He said this is what happens when you screw up your photos."

Earlier, sometime after returning from the April 15 drop, John Walker had confronted Whitworth with another version of what he said was the note from the Soviets. As Walker described what happened, after telling Whitworth he was getting no money, he showed Whitworth the note, from which Walker had cut references to Whitworth. Walker said later he wanted Whitworth to see that other people—referred to by letters of the alphabet—were receiving money for their services.

Whitworth, shocked, began complaining about how much work he had done for Walker. Whitworth grabbed a sheet of paper and started scribbling frantically. *I got all,* drawing several lines under *all. S* [for secret] . . . *C* [for confidential] . . . *General service traffic of the 12 months* . . . *Genser* [general service messages]. . . ."

Walker showed Whitworth a copy of a letter that he said he had sent to the Soviets, telling them that he had found "lower-cost replacements" for Whitworth.

Whitworth went back to Davis an angry, confused, and frightened man. He decided to write a letter of his own.

On May 9, 1984, Janet Fournier, an investigative assistant in the San Francisco office of the FBI, was on what the FBI called "complaint duty." "You have no idea how many nuts are in this country until you take a few hours of that kind of duty," an FBI veteran remembered about his days on that duty. "I had one that was always the same—'Adolf Hitler's in my living room again.' And then there are the nights of the full moon. . . ."

True to the tradition of responding to all who reach out to the FBI, Janet Fournier dutifully answered the phone calls of citizens who made generally groundless complaints and passed generally worthless tips to the FBI. She also handled letters to the FBI that resembled the phone calls: anonymous, useless. One of the letters she opened that day was addressed to "Agent in Charge, FBI, 450 Golden Gate Avenue San Francisco, California, 94118" and was postmarked Sacramento, California.

The letter inside was dated May 7, 1984. She glanced at its contents and, according to the official account of the incident, immediately took the letter to Special Agent John P. Peterson in Squad 14, the foreign counter-espionage squad that handles Soviet cases. Peterson read it and told Fournier to put a notice on the bulletin board alerting anyone who received a letter signed *RUS* to take the letter directly to Peterson. In the carefully constructed official FBI scenario on the Whitworth-Walker case, there is no explanation for Peterson's apparent prescience.

More letters did come. "We called them the RUS letters," Fournier recalled.

The first letter from *Rus Somewhere in USA* said:

> Dear Sir: I have been involved in espionage for several years. Specifically, I've passed along top secret cryptographic keylists for military communications, tech manuals for same, intelligence messages, and etc.
>
> I didn't know that the info was being passed to the USSR until after I had been involved a few years and since then I've been remorseful and wished to be free. Finally, I've decided to stop supplying material—my contact doesn't know my decision. Originally, I was told I couldn't get out without approval, this was accompanied with threats. Since then, I believe the threats were a bluff.
>
> At any rate, the reason for this letter is to give (FBI) an opportunity to break what probably is a significant espionage system. (I know that my contact has recruited at least three other members that are actively supplying highly classified material.) (I have the confidence of my contact.)
>
> I pass the material to my contact (A US citizen) who in turn passes the material to a contact overseas (his actual status —KGB or whatever—I don't know). That is not always the case, tho, sometimes US locations are used. A US location is always used to receive instructions and money.

If you are interested in this matter you can signal me with an ad in the Los Angeles Times classified section under "Personal messages (1225)." What I would expect to cooperate is *complete immunity* from prosecution and absolutely no public disclosure of me or my identity. I will look for an ad in *Monday editions only* for the next four weeks. Also, I would desire some expense funds depending on the degree that my livelihood is interrupted.

The Ad: Start with "RUS:", followed by whatever message you desire to pass. If your message is not clear, I'll send another letter. If I decide to cooperate, you will hear from me via an attorney. Otherwise, nothing further will happen.

Sincerely, RUS.

Julie Ann Garrison owned and operated a newspaper and tobacco store across from the University of California at Davis, where, in the spring of 1984, Brenda Whitworth was taking classes for her doctorate. One of the out-of-town newspapers Garrison sold was *The Los Angeles Times.* In May, usually on Mondays, she remembered, a tall slim man with a beard began coming in. He would buy a copy of the *Times* and usually nothing else.

On Monday, May 21, the FBI ran an ad in the *Times:*

RUS, considering your offer. Call weekdays 9:00 A.M. to 11:00 A.M. Telephone number (415) 626-2793, or write. Signed M. E., San Francisco.

The next letter was dated May 21 and postmarked May 25 in Sacramento.

Dear Sir, I saw your note today and was encouraged, however I'm not going to call for obvious reasons. I'll admit that my most earnest desire is to talk to someone (like yourself) about my situation, but I feel that I'm unable to trust any kind of personal contact—phone included. Nor have I begun to look for an attorney. Where does that leave us or specifically me?

I'll be very open. It took me several months to finally write the first letter. Yes, I'm remorseful and I feel that to come forward and help break the espionage ring would compensate for my wrong doing, consequently clearing my conscience. But there are other emotions: the difficulty of ratting on a "friend," and the potential of getting caught up in a legal mess (public disclosure of my involvement and a possible double-cross on immunity, assuming it was granted in the first place.)

I would guess that you are conferring with higher authority and possibly other agencies. I'm wondering if my situation is really considered serious enough to warrant investigation and to give me due consideration (immunity & etc.)!

I'm going to begin looking for an attorney, which will be tricky from my view, to discuss my situation. And I will keep an eye on the LA Times, Monday editions, for any additional word/instructions from you.

It would certainly be nice for people in my predicament to have a means of confidential consultation with someone in a position of authority without the possibility of arrest.

My contact will be expecting more material from me in a few months, if I don't, I'm not sure what his response will be. I'm going to come clean with him at that time (assuming no deal is made with you) and tell him I'm finished with the "business." And then get on with my life.

More info on him: He has been in "the business" for more than 20 years and plans to continue indefinitely. He thinks he has a good organization and has no real fear of being caught, less some coincidental misfortune; in that regard he feels safe also. I agree with his assessment.

Why haven't I discussed my desire to come clean (with you) with my contact and/or possibly convince him to do the same? It would be sure folly—dangerous to my health.

Sincerely, RUS.

On June 4 the FBI ran another ad:

RUS, understand your concerns, but we can help. Must have dialogue with you or proxy if you are serious. ME, San Francisco.

Nothing happened. On June 11 the FBI tried again:

RUS, considering your dilemma. Need to speak with you to see what I can do. This can be done anonymously, just you and I, at 10:00 A.M., June 21st, at the intersection of the street of my office and Hyde Street in my city. I'll carry a newspaper in my left hand. We will only discuss your situation to provide you with guidance as to where you stand. No action will be taken against you, whatsoever, at this meeting. Respond if you cannot make it or if you want to change locations. I want to help you in your very trying situation, but I need facts to be able to assist you.

The answer came in an undated RUS letter, postmarked San Jose, June 18.

Sir, I won't be meeting you the 21st. A letter will follow in a week or two.

On August 13, the FBI ran another ad:

RUS, haven't heard from you. Still want to meet. Propose meeting in Ensenada, Mexico,* a neutral site. If you need travel funds, we'll furnish same at your choice of location in Silicon Valley or anywhere else. Please respond to the above.

In response came another RUS letter, dated August 13 and postmarked August 17, Sacramento:

Dear Sir: I saw your note in today's L. A. Times. Since my last note to you, I've done a lot of serious thinking and have pretty much come to the conclusion that it would be best to give up the idea of aiding in the termination of the espionage ring previously discussed. To think I could help you and not make my own involvement known to the public, I believe is naive. Nor have I contacted an attorney. I have great difficulty in coming forth, particularly since the chances of my past involvement ever being known is extremely remote, as long as I remain silent.

Yes, I can still say I would prefer to get it off my chest, to

* A coastal town about fifty miles south of Tijuana.

come clean. The above notwithstanding, I'll think about a meeting in Ensenada. Funds are not the problem. My contact is pressing for more material, but so far no real problems have occurred. I haven't explicitly told him I'm no longer in the business.

It was the last RUS letter. By the time the FBI received that letter many pieces had shifted on the espionage chessboard, where the FBI and KGB often play several games simultaneously. One game involved James Harper, the engineer who had been passing the Soviets U.S. ballistic missiles secrets since 1979. What happened to RUS, to Harper, and to others on the espionage board of the 1980s illustrates how complex are the triumphs and the failures of America's offensive counter-espionage apparatus.

The case of James Durward Harper goes back to 1975, when a business associate, William Bell Hugle, introduced Harper, then a forty-one-year-old, self-employed electronics engineer, to two men identified as members of a Polish trade delegation shopping for U.S. electronics technology. The exporting of such technology, especially to an Eastern Bloc country, is sharply restricted by law, as part of a general U.S. policy aimed at keeping America's high technology, especially that with potential military use, out of Soviet hands.

Harper, during a two-year hitch in the Marines, had been trained in electronics. After he was honorably discharged in 1955 he worked in a series of jobs in electronics firms. He eventually struck out on his own, and when he met the Poles in 1975 his firm was making and marketing the world's first digital stopwatches. The technological information the Poles sought was not for stopwatches. The two men showed Harper what they said was a "shopping list" of high-tech information and devices Poland wanted. One of the items on the list was a tank-launched rocket.

Harper did not have security clearance, was not working on any defense contracts, and could not, at that time, provide the Poles with such shopping-list items as the rocket. But he did manage to deliver enough technological information to earn a trip to Geneva in November 1975, when he turned over the information for at least $5,000. He later described the information as unclassified, and he boasted that he had bilked the SB (Sluzba

Bezpieczenstwa), the Polish Intelligence Service. In reality, he had been recruited.

There apparently is no record of any Harper dealings with the Poles during the next four years. But by 1979, broke, newly divorced, and out of work, he was an outright agent, complete with code name, for the SB, whose American work was directly supervised by the KGB. Harper's value had greatly increased because of what he called his "business romance" with Ruby Louise Schuler, who held a secret clearance as executive secretary to Dr. Robert E. Larson, the co-founder and president of Systems Control, Inc. (SCI), in Palo Alto, California. Palo Alto was the unofficial capital of Silicon Valley, which the KGB had targeted for penetration by its intelligence forces, along with those of Eastern Bloc countries.

SCI* was one of many relatively small defense contractors doing research for the U S. Army Ballistic Missile Defense Advanced Technology Center in Huntsville, Alabama. The SCI research focused on efforts to make Minuteman missiles and other U.S. strategic missile systems less vulnerable to Soviet missiles, particularly in the most dreaded war scenario, a Soviet preemptive attack.

Some strategic analysts at the time believed that the early 1980s would be a particular "window of vulnerability" as new generations of Soviet land- and submarine-based strategic missile systems became operational while U.S. strategic forces, starved by the costs of the Vietnam War in the 1960s and early 1970s, and further degraded by President Carter's defense policies, would give the Soviets an opportunity to initiate or at least to threaten a nuclear war against the United States.

When Harper discovered that his girlfriend had access to missile defense secrets and would pass them to him, he contacted Hugle, who soon met with Harper in Geneva to plan strategy. In July 1979 the two men flew to Warsaw, Hugle via Vienna and Harper via Paris. In Warsaw, Harper and Hugle met with Zdzislaw Przychodzien, who was introduced as an executive of the Polish Ministry of Machine Industry. He actually was Lieutenant Colonel Przychodzien of the SB, assigned as head of an intelli-

---

* Ironically, in U.S. security circles, the initials also mean "sensitive compartmented information."

gence section, or Wydzial, that used the ministry as a cover for espionage against Western countries. Przychodzien spoke English fluently. In the 1970s he had been in the Polish Commercial Office in New York.

Before taking off for Warsaw, Harper had prudently placed copies of ten of his stolen documents in a safe-deposit box at the Citibank in Paris. He now showed Przychodzien copies of excerpts from each of the documents. Harper said he wanted $1 million for all the documents. The price startled Przychodzien, who shifted the subject to items on the Silicon Valley shopping list, especially tapes of computer data bases. Przychodzien saw the tapes as a wholesale acquisition of technology. All Harper had to do was get a tape, copy it, and deliver it to the SB, which could then scroll through the tape in search of wanted information, such as computer software. Harper, noncommittal about acquiring tapes, agreed to meet again with Przychodzien.

Hugle assured Przychodzien that Harper could be trusted, and the three men made a deal, agreeing that any money given to Harper by the SB would be split three ways: a third for Harper, a third for Hugle, and a third for Harper's source. They agreed to meet again in October.

Thus, that quickly and that simply, Harper's business romance had blossomed into a seemingly foolproof espionage operation. Ruby Schuler, who had been given the combination to Larson's presidential safe, had started regularly opening the safe after hours and systematically removing secret documents pertaining to U.S. missile defenses. She would put them in her pocketbook or strap them to her body and go home to Harper. Larson, who was away from SCI frequently on business trips, said he never noticed anything unusual about Ruby's behavior. But later he did remember that she told him she had read *The Falcon and the Snowman*, the story of Christopher Boyce and Andrew Daulton Lee, who had sold the Soviets secrets stolen from another California aerospace company, TRW.

Sometimes, taking advantage of Larson's frequent absences, Ruby became so bold that she would, on her own, request specific documents from the ballistic missile center in Huntsville. When they arrived she would log them into the safe and then take them home. Sometimes, especially on Saturdays, she would take Harper with her to fetch the documents. (She could do this because, under U.S. security regulations, he needed an escort. And her secret clearance authorized that role for her.) Harper acquired a large 3-M duplicating machine on which he copied the documents, which Ruby faithfully returned on the morning of the next workday.

In October 1979, Harper took Ruby along to Vienna, where he met Hugle and Przychodzien. This time Harper took the ten full documents and excerpts of others. Przychodzien accepted the SCI documents. "But a disagreement arose, or rather erupted, over the matter of payment," says an unusually dramatic report from U.S. intelligence analysts. "Harper and Hugle had come down a good deal from their original demands, but they understood that $15,000 would be paid for one of the ten documents. When Przychodzien declined to pay that much Hugle started a shouting match which quickly broke up the get-together, which was taking place in a public lounge at a hotel."

Harper and Ruby left Vienna immediately and returned to California. Believing that he might eventually find a buyer for the rest of the SCI documents, Harper took them from his and Schuler's apartment in Mountain View, a few miles south of Palo Alto, and buried them in the San Joaquin River Delta near Stockton. (Coincidentally, this is also the location of the Naval Communications Station where Jerry Whitworth had been temporarily assigned in December 1981.)

Harper decided that he no longer needed the brokerage services of the loudmouthed Hugle. So, through an intermediary in Switzerland, he reestablished contact with Przychodzien and returned to Warsaw in May 1980. He had with him the requested computer data-base tapes, which he had somehow managed to get, presumably without the help of Schuler. Przychodzien cordially apologized for the angry outburst at the Vienna meeting, paid Harper $10,000 for the tapes, and told him to go back to SCI and get some more documents.

Harper went to Stockton, dug up his cache, and was back in Warsaw in a month—with more than one hundred pounds of waterlogged documents. Przychodzien and other SB agents worked through the June night separating the pages and restoring the documents so that they were decipherable. The next day, says the U.S. counter-intelligence report on the case, "the documents were brought to the Soviet Embassy where a team of 20

KGB experts, flown in specially from Moscow, declared them to be genuine and extremely valuable." The report adds that Harper was paid $100,000 and that a month later "Przychodzien and his unit received a commendation for their efforts, directly from KGB Chairman Yuri Andropov" (who in November 1982 would take over leadership of the Soviet Union).

The intelligence report on Harper contains a partial list of the information he offered for sale. The secret documents included *Endoatmospheric Nonnuclear Kill Technology Requirement and Definition Study, Millimeter Wave Sensors; Discrimination Decoy Performance Requirements; Minuteman* [missile] *Defense Study; Report of the Task Force on U.S. BMD* [ballistic missile defense]; and *Summary of Soviet Growth Threat.*

At his next meeting in Warsaw in September 1980, Harper took along what amounted to an espionage order form—the register of the classified documents in the presidential security safe that Ruby Schuler so diligently kept raiding. Przychodzien and his aides went over the document register and selected from it exactly what documents they wanted for delivery in October and November. On delivery, Harper received $20,000. Like the KGB, the SB paid in cash (almost surely KGB cash). On one trip back to the United States from Warsaw, Harper had so many bills that he stuffed wads of them into the athletic tube socks and running shoes he wore on the plane.

When Przychodzien and Harper met in Warsaw in November, Przychodzien, for some reason, announced a change in procedures. He told Harper that the next meeting was to be on December 14 in Mexico City with a Polish agent Przychodzien said he knew only as "Jacques." Harper, with the code name "Jimmo," was to wear an "Irish Brotherhood" medallion. Przychodzien had Harper write a limerick on the back of a laundry list. Przychodzien tore it in half and handed one half to Harper.

At an appointed time on December 14, Jacques walked up to the cashier's cage of the Museum of Anthropology in Mexico City and showed Jimmo the other half of the laundry slip. Harper, surprisingly, had not brought any documents with him. He said that all he wanted to do on this trip was "get the feel of the city." Jacques amiably paid him $10,000 on account. Two months later Harper returned with copies of nine secret documents and was paid an additional $60,000.

At a subsequent meeting Harper gave Jacques eight documents and was paid $50,000. He also handed over tantalizing excerpts that previewed thirty more documents for future sale. But at the next meeting, in September 1981 at Guadalajara, Harper took a new tack: He arrived without documents, saying that he was not getting enough money for what he had been providing. Jacques, who had $30,000 ready for the thirty documents Harper had previewed, shrugged and told Harper to take his complaints to Przychodzien in Warsaw. Harper made arrangements to meet with Przychodzien in November.

By the time of this last meeting with Jacques, Harper had reached a crossroads in his espionage career. He and Ruby had married, bonding their joint spying venture. But they had to find a new source of secrets, for there would be no more easy picking from the president's safe. In August, Ruby had lost her security clearance because SCI had been acquired by a British firm. SCI's defense contracts were retained by a spin-off company. She remained an employee of the original corporation, now British-owned, and her clearance for secret information was "administratively terminated."

Incredibly, her own odd behavior had not cost her the security clearance. She was drinking heavily and was careless about displaying large sums of cash. For a long while co-workers had noticed that she carried a small bottle of vodka in her purse and would nip at her desk or slip off for a drink in the ladies' room. One day an SCI executive went with her to a bank and accompanied her to a safe-deposit box. Oblivious of her companion's startled gaze, she filled the box with fistfuls of $100 bills.

Harper knew that Ruby could not hold up much longer as a confederate. He wanted to find a way out. He began taking steps to extricate himself from the high-risk business of espionage. He did not know that each of his steps out of espionage was a step into a spiral of counter-espionage.

Sometime in September 1981, Harper called William Dougherty, one of Christopher Boyce's defense attorneys. Harper had probably been inspired by new headlines about Boyce. Sentenced to forty years in prison in 1977, Boyce had escaped in

January 1980. A month before Harper's call to Dougherty, Boyce had made news again by being captured.

Harper, calling himself "Jay," asked for a meeting with Dougherty. Refusing to identify himself, Harper told enough about his spying for the Polish Intelligence Service to convince the lawyer that the anonymous voice on the phone was telling the truth. In a way that has not been officially disclosed, Dougherty made contact with the CIA and proposed that the government grant the anonymous client immunity from prosecution in exchange for cooperation, including possible use of his client as a double agent.

While Dougherty attempted to open negotiations, Harper and his new wife drove to Tijuana and put the rest of their secret documents in a safe-deposit box. Then Harper went to Warsaw for an unsatisfactory meeting with Przychodzien, who curtly told Harper he would not get higher prices for the documents. Perhaps at another time the dispute could have been settled. But, like all intelligence officers in the Polish capital in November 1981, Przychodzien had other pressing matters on his mind, and even an espionage operation being run for the KGB had to be given low priority.

The Solidarity trade movement had burst into the streets, threatening open revolt against the government. Through the autumn of 1981 high Polish officials held secret meetings to plan a crackdown on Solidarity and the imposition of martial law. The plans were highly secret because premature disclosure would surely touch off an explosive reaction. At a strategy conference in Warsaw early in November, however, a Soviet official revealed to his Polish colleagues that detailed reports on the secret meetings had been leaking to the American government. A CIA mole in Polish intelligence, the Soviet official said, was informing the Americans of every secret move toward the plan to declare martial law on December 13.

The Soviet official did not say how his government knew that a Polish intelligence officer was working for the CIA. (One possibility, which has never been dispelled, was that the revelation about the Polish mole had come from a Soviet mole in the CIA.)

One participant at the meeting, Colonel Wladyslaw Kuklinski, needed no further details about the mole. After joining with the other Poles in a display of shock and anger, a cool but shaken Kuklinski made a prearranged emergency signal, and the CIA resident chief in the U.S. Embassy launched a smooth "exfiltration," as it is known, extracting not only Kuklinski but also his entire family. On November 6, 1981, when Kuklinski failed to report to his office, Polish intelligence officers, suspecting the worst, rushed to his home. They discovered it was empty, as were the homes of his two sons.*

Kuklinski's name has not been linked directly to the Harper case in official reports and off-the-record discussions of the tracking of Harper. But U.S. counter-intelligence officials have revealed that a high-ranking "Eastern bloc source" (also identified as "a source within the Polish Intelligence Service") provided the first leads that ultimately put the FBI on Harper's trail.

"The Source," as U.S. counter-intelligence officials label the mole, had first alerted them to the existence of an extremely valuable American agent when he passed them the news about the extraordinary 1980 Andropov commendation of SB officials. By one account the Source also heard that some of the American agent's handlers had even received cash rewards and medals. At a reception where SB intelligence officers had bragged about the achievement, the Source had also overheard the words *California* and *missile research*.

The Source was so reliable that FBI counter-espionage agents immediately began an intense and widespread investigation with two focal points—Silicon Valley, the most logical espionage site in California, and the Army ballistic missile complex in Huntsville, a logical place for spying on "missile research." The FBI searched records at Huntsville for suspects among local employees and among employees of California-based contractors who fit the sketchy description of the American agent. The number of suspects—*forty*—says much about the vulnerability of U.S. missile research. One by one, the forty suspects were ruled out.

What the FBI did not know was that the spy they sought had no *direct* connection with Huntsville's missile research—or Silicon Valley. Nor did he have a security clearance, which such a

* The family is reported to now live in the United States under new identities.

supplier of secrets would almost certainly possess. So checks of security-clearance files also led nowhere.

Although high-ranking FBI counter-intelligence officials say that Kuklinski was not the Source, they admit to the coincidental existence of *two* Polish double agents at that time. According to the official account provided the authors, it is only a coincidence that late in 1981, while the CIA was presumably debriefing Kuklinski in a safe house in the United States, the FBI came upon additional information about the American spying for the SB.

The Source said that on Przychodzien's office calendar for October 8, 1979, he had seen a note saying that a William Hugle had called about a meeting, leaving two call-back numbers in Vienna. The Source, suspecting that Hugle was involved in espionage in the United States, had jotted down the numbers. At some risk, the Source drew from Przychodzien details of the meeting that Hugle had arranged. Przychodzien could not resist boasting that Hugle had brought in an "American businessman" who offered to sell valuable documents about "American rockets." The Source said he got the impression that the American was in his fifties and apparently was a longtime friend of Hugle.

U.S. counter-espionage agents began comparing notes and discovered that two apparently separate espionage affairs now were beginning to merge. Many of the Source's details about the unnamed Americans seemed to coincide with information coming from the lawyer, who said he was representing an anonymous American who had spied for the Polish Intelligence Service. Still keeping the identity of the client secret, Dougherty provided his CIA contact with statements made from tape recordings transmitted to him by the client. In March 1982 the lawyer met with government agents and said that immunity for his client's wife must also be included in any deal.

The first wave of information concerned someone that "the Client," as he was called in reports, identified only as "the Big Man," who in Silicon Valley in 1975 had set up a meeting with Poles shopping for technology. Then the statement skipped to 1980 meetings in Europe. FBI agents analyzed such rambling statements as this description of the meetings:

> So I left Switzerland and went into Vienna and from Vienna I went into Warsaw, and the Minister picked me up. . . .

By this time now he has about six months to review that second list of abstracts I got. All the stuff I have got stashed over
here. He says that they have reviewed it and they want it all
and if I'll go back and get it and bring it to them they will give
me one hundred thousand for it. . . . I went back fairly
quickly, and I took him the documents and we went to the villa
again, just like before, and I gave him the documents. . . .
During the period that this stuff was stashed it became damaged. Some of the papers were kind of loose. I had a hell of a
time putting it back together. . . .

The Client said that the SB had told him to purchase a video
cassette recorder, video camera, and a large-screen television set.
SB technicians suggested the video arrangement as a way to expe-
dite the handling of the documents. The suggestion came after
the problems of the waterlogged documents, which, because they
had been reproduced on Harper's 3-M copier, were just as bulky
as the originals and much harder to smuggle than an innocent-
looking video cassette and video camera, an accessory of many
American tourists in Europe. (The KGB probably originated the
idea. Walker, who had used the small Minox still camera through
most of his career, in the mid-1980s began experimenting with a
cinematic camera to photograph documents.)

The Source, independent of the Client, had also told of
twenty KGB technicians being flown into Warsaw from Moscow
to work on damaged secret documents. And the Source described
a Vienna-Warsaw connection that resembled the one sketched by
the Client. U.S. investigators assumed that the Client's "Big
Man" was William Bell Hugle and "the Minister" was
Przychodzien. Another part of the Client's statement indicated
how valuable the Poles—and their sponsor, the KGB—considered the material the American was providing:

They just decided you didn't have to worry about the missing
pages. I said OK fine. So I got this big envelope with one
hundred thousand dollars in it and proceeded to count it and
got about a quarter of the way through it and said, Oh, the hell
with it. It has to be there. I can eyeball it, and it's one-hundred
hundred-dollar bills.

U.S. counter-espionage agents tracked the phone numbers seen on Przychodzien's calendar to two Austrians, Dietrich and Elizabeth Svoboda. Yes, they knew William Bell Hugle, and yes, he had used one of their Vienna apartments in October 1979. At the request of the FBI, the CIA asked its Austrian assets for a quiet check of Vienna hotel registers for October 1979.

The CIA told the FBI that Przychodzien, using his cover as an executive of the Polish Ministry of Machine Industry, had registered at the Intercontinental Hotel in Vienna on October 9 and 10. And a James D. Harper of Mountain View, California, had also registered at the same hotel from October 7 to October 9. FBI agents checked U.S. Customs Service records and found that the same Harper had arrived at Kennedy International Airport in New York City on October 19, 1979, a date tying into the Przychodzien calendar—and on May 21, 1980, and June 9, 1980, dates tying into the chronology that was being developed from the anonymous "Client" statements. Then came the tape-recorded words that would indisputably identify the anonymous Client as James Harper:

> First of all, they told me to lose my passport. Get a new passport. Do everything I could to get the passport under another name. Now, I destroyed my old passport and got a new U.S. passport. I was not able to get another passport under someone else's name. I kept screwing with that, and it's just too risky trying to do that, and I might do something to blow my cover on this thing, and I'm just going to quit my screwing around with it.

FBI agents, working with the chronology developed through the Client statements, checked State Department passport records and learned that on October 9, 1980, the same James Harper who had stayed at the Intercontinental had also filled out a "Statement Regarding Lost or Stolen Passport." The investigation now became a shuttling exercise between the inadvertently incriminating statements of the Client and the explanatory statements of the Source; between dates in the Client's statements and dates for a James Harper who had been indexed in the U.S. Customs Service computer records of all international airport arrivals.

The shuttling accelerated, driving the FBI toward the man named Harper. The Client, for example, said on the tape recorder that he had met with the Minister in a villa outside of Warsaw. The Source said Przychodzien had a villa in the small town of Zalesie Gorme, about twelve miles from the capital. The Client said he could enter and leave Poland without a visa by flying from Vienna to Warsaw and then making prearranged contacts with certain Polish customs officials. The Source said this was a standard SB procedure. The Client said that he had broken off with the Poles in November 1981. The U.S. Customs records showed that Harper's most recent international airport arrival was November 19, 1981, at Logan International Airport, Boston.

One admission from the Client spurred the FBI to close in on Harper:

> I have stashed probably about what I would guesstamate about 150–200 pounds of defense documents. . . . I have somewhere around forty secret documents and they all have to do with BMD ballistic missle [sic] defense. Out of Huntsville, Alabama, I think they call it the Data Processing Directory. I got these within the last year.

If ballistic missile defense secrets were in a stash somewhere, they had to be recovered as soon as possible. The time had come to turn from interpreting the rambling of the Client to building a case against this frequent traveler, James D. Harper. The FBI began looking into his background.

When the FBI starts closing in on a spy suspect, the first moves are routine: careful surveillance, cautious interviews with acquaintances, employers, and co-workers, and a checking of records that begins with a birth certificate and includes marriage licenses, divorce hearings, educational records, armed services personnel records, police and court records. That phase of the investigation turned up an interesting bit of information: In December 1980, Harper had been arrested for driving while under the influence of liquor. When police booked him he said that in case of emergency his *ex*-wife, Colleen Harper, was to be notified. Yet, he had been married two months before to Ruby Schuler. Local police also told the FBI that Harper had 150 Mexican pesos in his pocket. Jimmo would have been carrying pesos in December 1980.

As for the references to Colleen, investigators knew that Harper and Schuler had lived together at her apartment before they had been married and that they were still living there early in 1983, when the investigation had stepped up. Agents also learned about Schuler's connection with SCI. Was it possible that they had gotten married so that in a court of law neither could be compelled to testify against the other?

A woman named Ruby had accompanied Harper on at least one trip to Vienna. The FBI established that Ruby Louise Schuler had started working as a secretary-bookkeeper in 1972 and had left the company in 1982 because of illness, a year after SCI had been reorganized and had come under British control.

One of the companies that spun out of the SCI reorganization was Systems Control Technology (SCT). When FBI agents called on SCT in March 1983, they were relieved to know that the chief executive officer, John W. Pauly, was a man who understood counter-espionage. Pauly, a retired four-star Air Force general, had been Commander in Chief of the U.S. Air Forces in Europe and Commander of Allied Air Forces in Central Europe.

For nearly all of his thirty-five years in the Air Force, Pauly had dealt with classified documents. He knew the rules. With his cooperation the FBI began tracking backward to the time period when Ruby Schuler worked for SCI and Harper was beginning his "business romance." Inventories of documents ordered from Huntsville showed that material specifically described by the Client had been among the missile documents delivered to SCI. The FBI located many of the originals of these documents—originals that had at times been kept in the SCI presidential safe. Fingerprints on eleven of the documents matched Harper's fingerprints, probably obtained from his Marine service record.

In May the FBI raised the investigation to a new plateau by tapping Harper's phone. To reach that plateau the FBI had to enter the maze of U.S. espionage laws. In that maze the spy hunters take second place to the spy lawyers—the U.S. prosecutors who may or may not want to bring an espionage case into court and the defense attorneys who may want to make a deal for the client.

7

Bringing Spies to Justice

Authority to tap James Harper's telephone had to come from a clandestine court unique in American justice, a court that some legal observers have described as a modern version of England's notorious royal star chamber. No defense attorney can enter this court, for it serves only the federal government and admits before it only agents of the government. All briefs presented to the court are secret, as are all of its actions and decisions. Records of the proceedings of the court are sealed under security measures established by the Chief Justice of the Supreme Court and the Attorney General. The public cannot even go near the closed doors of this court, which convenes in an electronically secure room on the restricted sixth floor of the Department of Justice Building on Constitution Avenue in Washington, a couple of hundred yards from the National Archives, where the U.S. Constitution and Bill of Rights are enshrined.

The Constitution Avenue address of the U.S. Foreign Intelligence Surveillance Court is not ironic. The court's constitutionality stands virtually unchallenged by guardians of the Bill of Rights whether liberal or conservative. Democrats and Republicans across the political spectrum support the court. The leading architect of the secret court was Senator Edward Kennedy, who in 1976 introduced the court's legislative underpinning, the Foreign Intelligence Surveillance Act. The act, which became law in

1978, amended the U.S. Code by adding a new chapter, "Electronic Surveillance Within the United States for Foreign Intelligence Purposes." The law recognized the need to establish legislative controls over telephone taps and electronic bugging.

Paradoxically, the inspiration for the secret court emerged from congressional investigation of wiretapping abuses. Out of the 1975 inquiries came a decision to create a legal basis for the well-entrenched practice of wiretapping without a court order. The congressional solution, an attempt to balance the blessings of civil liberties against the menace of espionage, was the U.S. Foreign Intelligence Surveillance Court.

The unusual court, recognizing both police-power imperatives and democratic principles, finally put an end to the warrantless electronic bugging that had been going on in the United States since May 21, 1940. On that date President Roosevelt, in a secret memorandum to Attorney General Robert H. Jackson, authorized the FBI to "secure information by listening devices" that would detect "the conversation or other communications of persons suspected of subversive activities against the Government of the United States, including spies." The President, reacting to the threat of espionage at the start of World War II, said he believed that phone tapping and electronic bugging were constitutional because of the "grave matters involving the defense of the nation" at that time.

Roosevelt's secret memorandum became the basis for wiretapping through World War II. President Truman extended the practice into peacetime in July 1946 by endorsing a letter from Attorney General Tom C. Clark, who wanted to tap the phones of persons suspected of "subversive activities." Using this piece of presidential paper as its authority, the FBI tapped telephones and installed secret microphones, eavesdropping on American citizens and foreigners throughout the United States for nearly a quarter of a century. A wiretap law in 1968 tightened procedures but still gave the President unrestricted power to "take such measures as he deems necessary" to protect the United States. Under this provision Presidents Johnson and Nixon ordered taps during the Vietnam War. Congressional investigators said in 1975 that the FBI had placed about 6,000 wiretaps and planted some 1,500 electronic bugs.

In that same year the Rockefeller Commission, which President Ford had created to examine the activities of U.S. intelligence agencies, disclosed a secret agreement drawn up in 1954 by the Department of Justice and the CIA: If a CIA agent were suspected of a criminal act, the CIA would unilaterally decide whether the agent should be handed over to Justice for prosecution. If the CIA decided not to refer the case, that would be the end of it.

More details about that secret agreement came to light in 1976 from the Senate Select Committee to Study Government Operations with Respect to Intelligence Activities, headed by Democratic Senator Frank Church of Idaho. The committee said the agreement had been a "memorandum for the record" between Deputy Attorney General William P. Rogers, who became Secretary of State in 1969, and Lawrence Houston, general counsel of the CIA.

On February 18, 1976, President Ford, in Executive Order 11905, undercut the old memorandum by ordering intelligence officials to report to the Attorney General any "information which relates to detection or prevention of possible violations of law by any person, including an employee of the senior official's department or agency."

President Carter's Executive Order 12036 went further, ordering intelligence agencies to set up procedures to safeguard constitutional rights in the use of intelligence-gathering methods such as electronic surveillance. By taking away the secret shield that had protected intelligence employees from prosecution, the executive branch brought espionage proceedings into the open and set the legal stage for an examination of electronic surveillance.

A new-style, warrantless wiretap further inspired a look at counter-espionage legalities during the Carter Administration. The new kind of tap was a television bug, used to investigate what would be the only U.S. espionage case to emerge from the Vietnam War.

Attorney General Griffin B. Bell authorized the secret installation of a closed-circuit television monitor in the communications room of the U.S. Information Agency, where Ronald L. Humphrey, a career foreign service officer, was a watch officer. The FBI had tied Humphrey to the espionage activities of David Truong, a South Vietnamese working for the Vietnamese Communists. Truong's father, Truong Dinh Dzu, had run as a peace candidate in South Vietnam in 1967 against President Nguyen Van Thieu and had been jailed. David had moved to the United States to attend Stanford University and had become an antiwar activist, a source of information on Vietnam for many members of Congress, and a friend of many influential officials, including William Colby, Director of Central Intelligence.

David Truong founded the Vietnamese-American Reconciliation Center in Washington in 1975 and soon thereafter began passing intelligence to representatives of the Vietnamese Communist government in Paris. His courier, Dung Krall, the young Vietnamese-American wife of a U.S. naval officer, actually was a double agent working for the CIA. When President Carter, in May 1977, authorized a warrantless search of what she was carrying, investigators found classified documents containing information about U.S. policies that would be of interest to the Vietnamese. This, in turn, led to a warrantless wiretap of Truong's phone and, through an FBI investigation, to Humphrey.

Humphrey said he had been supplying documents to Truong in the hope that Vietnamese authorities would release his common-law Vietnamese wife, with whom he had lived when he had been stationed in Vietnam during the war. Truong said he had been working to try to improve relations between the United States and the new Socialist Republic of Vietnam. Although evidence in the espionage cases against both men had been gathered through warrantless surveillance, the Department of Justice decided to go ahead with a trial.

In the trial the jury sympathized with the men's motives for espionage, but both were convicted. In appeals, lawyers for the two men challenged the warrantless taps and searches that had produced the damning evidence. The appeals were in vain. Both men in 1982 began serving fifteen-year prison terms. But the court challenges exposed the shaky legal grounds for electronic surveillance and pointed up the need for a new judicial process.

In creating the Foreign Intelligence Surveillance Court—entering what Senator Daniel P. Moynihan called "virgin legislative territory"—Congress also wanted to protect from lawsuits and criminal charges those government officials and telephone company employees who had engaged in tapping. The new law, Moynihan said, was "an effort to provide legislative sanction in an area previously left virtually entirely to Executive discretion. But the form of sanction is modelled on the criminal law. The Act is therefore essentially a lawyer's document, complete with the norms of a judicial warrant issued by a special court."

One way to see how that warrant is issued is to follow the FBI as it moves to obtain what its counter-espionage agents believe is the vital evidence—incriminating phone conversations—needed to clinch the bureau's case against Harper.

Espionage, unlike other crimes, must be handled at the very highest levels of the Department of Justice. If a San Francisco bank were robbed, for example, the local FBI field office would work with the local U.S. Attorney in planning a case against the robbery suspects. But in an espionage case the field office must clear any proposed actions with Washington, where the Attorney General, through a designated Deputy Attorney General, approves or disapproves the field office's proposals.

The Department of Justice keeps an extremely close watch over FBI counter-espionage work. This was brought out vividly in the midst of an interview for this book. During the 9 a.m. interview with an FBI counter-intelligence agent in San Francisco, he repeatedly was called away to answer phone calls. "We always know when it's lunchtime in Washington," he said, explaining that Justice officials place the calls just before they go to lunch and want the answers by the time they come back. Most of the calls to the San Francisco field office around that time, March 1986, had to do with counter-espionage.

The intensive Washington involvement in espionage cases is not mere bureaucratic harassment or coaching. Each move in the nation's complex war on espionage must be analyzed by the principals in what is called, officially though loosely, "the U.S. intelligence community," and those principals cluster at the seat of power in Washington. The leading members of the community—which is nominally headed by the Director of Central Intelligence—are the National Security Agency, the Central Intelligence Agency, the State Department's Bureau of Intelligence and Research, the Defense Intelligence Agency, and the little-publicized National Reconnaissance Office, which administers U.S. satellites. The latter three entities are the responsibility of the Secretary of Defense. Other members of the community include the intelligence components of the Army, Navy, and Air Force, and, at least as occasional visitors to the community, such obscure intelligence gatherers as representatives from the Department of Energy (for nuclear intelligence) and the Drug Enforcement Administration (for narcotics intelligence).

The FBI is part of the intelligence community, but not as an intelligence gatherer, for the FBI has little opportunity to collect intelligence. Rather, the FBI is the nation's *counter*-intelligence (counter-espionage) agency. The FBI, restricted by law to activities within the United States, is mandated by federal authority as the "lead" or foremost agency of the U.S. effort against spies. But the bureaucratic designation as lead agency does not automatically confer on FBI agents and middle-level FBI officials a panoramic knowledge of the nation's continuous campaign against foreign spies and American moles. In fact, counter-espionage officers working in the field may have little knowledge beyond day-to-day surveillance orders. This is due, in part, to the FBI policy of rotating agents to make certain "all their tickets are punched" to make them eligible for promotion as fully rounded agents. Thus, as was recently the case, an agent who performed exceptionally well in the counter-espionage role at the Washington field office was forced to serve a tour in the public affairs office—for which he had some training but no inclination. He was then moved on to the budget office.

An FBI field office may be proposing to move against someone who is wittingly or unwittingly being controlled by U.S. counter-espionage operations unknown to the specific field office. A man who looks like a suspect from the vantage point of a San Francisco FBI surveillance team may in fact be an American working as a double agent, or a KGB officer in the process of being turned or being fed misinformation as part of a top-secret, multilevel counter-espionage enterprise. (Attorney General Bell tells of a behind-the-scenes debate between the CIA, which wanted to protect the identity of the double-agent courier in the Humphrey-Truong case, and the FBI, which wanted her as a witness in court. In this case the FBI's arguments prevailed.)

The Department of Justice—the FBI's parent organization —governs counter-espionage through coordinating mechanisms designed to assure cooperation between the FBI and other organizations, particularly the CIA. The Director of Central Intelligence (who is also, by statute, the head of the CIA) is the nation's supreme intelligence overseer.* He can, through the Justice Department coordination machinery, order the FBI to halt the *investigative* phase of an espionage case. But powerful as he and the CIA may be, he cannot, on his own initiative, initiate or halt the prosecution of a suspected spy, even one within the CIA. Only the FBI, a law-enforcement agency, has the power of arrest. Under federal law the FBI operates as an arm of the Department of Justice and only this police arm can bring a spy to justice.

(Investigative services in the armed forces can arrest suspects and recommend court-martial for espionage. But the Department of Justice can demand that a member of the armed services be brought into a federal court rather than be left to a military court-martial.)

In the Harper case the CIA had provided the leads, through the agency's initial contact with the Client and through the information that the Source in Poland provided to his CIA handlers. Once the Washington coordinators of counter-espionage policy decided that a case should be built against the anonymous spy, it was up to the FBI to develop the case, first by working to identify the spy, who was as yet unnamed. When the FBI decided that the probable name for that spy was James D. Harper, the next step was a relatively routine criminal investigation: surveillance and the discreet checking of records and people who knew him.

Then came the decision to push further, to seek Harper's actual words of espionage through telephone taps. The FBI began preparing what a veteran counter-espionage agent called "a mountain of paperwork" for presentation to the U.S. Foreign Intelligence Surveillance Court. "If every *i* isn't dotted and every *t* crossed, our technical agents won't even lift their tool bags," the agent said, referring to the FBI technicians who, under various

---

* When the National Security Act of 1947 established the position of Director of Central Intelligence (DCI), the director was to have "two hats." Wearing one, he would direct the CIA, the nation's intelligence agency, and wearing the other, he would coordinate overall U.S. intelligence activities—the work of other components of what became known as the intelligence community. However, because of a combination of weak or disinterested DCIs and the bureaucratic strengths of the other members of the community, the DCI's non-CIA functions have been severely limited.

guises, enter private and public premises to plant electronic bugs and tap phones.

Then FBI Director William Webster and members of his personal staff evaluated the Harper phone-tap application, as they did each application for an electronic surveillance warrant. "Polishing and shaping of the applications occurs as the paperwork moves through the approval mechanism," Webster has said. Webster signed the application—some may be forty pages long—and submitted it to the Attorney General for approval.

The warrant for electronic surveillance of Harper was one of 549 applications received and accepted by the court in 1983.* According to the FBI and other sources, none of the surveillance court judges has ever turned down an application. The Chief Justice designates the seven U.S. District Court judges, from various parts of the country, who take turns sitting in the secret court, which usually convenes for two or three days a month.

The FBI application for the tapping of Harper was submitted in May 1983 to the clerk of the court, who acts like a clerk in a conventional court except for the fact that everything he or she does is secret. In some ways the Harper application would look familiar to any court clerk, for it was a legal document containing the kind of language that would be contained in an application for an ordinary search warrant: a digest of the evidence obtained to date against Harper, a statement attesting to the need of the material for potential prosecution.

What makes such an application unique is that the authorization of need comes from the Attorney General,† who asserts that the officials submitting the application appear before the court as applicants. Their lawyers are attorneys from the Office of Intelligence Policy and Review, which Attorney General Bell had established as the Department of Justice's command post center in the nation's counter-espionage war.

Usually the court approves surveillance for ninety days. If

---

* The court approved 319 applications in 1980, the first full year after the act took effect; 431 in 1981; and 475 in 1982. In 1985, the Year of the Spy, the number was 635.

† The law allows the authorization to come from the President's national security adviser (officially, the Assistant to the President for National Security Affairs) or an executive branch national security official whose appointment requires the advice and consent of the Senate.

an agency wants more time, it must submit a new application. The government can conduct emergency electronic surveillance for twenty-four hours before requesting a warrant—but, simultaneously, the application must be applied for. "You can imagine the fun," a Justice Department official recalled. "And . . . you can imagine what it is like once we get the emergency authorization, which may be verbal, to then reduce that to writing, get it through all those lawyers and past all those Cabinet officers and to the court and signed in twenty-four hours. But we can do it and we have done it."

In such a case the government must go into the court not only to ask for approval but also to show that the emergency is real. If the court turns down a government request, the government can appeal the decision in a secret court of review consisting of three judges drawn from U.S. Courts of Appeal. All judges involved in that special appeals court and the surveillance court are given stringent security background checks under standards set up by the Director of Central Intelligence, who was Stansfield Turner when the Foreign Intelligence Surveillance Court was being set up. At that time Turner and Bell went to the Supreme Court Justices' conference room to discuss the proposed surveillance court with Chief Justice Warren E. Burger. Turner wanted lie-detector tests for the judges involved. Bell and Burger talked him out of it and decided that the judges need only to have strict FBI background investigations.

More than telephone taps and hidden microphones are involved in electronic surveillance. The court also authorizes the tapping of teleprinters and computers; the interception of radio transmissions; monitoring by closed-circuit television; the use of tiny transmitters that track the movement of vehicles; and "watch listing," the acquisition of telegrams and cables sent by or intended for the person being watched. In 1981, Attorney General William French Smith, deciding that the law covered more than electronic surveillance, added "physical entry" to the list.

In the Harper case telephone taps gave investigators all they wanted. While speaking with his ex-wife, Colleen, for example, Harper mentioned his new VCR and remarked that it had been purchased for a "different purpose." Colleen cautiously said that they should not discuss that purpose over the telephone. But because, through the Client's statements, the FBI already had information on the VCR's "different purpose," Harper's guarded mention of it was in itself incriminating.

Another innocent-sounding call that was incriminating came from a 3-M Company representative who wanted to know whether Harper needed any supplies for his copier machine. Harper said that for some time he had been using the copier so much he could not keep up with supplies. But, he added, he had not been using the machine much lately. What Harper told the 3-M representative closely resembled what the Client had said: He had copied thousands of documents but, after Ruby lost her security clearance, he had not had any documents to copy.*

"I've got a pretty good stash," Harper said in one of his frequent boasts about money. He mentioned Swiss bank accounts and deposits of cash into banks in the Cayman Islands, where "they don't ask a whole lot of questions." He also bragged about not having paid any taxes for the past ten years. When he started talking about foreign travel and making phone calls to Switzerland, FBI eavesdroppers began planning how and when to move in on him. By then it was too late to make a case against Ruby Schuler Harper.

In a call on June 4, 1983, Ruby had told a close friend, "There was a reason Jim and I got married that only he and I know. I can't tell you or anyone else, and I never will." Eighteen days after Ruby made that call she died from complications of cirrhosis of the liver.

On September 11 a woman named Penny Cook called her father from Harper's apartment and said that she and Harper would shortly be married and would have a European honeymoon. Six days later Harper and Penny, trailed by FBI agents, went to Carson City, Nevada, and were married. Harper would claim in a subsequent phone conversation that he was still richer than before, since he was the beneficiary of Ruby's $100,000 life

---

* The 3-M Company, ironically, had been unsuccesfully trying to get intelligence agencies and defense companies interested in a system designed to protect classified documents from being copied. The system, which could have thwarted many spies like Harper, uses a small security label that is firmly attached to the document; any attempt to remove the label will visibly damage the document. If someone tries to copy the labeled document, the loader cover on the copier snaps shut and an alarm goes off.

insurance policy. There was no such policy. He invented it as a way to explain some of the $250,000 that the Poles are said to have paid him.

When the FBI arrested Harper in October 1983 and showed him what the government knew about his espionage activities, he said, "Oh, my God! They know everything about it." He then collapsed.

Harper's own words, anonymously on the Client tapes and well identified on the FBI wiretaps, had effectively convicted him. After some sparring, he opted for a plea bargain instead of a trial. Three years before, William Bell, another Californian who had sold secrets to an agent of the Polish Intelligence Service, had also made a deal and had received an eight-year sentence.

The arrest of Harper and media speculation about the Harper and Bell deals apparently helped to inspire the RUS letters. FBI Special Agent Peterson of the San Francisco counterespionage squad had suspected exactly that when he had seen the first RUS letter, which had been written on May 7. By then Harper had pleaded guilty but had not yet been sentenced. On May 14, under a plea bargain, Harper was sentenced to life imprisonment, with a recommendation that he never be paroled. Still, RUS kept writing, asking for a chance for a deal, perhaps because, in the extensive media coverage of the Harper case, he had read that Harper's lawyer had held out the hope that Harper could be paroled after ten years. RUS knew, along with everyone involved with spying or catching spies, that the punishment for espionage did not always fit the crime.

Espionage generates a great deal of emotional rhetoric. "There can be no crime more serious than that of selling our country's defense secrets to a foreign government," said Judge Samuel Conti in sentencing Harper to life in prison. But espionage produces few trials. In hoping for a deal, RUS apparently assumed that the government would prefer to keep him out of a courtroom. RUS was somewhat behind the times, however. Once it had been true that espionage was a crime that did not go on trial, primarily in fear of the secrets that would be released through testimony. But times were changing.

From the early 1960s to the mid-1970s espionage cases had rarely reached courtrooms. During that period Soviet intelligence appears to have focused on recruiting spies in the armed services, particularly the Air Force. When servicemen were caught Pentagon officials tried to keep publicity subdued and sentences harsh. Air Force Captain Joseph P. Kauffman, court-martialed in West Germany in 1962 for having passed undescribed "military secrets" to East German intelligence, was sentenced to twenty years at hard labor. John Butenko, a civilian electronics engineer convicted in 1964 of conspiring to give information on the Strategic Air Command's communication system to the Soviets, received a thirty-year sentence. (So did Igor Ivanov, a Soviet agent tried with Butenko. Ivanov, who stayed out of jail through legal maneuvers, eventually was allowed to return to the Soviet Union.)

Air Force Sergeant Herbert Boeckenhaupt, in Air Force headquarters in the Pentagon, began meeting regularly with an employee of the Soviet Embassy in 1965. Arrested in 1967, he received a thirty-year sentence for passing secrets that were not revealed, or even hinted at, in public. Air Force Master Sergeant Walter Perkins, an intelligence specialist at the Air Defense Weapons Center at Tyndall Air Force Base, Florida, was arrested in 1971 on his way to deliver top-secret air-defense plans to a Soviet KGB officer in Mexico. He later said he had thought that he could swap secret documents for American prisoners of war in North Vietnam. In a prosecution handled by the Air Force, not the Department of Justice, Perkins was sentenced to only three years in prison. Another Air Force sergeant was taken into custody in 1973 as he headed for the Soviet Embassy to deliver what officials described as "classified counter-intelligence information," but neither his name nor the disposition of his case was disclosed.

What would appear to have been some of the most devastating espionage ever carried out in the Pentagon resulted in a relatively light sentence for Lieutenant Colonel William H. Whalen, a veteran Army intelligence specialist who was arrested in 1966 on charges of having spied for the Soviets for at least two years while he was in the Office of the Joint Chiefs of Staff. Whalen was charged with revealing "information pertaining to atomic weapons, missiles, military plans for the defense of Europe, information concerning the retaliation plans of the United States Strategic Air Command, and information pertaining to troop movements, documents, and writings relating to the national defense of the United States." He received only a fifteen-year sentence.

The few publicly acknowledged espionage cases of the late 1960s and early 1970s would cast their shadows deep into the 1980s. The concentration on servicemen distorted the real picture of espionage in the United States during that period, for spies, then and now, sought secrets not only in the armed services but also in the other two branches of the U.S. "intelligence triad": federal agencies (especially the CIA and FBI) and the defense industry. Senior officials and even lower-echelon bureaucrats in federal agencies could ward off the kind of surveillance and interrogation that, in the hierarchical command structure of the armed services, could lead to investigations and arrests. And defense plants were in the realm of private enterprise, where government investigators treaded warily.

Whenever investigators sought out spies—whether in the armed services, federal agencies, or defense plants—prosecution was unlikely. Espionage is a crime of double-edged secrecy. Spies, well experienced in clandestine procedures and operating not as individuals but as agents of a nation, are hard to detect by traditional police work. And the loot that they seek is not the kind of evidence that can be labeled Exhibit A in a courtroom. Secrets are no longer secrets if they become exhibits, and, if the cost of prosecuting a spy is the exposure of a secret, then prosecution may be too high a price to pay. And there is still another kind of secret that a trial reveals: the failings of the secret-holder's own security safeguards.

Espionage investigations are time-consuming and involve a great number of people. But often they are nothing more than "dangle" operations, in which a loyal American is trolled in front of an eager KGB officer in hopes that the Soviet will be hooked. A straight line can be drawn from these scams of the 1970s to the arrest in 1986 of American reporter Nicholas Daniloff by the KGB in cynical retaliation for the arrest by the FBI of Soviet UN employee (and spy recruiter) Gennadi Zakharov. These crisis-triggering incidents are driven by a choreography of espionage and counter-espionage that has nothing to do with the gathering of intelligence or the catching of spies. The incidents arise from a policy aimed at finding and tempting Soviet intelligence officers rather than tracking and convicting American betrayers.

In February 1972, as U.S. and Soviet negotiators were working on the antiballistic missile treaty and SALT I strategic arms limitations agreement, the FBI arrested Valery Markelov, a Soviet intelligence officer who worked under the cover of a translator at the United Nations. He was charged with receiving classified documents about the F-14A Tomcat fighter from a Grumman engineer, who turned out to be a double agent working for the FBI. Three months later, as Nixon was about to have a summit meeting with Brezhnev, the U.S. Government quietly quashed the espionage indictment and Markelov, who had been out on bail, was allowed to return to the Soviet Union.

The net result was the stinging of a KGB officer. No trial. No capture of a real spy. And that became the pattern: the use of U.S. counter-espionage resources on scams, the use of the U.S. legal system to keep the tricked KGB officers out of court.

By 1977, when Griffin Bell became Attorney General, the intelligence community "had come to believe that every time you prosecuted a spy, you would lose the secret, and that it was better public policy—the lesser of two evils—to let the spy go and keep the secret. But I had the idea that you could prosecute these cases without losing the secret."

Bell had successfully fought the intelligence community to put Humphrey and Truong on trial in 1978. And Bell successfully appealed directly to President Carter to end similar bureaucratic opposition to Bell's decision to prosecute William P. Kampiles, a CIA employee who in 1977 sold the Soviets the technical manual for the Keyhole (KH-11) reconnaissance satellite. The Kampiles case, a turning point for counter-espionage policy, put the U.S. intelligence community on warning: From then on spying was a crime that could be prosecuted in a courtroom. Kampiles, Bell later wrote, "would not have come to public notice had the 1954 Justice Department-CIA agreement been in force, because the prosecution revealed significant breaches in the CIA's own security."

Kampiles, then twenty-three, was a watch officer in the CIA's operations center. He had worked at the agency only for seven months and quit after receiving a letter chiding him for poor performance. He took with him the KH-11 manual, which, on a visit to Greece, he sold to a Soviet military attaché for $3,000. Kampiles, in effect, turned himself in, for he described his dealings with the Soviet in a letter that, according to Bell, "remained unopened for two months at the CIA." Although Bell won begrudging cooperation from the CIA, the Pentagon protested that information about the top-secret satellite project would be revealed. Kampiles was convicted of espionage and sentenced to forty years in prison. The Kampiles theft revealed, among other things, that the CIA's internal security procedures were "surprisingly lax," according to Admiral Stansfield Turner, who was DCI at the time. "When we learned that one [KH-11 manual] was missing, we also found we could not account for thirteen others!"

Bell was not yet sworn in as Attorney General when the espionage cases on his watch began. One night in December 1976, little more than a month after the election of Jimmy Carter, a hapless former CIA employee named Edwin G. Moore II threw several documents over the fence at a Washington apartment building housing Soviet Embassy families. A Soviet security guard, thinking the package was a bomb, called the Executive Protection Service, thus becoming the first known Soviet ever to assist in the arrest of a would-be American spy. Army explosives experts discovered that the package contained not a bomb but several CIA documents accompanied by an offer of "penetration into the headquarters operations of the CIA." A note asked for $200,000, to be left at a drop site in a residential suburban neighborhood.*

The FBI followed the directions in the note, left a dummy

* The call-for-the-cops-for-the-strange-brown-bag ploy can backfire in another way. When Vice Admiral James A. (Ace) Lyons found a brown paper bag on the doorstep of his home in the Washington Navy Yard one Christmas, he immediately called the yard police force, which in turn called Army explosives experts. The soldiers carefully conveyed the package to a cleared area where, with great caution, they blew up two bottles of Russian vodka. The bottles were a Christmas gift from Rear Admiral Ivan P. Sakulkin, the Soviet naval attaché. On his fourth assignment in Washington, Sakulkin, of course, was more than a career naval officer. He was also a GRU officer, and when the Reagan Administration kicked out a number of Soviet intelligence officials in the fall of 1986, Sakulkin was one of them.

package at the site, and hid agents nearby. A man across the street from the drop, raking the leaves on his own lawn, furtively looked around, put down his rake, and picked up the package. He was Moore.

Moore had not revealed anything to the KGB, but his arrest was to reveal more about the lax security practices at the CIA. Moore had been a staff employee, primarily in mapmaking and logistics studies, from 1952 to 1963, when he was fired after having been arrested for arson. Acquitted on that charge, he appealed for reinstatement and was rehired in 1967.

Moore retired in 1973, at the age of fifty-three, on a medical disability stemming from a heart ailment. "His career," said a later CIA report, "had been marked by marginal work performance, chronic work frustrations, and a general reputation of being miscast in an intelligence agency." In his home FBI agents found classified CIA directories listing names, addresses, and phone numbers of CIA employees. Among the hundreds of documents was material dating after 1973, indicating that he had had continual contact with people at the agency after his retirement.

Moore, convicted on two counts of espionage and three counts of unlawful possession of classified documents, was sentenced to fifteen years in prison in May 1977. He was paroled in 1979.

The Moore case introduced Bell to all of the elements of a touchy espionage case: a volunteer spy, an embarrassed agency, a tendency to deal leniently with would-be spies found within the intelligence community.

Bell's trials-for-spies policy, continued by his successor, Benjamin R. Civiletti, generated a rash of other prosecutions that involved the CIA. The trial that the CIA most hoped to prevent was not Moore's but that of David H. Barnett, a turncoat who worked for the agency from 1958 until 1970. Barnett's career as an agent for the KGB began in 1976, when his Jakarta-based exporting business was failing. He made contact with a Soviet intelligence officer and for $25,000—bargained down from his $70,000 initial selling price—he sold the KGB the names of at least thirty CIA agents and officers overseas.

Barnett also solved a mystery for the Soviet military by revealing why Soviet SA-2 surface-to-air missiles had been relatively ineffective against U.S. aircraft during the Vietnam War.

(Soviet-made surface-to-air missiles scored about one hit for every 100 missiles launched.) CIA covert operatives, by infiltrating the Indonesian Navy, obtained information about Soviet weapons given to Indonesia in the 1960s. Discoveries about how the SA-2 guidance system worked were passed along to U.S. electronics engineers, and they in turn developed jamming techniques that American planes used against the missiles. Barnett also provided names and psychological profiles of CIA employees who would be likely targets for turning by the KGB, along with the names of Soviet diplomats the CIA had been hoping to turn.

Barnett's information, though valuable enough to earn him $92,600, was dated. So the KGB urged him to use his CIA experience to get an appointment to the staff of either the Senate or House intelligence oversight committees. Other suggestions for employment as a mole were the State Department's Bureau of Intelligence and Research, the Defense Intelligence Agency, or, as a last resort, the CIA. Somewhat to the disappointment of his KGB handlers, Barnett managed only to be rehired by the CIA in 1979 as a contract employee to teach classes on how to resist interrogation. A year later, after what counter-espionage officials vaguely called "interception of communications" between Barnett and one of the handlers—Vladimir V. Popov, third secretary of the Soviet Embassy—the FBI confronted Barnett. Following the advice he had given his students (when all else fails, talk), he admitted his treachery.

CIA officials, aghast at the penetration of the agency, urged the Justice Department to make a deal rather than put Barnett on trial. Justice prosecutors pushed for a trial and built a case so strong that Barnett pleaded guilty. "The evidence was given under seal to the trial judge, thus keeping disclosure to what prosecutors regarded as the minimum," Bell wrote. Barnett was sentenced to an eighteen-year prison term.

Just as the Moore and Barnett cases revealed the vulnerability of the CIA, the exploits of Andrew Daulton Lee and Christopher Boyce underscored the sloppy handling of secrets in the defense industry. The two, both in their twenties, were convicted of selling information about U.S. reconnaissance satellites to the Soviets.

They were caught by a fluke. Mexican police saw Lee throw something onto the grounds of the Soviet Embassy in Mexico

City. While police were questioning him Lee hailed a U.S. diplomat, who had been to the embassy on business, and asked him for help. That U.S. diplomat called another, who accompanied Lee to police headquarters, where authorities found that he was carrying an envelope full of film strips. The police gave prints of the film to U.S. officials because the photos were of U.S. documents marked top secret.

FBI agents questioned Lee, who implicated Boyce, saying that they had stolen the material from TRW Systems Group, a space and defense communications company. At first the pair claimed that they were only fooling the Soviets by peddling worthless documents. But at their trials the government proved that they had sold, for about $70,000, invaluable secrets to the Soviets. Both were convicted of espionage. Lee was sentenced to life imprisonment, Boyce to forty years. They became celebrity spies, the subjects of a best-selling book, *The Falcon and the Snowman,* and a movie of the same name.

TRW is one of the many hundreds of high-technology firms that support U.S. defense programs. Boyce was given a security job with a highly classified satellite program at TRW. He not only had access to company and Department of Defense secrets but also to classified information relating to the U.S. intelligence community, which used some of the satellites.

Boyce's espionage was the work of a true agent, a walk-in who sold the Soviets vital secrets. Catching spies like Boyce is far more important than catching Soviet diplomats. But, down the years, U.S. counter-espionage has often involved espionage scams that presented hostile intelligence officers with tempting secrets proffered by bogus agents.

One scam, which dangled an Army warrant officer before Otto Attila Gilbert, a Hungarian intelligence officer (Chapter 3), went off well and resulted in a plea bargain and a fifteen-year sentence for Gilbert. But another FBI sting operation had repercussions that years later erupted into an international incident.

The scam began when Lieutenant Commander Arthur Lindberg, a Navy supply officer about to retire, agreed to become the dangle in an attempt to lure Soviet intelligence officers. Following an elaborate FBI scenario, Lindberg boarded the Soviet cruise ship *Kazakhstan* for a week-long, New York-to-Bermuda voyage in the summer of 1977. His FBI handlers expected that a ship's officer would attempt to make contact with him. None did. So Lindberg, as he was leaving the ship, handed an officer a note that said, "I am interested in making additional money prior to my retirement and can provide you with information which may be of interest to you." The note gave the number of a pay phone at a New Jersey diner.

For the next nine months Lindberg and his invisible Soviet contacts communicated by pay phones along the New Jersey Turnpike and Garden State Parkway. He provided them with information about underwater acoustics and detection techniques used in the hunting of Soviet submarines. Navy antisubmarine warfare experts doled out the information, which Lindberg photographed. He placed the film in empty orange-juice cartons and radiator hoses left at dead drops near New Jersey highways.

In May 1978, FBI agents staked out a drop in a Woodbridge, New Jersey, shopping center. The drop, containing Lindberg's latest delivery, was serviced by three Soviets, who were promptly arrested: Rudolf P. Chernyayev, a United Nations personnel official; Vladik A. Enger, an assistant to the Under Secretary General of the UN; and Vladimir P. Zinyakin, an attaché at the Soviet UN Mission. As employees of the UN, Chernyayev and Enger did not have diplomatic immunity but Zinyakin did. He was declared persona non grata—"PNG'd," as FBI counter-espionage agents like to put it—and quickly left the country. But his compatriots had to face trial, touching off a high-level policy fight that split the Carter Administration.

Both the State Department and the CIA, Bell recalled, "vigorously opposed prosecution" of Chernyayev and Enger, who, if they stood trial, would become the highest-ranking Soviet officials ever to be tried for espionage in a U.S. court. Secretary of State Cyrus Vance especially worried about the possible effect of the arrests on the forthcoming summit meeting between Carter and Soviet leader Leonid Brezhnev.

Director of Central Intelligence Turner had other worries. His CIA has a broader charter than the FBI's and stands watch over a broader horizon. What to the FBI was a successful espionage scam was to the CIA an escapade that could have wide, direct, and perhaps disastrous effects on CIA "legals," those intelligence officers who are under cover as diplomats on the rolls of embassies and consulates around the world. If a legal is caught doing his or her undercover job of espionage, the officer, by long custom, is merely PNG'd and does not have to face trial.

The arrangement reflects a professional courtesy that the KGB and CIA both understand. And it explained the CIA-State Department alliance on the issue, for the State Department (like the Soviet Foreign Ministry) has to tell the little white lies about intelligence officers masquerading as diplomats.

To the FBI and the Justice Department, all three Soviets were simply spies who did not warrant any special privileges. This hard-line approach, however, did not get official support from another likely source—the Department of Defense. The Pentagon found itself on the side of the State Department because the Navy submarine community, urged on by the powerful Admiral Hyman G. Rickover, lobbied against the trial. The submariners claimed that the so-called innocuous secrets passed to the Soviets by Lindberg (a supply officer and not a submariner) were *real* secrets, and disclosure in a trial could be a dangerous breach of security.

In the CIA-State Department view the FBI had done nothing more than give the intelligence community a headache. Zinyakin's arrest served no obvious purpose because he was immune to prosecution anyway. As for Chernyayev and Enger, the bureaucracies that were lined up against the FBI argued that, although the Soviets were not protected diplomats, they rated some special consideration because of the retaliation that their scam-style arrest could provoke. "I had argued against prosecution," Turner wrote, "largely because of the strong concern of the CIA's espionage branch that retaliatory actions might get out of control."

The decision was taken to President Carter, who approved of the prosecution of Chernyayev and Enger. "I'm told," Bell archly reports, "that when Admiral Turner pressed the point of potential harm to our agents if we prosecuted, the President responded that, based on the quality of information he had been receiving, he was surprised we had anyone working inside the Soviet Union."

The predicted retaliation came on June 11. F. Jay Crawford, an American who had spent nearly two years as Moscow service manager for International Harvester, was driving down a street in the Soviet capital. At a stoplight his car was surrounded by

KGB operatives in militiamen police uniforms. They pulled him from his station wagon and took him to Lefortovo Prison in central Moscow.

Soviet authorities charged Crawford with smuggling, an extremely serious charge. The State Department and CIA tried again to get Bell to change his mind and drop the charges against Chernyayev and Enger. Bell refused, saying, "I'm not about to trade two KGBers for any tractor salesman."

Brezhnev himself took the case of the tractor salesman seriously enough to announce his guilt before his trial began. While Crawford languished in prison and the KGB worked on fabricating a case against him, the Soviets stepped up the espionage war by revealing in extraordinary detail the KGB investigation and arrest of Martha Peterson, a CIA case officer under cover as a vice consul in the U.S. Embassy.

Peterson had been quietly PNG'd from the Soviet Union a year before. The Soviets, in diplomatic conversations, claimed that KGB counter-espionage agents had caught her servicing a dead drop. The United States, following diplomatic custom, had not acknowledged guilt but had acquiesced in her expulsion the day after her arrest.

The CIA officials were stoic about her arrest, but they were privately outraged at the way KGB interrogators had roughly handled Peterson. "She was not shown the usual courtesy expected by an intelligence officer," a retired CIA officer recalled. "They roughed her up—not injuring her, but playing rough." CIA debriefers later speculated that Peterson, whose husband also worked at the U.S. Embassy, had shown up the KGB. Soviet Embassy watchers had not spotted her as an intelligence officer and, when they belatedly did so, they took out their anger and frustration on her. "Unlike many intelligence officers," the retired CIA man said, "she had been 'living her cover' closely, working as a consular official, mostly on visa applications. People figured that the KGB had not spotted her as an intelligence officer for a long while, and someone was mad as hell."

At the time of Peterson's arrest the Soviet Union had refrained from publicizing the case, as was customary when someone protected by diplomatic immunity is accused of—or caught —spying. But with Crawford about to go on trial in Moscow and the two Soviet officials about to stand trial in Newark, *Izvestia* published a long and sensational report on Peterson. The Soviet newspaper said that her dead drop was a crevice in a bridge over the Moscow River near the Luzhniki sports stadium. In *Izvestia's* description of her arrest she was portrayed depositing gold, Russian currency, cameras—and ampules of poison to be used by one of her agents to kill a Soviet citizen who was impeding CIA espionage. Accompanying the story was a photograph showing her with a U.S. Embassy official at a table spread with the objects said to have been found in the dead drop.

Chernyayev and Enger were tried and convicted and each was given a fifty-year sentence. But, in an unusual legal move, they were released from prison while their cases were under appeal. They were soon traded to the Soviet Union for five Soviet dissidents and, Bell mysteriously adds, "for other considerations I cannot discuss." (Some intelligence sources say the "considerations" included a Soviet promise not to execute an imprisoned CIA agent.)

The charges against Crawford, meanwhile, underwent an abrupt change, from smuggling to currency violations. His American lawyer said that KGB officials stage-managed the change when they discovered they could not concoct "even a halfway plausible case on smuggling." But the black-market currency accusation tottered in court. A would-be confederate testified to having met Crawford in Moscow when he was actually in Chicago; documents were ineptly falsified by someone using two different inks; the major witness stumbled in his testimony and had to be prompted by the judge. Nevertheless, Crawford was convicted and given a five-year suspended sentence. He was allowed to leave the country on September 8.

It may appear that the tides had thus rolled over the whole event and all was the same as before. But powerful currents were working unseen. The KGB, by making the ugly claim that Peterson had ordered a murder, had issued a warning to the CIA that dirty work might break out in the secret world of professional espionage, where amateurs were dangerously afoot. Bell showed the extent of his own naiveté about the KGB with a proposal he made behind the scenes: "Both sides would agree to use as spies only their people with diplomatic immunity. If they were caught, the most that could be done would be to send them home. Anyone else caught spying would be prosecuted to the full extent of the law." U.S. counter-espionage experts politely turned down the idea; it is not officially known what the KGB thought of the proposal.

The incident, which had begun with the Lindberg dangle, should have taught the U.S. counter-espionage establishment that resources are better spent finding real American spies rather than running fake ones. But the FBI, enamored of scams in exposing bribe-prone congressmen and other domestic crooks, continued to stage such sting operations. The Army, on its own, was doing the same, dangling soldiers who pretended to work as spies for the Soviets. U.S. counter-espionage efforts again settled into a routine of scam and swap that periodically produced international incidents—but did not produce the American spies in our midst.

A 1986 scam-and-reprisal episode that flared into a Washington-Moscow confrontation had its beginnings in late 1982 when Gennadi F. Zakharov arrived in New York from Moscow to assume his post as scientific affairs officer assigned to the Center for Science and Technology for Development, part of the United Nations Secretariat. The FBI counter-espionage squad assigned to the Soviet UN Mission and the Soviet Consulate logged Zakharov in as a new man on the Soviet KGB unit operating out of those legal spy nests.

Under the rules of the UN-cover game, Zakharov was expected to be assigned the role of spotter—an intelligence officer who discovered and recruited potential agents. The actual exchange of information and money, directly or through dead drops, was, according to the rules, supposed to be handled by Soviets with diplomatic immunity. If they were caught, they would be expelled but not tried and jailed, and the game would go on without incident.

Surveillance teams assigned to "Group 3," the Russian Counter-Intelligence Division, watched Zakharov make his rounds, concentrating on college campuses in the New York area. Several students he approached reported him to the FBI, but, for various reasons, none of them could be developed as double agents. Then, in April 1983, the FBI recruited one of Zakharov's recruits, Leakh N. Bhoge, a twenty-five-year-old man from Guyana (formerly British Guiana), a small country whose government is friendly to the United States. Bhoge was a permanent resident of the United States. The FBI code-named him "Plumber." The KGB name for him was "Birg."*

Bhoge was in his third year at Queens College, New York, where he was majoring in computer sciences. Bhoge said that Zakharov had appeared on the campus one day, claimed that he worked as a scientific researcher at the UN, and asked for help in getting information on robotics and computer technology. He said he would pay Bhoge for the research. Then began a classic KGB espionage courtship. Bhoge was asked first for easily accessible information, which he photocopied for Zakharov on library copier machines, usually making an extra copy for the FBI. Next came requests that would more deeply enmesh him with Zakharov, who asked Bhoge to steal microfiche from the college library.

As Bhoge's graduation neared in late 1984, Zakharov gave Bhoge a list of employment agencies and urged him to get a job working on artificial intelligence or robotics. To help in his job search, Zakharov paid for Bhoge's professionally prepared résumés. He also said the Soviet Government would underwrite graduate school if Bhoge wanted to continue his education. The FBI helped Bhoge even more than Zakharov did by actually finding him a job. He was advised to answer a help-wanted advertisement in the *Daily News*. The cooperative employer, willing to hire a double agent, was a machine shop that manufactured precision parts for radar and the engines used in military aircraft. The shop was owned by the father of an FBI agent.

Soon after Bhoge began work, Zakharov, with the vague explanation that he needed the technical information for his own research, asked his protégé to photograph operating manuals for the machine that the shop used in the production of engine parts. By now Bhoge was usually wired when he met with Zakharov. He had a tape recorder taped to his back. Connected to the recorder were two tiny transmitters and microphones on his chest

---

* Neither the FBI nor the KGB identified Bhoge. He came forward in 1987 at a news conference, following publication of his story, "I Spy," in *New York* magazine. He said he had expected "well over $100,000" for his services as an FBI double agent, but had been paid only $20,000.

and arms. The transmitters relayed conversations to shadowing FBI agents in vans and cars.

During a meeting on a subway platform in Queens in May 1986, Zakharov dictated an agreement, which Bhoge wrote down on a piece of paper, signed, and handed to Zakharov, who paid him some money to seal the bargain. Under the agreement Bhoge would work as a spy "for seven to ten years, and after that, if I am willing, then the contract can be renewed or extended." Payment would depend upon the quantity of the information provided the Soviets.

Zakharov asked his agent to remain unmarried and apply for graduate school at Brooklyn Polytechnic Institute. By now it was clear that Zakharov was not merely a spotter. He acted more like an active case officer. From the way he parked his blue 1982 Plymouth and then walked to his meetings, FBI surveillance specialists believed that the car was equipped with scanners that could detect electronic surveillance devices.

Zakharov was not playing by the rules. He was an officer actively running an agent. He was paying money, making agreements, and he had all the paraphernalia of espionage—the code pads, the secret writing paper, the microdots. His microdots appeared to be designed for greeting cards; a real dot in a printed felicitation could be covered with a microdot, which looked like a period but actually was a typewritten message reduced 200 times, a photographic process perfected by the Germans in World War II.

Surprised counter-espionage agents believed that a strong case could be made against the overreaching Zakharov, who, because he lacked diplomatic immunity, could be tried, convicted, and jailed. The agents had been pressing for the arrest of someone in the large New York KGB contingent employed by the UN, to at least provide an example to the others. The FBI, knowing that the State Department would oppose such an arrest, started lobbying in Washington for a UN arrest.

In June, FBI counter-espionage agents from the Washington, D.C., field office had arrested Vladimir Makarovich Ismaylov, a GRU officer assigned as an assistant air attaché in the Soviet Military Office in the capital. About a year before, Ismaylov had walked up to a U.S. Air Force officer in a bar near the Pentagon and asked him to spy for the Soviet Union. The American reported the approach to the FBI, volunteered to work as a double agent, and for months had strung Ismaylov along with phony secret documents.

The arrest of Ismaylov at a Maryland dead drop had been relatively routine and had not required the kind of lobbying the New York FBI had to do in the Zakharov case. Ismaylov, as an attaché, had diplomatic immunity and his arrest resulted only in expulsion. The FBI agents in Washington had been able to convince administration officials that Ismaylov had to be arrested because he was "an extremely aggressive officer" who needed to be curbed quickly. And espionage experts knew from experience that the arrest and expulsion of a military attaché, as part of the game, did not cause trouble at the White House-Kremlin level.

The FBI's Russian squad in New York argued that Zakharov, though a lightweight and not a particularly dangerous spy, provided the United States with an opportunity to show its displeasure about the flagrant use of the UN for spying. The FBI had another, unstated reason for wanting to make an espionage arrest. On August 7, Edward Lee Howard, a former officer of the CIA, had surfaced in Moscow. A year before, Howard had slipped away from FBI agents who had him under surveillance. The FBI had been embarrassed then, and now, with Howard's escape back in the headlines, the FBI was embarrassed again.

In mid-August, with key State Department opponents to the Zakharov arrest on vacation, the FBI sought approval elsewhere. One champion was Vice Admiral John M. Poindexter, the President's national security adviser. Poindexter, one of the officials empowered to authorize wiretap applications, was intensely concerned with security matters and stalked the National Security Council in search of leaks. He was fanatic about keeping secrets and was proposing what would have added a new category to the nation's security labels: "sensitive, but not classified, information." With Poindexter reportedly the principal proponent, the FBI request went through the White House bureaucracy and won approval.

FBI counter-espionage agents had often heard that the KGB thought they were lax on weekends. Perhaps that is one reason why the arrest was made on a Saturday—August 23. Two agents, a man and a woman posing as a pair of joggers, arrested Zakharov as he talked to Bhoge on a Queens subway platform.

The FBI charged that Zakharov was a KGB intelligence officer who had paid Bhoge $1,000 for three classified documents showing the design of U.S. Air Force jet engines. The FBI provided the documents to Bhoge, who did not have access to any such documents on his job. They were the first classified documents Bhoge had ever given Zakharov.

Exactly a week later KGB agents arrested Daniloff, a correspondent for *U.S. News & World Report,* in Lenin Hills, a Moscow park near his apartment, after a Soviet acquaintance handed Daniloff an envelope containing maps, photographs, and military documents. The Soviets later linked Daniloff to Paul M. Stombaugh, a political officer at the U.S. Embassy who had been expelled as a spy in 1985, and Murat Natirboff, an embassy officer the Soviets identified as the CIA station chief in Moscow. He had left the Soviet Union shortly before the Daniloff arrest.

As in previous such cases, a Soviet leader (Mikhail Gorbachev this time) condemned the American (Daniloff this time) as a "spy who was caught in the act." Daniloff angrily denied the charge. And Zakharov said he was no spy. "I was set up," he said.

Talk of spy swapping immediately began, but American officials, from President Reagan down, sternly declared that no deal could be made because Daniloff was not a spy. That was certainly true. But his arrest raised a question: Why didn't the Soviets arrest a *real* spy? Possible answers came in the wake of Howard's defection: He had revealed so much information about the CIA's intelligence operations in the Soviet Union that it was in shambles. (In October the Soviets would announce the execution of Adolf G. Tolkachev, a Soviet defense analyst, who was identified as a CIA spy. The Soviets said that he had been caught passing secret information to Stombaugh, who also had been exposed by Howard.) Another possibility: The Soviets had learned so much about U.S. intelligence that the KGB was running its own scams and did not want to give up one of its controlled U.S. agents.

The end of the Zakharov-Daniloff affair came on September 30, when the United States and the Soviet Union announced that President Reagan and Gorbachev would meet for a summit conference in Iceland on October 11 and 12. As had happened prior to the Nixon-Brezhnev summit in 1972, the bothersome espionage problem had become a nonproblem.

The announcement about the summit was made by Tass, the Soviet news service, at 9:50 a.m. Four minutes later Zakharov entered a plea of no contest to the espionage charges in Federal Court in Brooklyn.* He then left for Washington, where he boarded a Soviet Aeroflot flight that left Dulles International Airport at 3:15 p.m. Daniloff arrived in Washington at 4:40 p.m. on the last leg of a journey from Moscow that had begun the day before. A Soviet dissident and his wife were also released as part of the exquisitely timed swap—which the Reagan Administration officially described as not a swap.

Donald T. Regan, the White House Chief of Staff, made it appear that policy decisions do not surround espionage cases. "We don't go around approving what the FBI and the court system do," he said. "The courts of the United States and the prosecutors of the United States act under the laws of the United States. The White House hasn't anything to do with spies and catching spies. That's not our job." He was right, of course, about *interference* with courts, which would be illegal. But the point was *control* of counter-espionage, which is a vital, though rarely acknowledged, responsibility of the executive branch.

Attorney General Bell had brought espionage back into the courtroom with genuinely bolt-from-the-blue spies—Humphrey, Truong, and Kampiles. These cases were greatly different from the FBI scams that climaxed with the Zakharov-Daniloff deal. The scams had made intelligence and counter-intelligence appear to be a kind of game played by cynical operatives on both sides. Spy swapping, by whatever name, was part of the game. The ultimate beneficiary of such public perception is the Soviet Union, for, instead of being viewed as a totalitarian nation unlike the United States, it is seen as a competitor of equal status. In this view, the two superpowers mirror each other as they play at espionage, a dirty little pastime of the Cold War.

The crime of espionage has been diluted in other ways as well, for spying no longer necessarily means betrayal of the nation to an enemy. Historically, espionage has involved the passing of secret information from one person to another, with harm to the nation as the result. Usually spies passed a specific secret—

---

* In November, Bhoge took the oath of U.S. citizenship in the same courthouse.

the disposition of warships at a certain moment, the sailing date of a convoy of merchant ships laden with important war supplies, information on a country's aircraft production, a map of the berths at Pearl Harbor, technical details of the atomic bomb.

Today, however, the espionage law may be invoked against someone who leaks information for political reasons or to support a specific program, such as revealing the existence of a new Soviet bomber in an effort to get Congress to fund a defensive missile. Under the law this almost daily Washington occurrence is technically a form of espionage. Proceeding under this theory of espionage, prosecutors put on trial Samuel Loring Morison, a Navy employee who sent satellite photographs of a Soviet shipyard to a British magazine.

But while Morison was put on trial for selling the photos to one of the Jane's publications, a U.S. Air Force general who similarly revealed classified photographs was not punished under the espionage laws. He was not even censured.

Lieutenant General Lawrence A. Skantze, testifying before the House Armed Services Committee in 1983, showed photographs of the new Soviet MiG-9 Fulcrum and Su-7 Flanker fighters. The views were taken by satellite. The published hearings—which Skantze's staff had reviewed before publication—contained reproductions of the photos, which U.S. magazines were quick to publish. Today, years later, those photos are still classified by the Department of Defense.

Skantze showed these photos to Congress in an effort to garner more funds for Air Force programs. He was subsequently promoted to full general, even though, according to a senior Air Force intelligence officer, referring to the photos, "The unauthorized disclosure of such information could reasonably be expected to cause damage to the national security."

The FBI, also operating under espionage laws, has established a special squad to investigate the disclosure of government information to American news organizations. Agents of the Defense Criminal Investigative Service in 1986 got a search warrant to seize "improperly held classified documents" on loan to an American newsletter editor. Officials may think these actions have something to do with espionage but their definition beclouds the public perception of spying as a deliberate betrayal of the nation.

* * *

The modern era of espionage began with the fading of ideology as a motive for spying. The turning point came in the 1950s with the smashing of what headlines dubbed the "Atomic Bomb Spy Ring." The Soviet intelligence apparatus skillfully built the ring specifically to obtain the secrets involved in the development and manufacture of America's first nuclear weapons. The Soviets, using ideology as a motive, recruited Americans, Canadians, and British subjects to work as zealots who would put faith in communism and world peace above loyalty to their countries.

That spy ring did not succeed. The Soviet Union did get the bomb long before Soviet scientists would have been able to develop it on their own. But the ring also failed, for it spawned the trials of Julius and Ethel Rosenberg and the other members of the ring in courts in the United States, England, and Canada. And those trials publicly revealed the Soviet Union not only as a recruiter of people who would betray their nations but also as a country that itself was a betrayer of its wartime allies.

Espionage trials as a form of public education was a phenomenon that coincided with the era of the ideological spy. As spies became motivated by dollars rather than ideals, show trials simultaneously gave way to back-room plea bargains. When all that could come out in a trial was the defendant's own treachery, when the government could not portray an ideology-inspired plot, then espionage often was handled as just another crime. And bureaucrats, angry over leaks to the press, could cry "espionage," diminishing a word that once meant "betrayal of country."

In the bureaucratic world of plea bargaining, a traitor can be treated like a white-collar criminal. But in the world outside court and prison, people still know what real espionage is. They call it treason.

Treason is the ultimate word of betrayal. Treason means stabbing your country in the back. But in legal terms, treason, the only crime that is defined in the U.S. Constitution, has a narrow meaning: "Treason against the United States shall consist only in levying War against them, or in adhering to their Enemies, giving them Aid and Comfort." The Founding Fathers, well aware of the political use of treason charges by kings of England, wanted to restrict the crime to one that could not be used as an excuse for the elimination of political rivals.

So the American view of treason traces to British law, which itself is rooted in the attitude of Romans to treason: a crime against the ruler, punishable by an ingeniously horrible form of death. In the Treason Act of 1351 the British legally define high treason as crimes against the king and realm, including the crime of counterfeiting. A man could lose his head even for "imagining the death of the king." Mary, Queen of Scots and Sir Walter Raleigh were among the many British subjects tried under this act, which was also invoked in modern times to try British traitors during both world wars.

The United States Government, even in war, has been reluctant to prosecute crimes of treason. Aaron Burr, charged with treason after he hazily conspired to carve a nation in the Southwest, was acquitted. A presidential pardon wiped out any thoughts of treason stemming from the actions of Southerners during the Civil War.

Although treason still flickered as a crime during the patriotic fervor of World War II, the Department of Justice chose espionage as a more practical crime to prosecute. Not until World War II did the Supreme Court get its first treason cases. The defendants were charged with treason for aiding German saboteurs. The court ruled that the acts, though traitorous, were not treasonable within the strict confines of the Constitution's definition.

Spies may be traitors but they are not necessarily practicing treason under the Constitution. Government prosecutors have held that the Espionage Act of 1917 is powerful enough to try and punish spies. Ethel and Julius Rosenberg, the first civilian Americans ever executed for espionage, were proof of the law's power—at least in time of war.

The issue of war is complex in the case of the Rosenbergs. They committed espionage during World War II, but the secrets they stole went not to an enemy but to the Soviet Union, an American ally in that war. By the time they were tried in 1951, however, U.S. forces were fighting in another war, and, although the enemy was not the Soviet Union, that nation supported both of the Communist enemies that U.S. forces were fighting, North Korea and the People's Republic of China.

In sentencing the Rosenbergs to death, Judge Irving R. Kaufman said their crime, "worse than murder," was actually treason. Because they had given "the Russians the A-bomb years before our best scientists predicted" that the Russians would have it, he said, this "has already caused, in my opinion, the Communist aggression in Korea, with the resultant casualties exceeding fifty thousand and who knows but that millions more of innocent people may pay the price of your treason."

Kaufman also said that he had given the Rosenbergs the death penalty to "demonstrate with finality that this nation's security must remain inviolate; that traffic in military secrets, whether promoted by slavish devotion to a foreign ideology or by a desire for monetary gains, must cease."

When the Rosenbergs were tried, the Espionage Act provided that anyone convicted of espionage "in *times of war* [emphasis added] shall be punished by death or by imprisonment for not more than thirty years." Congress in 1954 amended the espionage law by making the punishment for *peacetime* spying death or "imprisonment for any terms of years or for life." In 1986 a presidential order amended the Uniform Code of Military Justice, the law that governs the conduct of all members of the armed services. The amendments made espionage in war or peacetime a crime punishable by death if the espionage involved betrayal of secrets pertaining to nuclear weapons, military spacecraft, war plans, cryptographic information, communications intelligence, warning systems and other strategic systems, and other major defense matters.

Theoretically, members of the armed services can be prosecuted under civil law. The presidential order, however, seemed to distinguish between espionage by civilians and by service personnel and then implied that the latter would get harsher punishment in military courts-martial.

But there is little reality behind all of this conjuring up of the electric chair or the gallows, for civilians or for soldiers and sailors. In peace, or what has been called the Cold War's era of violent peace, prosecutors have zealously kept the death penalty out of espionage cases. And, ever since 1972, when the Supreme Court ruled the death penalty unconstitutional for federal crimes, Congress has turned down proposals to restore execution as a punishment for espionage and treason.

Courtroom moves to invoke the death penalty in spy cases have been repeatedly made, often by a conservative organization, the Washington Legal Foundation, in concert with several congressmen who champion execution for spies. The foundation, which describes itself as a nonprofit public interest law center with more than 200,000 members and supporters, has argued for the death penalty in murder cases as well as in espionage cases. The foundation's basic contention, which parallels most death-to-spies arguments, is that the Supreme Court did not intend to outlaw the death penalty in espionage cases. By this view the Court was concerned only with injustice for reasons of race or poverty in murder and rape trials held in state courts. Chief Justice Warren Burger, in his dissent, however, said that the decision "casts serious doubt upon the constitutional validity of statutes imposing the death penalty for a variety of conduct which, though dangerous, may not necessarily result in any immediate death, *e.g.*, treason, airplane hijacking, and kidnapping."

Despite the Burger admonition, in 1974 Congress included the death penalty in anti-hijacking legislation. And so the matter stood in 1984, when, in a pretrial order, Judge Samuel Conti of the U.S. District Court for Northern California, where Harper would have been tried, issued a surprise ruling that said the death penalty could be invoked if Harper were put on trial and convicted.

Like Kaufman more than thirty years before, Conti said that espionage was so extreme a crime that its punishment must also be extreme. "Given the potential consequences of a serious breach of our national security through espionage, which may threaten the lives of all citizens of the United States," the ruling said, "this court finds that capital punishment for espionage is not uniformly disproportionate to the severity of the offense. Accordingly, the punishment of death for espionage is not unconstitutional *per se* under the Eighth Amendment [prohibition of cruel punishment]."

Harper never faced the death penalty because *both* Harper and the government appealed Conti's ruling, which the Ninth Circuit U.S. Court of Appeals overturned. Although a trial never took place, Conti's words would become part of the legal lore about espionage and would echo in other cases.

In a footnote in his ruling Conti noted that treason "can be characterized as a cousin of espionage." Although "the elements of the crimes are distinct, and the problems of proof different," he remarked, "public attitudes towards treason and espionage are assumed to be similar." It is this popular conception of espionage as a cousin of treason that influences the attitude of the public—and thus the attitude of jurors—when spies go on trial.

8
Spies on Trial

James Harper sold stolen top-secret documents to the Soviet Union. Samuel Loring Morison, a Navy intelligence analyst, gave satellite photographs of a Soviet shipyard to a British publication. The Department of Justice charged both Harper and Morison with espionage. Morison went on trial. Harper did not. John A. Walker, a former Navy radioman, sold U.S. cryptographic secrets to the Soviet Union for at least seventeen years. Jerry Whitworth, also a radioman, was Walker's most valuable spy. The Department of Justice charged both Walker and Whitworth with espionage. Whitworth went on trial. Walker did not.

Espionage, unlike other serious crimes, does not readily find its way into a courtroom. Murder, rape, and burglary are crimes with visible victims and witnesses to a violent act. Espionage is fundamentally different. John Martin, head of the Department of Justice's Internal Security Section and an architect of government espionage policy, makes the distinction. "Unlike the ordinary street crime in which there's a victim, a weapon, or missing property," he says, "an act of espionage involves a witting and willing person who leaves no footprints." A spy's victim is a sovereign nation, which, like a betrayed king, can call forth its own forces to strike down the spy. Or, like a betrayed king, a nation can have its special and perhaps secret reasons for making a deal with the traitor.

During the espionage trial of Ronald W. Pelton, a former
National Security Agency employee, the federal prosecutor told
the jury, "My client is this nation." But the judge who presided
at the trial, in his charge to the jury, corrected the prosecutor,
making a distinction that hovers over all espionage cases. The
defendant, the judge said, had been put on trial by the United
States Government, not by what we all think of as the nation.

The United States Government decides whether someone
goes on trial as a spy. And the government in spy cases is the
Department of Justice, just as in foreign affairs the United States
Government is the State Department. The difference, however, is
this: Foreign affairs develop from high-level policy decisions,
while the settling of an espionage case typically is handled by the
bureaucracy. The process is usually hard to follow, especially
since decisions are made not only inside the bureaucracy but also
are cloaked from view because national secrets must be protected.

From the beginning of 1984 to the spring of 1987, twenty-
eight people, nearly all of them Americans, were accused of espionage. One slipped away from an FBI surveillance team and fled
the United States. Of the others, seven stood public trial. (Many
of the others were members of the military. Accused military
spies are subject to closed-door military justice, which could call
for a secret court-martial or a quick discharge.) All but one of the
accused who were put on trial were convicted. All who did not
stand trial pleaded guilty and nearly all of them received long
prison terms.

In the one trial that ended in acquittal, justice and national
security collided. The case produced not only an acquittal but
also a bizarre example of the entanglement that results from the
conflicting actions of government agencies concerned with espionage and counter-espionage. A man who claimed to be working
as a double agent for the United States was accused of spying
against the United States. By the end of the trial the agencies
involved stood guilty of at least confusion, certainly incompetence, and definitely deception.

Mr. Smith Goes to Tokyo

In April 1984, Richard Craig Smith, a forty-year-old former
intelligence officer in the Army's Intelligence and Security Command, was arrested at Washington's Dulles International Airport
by the FBI and charged with accepting $11,000 from a Soviet

agent in payment for the identities of six U.S. double agents. Smith admitted taking the money but said that he did so as part of a CIA plot to infiltrate the KGB with double agents.

From 1973 to 1980, Smith had worked for the Army's Intelligence and Security Command, where he managed U.S. double agents and developed cover stories for them. He had left the Army in 1980 to spend more time with his family and start a video company in his home state of Utah. He had learned Japanese while in the Army and in June 1981 went to Tokyo as a representative of several American firms that were looking for Japanese investors.

According to the story that Smith eventually told the FBI, while he was in Tokyo two men approached him, identified themselves as Ken White and Danny Ishida, and told him they were from the CIA. Apparently aware that he had been in Army counter-intelligence, they asked him to cooperate with them in a plan they had for penetrating the KGB through Tokyo. Two years before, KGB Major Stanislav Aleksandrovich Levchenko had defected from the large KGB Residency in Tokyo, where he had worked for five years. He had given the CIA a great deal of information about Soviet espionage activities in Japan.

The mysterious CIA operatives, according to Smith, had given him a cover story as imaginative as any he had ever concocted. He said they had instructed him to pose as an American businessman who was in Tokyo on a mission of treachery and despair: Because he was broke and dying of cancer, he was willing to sell anything—including secrets he possessed—so that he could provide his widow and four children with a legacy. The basis of his cover was true. He did have four children and his video business was bankrupt by the time he carried out the plot by meeting with Victor I. Okunev, a KGB officer, at the Soviet commercial compound in Tokyo in 1982 and 1983.

Concerned that he had not heard back from the CIA and wondering if U.S. counter-espionage agents had learned of his dealings with Okunev, Smith went to the FBI and told agents what he had done. At first he did not tell the FBI about the CIA, he later explained, because a CIA agent had told him, "Keep your mouth shut."

To demonstrate to the FBI that he knew how to operate with the KGB, he revealed an elaborate KGB contact ritual. To test it the FBI sent a note and a flower arrangement to the Soviet Consulate in San Francisco. Next, the fictitious name was paged in the lobby of the St. Francis Hotel. The FBI followed the subsequent directions, and an agent made telephone contact with a Soviet who attempted to set up a rendezvous in Tokyo. When the agent asked about travel expenses he was told he would get reimbursement in Tokyo, the Vienna of West Coast KGB agents. Apparently the demonstration rendezvous never took place.

After ten months of intermittent discussions, the FBI finally decided not to believe Smith, who was arrested and then indicted for espionage, largely on his own story because he had started the case himself by going to the FBI. Facing a life sentence if convicted, Smith awaited trial in U.S. District Court in Alexandria, Virginia, the Washington suburb where the Intelligence and Security Command is located. Because of government actions, it would be two years before Smith, who lived in Bellevue, Washington, went on trial.

The trial called for the use of the Classified Information Procedures Act (CIPA) of 1980, which protects security information by allowing a judge to decide on ways to keep secrets out of trials. Under the act, a judge, in a closed hearing, can decide how to balance protection of secrets with the standards for a fair trial. Enactment of CIPA was inspired by fears of what legal observers call "graymail," a veiled threat by the defense that the cost of prosecution would be the exposure of secrets in the courtroom. Graymail can thwart justice by forcing the Department of Justice to drop the case or arrange a plea bargain beneficial to an admitted spy.

Through CIPA, secrets may be examined, under tight security arrangements, by defense attorneys, clerks, and others involved in the trial; the examination takes place in closed hearings, and those handling the classified documents must swear oaths of secrecy.

Smith, who said that the CIA had left him out in the cold, wanted for his defense classified documents that would prove his story. The government, however, dragged out the process of producing the documents and, in an extraordinary move, attempted to get A. Brent Carruth, one of Smith's attorneys, disqualified, claiming that Carruth was in a conflict of interest.

Carruth also represented Ronald R. Rewald, who had operated the Honolulu investment firm of Bishop, Baldwin, Rewald, Dillingham & Wong, which, Rewald had claimed, had been used by the CIA as a front. Smith said one of the two men who had recruited him and identified themselves as CIA agents had given him the phone number of BBRD&W and a BBRD&W business card that also carried the name of a subsidiary, CMI Investments, Inc., and the name "Richard P. Cavannaugh."

Four months after Smith was indicted for espionage, a Honolulu grand jury returned a one hundred-count indictment against Rewald, charging him with mail fraud, interstate transportation of stolen securities or money, false statements to a federal officer, perjury, securities fraud, fraud by an investment adviser, and tax evasion. Rewald insisted that all of his troubles stemmed from his firm's role as a CIA front. He also claimed that he was the target of an intended assassination.

The government tried to shoulder Carruth out of both the Smith and Rewald cases because of CIPA. Through CIPA, Carruth could see the classified documents obtained for one case and use knowledge gained from them in the other case. The CIA had initially reacted to Rewald's claims by refusing to confirm them. Classified documents obviously would prove or disprove Rewald's allegations. Similarly, Smith could get confirmation of his story about "Richard P. Cavannaugh" through such documents.

In one of the many hearings preceding the trial, U.S. District Judge Richard L. Williams noted that Carruth, in a CIPA motion, had said that "Cavannaugh" would be named in the requested documents—as would the name of a hired assassin. Judge Williams ruled that Smith would be allowed, through CIPA, to use specified classified information for his defense.

The Department of Justice, apparently at the urging of the CIA, challenged the judge's ruling and appealed to the Fourth U.S. Circuit Court of Appeals, which, in a divided opinion, sharply narrowed the amount of information that would be made available to Smith. The appellate court's ruling, an amazing document in an espionage case replete with amazing documents, includes footnotes that are themselves *classified*. The appeals court's ruling does not explain why the footnotes must remain secret.

By the time Smith went on trial in April 1986, Rewald had

been convicted on ninety-four counts and sentenced to eighty years in prison. The government's position, as stated by Assistant U.S. Attorney Joseph J. Aronica, was this: "The idea that the CIA would have [Smith] working as a double agent and that another agency of the same government [the FBI] would bring him in here to prosecute him is preposterous."

The judge ordered the government to produce "Cavannaugh" and it was the judge himself who put the shadowy witness on the stand. He turned out to be Charles Richardson, a former CIA intelligence officer who said he had been involuntarily retired from the CIA because of unauthorized business dealings with BBRD&W. Richardson said he did not know Smith, and the CIA said it had no record of "Ken White" and "Danny Ishida."

"Is this man a spy?" A. Brent Carruth asked the jury. "Yes —for the United States of America," Carruth answered for himself. Carruth said that the motives sketched by the prosecution— personal debt, the bankruptcy of Smith's Utah video company— were all part of the plot concocted to convince the KGB that Smith was a potential recruit for espionage. The plot that enmeshed Smith was never revealed, although some sources speculated that Smith had been caught up in one of the "off the books" operations engineered by DCI William Casey. Marine Lieutenant Colonel Oliver North, testifying during the Iran-Contra hearings, said that Casey had wanted to operate covert projects completely outside the CIA. The Hawaii-Tokyo dealings disclosed in Smith's trial at least faintly resembled some of the Iran-Nicaragua activities Casey had covertly directed.

The jury believed Smith and acquitted him. And the Classified Information Protection Act was given a new legal twist that likened the law to an informer-protection law. The appellate court had ruled, "The government has a substantial interest in protecting sensitive sources and methods of gathering information [which] resemble closely the gathering of law enforcement information. . . . Law enforcement domestic informers generally know who their enemies are; intelligence agents ofttimes do not. To give the domestic informer of the police more protection than the foreign informer of the CIA seems to us to place the security of the nation from foreign danger on a lower plane than the security of the nation from domestic criminals. In our opinion the national interest is as well served by cooperation with the CIA as with the domestic police."

A Leak—or Espionage?

The four trials that ended in convictions illustrated older, more fundamental points of espionage practices and espionage law. *The Show Trial:* Jerry Whitworth, author of the RUS letters, tried to make a deal but got a trial instead because a trial was needed to portray the crimes of the Walker spy ring. *The Punishment Trial:* Richard W. Miller, an FBI counter-espionage agent, was twice tried to demonstrate publicly the bureau's determination to discipline a man who betrayed the FBI as well as his country. *The Reluctant Trial:* Pelton sold the Soviets secrets from his own memory. Lacking the physical evidence for a potentially successful trial or plea bargain, the government had to take a chance on a weak trial and the possibility of acquittal. *The Warning Trial:* Samuel Morison was brought to court in another version of the show trial: to demonstrate that the espionage laws can be used on those whose crime is not spying but rule-breaking.

Samuel Loring Morison, grandson of the distinguished naval and maritime historian Samuel Eliot Morison, was arrested in 1984 for giving satellite photographs to a British defense magazine. Morison at the time was an analyst at the Naval Intelligence Support Center (NISC), the Navy's ultrasecret facility in the Washington suburb of Suitland, Maryland. The photographs showed a nuclear-powered aircraft carrier under construction at a Black Sea shipyard. Morison, who was a liar and a thief but certainly not a spy, was tried for espionage as a lesson to leakers of information.

Morison served briefly as an officer in the Navy during the Vietnam War, and then worked as a civilian employee for the Navy's history office before going to work as a junior analyst at NISC in 1974. In 1976 he became Washington representative for *Jane's Fighting Ships,* a $140-a-copy British-published reference annual containing unclassified information about all the world's navies. The Jane's organization paid Morison for photos and information about U.S. Navy ships. His work for *Jane's* was done with the approval of his superiors, although the conflict-of-interest issue was apparent, since Morison held a top-secret clearance and certain compartmented (code word) clearances.*

So, while working full-time in a high-security facility where he dealt with classified intelligence data about Soviet ships, Morison was simultaneously sending to his other employer information that was theoretically unclassified. In July 1980 Morison received the first of five "letters of requirement" warning him about his violations of Navy regulations covering the misuse of materials, information, and equipment. Evidence was found that he was writing for *Jane's* on Navy time.

When his co-workers would ask questions about apparently classified material that he was supplying to *Jane's,* he would intimidate them by flaunting his approval from the higher-ups. And when his immediate superiors at NISC became unhappy with the amount of time he was spending on *Jane's,* Morison had the publisher obtain a letter from the Pentagon supporting his work on the reference book.

Morison's security violations were blatant. For example, he once sold a used copy of *Jane's Fighting Ships* to a civilian who found several classified documents stuck in the book and called the FBI. Morison visited Norfolk and used his NISC identification to get on the base and take ship photos for *Jane's;* when stopped by base security officials, he claimed, falsely, that he was taking the photos for naval intelligence. In February 1984 Morison was told to sign a memorandum that set down the prime rule for continuing to work for both the Navy and *Jane's:* He could not "obtain classified information on the United States Navy and extract unclassified data for inclusion in *Jane's.* . . ." Morison began looking for a full-time job at *Jane's.* In a letter to an editor, he wrote, ". . . my loyalty to Jane's is above question. I'd rather quit here than there."

A new publication, *Jane's Defence Weekly,* had just been launched. Morison started submitting unclassified, but unre-

---

* *Jane's Fighting Ships* also figured in the real espionage of John Walker and Jerry Whitworth. They both claimed at various times that the information they were garnering from Navy communications was for *Jane's.* Once, for instance, a woman sailor Walker was dating asked Whitworth where Walker got all of his money. Whitworth replied that Walker was a spy. A day later Whitworth contacted the woman to tell her that Walker's spying was for *Jane's* and nothing as sinister as a real enemy.

leased, Navy information to the magazine. Then, in July 1984, on a colleague's desk he spotted four black and white satellite photos of the Soviet aircraft carrier under construction. Morison stole three of the photos and removed from them the NISC logo and date, along with these notations:

NICKOLAYEV SHIPYARD SECRET/ Warning Notice: Intelligence Sources or Methods Involved. REL TO UK AND CANADA [releasable to the United Kingdom and Canada].

He then sent the photographs to *Jane's Defence Weekly.* Publication touched off a frantic search and Naval Investigative Service investigation at NISC. Morison, the leading suspect, told his superior, "on my honor," he had nothing to do with the theft of the photos. He even volunteered to try to retrieve the photos from the magazine.

Meanwhile, though, investigators analyzed the cartridge of Morison's typewriter and reconstructed a letter he had written to the editor of the magazine about the "shipment" of undescribed materials. He also warned the editor not to phone him at NISC because all the phones were "bugged."

The Navy got the photos back not through Morison's efforts but with the cooperation of *Jane's* and the British Ministry of Defence. Morison's thumbprint was on one of the photographs. Morison, still denying involvement, named two coworkers as possible perpetrators, infuriating investigators who knew that Morison was the thief.

On October 1, 1984, as he and a girlfriend were about to board a flight to London from Dulles International Airport, the FBI arrested him. He denied he was fleeing the country. As his companion pointed out to investigators, he had bought a round-trip ticket and he had put his cat in a kennel for only a week.

A search of his apartment turned up a collection of some 3,600 documents and 4,200 photographs, all of them marked secret and confidential. This led to an indictment for theft of government property. The more serious charge was espionage. While insisting that he was not a spy under the law, Morison did concede that he had "leaked" the photos to demonstrate the increasing threat of the Soviet Navy.

The leak did damage, not to national security but to Pentagon credibility. The satellite photos showed that the Soviet carrier was not as near completion as Secretary of Defense Caspar Weinberger had claimed through drawings and a description in his annual unclassified public relations report, *Soviet Military Power,* published in April 1984. Incensed because the intelligence community had advised him not to use satellite photographs that *Jane's Defence Weekly* somehow managed to publish, Weinberger reportedly ordered that Morison be prosecuted to the full extent of the law.

"Full extent" meant espionage, not theft. The government machinery moved quickly and Morison was indicted under a section of the 1917 espionage statute that prohibited people with *lawful access* to U.S. military documents from disclosing them to an unauthorized person. Morison would be the only person in U.S. history to be tried under the statute. Daniel Ellsberg and Anthony Russo, who had given the "Pentagon Papers" on the background of the Vietnam War to the press, had been charged under the law. But a federal judge had dismissed the case against them because of Watergate-era government misconduct. The dismissal was not based on any deficiency in the espionage law.

Defense attorneys moved to have the indictment dismissed, arguing that the espionage law was intended by Congress to prevent the passing of secrets to foreign powers, not publications. U.S. District Judge Joseph H. Young upheld the indictment, ruling, "If Congress had intended this situation to apply only to the classic espionage situation, where the information is leaked to an agent of a foreign and presumably hostile government, then it could have said so. . . ." So the law was—and still is—applicable to leakers like Morison.

Morison was paid $5,000 a year by the Jane's organization for the routine information he gathered for *Jane's Fighting Ships.* Although he received a $300 bonus for the satellite photos, he had sent the secret satellite photos not for immediate payment but to ingratiate himself with *Jane's* in the hope of obtaining a job with the firm. Working for naval intelligence, he told the editors at *Jane's,* was "the pits," and he anxiously desired full-time employment with *Jane's.* He openly told colleagues that someday he would be the editor of the prestigious *Jane's.*

The FBI search of Morison's apartment also turned up clas-

JANE'S

DEFENCE WEEKLY

VOLUME 2 NUMBER 5   11 AUGUST 1984

EXCLUSIVE
SOVIET CVN
PROGRESS

The cover of the August 11, 1984, issue of *Jane's Defence Weekly,* with a satellite photo of a Soviet aircraft carrier (and other ships) under construction at the Nikolayev shipyard. The secret photos in this issue of the British magazine were stolen by Samuel L. Morison—an admitted thief, but was he a spy?

The U.S. intelligence-collection ship *Pueblo* was the victim of U.S. naiveté and a commanding officer's indecision as much as North Korean gunboats and soldiers. The designation "GER" on the bow indicated that the *Pueblo* had the cover of a miscellaneous auxiliary ship (AG) for environmental research (ER). (U.S. Navy photo)

No disguised fishing craft, Soviet intelligence-collection ships—AGI in Western intelligence parlance—are large, sophisticated naval ships. This is the SSV-493 of the Bal'zam class—she is 346 feet long and displaces 5,000 tons. This photo was taken from the U.S. strategic submarine base at Bangor, Washington. (U.S. Navy photo)

The Soviet Embassy on 16th Street in northwest Washington is four blocks north of the White House, in a mansion built by the Pullman family and purchased by the Czarist government for use as the Russian Embassy.

The Soviet Military Office on tree-lined Belmont Road in northwest Washington provides offices for the GRU contingent in Washington, D.C.

The rear of the new Soviet Embassy complex in Washington, as viewed from Tunlaw Road, shows part of the mass of structures.

The new Soviet Embassy complex in Washington, as viewed from the main entrance on Wisconsin Avenue. The view belies the size of the complex, which cannot be occupied until the new American Embassy in Moscow is ready for occupancy.

The roof of the Soviet Embassy on 16th Street bristles with antennas—for communications with Moscow and, according to FBI sources, for the interception of U.S. government communications.

Convicted spy Ronald Pelton passed the Soviets no secret papers—he gave them secrets of U.S. communications intercepts that he kept in his head. (AP/Wide World Photos)

Convicted spy Samuel L. Morison was not really a spy but a thief and liar who essentially gave away secret satellite photos to ingratiate himself with a British publisher. (AP/Wide World Photos)

Retired Navy Chief Radioman Jerry Whitworth gave the Soviets the keys to U.S. military communications for several years, flaunting his rewards while he did so. (UPI/Bettmann News-photos)

Master spy John A. Walker, in the firm grip of the law. He sold top secret communications information to the Soviets for almost two decades, while seducing son, brother, and friend into espionage, and attempting to have his daughter join his "way of life." (UPI/Bettmann Newsphotos)

One of the youngest spies in American history—Michael Walker, age twenty-two when arrested, followed in his father's footsteps to steal Navy secrets. (UPI/Bettmann Newsphotos)

Some mystery remains as to Arthur Walker's full role in the Walker-Whitworth spy ring. Convicted and sentenced to life imprisonment for espionage, he claimed that he was recruited when he was retired from the Navy. But some observers contend that he began spying while on active duty. (UPI/Bettmann Newsphotos)

Barbara Walker—mother and ex-wife of confessed spies—participated in some of John Walker's secret "drops" but was never charged with espionage. (UPI/Bettmann Newsphotos)

Convicted spy Jonathan Pollard stole secrets from several government agencies for the Israelis—and sought to excuse his actions on the basis of helping a beleaguered ally. (UPI/Bettmann Newsphotos)

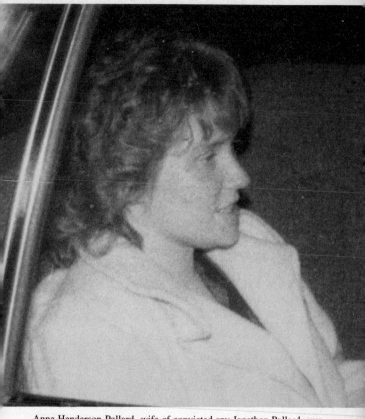

Anne Henderson-Pollard, wife of convicted spy Jonathan Pollard, was sentenced to five years' imprisonment for her part in the Israeli spy operation. (UPI/Bettmann Newsphotos)

Larry Wu-Tai Chin spied against the United States for China while he worked for the CIA. He apparently killed himself while awaiting sentencing after his espionage conviction. (UPI/Bettmann Newsphotos)

Marine Sergeant Clayton Lonetree became the focus of charges of extensive Soviet penetration of the American Embassy in Moscow, where he was a guard. He was convicted of espionage and sentenced to thirty years in prison. (UPI/Bettmann Newsphotos)

An FBI surveillance photo shows FBI agent Richard Miller (wearing white shirt and dark trousers) walking with Svetlana Ogorodnikov (with sunglasses and warm-up jacket). Miller was convicted of espionage and sentenced to life imprisonment. (UPI/Bettmann Newsphotos)

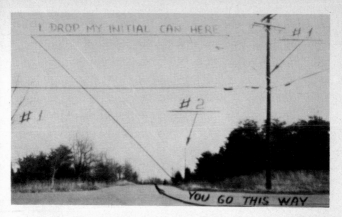

Soviet agent instructions, provided to John Walker for the ill-fated drop and payoff of May 1985, include detailed, annotated photos of the sites. This photo of the Poolesville, Maryland, area—twenty-odd miles from the center of Washington—was taken in winter. When John Walker drove this route in the spring there was much more foliage. (Courtesy Federal Bureau of Investigation)

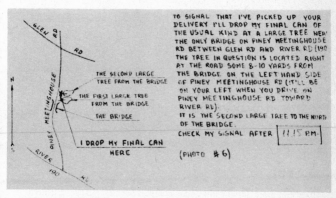

The large agent instructions and detailed maps were repeated on the reverse of the photographs showing specific points in the "spy trail" that Walker was to follow in May 1985. The intricate details demonstrate in-depth and detailed site reconnaissance by the Soviet spymasters of the KGB and GRU. (Courtesy Federal Bureau of Investigation)

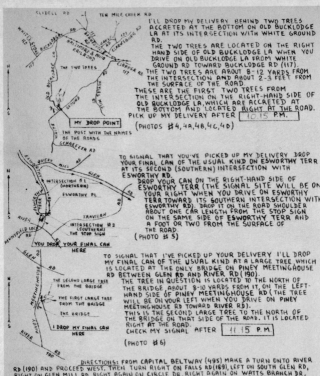

Soviet agent instructions are intricately detailed. This is one of several pages of Soviet directions for John Walker's May 1985 operation, with hand-printed instructions, detailed area maps, time to be at each point indicated, and supporting photo numbers noted. (Courtesy Federal Bureau of Investigation)

sified copies of "Weekly Wires," summaries of current intelligence that were distributed throughout the Navy. Drawing from
the "wires," Morison had sent *Jane's* magazine information
about mammoth explosions at Severomorsk, the main ammunition depot for the Soviet Navy's Northern Fleet. The incident
was no more a secret than the construction of the Soviet aircraft
carrier. Revelations about the destruction of the dump had been
leaked by Pentagon officials in June 1984. Morison's leaking,
however, was unofficial and unauthorized.

Leaking, official or otherwise, has long been as much a part
of Washington as the Redskins. Every administration has engineered self-serving leaks. Officials continually leak information
that helps their policies and programs, regardless of the classification.

Some leaks have been nothing less than sanctioned, intramu-
ral espionage. One of the most blatant examples of the latter also
involved a Navy leaker. But he, unlike Morison, was not punished.

In late 1971 and early 1972 columnist Jack Anderson published direct quotations from top-secret documents prepared for
the National Security Council, Joint Chiefs of Staff, CIA, State
Department, and U.S. Mission to the United Nations. A congressional committee launched an investigation into this "serious
compromise to national security decision-making" and turned up
a Navy yeoman who had acted as a spy—for the Navy. The
yeoman made copies of texts, such as "Eyes Only" or "NODIS"
(No Distribution) National Security Council documents, which
wound up in the hands of Admiral Thomas Moorer, Chairman of
the Joint Chiefs of Staff.

The yeoman also sometimes served Henry A. Kissinger,
then President Nixon's national security adviser. The yeoman's
services, according to an enraged Kissinger, included "going
through my briefcase, reading or duplicating whatever papers he
could get his hands on, and sometimes retaining discarded car-
bon copies of sensitive documents that were intended to be dis-
posed of in the 'burn bag.' " The yeoman's connection to Anderson was suspected; his work as a sanctioned Navy spy was
confirmed. He was transferred from the liaison office between the
Joint Chiefs and the National Security Council and the office was
abolished. No legal action was taken against him.

Suspicions of similar deliberate leaking flitted through the Morison trial. His superior at NISC, Navy Captain Thomas Fritz, admitted that he had not begun investigating the publication of the satellite photos until he asked the director of naval intelligence whether high-ranking Pentagon officials had, for some reason, leaked them. John E. Moore, editor of *Jane's Fighting Ships,* told the authors that when the photos arrived at the publisher, editorial employees had assumed that the photographs had been leaked. The practice of unofficially leaking material to *Jane's* had been going on for years.

Jane's Fighting Ships has always had a special relationship with the U.S. Navy. A high-priority supply of the annual was shipped to Washington every year. Morison would then personally distribute copies of the expensive book to high-ranking Pentagon officials. Admiral James D. Watkins, the Chief of Naval Operations, inscribed a photograph showing Moore and Morison presenting Watkins a copy.

Because of this history of cooperation with *Jane's,* many knowledgeable observers who saw the satellite photographs assumed an official leak. That was the initial belief of Roland S. Inlow, who for ten years had been chairman of the Intelligence Community's Committee on Imagery Requirements and Exploitation. The committee, known as COMIREX, sets priority for the use of reconnaissance satellites and the distribution of their photographs. Inlow was in charge of the damage assessment after the CIA learned that William Peter Kampiles had sold a KH-11 manual to the Soviets. Since 1980, Inlow had been doing classified consulting to the CIA.

The American publication *Aviation Week & Space Technology* picked up the satellite photos and published them after the British magazine did. When Inlow opened his copy of *Aviation Week* he immediately recognized the photograph as a KH-11 product. "My initial reaction," he testified at Morison's trial, "was that somebody had decided to release these photographs. I was somewhat surprised. But in all honesty my reaction was much more 'ho hum' than 'Oh, my God.'"

Believing that what he saw was a deliberate leak, "I said to myself that if a policy official came to me and said he wanted release, I would have said, 'Yes.' In my opinion the disclosure of these three photographs would do no damage to the United

States." He went on to explain in his precise way—and "soberly, with a great deal of reflection"—that damage could come in three ways: through revealing to the Soviets that satellites were watching them; through revealing technology that could be implied from the photographs, and through the "information content" of the photographs. The Soviets knew that they were being watched by U.S. satellites as well as they knew they were building an aircraft carrier.

As for the satellite technology, he noted that, thanks to Kampiles, the Soviets also knew about the KH-11's basic technology. Changes that had improved the resolution of the photography, he added, were not disclosed by these photos, which were at least six or seven generations removed from the originals. Another retired CIA officer familiar with satellite photos disagreed. He told the authors that *any* photographs could disclose intelligence information. "There's a great difference," he said, "between leaking *information* and giving away physical documents."

Inlow's testimony as a witness for Morison surprised the prosecution and angered Navy and Justice officials, who had apparently expected that the government would close ranks for the trial—one of four espionage cases that would be staged in federal courtrooms in that same Baltimore building. (There John and Michael Walker would hear their fate and there Ronald Pelton would be tried.) The Navy produced a parade of officers who seemed to lump Morison with the Walkers. The Justice Department treated Morison as a true spy, underlining this attitude by the way the prosecutors* staged the trial.

The Department of Justice decided to invoke the Classified Information Procedures Act. For Morison the government went far beyond the ordinary CIPA procedures in which attorneys who will be seeing classified material simply agree to a "protective order" issued by the presiding judge and sign a pledge never to divulge the secrets in the documents they have seen. In the Morison case the government demanded that his lawyers be fingerprinted, get full-scale security clearances, and allow FBI inspection of confidential records "including, but not limited to,

---

* Assistant U.S. Attorney Michael Schatzow, the prosecutor at the Morison trial, had been selected for the Walker prosecution team.

academic, achievement, attendance, athletic, personal history and
disciplinary records, medical records, and credit records."

The extraordinary demands, which the lawyers considered
demeaning and unwarranted, were also superfluous. No secrets
were revealed during the trial, which lasted seven days and ended
with the jury finding Morison guilty. Judge Young, saying that
Morison knew "what was protected and what was not," handed
down a two-year sentence, an extremely light penalty for what
was, legally, espionage.

Inlow, who emphasized he had no sympathy for what Morison did, later questioned the verdict. "While 'leaking' is an unsatisfactory and haphazard method at best for the release of previously classified information," he wrote, "an exaggerated
conviction of espionage in a case that was weak on its merits will
solve little. If the verdict is upheld on appeal, I believe the consequences will be damaging for both the government and the public."

Morison was free on bond and his case was on appeal as this
was written. Whatever the final outcome, many legal observers
believe that *United States of America* v. *Morison* will have the
effect of weakening U.S. espionage statutes until Congress up-
dates an antiquated law that can be used to punish errant, low-
level leakers as well as genuine spies.

A Bargain for Walker

There are several options for handling a captured spy. He or
she can be tried, convicted, and sentenced to prison (or, in wartime, to death). A spy can be given a plea-bargain deal: a prison
sentence without trial in exchange for certain information. A spy
can be "turned"—converted into a double agent whose spying is
controlled by the country the spy is supposed to be spying on. A
convicted, imprisoned spy can be traded to another country in
exchange for one of your own spies. This has modern historical
precedence, beginning with the exchange of Soviet KGB officer
Rudolf Abel for the U-2 pilot Francis Gary Powers. And, as has
happened a few times, an imprisoned spy's controllers can stage a
jailbreak to get their man out.

For the Department of Justice the options usually come
down to two: a trial or a plea-bargain deal. But the arrests of
John, Michael, and Arthur Walker in May of 1985—and the

spate of espionage cases that continued to surface from then until 1987—compounded the decision-making.

Arthur Walker, a retired Navy lieutenant commander, solved one part of the government's problem by setting up his own trial before he was even arrested: He waived his right to remain silent and gave two FBI agents a confession. Arthur had worked for a small defense contractor and had supplied his younger brother with relatively low-level documents. One was the damage-control manual of the amphibious command ship *Blue Ridge*. On August 5, Arthur went on trial in the Navy town of Norfolk, Virginia. The highlight of the government's testimony was adultery rather than espionage. Arthur's wife, Rita, testified that after John was arrested, Arthur, in a confessional mood, had told her that in the late 1960s and early 1970s he had had an affair with John's wife, Barbara. Arthur's defense rested without calling any witnesses. On August 9, Arthur was convicted. He was later sentenced to three life terms and fined $250,000.

Now the Department of Justice had to decide about John and Michael Walker, about Jerry Whitworth, about the fate of others who had known of their spying or had aided them, and about the shadows that these decisions would cast over the ever-growing list of espionage cases. Hampering the decision-making were jurisdictional jealousies and logistics. Whitworth was to be tried in San Francisco, John and Michael in Baltimore. Other espionage trials loomed in Los Angeles and Virginia.

Preparations, meanwhile, had been going on for putting John and Michael Walker on trial in Federal District Court in Baltimore before Judge Alexander Harvey II. The grand jury had swiftly indicted them for conspiring to deliver information relating to national defense to a foreign government, "that is, the Soviet Union." They were also charged with attempting to deliver information relating to national defense to a foreign government (specifically Aleksey Gavrilovich Tkachenko, vice consul in the consular office of the Soviet Embassy); unlawfully obtaining, receiving, and transmitting information relating to national defense; and aiding and abetting in the obtaining, receiving, and transmitting of that information.

Assistant U.S. Attorney Schatzow and the rest of the prosecution team believed that a strong case could be built against

John Walker, who had squirreled away an incredibly incriminating hoard of documents in his two-story brick-and-clapboard Norfolk home, and against Michael, who had waived his rights to investigators and presented them with a detailed confession that appeared to meet all the criteria for admission in court. Prosecutors in San Francisco might not have as tight a case against their spy Whitworth, but that was their problem.

The Departments of Justice and Defense had a higher vantage point and more concerns than how to prepare for a good espionage trial. High-ranking officials in Justice and the Pentagon wanted information more than they wanted justice or retribution. Talk of a plea bargain was going on even before the conviction of Arthur Walker.

A plea bargain offers a criminal a specified sentence in exchange for a plea of guilty. About 90 percent of all criminal defendants take the plea-bargain route rather than go on trial, saving themselves the risk of a maximum sentence and saving the justice system time and trouble. The maximum sentence John and Michael Walker faced was, theoretically, the death penalty. In reality they faced life imprisonment. A plea bargain certainly would be to their advantage. What had to be shown to Judge Harvey was the advantage of a plea bargain to the public and to justice.

John Walker had pleaded poverty when he was arraigned, and the court had routinely assigned a public defender. When Harvey heard that John Walker had a net worth of $182,785, he asked for a check of his finances and was told that the Internal Revenue Service had already filed a $252,487 tax lien against Walker.* Harvey let Walker keep the poverty plea, and as a result John Walker kept his shrewd defender, Attorney Fred Warren Bennett.

Bennett sensed the government's inclination toward bargaining, although he knew that any overt moves would come when the trial date neared. He also knew that the government's two-for-the-price-of-one trial was an easy target. He and Michael's

---

* In December 1986 the IRS auctioned off Walker's house for $27,500 (the new owners assumed a $50,000 mortgage) and got $25,440 more for the rest of his possessions, including his Navy medals and an oil painting of him in his Navy uniform.

defense attorney moved for severance of the two trials, and Judge Harvey agreed. Now the prosecutors had double trouble. They still had a good case with John, who could easily be shown to be an evil, treacherous warrant officer who betrayed the Navy and his country. But Michael, a twenty-two-year-old, cherub-faced sailor with a pretty young wife, could be portrayed before a sympathetic jury as a misguided, dutiful son who succumbed to a domineering father's insidious demands.

Bennett continued to bombard Harvey through the summer. The judge and the prosecution team could see a pattern—and a nightmare: the overturning of a conviction, a spy set free.

Bennett had laid the foundation for a biased-trial appeal by boldly claiming that the publicity was so unfair when the Walkers were brought before the grand jury that the indictments ought to be dismissed. Harvey turned down that motion, but he saw what Bennett was planning.

The defense was using the government's own words to build a claim of prejudicial pretrial publicity. Through press conferences, leaks, and background briefings, federal officials had been flagrantly trying the Walkers in print and on television. Secretary of Defense Weinberger, himself a lawyer, even stoked the mood by introducing the highly unlikely possibility of a death sentence, saying that if the Walkers were convicted they "should be shot," though hanging was the "preferred method."

Such inflammatory publicity could so prejudice a trial that an appellate court might dismiss a conviction on the basis that the jury was unfairly biased. Harvey took this threat quite seriously. The Supreme Court had twice reversed criminal convictions on these grounds. Even a change of venue—the usual judicial remedy for extensive, prejudicial publicity—would not diminish the threat because the espionage case had been given national coverage. Harvey ordered everyone connected with the Walker cases to refrain from commenting about it publicly.

On August 15, Judge Harvey set John Walker's trial for October 28, with the separate trial of Michael Walker to begin immediately after his father's ended. The scheduling of the trial stepped up the plea-bargain negotiations. So did pressure from U.S. prosecutors in San Francisco, who desperately wanted John Walker as a witness to buttress the largely circumstantial case against Whitworth. That trial was to begin on November 12.

As the trial date neared, representatives from the FBI, CIA, Pentagon, Department of Justice, and State Department began meeting with Harvey. The officials wanted to avoid reporters assigned to the Federal Building in Baltimore. So, instead of meeting in the offices of the U.S. Attorney, the officials were escorted to Harvey's highly secure seventh-floor chambers, which are off limits to reporters. Participants heading for meetings stepped before a closed-circuit television camera mounted in the public area of the seventh floor, identified themselves, and then heard the click of admittance at the locked doors that seal off the judges' hushed precincts from the public corridors.

During the meetings Harvey sat at the head of a long table in a conference room that overlooked downtown Baltimore and the city's bustling harbor. Behind him was a bookshelf. Among the books was the blue-covered *Federal Rules of Criminal Procedure,* which he and the prosecutors frequently referred to. It was obvious from the start that the Department of Justice wanted to make a deal with John Walker in order to get as much information as possible about his years of espionage and to use him as the star witness in the Whitworth trial.

Ordinarily plea bargains are worked out between defense attorneys and prosecutors and then submitted to the presiding judge with the understanding that the judge may modify the agreed sentence. But in this case the government wanted something rare, an agreement that one court official called "hardwired"—a plea bargain that curbed the judge's sentencing power.

Lawyers referred to the rare agreement as a "C-type" plea, for it was covered under Rule 11(e) (1) (C) of *Federal Rules of Criminal Procedure.* Rule 11 said that attorneys could (A) negotiate a motion for dismissal; (B) make a recommendation for sentencing but leave the actual sentence up to the judge; or (C) submit to the judge a plea agreement that contained the actual sentence, leaving the judge no alternative but to accept or reject the deal. The C-type is rare because it takes from the judge the right to hand down the sentence.

Officials urging the C-type on Judge Harvey were driven by the intelligence community's bureaucratic turmoil. As the worried officials saw it, here, leading the lengthening parade of American traitors, were four spies who could march off without punishment. This was the worst-case analysis: a Whitworth acquittal in California, a mistrial or a dismissal of the convictions of John and Michael Walker in Baltimore, and, finally, reversal of Arthur's conviction as a result of the failure of the other convictions.

Finally, days before John Walker's trial was to begin, Justice officials, acting in deep secrecy, put the worst-case analysis to rest by deciding on the strategy: make a deal with John and Michael Walker and develop the technically weak case against Whitworth by making John Walker the star witness against his erstwhile friend. Judge Harvey said he would accept a C-type plea. On October 24, Schatzow formally sent a letter to the defense attorneys setting forth the terms of the agreement.

John Walker, agreeing to plead guilty to espionage and conspiracy, received a life sentence in consideration for a lighter sentence for his son. Michael, who had faced a life term, accepted a twenty-five-year sentence. Walker also agreed to cooperate with the government by answering all questions truthfully, with the aid of a polygraph if necessary. He also said he would testify before any grand juries and at any trial the government sent him to. The government agreed not to charge Walker with any other crimes, including any violations of federal income-tax laws.

The judicial stage now was set for the trial of Jerry Whitworth, which, after several postponements, began in March 1986.

A Surprise for RUS

FBI agents began accumulating connections between Jerry Whitworth and John Walker soon after the arrest of Walker early on the morning of May 20, 1985. The night before, hidden FBI agents had watched Walker making a drop in suburban Maryland. In the plastic garbage bag he left for pickup by Aleksey Gavrilovich Tkachenko were classified documents and three letters.

"Dear Friend," one letter began:

"D" continues to be a puzzle. He is not happy, but is still not ready to continue our "cooperation." Rather than try to analyze him for you, I have simply enclosed portions of two letters I've received. My guess? He is going to flop in the stock-broker field and can probably make a modest living in computer sales. He has become accustomed to the big-spender life-style and I don't believe he will adjust to living off of his wife's income. He will attempt to renew cooperation within 2 years.

Accompanying the notes to "Dear Friend" (the traditional term used by Soviet spymasters and their spies) were two "Dear Johnnie" letters from D. The bottoms of the letters were cut off, apparently to shield the name of the writer. One letter said:

I realize this doesn't fit in with your advice and counseling over the years. Your help has been rewarding and I greatly appreciate all that you've done for me in the past. I can't specifically say what it was, but I believe it relates to psychological benefits one gains from autonomous decision making. In other words striking out independently in pursuit of ones own goals. In all honesty, I was happier in the 60's and early 70's than I've been since. I have agonized over this decision. I hope you can understand and respect it.

In the other "Dear Johnnie" letter, written on March 25, 1985, Johnnie's unnamed friend writes "news about Brenda's job prospects" and refers to being back on the track of becoming a stockbroker and entering "computer sales."

When it gets to the bottom line though, I believe that once Brenda and I are into our new careers that I'll be happy with my strategy and that it will succeed. This period (October '83) to now, has been rough on my mental health at times.

In a search of Walker's home the FBI found two pages of handwritten notes, unsigned and undated, from what seemed to be D, who was agonizing over what he was going to do in civilian life. His first notion was civil service, but he felt that the paperwork would take too long. The letter continues:

2. Get a position at NCSS [Naval Communications Station, Stockton, California] hopefully in near future. Most likely that it would be a GS5/6 [a reference to the probable government employee pay grade] crypto operator in the Tech [illegible word] Control Division.
3. Also I will check out the AF in [followed by three letters,

which Walker translates as "sec" for "security" and some authorities translate as "SAC" for "Strategic Air Command"] area.

4. I plan to make myself known to a larger segment of government and civilian organizations just to see what is out there, an example: CIA.

5. Brenda's situation. Graduate [illegible] DEC 84 (Ph.D.). I'm committed to giving her first options on location (within reason), consequently where we go from Davis is unknown at present.

6. In sum: there are a lot of ifs but I won't bite off my nose.

The FBI had been investigating Walker long enough to know that one of his former Navy buddies was a California man named Jerry A. Whitworth. *D* seemed very much like Whitworth. When two agents called on Whitworth in Davis, California, on May 20, he broke off the interview because he said he wanted a drink of water. Instead, he walked by his computer, and an agent, craning his neck, saw Whitworth pull two sheets of paper from the printer next to his computer and hide them under the computer keyboard. When he allowed the agents to search his mobile home, one of them found what he had so ineptly hidden: the printout of a letter to Walker, written that day.

A later search turned up a rough draft of one of the notes that *D* had sent to Walker. *D*'s Brenda was obviously Brenda L. Reis, Whitworth's wife since 1976. The searchers also found an envelope marked *Job Ads.* The "Help Wanted" advertisements bore out *D*'s employment plans, for the ads included one in the *Navy Times* for radio operators and communications specialists at the CIA.

The FBI did not immediately arrest Whitworth, although agents kept him under highly visible surveillance. He was allowed to surrender on his own on June 3. By then the FBI was convinced that both *D* and RUS were Whitworth. One odd bit of investigative trivia gave agents intuitive confirmation. Agents had turned up a civilian communications specialist named Russell H. Salvi who knew Whitworth. Salvi was called Russ, but messages to and from Whitworth, a bad speller, were addressed to *Rus,* not Russ.

Agents were also convinced about the RUS connection

when, before Whitworth's arrest, an agent showed him a copy of one of the letters and asked him if he had written it. Whitworth, the agent said, "stared at the letter for . . . what seemed like a long time, about ninety seconds . . . and said he did not want to answer that question."

Investigators later discovered a link to the "stockbroker" remark in one of the "Dear Johnnie" letters: Whitworth had taken a course in stockbroking and on April 20 had flunked an examination required for dealing in securities.

On the basis of such strong circumstantial evidence—but without the solid kind of evidence a prosecutor always wants— the government convinced a grand jury to indict Whitworth for conspiring to commit espionage under a section of the U.S. Code that makes it a crime to conspire to commit a crime described elsewhere in the code. He was also charged with the crime of espionage itself and with copying and taking a document in violation of another section of the Espionage Law of 1914.

Five other counts had to do with income-tax-law violations that essentially amounted to failing to report his espionage earnings, which the government estimated to be at least $332,000. The counts were legally entwined, so that Whitworth had to be tried simultaneously for both spying and tax cheating. The defense implied that Whitworth would take the stand in his own defense only if the tax charges were dropped. A defense motion to separate the two crimes was rejected.

The defense attorneys, James Larson and Tony Tamburello, both had impressive records for defending unpopular defendants —from draft resisters to men accused of terrorism and politically inspired, anti-Establishment murder. Neither lawyer had ever defended an accused spy. Assistant U.S. Attorney William S. Farmer, who had worked on the James Harper case, would put Whitworth on trial. The other members of the prosecution team were Assistant U.S. Attorney Leida B. Schoggen, John J. Dion, an attorney representing the Department of Justice, and Navy Lieutenant James Alsup, a Navy lawyer with an intelligence background who had been deputized a Special Assistant U.S. Attorney. They all knew they had a weak case that could be strengthened only by an infusion of Walker testimony. What ultimately happened in San Francisco would depend on what happened with the Walker plea-bargain negotiations.

Soon after John and Michael Walker pleaded guilty and accepted the plea bargain, Walker was taken to San Francisco, where he testified before a grand jury recalled for the purpose of seeking new indictments against Whitworth. From Walker's testimony came many more details of their operation, including specifics on some forty meetings. "This grand jury has become a farce," Larson, Whitworth's lead attorney, complained. Walker, he said, is "dancing to the government's tune in order to benefit from the bargain that he made." The government's big benefit would be at the trial, where Walker's words would shore up the circumstantial evidence.

Well aware of this, Larson and Tamburello secretly tried to launch plea-bargain negotiations just before the trial started. They offered a guilty plea in exchange for a government agreement to recommend a life sentence and no fine. They also asked for a guarantee that charges would not be brought against Brenda Reis, who had jointly signed income-tax forms with her husband. Through his attorneys, Whitworth also promised the kind of damage-assessment cooperation that Walker was reputedly giving.

"It is the position of the Department of Justice," the prosecution team formally replied, "that the only acceptable disposition of this case without trial is an open plea by Mr. Whitworth to the entire indictment with no conditions whatsoever. . . . [W]e believe that a full exposition of the entire conspiracy in a public trial is of paramount importance. . . ." If Whitworth wanted to offer information, it would be accepted, the secret rejection letter continued. But there would be a trial, not a deal. To Larson this meant the government simply wanted what he later labeled "a show trial."

During the long, repetitious process of jury selection, one of the routine questions asked each prospective juror was whether he or she or any close relative had been a victim of a crime. A surprising number had been robbed or were related to people who had been robbed. If they had, they were not necessarily discharged. But exposure to violent crime was viewed by both the prosecution and the defense as straining the quality of mercy in a prospective juror.

The defendant facing the potential jurors, however, was not an accused robber, murderer, or rapist. He was charged with committing a crime that the average juror could know about only by reading spy novels. "I believe in my country," one said and disqualified himself with his own fervent and inaccurate words: "Espionage is treason."

Of the scores of prospective jurors examined, only one came close to being a juror whose background would have given him a special understanding of an espionage case. He was an engineer at Lockheed with top-secret clearance. He worked on weapons systems that he did not describe. Asked whether he had cryptographic knowledge, he said that he could not respond to that question, presumably because his security clearance prohibited him from doing so. He was excused, with no objection from either prosecution or defense.

Lieutenant Alsup, in uniform, sat at the prosecutor's table during the trial, a visible symbol of the nation. The Navy supplied witnesses ranging from three-star admiral to petty officer, all in uniform. FBI agent followed FBI agent to the witness chair, each one well groomed, articulate, solid. The best of America testified against a traitor to America. Howard J. Varinsky, a "trial behavior consultant" hired by the defense attorneys to advise them on juror selection, said afterward that he wondered if a fair, unbiased jury of peers could ever be selected for an espionage trial.

Some of the testimony ranged over terrain any juror could recognize: Whitworth's spending spree. The jurors could easily follow the IRS accountants and the automobile dealers and the shop clerks as they reconstructed the high-living style of the big-spending sailor.

Then there were the secrets, cautiously revealed by witnesses who seemed reluctant to testify. Here in public they were talking about code machines and communications procedures they long had been ordered to hold close. This was another compulsion inspired by the weakness of the case. "We had to produce this trial because so much rests on circumstantial evidence," Alsup said at the beginning. He shook his head. "We have never revealed this much before."

The vocabulary of the Navy's secret world was hard to follow: crypto access, keylist, genser, CMS, KW-7, KG-36. . . . The trial needed a star, and the government found him in John Walker, a real spy, telling about the Vienna Procedure and the

Minox camera, remembering the talks with his gullible friend Whitworth in the *Dirty Old Man,* describing the meetings in exotic Hong Kong and Casablanca. Whitworth sat still, never seeming to move, his thick beard hiding whatever expression his face may have borne. He looked detached, oblivious.

Walker the star had his own supporting cast, each of whom had a turn in the witness chair, although none had a direct espionage connection with the man at the defendants' table. Arthur Walker said all he knew was that his brother was involved somehow with an old Navy friend on the West Coast. Barbara Joy Crowley Walker talked guardedly about her ex-husband's espionage, skirting around how much she knew and when she knew it. Michael Walker told his story of a son following his father's trade. And Laura Walker Snyder recalled some of her talks with her father, who urged her to end her pregnancy with an abortion so she could stay in the Army and become a spy. "He told me I was stupid for quitting [the Army], that I had no hope for the future, that I would never amount to anything. I was an idiot."

At times it seemed that the despicable Walker, not the stoic Jerry Whitworth, was on trial. Walker proudly testified about the Walker spy ring, trying to make it sound more like an espionage organization and less like a creature of John Walker's greed and cunning.

In cross-examination Larson opened an issue that would threaten the prosecution's case. He began questioning Walker about his recruitment techniques. Then he asked:

"Now, in each of these situations, you essentially—and I'm referring to Mr. Whitworth, your brother, your daughter—you essentially used the same approach, that is that you talked about your man in Europe or a private intelligence organization that disseminated classified information to allies, or the *Jane's Fighting Ships,* and that sort of thing; is that right?"

"That's right," Walker answered.

"Where did you develop or come up with this notion of how to approach a potential recruit?"

"It was my own idea."

"And something that you consistently utilized throughout your career in espionage, correct?"

"Yes."

The testimony set up a legal problem that would appear in

two other espionage trials, raising further questions about the use of the Espionage Law of 1917 in the complex world of the 1980s. The government had charged Whitworth with "knowingly and willfully" passing to Walker—a "representative, officer, agent, and employee" of the Soviet Union—documents, photographs, and information concerning cryptographic equipment, keying material, and messages "with intent and reason to believe that they were to be used to the injury of the United States and to the advantage of a foreign nation, that is, the Union of Soviet Socialist Republics." The indictments cited the Soviet Union thirty-nine times.

Under the espionage law all the government had to prove was that Whitworth had passed secrets with the intent of injuring the United States and giving advantage to a foreign nation—*any* foreign nation. For Morison the nation had been the United Kingdom; for Jonathan Jay Pollard (Chapter 11) the nation had been Israel.

The defense, giving up all pretense of Whitworth's innocence as a supplier of secrets to Walker, contended that Whitworth did not know where the secrets were going. Larson and Tamburello argued that the government, by specifically identifying the "foreign nation" as the Soviet Union, had added an accusation that had not been proved. Over prosecution objections made in an unusual, trial-interrupting government appeal to a higher federal court, U.S. District Judge John P. Vukasin, Jr., accepted the defense argument and mentioned it in his instructions to the jury. At the same time attorneys for Arthur Walker vainly appealed his conviction, claiming that he had no specific knowledge that the secrets he passed to his brother went to the Soviet Union.

Although the foreign-nation issue still was not legally settled, the raising of the issue did Whitworth no more good than the belated citing of it did Arthur Walker. The jury found him guilty.

Judge Vukasin sentenced Whitworth, who was forty-six years old, to 365 years in prison and fined him $410,000.* Under the formula that Vukasin incorporated in the sentence, it would

---

* The prosecution said it would have asked for the death penalty, "but the ultimate punishment is not enforceable, in light of constitutional decisions, as this Court previously recognized."

be sixty years before Whitworth could be paroled. Jerry Whitworth, the judge said, is "a man who represented the evil of banality . . . a zero at the bone. He believes in nothing. His life is devoted to determining the wind direction and how he can make a profit from the coming storm."

Whitworth's sentencing was supposed to set the stage for the sentencing of John and Michael Walker. John Walker, who had sworn to tell the truth when testifying against Whitworth, repeatedly failed polygraph tests administered by government interrogators during debriefing sessions. The questioners were particularly not satisfied with Walker's answers about the origin and dimensions of his spy ring. The debriefing of Walker went on under ever-increasing pressure. If Walker continued to lie, the plea bargain would collapse, for deception could hardly be justified in the acceptance of a not-guilty plea. And worried Justice officials knew that Judge Harvey was growing impatient over postponements of sentencing.

The officials also knew that withdrawal of the plea agreement could have a domino effect on the other trials, for dropping the plea agreement because of Walker's deceit would becloud his testimony at the Whitworth trial, providing grounds for appeal. A similar possibility could aid court appeals of Arthur Walker, whose own confession was linked to his brother's statements. Withdrawal of the agreement also meant that Justice would have to grovel before Navy officials, particularly Secretary of the Navy John Lehman, who had denounced the plea bargain as "treating espionage as just another white-collar crime."

On November 6, 1986, federal marshals brought Michael and John Walker before Judge Harvey in the Baltimore courtroom where they would have been tried. Judge Harvey methodically reviewed the charges, making sure that the Walkers knew the crimes to which they were pleading guilty. He also reviewed the plea bargains, which set the sentences—life in prison for John Walker, a sentence of twenty-five years for his son—and, in almost impenetrable legalese, held out the promise of parole for both of them. "Within ninety (90) days from the sentencing in this case," each agreement said, "the government will notify the United States Parole Commission of the nature and extent of Mr. Walker's cooperation in this case."

What this meant was that it was highly probable that Walker had put his friend Jerry Whitworth in jail for many more years than Walker would serve. Congress abolished the U.S. Parole Commission in 1987 in a reform action that dismantled the federal parole structure, replacing it with a system of firm sentences. But parole procedures will continue to prevail for federal prisoners sentenced while the commission existed.

Under the law establishing the commission, anyone who receives a sentence of more than thirty years in a federal court is technically eligible for parole in ten years. Thus, the sentences of the Walkers and Whitworth—and all the other spies jailed in recent years—will be subject to the old algebra of parole, which is difficult to calculate. Theoretically, John Walker and Arthur Walker could be paroled after serving ten years, Michael after serving eight years and four months. A ten-year "life sentence" is possible because a disputed section of the federal code seems to limit a judge's power to control parole practices. The section does not allow a federal judge to raise the minimum eligibility beyond ten years.

After the sentencing of Whitworth, Larson had claimed that, because of this limitation, the sixty-year parole order Judge Vukasin had attached to the 365-year sentence was unlawful. Appeals of parole-thwarting murder and kidnapping sentences, based on this legal question, were winding through the federal court system when Judge Vukasin sentenced Whitworth. In a kidnapping case, for example, a federal judge handed down a 300-year sentence and set a parole eligibility of 99 years.

A ten-year sentence seems unlikely for John Walker because the parole commission looks not merely at the authorized jail/parole ratio but also at the gravity of the crime. Espionage stands alongside murder at the end of the sentencing scale. But a life sentence is relatively rare in federal courts and there is not much experience to draw upon. One study of life sentences for murder and kidnapping showed that convicts eligible for parole at ten years usually spent twenty-five to thirty-five years behind bars.

Judge Harvey, well aware of the parole-limitation dilemma in federal cases, was bound to the plea agreement. Talking about it later, he seemed to treat the agreement as a necessary evil in the malignant world of espionage.

"I concluded that there were exceptional circumstances in

this case," he said at the sentencing. John Walker stood before the high dais. Judge Harvey looked down, and in a low, firm voice, continued, "Your motive was pure greed, and you were paid handsomely for your traitorous acts. It has been estimated that over this eighteen-year period, you received from the Soviet Union approximately $1 million in cash.

"Throughout history, most spies have been moved to betray their country for ideological reasons. You and the others who participated in this scheme were traitors for pure cold cash. Whether this says something about today's society and its values, I leave for the sociologists to determine.

"In reviewing the details of this offense and your background, I look in vain for some redeeming aspect of your character. When one considers the facts, one is seized with an overwhelming feeling of revulsion that a human being could be as unprincipled as you.

"Certainly everyone who has ever worn a uniform of the armed services—and I served my country overseas in combat during World War II—must feel utter contempt and disgust that a serviceman could bring the ultimate disgrace to the uniform that you have."

Walker's wife and daughters, sitting among the spectators, cast down their eyes. Michael Walker, seated at a table with his lawyer, turned his head and looked away from his father, who stood next to Michael's chair. John Walker showed no emotion as the judge continued his devastating denunciation, in soft, measured tones.

"You showed your stripes early," he said. "When you needed money for your failing bar in Charleston, South Carolina, in 1966 and 1967, you suggested that your wife turn to prostitution. Shortly thereafter, you decided that more money could be made by betraying your country. To increase your earnings from espionage, you enlarged your operation and recruited members of your own family. It made no difference to you that your own flesh and blood would be exposing themselves to extreme risks by engaging in these traitorous activities.

"Your brother is now serving a life sentence. Your son is a young man who will be spending the next twenty-five years in federal prison. Your daughter Laura, to her everlasting credit, refused to join you when you sought to recruit her. Your good friend Jerry Whitworth will spend the rest of his life in federal prison.

"None of this apparently mattered to you so long as the cash was coming in. You, a twenty-year Navy man, have betrayed your country so that you might enjoy luxuries such as an airplane, a houseboat, cars, and sailboat."

The judge said that it was difficult for him to believe that any parole commissioner would ever give Walker an early release. But, he added, "I shall do everything in my power to see that this does not occur." He said he would "strenuously recommend" to the U.S. Parole Commission "that you not be released on parole at any time during the rest of your life." He then formally sentenced John Walker to "imprisonment for the remainder of your natural life."

Walker's attorney, Fred Bennett, seemed stunned and acted as if he were about to speak. But Judge Harvey turned to baby-faced Michael, who still had a close, military-style haircut. The judge quickly reviewed Michael's plea agreement and then addressed the young man who stood where his father had stood moments before.

"Unlike your father's case," the judge said, "there is at least something that can be said on your behalf. You unfortunately looked up to your father. As an immature twenty-one-year-old, you were easily led into these traitorous activities. . . . However young you were, Mr. Walker, you were nevertheless an enlisted serviceman in the United States Navy, from which you have now been dishonorably discharged. Your duty was to defend your country. You chose to betray it.

"One does not need much maturity or education to understand that being a traitor is perhaps the ultimate of all crimes. It is therefore appropriate that you receive this lengthy term of imprisonment, and I will likewise recommend to the Parole Commission that you not be paroled at any time during your twenty-five-year term."

Bennett now moved to speak. He protested the judge's decision to recommend no parole to the Parole Commission. "We think," Bennett said, "that this, in effect, literally amounts to an amendment of the plea agreement . . ."

"You can think what you want, Mr. Bennett," the judge replied. "That is what I will do."

Michael's mother seemed disoriented. She left the sloping general-attendance seats in the huge courtroom and walked toward the defendants' table. But John and Michael Walker had already been briskly escorted through a door behind the high dais. Even as the door was closing a marshal was reaching in his pocket for the handcuffs that had been removed from the Walkers for their brief courtroom appearance.

Barbara Walker spoke to Bennett, and then, convoyed by her three daughters, Laura, Cynthia, and Margaret, she left the first-floor courtroom and entered the Federal Building's modernistic lobby. Through the double set of glass doors she could see the gauntlet of reporters, cameras, microphones, and lights arrayed along the sweeping driveway in front of the building. A large sculpture—a crisscross of bright-yellow steel beams—dominated the patch of lawn near the doorway.

A television reporter, a slim blond-haired woman in a blue suit, ran up to Barbara, began walking rapidly alongside her, put a microphone in front of Barbara's pudgy face, and began questioning her: "You said before that if you knew what would happen to Michael you never would have done it. Still feel that way?"

"Yes," Barbara Walker said, hardly moving her lips. And she hurried on. Laura, acting as the family spokesperson, lingered and answered questions shouted through a tumult of impromptu press conferences being held in front of the building.

"What my father did to my brother was horrible," she said, and, to a question about her father's motives, she answered, "Greed. Selfishness and greed. No parole. Now that came from somewhere out in left field."

"He has expressed remorse to me," Fred Bennett was saying, a few feet away. "I wish he had spoken in court today. I do think he is psychologically able to deal with the enormity of the crime, to express himself, and survive emotionally. He expected the harsh words. He expected fully the sentence that was imposed. He is surprised and disappointed in regards to the judge's comment about what the judge intends to do on his written form to the Parole Commission." Bennett said that Walker had counted on parole at "some time in his old age—depending on the political climate" and "a good institutional record."

Michael's attorney, Charles G. Bernstein, said of his client,

"He is so scared. I think his words to me were, 'If I try to say anything, I'm afraid I'm just going to squeak.' His remorse is real. He's been through a personal tragedy."

In still another press conference, Robert W. Hunter, the Norfolk-based FBI agent who had managed the case against John Walker, said that he believed the case was 98 percent complete. "The questions that were still unanswered," he said, "were exactly the ones that were there when the spy case began."

Finally, Schatzow, the Assistant U.S. Attorney who had prosecuted Morison and would have prosecuted the Walkers, had something to say about John Walker's future: "People accused or convicted of espionage are less well received in confinement than any other type of offender, with the possible exception of child molesters."

Judge Harvey did send to the U.S. Parole Commission a transcript of the sentencing hearing, along with his no-parole recommendation. It was warmly received, he later said. Bennett questioned the judge's remark in a formal brief to an appellate court, which let the judge's decision stand. If John Walker never walks out of prison, it will be because of the recommendation of a former lieutenant in the U.S. Army field artillery who fought in World War II, went to law school, became a federal judge, and one day looked down upon a man who had disgraced his uniform.

A Duel of Q & A

The phone call to the Soviet Embassy in Washington was made at 4:53 p.m. on January 14, 1980, and routinely recorded by FBI wiretappers:*

First person: May I know who is calling?

Caller: I would like not to use my name if it's all right for the moment.

First person: Hold on, please. Sir?

Caller: Yes, um.

First person: Hold the line, please.

Caller: All right.

Second person: Hello, sir.

* The government does not officially acknowledge that it taps any embassies. The source of the conversation is labeled "targeted premise" and is not named.

Caller: Ah, yes. I would—

Second person: Ah, Vladimir Sorokin speaking. My name is Vladimir.

Caller: Vladimir. Yes. Ah, I have, ah, I don't like to talk on the telephone.

Sorokin: I see.

Caller: Ah, I have something I would like to discuss with you I think that would be very interesting to you.

Sorokin: Uh-huh, uh-huh.

Caller: Is there any way to do so in, in, ah, confidence or in privacy?

Sorokin: I see. I understand. . . . Maybe you can, ah, name yourself?

Caller: Ah . . . ah, on the telephone it would not be wise.

Sorokin: I see. . . .

Caller: I come from—I, I, I am in, with the United States Government.

Sorokin: Ah, huh, United States Government. . . . Maybe you can visit.

The Caller said he would visit the next night—"so that it will be dark when I come in."

But at 2:32 p.m. on January 15 the Caller phoned the embassy and said he would be there in two minutes. The FBI had expected more warning. "We saw him go in, saw his backside, and we could not identify his exit," FBI Director William H. Webster said later.

The Caller's name was Ronald William Pelton, although it would be five years before the FBI discovered that name in the kind of an investigation the FBI does so well, burrowing through a great haystack of superfluous information for that needle of accusation. And the investigation would be topped off by two psychological duels—first a fascinating encounter between Pelton and two shrewd FBI agents and then an amazing trial, with no physical evidence, no witnesses, no solid proof of espionage.

Pelton had worked as an intelligence analyst for the National Security Agency for fourteen years by 1979, a troubled year. He had piled up so many debts while building a house for his family that he was forced to declare bankruptcy. He knew that this could endanger his clearances for top secret and beyond, for a man in heavy debt is a security risk. He resigned from his

$24,500-a-year job and, a few months later, dialed the Soviet Embassy.

When he walked in, all he took with him was a certificate showing that he had satisfactorily completed an NSA course and a photograph showing himself among the graduates of the course. Pelton had had a top-secret clearance with additional clearances "for special compartmented information relating to signals intelligence." What he had to offer were not documents but what he carried in his remarkable mind. He had what co-workers at NSA called a photographic memory, an ability to summon up bits of information from many sources and produce a mosaic of intelligence. He was the author of an NSA eavesdropping encyclopedia that listed some sixty Soviet signals that the agency's listening posts regularly intercepted, analyzed, and decrypted.

The NSA table of organization would show Pelton as having "compartmentalized" knowledge, in keeping with the standard intelligence practice of confining sensitive information only to those who need to know it. In reality, Pelton was what a colleague called a "wheeler-dealer," a busy bureaucrat who knew so much, especially about making budgets and buying equipment, that frequently he was invited into other compartments to share his knowledge.

The KGB officer who greeted Pelton at the embassy on January 15 was Vitaly Yurchenko. He accepted Pelton as a genuine walk-in and listened to his major disclosure: The United States used submarines to tap an underwater military communications cable in the Sea of Okhotsk between Soviet installations on the Kamchatka Peninsula and the Soviet far east coast. The project was code-named "Ivy Bells."

A bearded Pelton had entered the embassy through the front gate. Yurchenko had the neophyte spy shave off his beard. Dressed in bulky work clothes, Pelton slipped out of a side door with a group of Soviet employees. The group entered the van that regularly shuttled workers between the embassy and the apartment complex used as a Soviet residence. Like Walker in 1968, Pelton was not spotted by FBI surveillance agents.

In August 1985, Yurchenko began what turned into a two-way defection—first to the United States and then, three months later, back to the Soviet Union. When CIA intelligence officers questioned him, he gave them a few counter-espionage nuggets, including what he said he knew about the former NSA employee he had met in 1980 and never seen again.

FBI director Webster, recounting the investigation that followed, said that the initial information from Yurchenko produced a list of about five hundred names. "Through an interview with Yurchenko granted by the CIA," Webster says, "we almost inadvertently learned that the man we wanted had red hair. When we pushed Yurchenko to describe the exact shade of brown hair he had earlier identified, Yurchenko pointed to a red color. And with this critical piece of information, we made the identification —and confirmed it when NSA employees identified Pelton's voice on calls to the Soviet Embassy in 1980."

The FBI believed it had enough on Pelton to apply on October 15 to the Foreign Intelligence Surveillance Court for taps on the suspect's business phone at an Annapolis boat company and the phone in his girlfriend's apartment in northwest Washington. The taps were authorized, along with bugs in the apartment and on Pelton's car.

No incriminating espionage information turned up on the taps, although there were many references to illegal drugs. Pelton did not seem to be doing much spying. Six years out of NSA and not in regular contact with Soviets, he was a suspect against whom the FBI had the flimsiest case imaginable. They had a voice on a tape and they had the word of a defector who, on November 4, announced, at a press conference in the Soviet Embassy, that he was returning to the Soviet Union.

All the FBI could do was try to make Pelton incriminate himself in a legally delicate and psychologically challenging encounter with skilled FBI interrogators. The plan called for the encounter to take place in neutral space, so, under the name "John Francis," the FBI rented six rooms at the Annapolis Hilton. A polygraph examiner took over Room 410. FBI supervisors set up a command post in rooms 418 through 420. Room 411 became a bunk room. And Special Agent David Faulkner stage-managed the laying out of Room 409.

The bed was moved out, a small refrigerator and coffee maker were moved in. Faulkner gave great care to the placement of·three chairs.

Agents had Pelton under twenty-four-hour surveillance.

They knew that he and his girlfriend, Ann Barry, bought street drugs in Washington and spent weekends drinking and getting high. As many as forty FBI surveillance agents were sometimes needed to keep watch on Pelton's wanderings. The plan called for getting Pelton to what would appear to him to be neutral grounds, which meant neither an FBI office nor his business office. Faulkner, the stage manager, wanted the questioning of Pelton to be on a weekend. But Faulkner wanted his man sober. On Saturday, November 23, Pelton spent the night on his employer's yacht in Annapolis, alone. Faulkner knew that the best way to set up his suspect was to surprise him when he was by himself.

About 9:30 on Sunday morning, November 24, Pelton was in the boat company office in Annapolis when he got a telephone call from Faulkner, who identified himself and asked Pelton to come to the Annapolis Hilton to discuss a matter of "extreme urgency." Pelton had no one to turn to. On his own, he stammered a suggestion that Faulkner come to the boat office. Faulkner, who had to be in charge, turned down the idea, saying that sensitive national security information was involved. Pelton agreed. He drove the short distance to the hotel and was met in the lobby by Faulkner and Dudley F. Hodgson, another agent. The agents were wearing open shirts and sport coats, open to show they carried neither weapons nor handcuffs. The three men took the elevator to Room 409.

Faulkner offered Pelton coffee and doughnuts and directed him to one of three chairs in the room. The chair was in front of the window, facing toward the room so that Pelton would not be distracted. Faulkner took a chair directly in front of Pelton. Hodgson's chair was to one side, just at the edge of Pelton's vision. To talk to Faulkner, Pelton would have to face him. To talk to Hodgson, he would have to turn his head.

"Agent Faulkner then told me that he was going to tell me a story and . . . he asked me to remain silent during the story, and to withhold any comments until the story was finished," Pelton later recalled. "The story started off with a young man who grew up in the city of Benton Harbor, Michigan." That was Pelton's hometown. The story was about him, about a man who joined the Air Force, which taught him Russian and sent him to Pakistan as an electronic eavesdropper. This led to his next career at the NSA, where he worked until 1979. The story went on about the man who quit the NSA and then, a few months later, called the Soviet Embassy.

Faulkner next played tapes of conversations between two men speaking on the phone on January 14 and 15, 1980. He showed Pelton a photograph of Yurchenko and said that he was one of the men speaking on January 15. Faulkner said that Yurchenko spent three hours speaking to the hypothetical man in the story. The man went into the embassy with a beard and came out clean-shaven. Then Faulkner asked Pelton to finish the story.

"I responded to the effect that it was a nice story, and that it was obvious that he was implying that it was me, but that it was not," Pelton remembered.

Hodgson said it was obviously Pelton's voice on the tape. "I said basically that . . . they had no case, that this was nothing but a tape. They had no case."

Pelton asked if there were any recording devices in Room 409. Faulkner honestly answered that there were none. He had decided not to take the chance with Pelton, in order to create more trust. Anyway, Pelton, who had been an expert on electronics, probably would have spotted any ordinary recording equipment. Faulkner casually asked Pelton about the .38-caliber pistol he owned. Pelton said it was at home. Faulkner and Hodgson relaxed about being unarmed.

Pelton and the agents sparred about how much "cooperation" he would give them, about whether he would travel around with the agents, perhaps even to Vienna, to show them the places where he had met with Soviets. Pelton later recalled that he said he would have to talk to an attorney before he made any decision about helping the FBI. Faulkner was skimming close to the limitations of legally acceptable interrogation. If Pelton had said he had *wanted* a lawyer to protect his rights as a suspect, Faulkner would be obliged to stop the questioning until a lawyer was present.

Faulkner said that an attorney would just complicate matters at the moment because the two agents and Pelton were going to discuss national security matters and anyone who heard the conversation would need to be cleared.

At that point Pelton began responding the way Faulkner had hoped he would: It had begun to dawn on Pelton that perhaps the FBI wanted him to become a double agent. "I sort of corroborated that with a fact we were sitting in a hotel room, not the FBI office."

Pelton, warming to what he thought was his new role-to-be, asked whether the agents had high enough clearance to discuss what he knew. Faulkner replied that he and Hodgson had been cleared by NSA for whatever level Pelton had been cleared for and that access had been authorized in writing.

Faulkner said that his superiors in the FBI had been pressing for a full investigation, which would have meant embarrassing Pelton because agents would have to interview his friends and business associates and let them hear the embassy tapes.

"I said that it is possible—isn't it?—that this whole area could lead to prosecution. He [Faulkner] again responded that this was a possibility but it wasn't their decision. They didn't make those kinds of decisions. Their job was in counter-intelligence, and prosecution was a decision made by another group in different and higher authority. . . .

"Agent Hodgson spoke up and said, 'You know, Mr. Pelton, many cases involving national security just do not end up in prosecution.'

"Well, I asked him what good it was going to do me to cooperate if they still ended up going to prosecution.

"Agent Faulkner responded that I would have two FBI witnesses on the—telling—on the stand, that I, in fact, cooperated from the beginning."

When Pelton began acting guarded, the agents switched to other subjects, such as Pelton's bankruptcy and income-tax problems. The agents called these matters "liabilities." They asked him if he had other liabilities.

"And I said, no, I didn't know of any. And then Agent Faulkner said, 'Well, what about drugs?'

"And I said, yes, I guess there is a potential problem there, that I admitted that I do use the drug Dilaudid. I indicated to them that I used it recreationally, that is, that I wasn't addicted to it."

Faulkner then "asked me whether I didn't think it would be kind of risky buying drugs and the potential of getting caught doing so. And I had indicated that, no, I had not had any problems so far, that I knew where to go, and whom to see, and didn't see a problem."

Hodgson interrupted Pelton, saying, "For Christ's sake, don't get caught copping drugs in D.C. because we can't help you if you do."

Pelton thought that the agents were, as he put it, sizing him up, trying to find "if there were errors in my life" that would rule him out as a double agent. Soon the conversation drifted back to Pelton's "cooperation." And Pelton brought up John Walker.

"I mentioned to the agents that I understand that John Walker is now cooperating with you and that he, in fact, received a life sentence." He said later that he saw himself cleverly switching control of the situation, that by mentioning Walker as an example he would force the agents to "clarify what they meant by 'cooperate' "—ironically, the very term that the KGB uses as a polite way of saying betrayal.

"Well, they had responded that John Walker was quite a bit different from myself. They explained that he had been involved in this sort of activity for something like twenty years, he had made considerable sums of money, that he had involved his family, and associates, and some friends, and that basically he was just, in their opinion, a bad guy. But they felt that I was not anything like him."

And, the agents implied, Walker had not "cooperated." If he had, perhaps things would have gone much differently.

Now came the moment that Faulkner and Hodgson had psychologically created: Pelton had convinced himself that he had outwitted them. He said he thought, "If I cooperated at the beginning perhaps things would have been different for me than they were for John Walker." Pelton quoted Faulkner as saying that, while working with Walker would have been "quite distasteful," he "didn't feel like that" about the possibility of working with Pelton.

Faulkner, without saying where he was going, excused himself from the room. While he was gone Pelton telephoned Ann Barry to tell her he might be late for their Sunday brunch date. Faulkner returned to say that he had talked about Pelton with his superiors. "He indicated," Pelton recalled, "that they had to have enough information to know what it was that they were being asked to provide guarantees for. Without the information they weren't going to give me a carte blanche. . . . He asked me, for example, was I working alone, and was I working with other people.

"Well, it was kind of a catch-22. If I didn't give him information that he needed in order to—that the superiors needed, rather—in order to make their decisions, then there was no way to get guarantees, and if I didn't, so that meant that I would not cooperate. If I didn't cooperate, then the other option was, it appeared to me, that I would simply be arrested. . . . So I was caught in a catch-22. So I think the bottom line is—why I continued to give information—was, basically, I trusted the agents."

Faulkner began asking questions: Did Pelton work alone? Had he attempted to recruit anyone? When was his last contact with the Soviet Union?

Pelton said he had last gone to Vienna in April 1985, walked around his meeting site—the gardens of the imperial summer palace, Schönbrunn—for about three days, but was not contacted. He had then returned to the United States. He also said that he had been worried lately because he thought the Soviets had found his unlisted telephone number. Faulkner told him that, in fact, his residence had been under Soviet surveillance. Pelton asked if he should attempt to recontact the Soviets. Faulkner, who was sure that, because of Yurchenko's defection and redefection, the Soviets had abandoned Pelton, advised him not to try to contact them again. Pelton did not know that he was a spy left out in the cold, a spy who was about to be brought in by the other side.

Faulkner turned to questions about what NSA projects Pelton had revealed to the Soviets. Pelton balked at answering these questions until he got some "guarantees." Then, quite casually, Hodgson asked how much money was involved. Caught off guard, Pelton replied that he could not remember whether the amount was $30,000 or $35,000. Any expense money? About $4,000 or $5,000, he replied. How did you get the expense money?

Pelton, falling into the give and take of question and answer, said that on the last Saturday of the month he was to go to a restaurant in suburban Virginia and await a telephone call. That call sent him to a nearby pay phone where he found money crammed into a magnetic Hide-A-Key box under a shelf.

Prodded by a few questions, Pelton rattled on about his

meetings in Vienna. He said he was questioned at the residence of the Soviet ambassador to Austria and that a greatly annoyed ambassador had to move elsewhere during the sessions. Pelton said he spent as long as eight hours a day, three or four days at a time, answering, in writing, written questions about NSA. The agents showed him a photo of Anatoly Slavnov, a Moscow-based KGB officer, whom Pelton identified as his leading interrogator in Vienna.

By then "I felt that we had developed a rapport. There was a very friendly attitude back and forth, of getting along with each other. There seemed to be a chemistry. I felt very secure in the fact that we were going to be doing something together."

The agents now told Pelton he could go off for his date with Ann Barry. Pelton agreed to meet the two agents for lunch the next day. They escorted him out of the hotel and to his car, a 1979 Lincoln. When he opened the door he was somewhat embarrassed to see on the seat two bottles of Grand Marnier and a bottle of vodka. His passport was in the car. The agents examined it, talked to him about the entries in it, and asked if they could hold on to it for a while. Pelton felt so secure that he gave it to them.

He then drove off in a car that had a legally authorized electronic bug to an apartment that also had one. His every move was under FBI surveillance.

When he got to Ann Barry's apartment she told him she needed hair spray and cat food, so he went down to a grocery store, bought those items, eggs and other groceries, and returned to the apartment, where he cooked himself an omelet. As he settled back with the Sunday papers, TV, and a glass of Grand Marnier, Ann said she wanted to go out and buy some Dilaudid. But, in his expected role as a double agent, Pelton did not want to be seen buying drugs. So he told her to go buy the drugs herself. They began arguing.

He finally explained that the FBI wanted him to work for them and so, although he could not buy drugs, he would drive her from Georgetown to Eleventh and O Street, a notorious Washington drug bazaar, and let her buy them. This she did, paying $80 for "two fours"—two four-milligram tablets of Dilaudid.

Back at Ann's apartment, Pelton "cooked" the tablets, reducing them to a liquid. He injected half, Ann the other half. He poured himself another Grand Marnier and, having downed that, switched to vodka and orange juice.

Ronald Pelton, who had just turned forty-four, had, in the past few years, changed from a sober, born-again Christian—a solid, churchgoing married man with four children, ranging in age from sixteen to twenty-one—to a man who regularly took drugs, drank heavily, and had a girlfriend who did the same. After quitting NSA in 1979, Pelton had gone from job to job, the latest one being a salesman for an Annapolis boat company. He had left his wife in April 1985 and moved in with Ann Barry, whom he had met about a year before. He soon began seeing her regularly and using drugs, first marijuana and cocaine, then Dilaudid. He described it as "an opiate that leaves one with a feeling of some euphoria." The "word we use on the street," he added, "is a lazy mellow. It makes you quite relaxed."

The Sunday afternoon evaporated into a hazy Sunday evening. Pelton and Ann went out to do the laundry and have a few drinks at a neighborhood restaurant. About 9:30 they returned, and five or so minutes later the phone rang. It was Faulkner, asking Pelton to return to Annapolis for an urgent talk.

Pelton and Ann began arguing again, this time over his giving her unlisted telephone number to the FBI. He had not given it, but apparently he did not realize that the FBI had the number and a great deal more. He had not even noticed that the call from Faulkner, so soon after their return, indicated that he was under close surveillance.

"There's a deal I might be able to make," he told Ann. On the somewhat unintelligible wiretap recording he also says something about "twenty years in jail" and adds "there's no promises for that."

He drove to Annapolis, with the FBI agents who followed his Lincoln hoping that Pelton—"mellow. I was feeling pretty mellow"—still was able to drive. He made it without incident back to Room 409, where Faulkner resumed questioning about what was to be referred to only as Project A. This was the NSA-Navy tap on the Soviet military communications cable in the Sea of Okhotsk. Faulkner handed Pelton a map and asked him to show where he had located Project A when he told the Soviets about the supersecret tap. He drew a circle around the spot. (Offi-

cials said afterward that he was off by a considerable distance.)
Pelton assumed that the FBI was making a "damage assessment"
and that the information he had given the Soviets was "a bargaining chip" for negotiating with the FBI.

Faulkner started asking more and more questions. "It was
going pretty rapid," Pelton recalled. One question was crucial to
Faulkner's psychological plan and to Pelton's eventual trial.
Faulkner and Hodgson asked it in various ways. It came down to
this: Didn't you feel that giving up this kind of information
would be harmful to the United States?

Pelton, after some skirting of the answer, finally admitted
that he had known that the information in Soviet hands would be
harmful. This was a key element in an espionage charge. The
accused must give information whose disclosure not only will aid
the foreign country but which will also harm the United States.
The agents pressed on, showing Pelton documents, asking what
he had told the Soviets. Pelton sensed that a change had come.
He said he already had had enough trouble for the day and that
he was tired of answering questions without what he called
"guarantees." Faulkner abruptly left the room and returned with
Form FD395, a document the FBI calls a "waiver-of-rights
form." Whitworth had signed one the day the agents called on
him. It says:

> You have the right to remain silent.
>
> Anything you say can be used against you in court.
>
> You have the right to talk to a lawyer for advice before we
> ask you any questions and to have a lawyer with you during
> questioning.
>
> If you cannot afford a lawyer, one will be appointed for
> you before any questioning if you wish.
>
> If you decide to answer any questions now without a law-
> yer present, you will still have the right to stop answering any
> time. You also have the right to stop answering at any time
> until you talk to a lawyer.

Pelton read and signed it, even though "I felt at this point
that whatever I had felt that was going to be happening in terms
of cooperation at that point was disappearing and that, in fact,
this indicated to me that the whole thrust of the events were now

headed toward prosecution and that, in fact, I would be arrested."

He was.

The court gave the penniless suspect a lawyer—Fred Warren Bennett, the skilled public defender who had so well defended John Walker without going to trial. For his next espionage case, Bennett would go to trial. His learned opponents also had espionage experience. Assistant U.S. Attorneys John G. Douglass and Robert N. McDonald had been involved in the Walker cases. U.S. District Court Judge Herbert F. Murray, who would preside, was, like Judge Harvey, a veteran of World War II.

The defendant and counsel for both sides signed a document that acknowledged CIPA procedures for the protection of classified information. Pelton, ironically, had to agree, for the good of the country, not to reveal in court the secrets he was accused of selling the Soviet Union. He agreed not to use any NSA code names for the projects he had worked on, sold to the Soviets, or discussed with the FBI. He could look at the FBI FD302 Report, which recounted, in great detail, his conversation with Faulkner and Hodgson. But the 302 was itself to be a classified document. The secrecy also extended to the "targeted premise" source of the January 14 and 15 telephone tapes, which Faulkner had played at the end of his story about the hypothetical man who entered the Soviet Embassy.

The government produced several witnesses from the hidden world of NSA (sometimes called "No Such Agency" in recollection of the time when its very existence was officially unacknowledged). Testimony came so close to the revelation of secrets that high-level Reagan Administration officials contemplated prosecuting news organizations for speculating beyond the carefully controlled admissions. The proposed prosecution for speculation was not to have been under the espionage law, as in Morison's case, but under a 1950 statute designed to protect U.S. intelligence communications, particularly NSA's. There was no prosecution, but the media felt a long-lingering chill.

In the trial Bennett focused his defense on the prosecution's gamble: the decision to prosecute without physical evidence. Pelton was accused of selling his memory, not documents, to the Soviets. So the only evidence was intangible: first, testimony that showed Pelton had known secrets, and then testimony, primarily from Faulkner, that in Room 409 Pelton had admitted spying, had admitted getting money, and had conceded that he had done harm to the United States. The government was hoping to convict Pelton with his own, voluntarily given words.

Bennett tried another tack: Pelton, mellow on Dilaudid and alcohol, could hardly be expected to act rationally or remember what he had done on that presumably bleary Sunday. But Pelton, testifying in his own defense, was defeated by his own remarkable memory. He went over what he had done that day, minute by minute, admission by admission. What he remembered coincided with what Faulkner and Hodgson had reported. The man whose memory made him a spy without fingerprints convicted himself by remembering and accurately retelling his own confession.

The jury certified his memory by finding him guilty. Judge Murray, saying that Pelton's sellout to the Soviets had done "inestimable damage," sentenced him to three concurrent life sentences.

The FBI Agent and the KGB Blonde

This is the unlikely first scene in a spy drama that ended in a courtroom not once but twice: It is August 1984. A sedan is speeding north from Los Angeles on the freeway that Californians call I-5. An FBI counter-intelligence agent is driving. At his side is a slim, dark-eyed blond woman who speaks with a Russian accent made even thicker by the cognac she is sharing with the driver. She throws an empty out the window. "Oh, for me it was extraordinary," the agent, Richard W. Miller, later says, describing his trip to San Francisco, where his companion, Svetlana Ogorodnikov, would meet with one of her colleagues in the KGB.

"I had never drunk before in my life. She had brought some margaritas and cognac. That cognac is the awfullest tasting stuff in the world. I thought—I thought, 'Man, this is my chance to be worldly,' and I was gonna just take the opportunity. And we were driving up I-5, just singing songs, and having a great old time throwing bottles out the window. I tried to stop her from throwing the bottles out the window."

The trip ended at the Soviet Consulate in San Francisco. Svetlana, a thirty-four-year-old Soviet émigrée, went in, taking with her Miller's badge and credentials to prove that the fat, red-faced man in the car parked outside was indeed an FBI counter-intelligence agent. She also took with her a copy of an FBI manual on the gathering of intelligence information. Miller had made the copy of the manual on the field-office copying machine. The FBI later described the twenty-four-page classified manual as a guide that could give the Soviets "a detailed picture of FBI and U.S. intelligence activities, techniques, and requirements." He is also accused of having given her at least one other classified document.

The consulate was certainly familiar to Miller. The San Francisco FBI field office, charged with keeping the Soviet spy nest under surveillance, had even once tried to dig a tunnel under it. The burrowing had been detected, and so the counter-intelligence agents had to be satisfied with conventional surveillance techniques—tapping phones, following Soviets believed to be KGB officers, photographing people who entered and left the consulate, which had become KGB West.

On that very worldly day with Svetlana, Miller apparently forgot that he himself would be under surveillance by FBI agents based in San Francisco. Miller, a forty-seven-year-old agent with an incredibly bad record, worked out of the Los Angeles field office, which had relatively little counter-espionage work compared with the San Francisco office with its responsibility for KGB West. Given the intense competition between FBI field offices, he stood out even more when puzzled local agents first learned that he had been seen near the Soviet Consulate. The L.A. field office had no business sending a man to San Francisco. FBI field offices sometimes slyly manipulate an important case so that it will come into the jurisdiction of one rather than the other.

If, for example, Whitworth had been arrested in Davis, where he lived, the San Francisco field office would have lost him to the Sacramento field office. By following San Francisco field-office instructions and driving to that city to give himself up, Whitworth put himself into the jurisdictional territory of the FBI office there. Similarly, the FBI arranged the Pelton case so that he was arrested and tried in Maryland, rather than the District of Columbia, where he lived and where he began his espionage, because, for undisclosed reasons, the FBI field office in Baltimore ran the case. (Traditionally, the FBI has covertly campaigned to keep major cases out of the District of Columbia because of a distrust of the judgment of juries that are made up of black middle-class and lower-class residents.)

For Miller, a twenty-year FBI veteran, the competition ran along a different track. When it came time to decide the jurisdiction of his case, neither the Los Angeles nor the San Francisco field office wanted it. Agents in the Los Angeles office called it "the flagship of the FBI."

Soon after the boozy trip up I-5, the San Francisco FBI learned, apparently through an informer, that Miller and Svetlana were having an affair. The FBI now began tracking one of its own, videotaping Miller's meetings with Svetlana, tapping phone calls, quietly checking Miller's case load, and simultaneously building a case against Svetlana, who was believed to be working for the KGB.

Miller, who could have won a contest as the FBI's worst agent, nevertheless had been assigned to counter-espionage in 1982, in a move that seemed inspired by his superiors' need to keep Miller away from anything really important. The assigning of an agent as hopeless as Miller to counter-espionage illumines a dark little FBI secret: counter-espionage work is often a career dead end, with the possible exception of New York and Washington field offices.

Miller once lost his gun. And his credentials. One night, when he locked up the Los Angeles field office, he left the key in the lock. It was still there the next morning, and an investigation disclosed that the agent most likely to have done it was, indeed, the agent who had done it. Miller's reputation, as he himself put it, "wasn't very good, to say the least." Yet Miller usually received an "excellent" rating—as do about 90 percent of all agents.

He was constantly behind on paperwork, which usually is a cardinal sin in the FBI. He peddled Amway products out of his FBI car, used his badge to cadge candy from a 7-Eleven store, and sold FBI information to a private investigator. A former colleague described him as "lunchy," meaning "a guy that's unkempt, disheveled. Looks like he's got bread crumbs and soup spots on his shirt and tie." His own lawyer said of him, "He was certainly no Efrem Zimbalist, Jr., and he was, in fact, much closer to an overweight Inspector Clouseau."

The father of eight children, he was always scrabbling for

money. He lived alone in Lynwood, a Los Angeles suburb, during the week, and on weekends drove more than one hundred miles to northern San Diego County, where he and his wife tried to run an avocado ranch that produced more debt than fruit.

The FBI physical standards for an agent of Miller's height—five feet, ten inches—was a maximum weight of 193 pounds. When Miller's weight reached 250 pounds he was suspended for two weeks and told to lose his excess pounds. A few weeks after this low point in his career, Svetlana asked him if he wanted to become a spy.

When Miller began as a counter-espionage agent in 1982, Svetlana Ogorodnikov was the responsibility of another counter-espionage agent, John E. Hunt, whose record of contacts with Soviet émigrés would show fifty-five meetings with Svetlana in 1982 and 1983. One of these meetings consisted of a visit to a Los Angeles physician. Hunt said the purpose of the visit was to have Svetlana examined for "a rare blood disease." Svetlana said that Hunt took her to the physician for an abortion. She strongly implied that Hunt was the father, apparently not knowing that the agent had had a vasectomy in 1960. Hunt, at age fifty-two, retired from the FBI in 1984.

Hunt reported that he had spent time with Svetlana in an unsuccessful attempt to turn her. Svetlana was believed to be a KGB "contact agent," a low-level operative who spotted potential recruits and linked KGB officers under diplomatic cover with American spies. She tantalized the FBI by sometimes giving bits of information about pro-Soviet activity among the émigrés. The field office kept track of her because, whatever she was, she obviously was not an ordinary Russian émigrée.

She and her husband, Nikolay Ogorodnikov, had emigrated to the United States in 1973 and ostensibly were members of the Soviet émigré community in West Hollywood. But other émigrés treated them as pro-Soviet informers working for the KGB. "They were like puppets," one émigré said of Svetlana and Nikolay. Svetlana in particular had what seemed to be an amiable relationship with officials of her erstwhile homeland. She received from Moscow, Soviet-made films, which she rented to a neighborhood movie house that paid her a percentage of the admissions.

She distributed Soviet magazines and boasted of her connections with the Soviet Consulate. She also managed what suspiciously seemed to be the impossible by traveling back and forth to the Soviet Union.

Svetlana, thirty-four, worked off and on as a day nurse. Nikolay, fifty-one, was a meat-packer. A Russian-language weekly published in Los Angeles once had accused the couple of being pro-Soviet. A story about them was accompanied by a photograph showing Nikolay Ogorodnikov taking photographs of an anti-Soviet demonstration. A Russian Orthodox priest said he had asked Svetlana not to bring her thirteen-year-old son to church school because she had talked one of the parish's families into returning to the Soviet Union. The son, Matvei, spent his summers at a Communist Party youth camp on the Black Sea. His parents talked of sending him to a military school in the Soviet Union.

Sometime around May 1984, Miller met her and, without official sanction, began what the FBI later described as "numerous personal meetings." They became lovers, although each later had a different recollection of the affair. Svetlana said she tried to resist Miller's sexual advances and submitted only "because he scared me." Miller said in response, "Let's put it this way. I was more inclined toward lovemaking than she was."

As the months went by, Svetlana began hinting at giving Miller more than sexual favors. She said she was a KGB major and she promised $65,000 in gold and money if Miller would spy for the KGB. Perhaps because she could see that he fancied himself as needing the trappings of a spy, she also promised him a $675 Burberry trench coat. She introduced her husband to Miller as "Wolfson," the KGB treasurer for the operation. Miller may not have known that Wolfson was actually Svetlana's husband.

To earn his money and trench coat, Miller would be given specific tasks. Svetlana had two particularly sinister requests. She asked Miller to learn the whereabouts of KGB Major Stanislav Levchenko, who defected from Tokyo, and Victor Belenko, a Soviet pilot who flew a MiG-25 to a civilian air field on the Japanese island of Hokkaido in 1976. Both of them had been condemned to death in absentia in the Soviet Union and presumably would be targets for KGB assassins.

Luckily for Levchenko and Belenko, Miller was no better a spy for the KGB than he was a counter-espionage agent for the FBI. He did not provide the information. But when he supplied

Svetlana with the FBI intelligence-gathering manual, she knew he was worth developing. She called the Soviet Consulate in San Francisco and talked to Soviet Vice Consul Aleksandr Grishin about a valuable, unnamed "friend." FBI eavesdroppers were convinced the friend was Miller, now the target of an FBI counter-espionage operation bitterly code-named "Whipworm."

Agents stepped up surveillance on Miller and Svetlana while high-ranking officials pondered the inevitable decisions that must be made at this stage in a counter-espionage case. Investigators had several options. They could let Miller play out his betrayal while giving him, without his knowledge, safe or deceptive secrets to pass on to the Soviets. They could try to turn Miller. They could try to turn Svetlana, which, given Hunt's experience, was unlikely.

Two breaks in the case interrupted the strategy planning. Svetlana and Grishin began talking about trips to Mexico, Warsaw, and the KGB's favorite city, Vienna. She told Grishin that she would make sure that her unnamed traveling companion would bring "all the baggage with him." FBI officials feared that if Miller left the country they might lose him. But there was also discussion about letting him go so that U.S. counter-espionage experts would get insights into KGB training techniques. The next break, however, settled matters, for Miller had his own strategy.

On Thursday, September 27, Miller told his immediate superior, P. Bryce Christensen, supervisor of the office's counter-espionage squad, that for months he had been working on his own to penetrate the KGB by becoming a double agent. He said that he had hoped to trick Svetlana—and the KGB—into thinking that he was a traitor as part of his plan. He had another motive, he said later: "I had to prove to myself and to the rest of the FBI that I wasn't the klutz that everybody thought I was." Miller claimed that he had revealed his association with Svetlana because he wanted FBI help in arranging the trip to Vienna. The FBI believed that he had turned himself in because he had somehow discovered that he was under FBI surveillance.

Christensen, along with counter-espionage experts flown in from Washington, began questioning Miller, confronting him with the information they already had. The marathon interrogation, augmented by polygraph tests, continued through Friday, went into the weekend, and finally ended on Monday, October 1. FBI director Webster was notified. It was apparent that the FBI faced a public relations disaster, for the publicity would reveal Miller not only as an accused spy but also as a bumbling klutz who had somehow managed to remain in the FBI and had even been made a counter-espionage agent.

There was also the "Mormon Mafia" problem. Christensen was a Mormon. Richard T. Bretzing, the agent in charge of the Los Angeles office, was a bishop in the Mormon Church. Miller, also a Mormon, had been excommunicated a few months before. Charges of Mormon favoritism had circulated among non-Mormons in the office for some time. The continuance of the hapless Miller as a counter-espionage agent had added to the claims. A non-Mormon agent had even made a formal complaint of favoritism to the Equal Employment Opportunity Commission. The bureau consistently denied a Mormon bias in the field office.

On Tuesday, October 2, Webster agreed that the FBI had no choice but to arrest Miller and the Ogorodnikovs. A decision was also made to dismiss Miller so that when he was arrested the following day he would be, as far as dismayed FBI officials were concerned, a *former* FBI agent. No one outside the FBI bureaucracy would, of course, note the distinction. Miller and the Ogorodnikovs were arrested on Tuesday night. On Wednesday, Webster held a Washington news conference to describe the arrest and lament a "very sad day for the FBI."

Sadder days were to come. Initial investigation showed that Miller had helped himself to many secrets. FBI agents armed with search warrants discovered secret and confidential documents that Miller had taken to his bachelor apartment. They had been easily slipped out of the office he had at least once left unlocked.

Security was so sloppy that he was able to remove stored records—such as the FBI file on Svetlana—without even filling out a checkout slip. In the Ogorodnikov apartment, where Miller and Svetlana had dallied in Nikolay's absence, agents found such standard tradecraft tools of KGB espionage as one-time-use cipher pads, secret-writing instruments, and photographic equipment for concealing material in microdots.

The Soviets involved in the case followed a typical KGB strategy by avoiding possible disclosures in a courtroom. Vice

Consul Grishin, named as a co-conspirator in the espionage charges against Miller and the Ogorodnikovs, took advantage of his diplomatic immunity, warding off prosecution simply by quietly returning to Moscow. Svetlana and Nikolay interrupted their trial by pleading guilty in a deal that handed Svetlana an eighteen-year sentence and Nikolay an eight-year sentence. They sent their son back to the Soviet Union, where he may carry on the family tradition. He is believed to have taken the first step toward an intelligence career by entering a military school.

During plea-bargain negotiations, Svetlana agreed to testify at Miller's trial. But she told confusing, often contradicting stories about her involvement with Miller and failed a polygraph test. Although she has publicly said that she was not a spy, Justice officials believe that she and her husband would agree to a spy swap if one developed. In her cell at Pleasanton Federal Prison near San Francisco she has a picture of Soviet leader Mikhail Gorbachev over her bed.

The Department of Justice spent several months preparing to prosecute Miller. The trial moved smoothly. The prosecutors produced videotapes and audio tapes of Miller's dealings with Svetlana. Miller's defense attorneys virtually conceded the FBI case against their client, claiming, however, that he had merely bumbled trying to carry out his self-appointed mission as a KGB mole for the FBI. The jury could not agree on his guilt. The three-month trial was declared a mistrial in November 1985, after the jury, voting ten-to-two for conviction on some counts and eleven-to-one on others, reported a hopeless deadlock. Some jurors said afterward that they wished that the government had put Svetlana on the stand.

The failure to convict Miller devastated the Los Angeles field office. Every U.S. Government espionage trial up till then had ended in a conviction. Besides the Miller loss there had also been, a short time before, in the same Los Angeles Federal Courthouse, the humiliating acquittal of John Z. DeLorean. The automaker had been found not guilty of charges that he had dealt in drugs to finance his failing automobile company. To convict DeLorean the FBI had set up a scam, with agents secretly filming a deal in which a convicted narcotics smuggler, working for the FBI, appeared to have sold DeLorean cocaine. The jury's foreman said he believed that the verdict in the DeLorean case "would indicate to the government that they should reevaluate their investigative techniques."

Miller's second trial began three months after the first. Again the FBI's two major California field offices found themselves in competition—Miller on trial in Los Angeles, Jerry Whitworth on trial in San Francisco. This time Svetlana testified —as a defense witness. Sometimes a translator transformed her throaty Russian into English; at other times she spoke in thickly accented English.

She now insisted that she was innocent. "I was close to going crazy," she said, trying to explain why she had confessed to being a spy. "When I told the truth no one would believe me. When I tell lies people believed me . . . I would be suffering all my life if I didn't say these things today." She said that she accepted a plea bargain rather than face a life sentence.

Under cross-examination, prosecutors demolished Svetlana's story, for they revealed that she had confessed secretly to Federal District Judge David V. Kenyon, who had presided over her interrupted trial and had ratified her plea bargain. The confession in the judge's chambers ostensibly had been arranged to protect Svetlana's family in the Soviet Union. The arrangement also had the advantage of keeping information about the KGB private.

This time the jury found Miller guilty of six counts of espionage. The jury reported that it had deadlocked on a seventh count—accepting the Burberry trench coat from Svetlana. Judge Kenyon sentenced Miller to two life terms plus fifty years and fined him $60,000. "As I see it," the judge said, "Miller's fundamental problem is he didn't realize that he had everything.

"He had eight children he helped bring into this world. He had the lesson of watching them grow, helping them to achieve their potential. He had a wife, and although they had problems, she stuck by him. He had a church that was loyal to him."

The judge, noting that Americans were beginning to take espionage too lightly, said, "It seems to me a person who deliberately, for their own personal gain, betrays their country should not walk again in this country as a free man. It is this court's intention to sentence the guilty with that in mind."

Miller's conviction ended the tragicomic journey that had begun with the rollicking drive up I-5. But questions raised by this soap-opera espionage case linger like a Los Angeles smog:

How typical an FBI counter-espionage agent was this slovenly, unsupervised bumbler? What would have happened if Miller had not given himself up? Why did the Department of Justice approve a plea bargain for a Soviet spy who ended up testifying *against* the government?

And, finally, what effect did the arrest of Miller have on the decision to arrest John Walker? The answer to this last question may be found by comparing the official FBI story about the Walker spy ring with what really happened.

9

The Spy Who Saved the FBI

On Sunday, May 19, 1985, the Federal Bureau of Investigation launched the most elaborate arrest the bureau had ever staged. The arrest was to be the triumphant climax of an epic espionage case that had been code-named "Operation Windflyer." But the arrest was also the result of a desperate decision to end an espionage case gone wrong. The FBI, tarnished by the handling of the DeLorean scam and shamed by the defection of Special Agent Miller, could not afford another disaster. Windflyer could be that fatal disaster if the operation were not quickly ended with a smoothly dramatic arrest.

There are two versions of Windflyer—the "Official Story" and the "Mystery of the Spy Who Almost Got Away." The mystery involves not only the Department of Justice and the FBI but also the Navy and its little-known band of investigators, the Naval Investigative Service (NIS). Their clash over Walker exemplifies the disruptive rivalry and the all too frequent amateurism that have often marred U.S. counter-espionage. The clash came at a time when Soviet intelligence was scoring its most sensational successes.

The central mystery is why there is one, why it is necessary to keep secrets about a traitor like John Walker, why shrouds of official secrecy must be cast around what should have been a very straightforward counter-espionage case. The final answers seem likely never to be known, for, in the words of one of the attorneys involved in the Walker-Whitworth case, "the murky world of espionage" is "a wilderness of mirrors, because deception is so much a part of the structure that nothing is as it seems."

What follows is the authors' attempt to penetrate that murky world and explore the official story to see how much reality it reflects and to separate the image from reality. The official story, which focuses on Walker's arrest, must be told before the mystery can be examined.

The story began at 12:30 p.m. on Sunday, May 19, 1985, when a new blue-and-gray Chevrolet Astro Van pulled out of the driveway of a home at 8424 Old Ocean View Road in Norfolk, Virginia. The van, which bore temporary Virginia tags X076-291 issued ten days before, was registered to Associated Agents, Inc., a private investigative firm. It was owned and operated by a retired Navy warrant officer named John A. Walker, Jr.

A month before—on April 11—the FBI had begun tapping Walker's phones under an authorization from the Foreign Intelligence Surveillance Court. Reports on each day's taps went to Joseph R. Wolfinger, a supervisory special agent in charge of foreign counter-intelligence investigations in the FBI's Norfolk field office. Not much had shown up on the taps until mid-May, when agents began hearing Walker guardedly talking about taking a trip. Walker told both his mother and his brother Arthur that he would not be able to go to an aunt's funeral because he had important business on the coming weekend. He told another caller that he would be going to Charlotte, North Carolina.

Wolfinger, knowing the KGB's penchant for weekend drops, ordered a continuous FBI watch on Walker, beginning on Saturday morning, May 18. Nothing happened until the next day, Sunday, when Walker got in his van and took a roundabout route to Interstate I-95. He then headed not south to Charlotte but north toward Washington. Wolfinger instantly alerted the Washington field office, which started ordering scores of agents to take up previously planned surveillance assignments in the Washington area.

David W. Szady, a special agent supervisor in the intelligence division of the FBI, was just coming off the eighteenth hole of a golf course. Instead of going to his office in the J. Edgar Hoover Building, the massive FBI headquarters building on

Pennsylvania Avenue in Washington, he headed for the Washington field office, in a run-down neighborhood about four miles away. There Szady would supervise the tactical command center that ran the Walker arrest.

FBI Special Agent Stephen Ramey was waxing the kitchen floor in his northern Virginia home when his call came. Still wearing a white knit shirt and jeans, Ramey drove to a rendezvous point, where he and other agents got into a set of unmarked cars with random Virginia license plates. In the car trunks were similar, nonofficial tags for Washington and Maryland.

Nearly all of the more than forty Windflyer agents were stationed within a twenty-five-mile radius marked from the "zero milestone" located on the Ellipse, just south of the White House. Under the gentlemanly rules of espionage, KGB officers scrupulously obeyed the travel rule rather than be found in an illegal area and get PNG'd on a technicality.

An FBI airplane went aloft to keep Walker's van under surveillance as it headed north on I-95. A variety of unmarked cars trailed Walker and sometimes even pulled alongside him. The FBI's Windflyer strategists expected Walker to rendezvous with the Soviets in a Virginia suburb. As he approached Washington on I-95, Walker turned onto the Washington Beltway, going west onto I-495. But instead of taking an exit in Virginia, he continued on the Beltway and crossed the Potomac River on the American Legion Bridge into Maryland. He left the Beltway at the River Road exit. (FBI cars would later converge behind a shopping center in Potomac, Maryland, where Virginia license plates were quickly removed and replaced with Maryland plates.)

As soon as Walker entered Maryland he began following a series of minutely detailed instructions given to him by his KGB handlers. Most of the instructions, which were accompanied by black-and-white photographs, were carefully printed in one hand; a kind of postscript appears to have been in another hand. Some instructions were written in red, others in blue. Szady, a veteran FBI counter-espionage agent, later called the instructions "the most complicated and exact operational directions that I've ever seen."

The delicate art of the dead drop involves the transfer of extremely sensitive and dangerous information from one party to another. Neither party can risk meeting the other, but the procedure must be utterly reliable and undetectable. The Walker drops were designed by a master so concerned about protecting Walker's delivery that drop arrangements, which usually cover a few miles, for Walker's last drop encompassed more than sixty miles of suburban Maryland roads—a record, to FBI knowledge. The written instructions of the drop clearly showed that the KGB dead-drop architect had been well trained.

The redundancy, the use of neat block printing, and the use of cut-out maps were all KGB touches that U.S. experts on espionage tradecraft had seen many times. But Walker's instructions were in color and original, a rare occurrence in such documents. Usually they are reproduced so as to take them one step from the original, making them that much less informative to counterespionage officers who may obtain them and seek answers about the masters who created them. A photocopy, for example, does not reveal fingerprints or indentations left by erasures in the original paper. The block printing represents a more typical piece of tradecraft. It is nearly impossible to trace a person's normal handwriting from block printing.

The paper itself, 25 percent cotton watermarked Gilbert bond, was made in the United States. Some U.S. counter-espionage officials believe that the instructions may have been written by an American in Moscow and then sent by diplomatic pouch to the Soviet Embassy in Washington, where a local KGB officer added his words. Other officials say that an American wrote them in America.

The instructions begin:

FOR OUR NEXT EXCHANGE, WE'LL USE THE FOLLOWING SITES IN MONTGOMERY COUNTY, MARYLAND:

TO SIGNAL THAT I AM READY TO EXCHANGE I'LL DROP MY INITIAL CAN OF THE USUAL KIND AT A UTILITY POLE ON WATTS BRANCH DR NEAR ITS INTERSECTION WITH CIRCLE DR AND RIDGE DR.

THE UTILITY POLE IN QUESTION IS THE SECOND ONE TO THE EAST OF THE INTERSECTION (THE FIRST UTILITY POLE IS LOCATED RIGHT AT THE INTERSECT OF WATTS BRANCH DR AND CIRCLE DR).

MY SIGNAL SITE WILL BE ON YOUR RIGHT WHEN YOU DRIVE

ON WATTS BRANCH DR FROM CIRCLE DR TOWARD VALLEY
DR.
I'LL DROP MY SIGNAL ON THE ROAD SHOULDER A FOOT OR
TWO FROM THE SURFACE OF THE ROAD.

On a hand-drawn map, the anonymous giver of directions
had written *I start here.* The next instruction—*check my signal
after* is followed by a rectangular box; it looks as if *8:00 P.M.* was
written in the box by another hand. The initial signal, which
espionage experts call the "ready-for-action signal," was a 7-Up
can.

On his Sunday afternoon drive through the Montgomery
County countryside, Walker was not making a drop; he was re-
connoitering, getting the feel of the winding country roads in late
afternoon in preparation for the real run under the cover of darkness. This was the dry run, taken while it was still light so that he
could see his two sites—the one where he would drop off his
package of secrets and the one where he would pick up the packet
of cash left by his Soviet controllers.

When Walker began the circuitous drive his FBI shadowers
were certain that he was embarked on a classic dead-drop operation. Now both watchers and watched entered a labyrinth of surveillance, counter-surveillance, and counter-counter-surveillance.
Walker would follow a route laid out with long straightaways and
tight turns so that he could easily spot a car that was trailing him.

The FBI would keep track of Walker not by following him
but by coordinating the spotter plane's observations with about
twenty cars stationed at places—such as gas stations and rural
driveways—where, hopefully, Walker would not notice them
watching him go by. And somewhere in the labyrinth would be
the KGB officer in his car, doing his surveillance of any possible
surveillance of Walker. The elaborate instructions Walker carried
were designed so that he and the KGB handler would be able to
detect each other's presence without meeting.

TO SIGNAL THAT YOU ARE AVAILABLE FOR OUR EXCHANGE
DROP YOUR INITIAL CAN OF THE USUAL KIND AT THE BOT-
TOM OF A UTILITY POLE ON QUINCE ORCHARD RD AT ITS
INTERSECTION WITH DUFIEF MILL RD.
THE UTILITY POLE IN QUESTION WILL BE ON YOUR LEFT

WHEN YOU DRIVE ON QUINCE ORCHARD RD FROM DUFIEF
MILL RD TOWARD DARNESTOWN RD. IT IS THE FIRST UTILITY
POLE FROM THE INTERSECTION ON THAT SIDE OF QUINCE
ORCHARD RD.
I'LL CHECK YOUR SIGNAL AFTER 8:30 P.M.

By late in the afternoon the FBI plane that had trailed the
van out of Norfolk was running low on fuel and had to land. A
second plane took over the surveillance a little after 4 p.m. The
plane flew obliquely over the site; if Walker happened to look up,
he would see a plane far off to his left or right, never directly
overhead. But the KGB route designer, probably anticipating ae-
rial surveillance, had included stretches of road crowned by
thickly foliaged tree branches. The designer seemed to have a
special interest in trees as markers for drops.

I'LL DROP MY DELIVERY BEHIND TWO TREES ACCRETED AT
THE BOTTOM ON OLD BUCKLODGE LA AT ITS INTERSECTION
WITH WHITE GROUND RD.
THE TWO TREES ARE . . . ABOUT 8–12 YARDS FROM THE
INTERSECTION AND ABOUT 2–3 FEET FROM THE SURFACE OF
THE ROAD. . . .

If Walker was as arboreally illiterate as others who have
since read the instructions, he would have had to look up *accreted* to find out it means "to grow together." Investigators who
have studied the instructions sometimes picture the conscientious
KGB route designer going to a forestry reference book for the
precise word. Investigators who question the American-author
theory say that an American writer would have simply written
"two trees connected at the trunk."

But those who believe an American wrote the instructions
point out that a Russian driving a car with diplomatic plates
would be far more conspicuous on country roads than an American. Someone had spent a great deal of time prowling those roads
and taking the fourteen photographs given with the instructions.
It was the kind of a compartmentalized task that might be given
an illegal agent who would never know anything about the serving of the dead drop.

About the time that Walker's van turned down a tree-

bowered road, the spotter plane lost its quarry. Fearing an interception of his radio transmissions, the pilot landed and phoned
the Windflyer command center at the Washington field office.
Walker was lost for about three hours. "I remember every minute
of it," Szady said later.

The command post did not send out a query to the surveillance cars scattered around the area because, like the FBI pilot,
the command post distrusted the radio. The FBI had reason to be
careful of its radio traffic. The Soviet Embassy is believed to routinely monitor FBI communications, even though operational
messages are terse and go through voice scramblers. The Soviets
may not be able to read the messages, but they can pick up the
"squelch breaks" when an agent turns a microphone on or off. A
surge in the number and intensity of the breaks would tip off
Soviet listeners to a concentration of agents coincidental to the
serving of a dead drop. The KGB handlers would then play it
safe by calling off the drop.

The plane took off again and, at 3,500 feet, flew parallel to
various roads in a search pattern. On the ground, FBI cars cautiously looked for the lost van. At 7:48 the pilot spotted the van
and took the chance of notifying his partners below. According
to plan, if the pilot saw the van stop, he would order all FBI cars
to stop and would then order the safest arrangement of trailing
cars. Some would follow him; some would take up a parallel trail;
some would stay parked.

Steve Ramey, the agent who had been waxing the kitchen
floor that morning, was in a car three quarters of a mile behind
Walker's van on White Ground Road. The van stopped and then
turned down Old Bucklodge Lane, site of the accreted tree, where
the KGB servicing officer would make his drop off—cash and
further instructions. The FBI car passed the intersection, continued on White Ground for another three quarters of a mile, turned
around, and parked, its engine running.

Then from the surveillance plane came the report that
Walker had left the intersection and was retracing his route. "We
pulled in and parked where he had parked," Ramey recalled.
"We got out with a hand-held radio and a searchlight, a sealed-
beam light, and searched around this tree, that tree, poking at
debris, picking up cans, still thinking that this was Walker's

pickup point, but not knowing for sure. It might have been his put-down point."

Ramey and most of the other counter-espionage agents well knew the fringe of the twenty-five-mile zone from other stakeouts and other arrests. (Lieutenant Colonel Yevgeny Barmyantsev had been caught at a rural Maryland drop site in 1983; Colonel Vladimir Makarovich Ismaylov would be arrested at another one in June 1986.) The agents also knew the crucial steps in the choreography of a dead drop.

One: The KGB officer puts down the ready-for-action signal. (This time it was a soda can; it could be a chalk mark on a utility pole or orange peels or any one of several other signals.) *Two:* The agent signals that he is ready (another can on the road). *Three:* The KGB officer drives past that signal, sees it, and proceeds to the pickup point, where he leaves the money and the message. *Four:* The agent drives to his put-down point and makes his delivery. *Five:* The agent goes to the pickup point, collects the KGB officer's delivery, and, at a designated site, drops a can to signal that he has collected. He then drives out of the area. *Six:* The KGB officer, seeing the final okay signal, goes to the put-down point, picks up the agent's delivery, and drives off by another route.

The steps are choreographed so that the KGB officer—sometimes called "control"—and the agent do not cross over each other's paths. A control, especially a known KGB legal, has to assume that he is not "clean," that he may be under surveillance from the time he left the embassy or his home. He does not want to "drag" his possible trail across the path of his agent. He watches for signs of surveillance in the area. He assumes that his agent is "black"—secret and unknown.

Ramey and his partner did not know whether Walker was delivering or picking up. Nor, in the darkness, did they know that they risked one of the hazards of a rural dead drop—poison ivy.

"We're looking around the area, searching through weeds and stuff on the ground," Ramey continued. "The aircraft said, 'He's coming back again.' So at this time I said, 'Joe, you leave the area. I'll stay in the woods.' "

Ramey got behind one of the small trees a few yards from the road and drew his service revolver. Walker was believed to be armed. "He came back again," Ramey recounted. "He parked his car at the same spot, turned on the parking lights, got out of the car with a flashlight." Ramey could see that Walker was reading instructions, looking up at a road sign, and returning again and again to a certain tree, one that Ramey thought was unusual because it had a double trunk. Walker was only a couple of feet from Ramey at this point.

"Then he gets back in his car and leaves the area again. At this time another agent drives up." The second agent and Ramey start searching both sides of the road. "Although we were certain it was that tree, something could have gotten screwed up in the agent's instructions. Or the Soviets may have gotten mixed up. Or he may have gotten mixed up.

"Again we heard over the radio that he was coming back." The other car got out of the area. Ramey and a second agent, guns drawn, hid behind trees while Walker once more searched around the double-trunk tree, looking for something, acting as if something might have gone wrong.

Something had gone wrong, but the only person on earth who knew it for certain was Aleksey Gavrilovich Tkachenko, vice consul of the Soviet Embassy. Tkachenko was driving a blue 1983 Chevrolet Malibu with the distinctive red-white-and-blue diplomatic license plate DSX-144.* In the car with him was a woman and a child. FBI agents who spotted his car at 8:20 on Dufief Mill Road noted the classic use of innocent-looking passengers to disguise a dead-drop mission. But what they did not realize was that Tkachenko, knowing that all was not well, was extricating himself from the mission and leaving Walker on his own.

Tkachenko, like Walker, had been following the strict, detailed instructions. "To signal that you are available for our exchange," Walker's instructions had begun, "Drop your initial can of the usual kind at the bottom of a utility pole on Quince Orchard Rd at its intersection with Dufief Mill Rd." There was

---

* D means diplomat and SX signified the Soviet Union. The SX became so notorious that in 1986, at the request of the Soviet Embassy, the State Department switched the designation on about two hundred Soviet cars in the United States to FC.

no 7-Up can, signaling "ready for action," at the pole when Tkachenko drove by—because an FBI agent had removed it.

According to the official story, "FBI agents searched the area on the left-hand side of Quince Orchard Road where John Walker had been. There they found a 7-Up can, which they seized." What actually happened, according to another FBI version, was this: Agents in one surveillance car had seen Walker stop on Quince Orchard Road, get out of his van, and then get back in. When he got out of sight the agents spotted a 7-Up can at the side of the road. Using care not to touch it with bare fingers, they examined the can, found that it was empty, and, believing that it was a signal, put it back on the side of the road. Over the radio one FBI agent remarked not to forget to pick up the can . . . before the operation was over. Agents in a second car behind them misunderstood the message, stopped, and picked up the can. As a result, Tkachenko, never having gotten the signal to leave the money and additional instructions, drove back to Washington.

As Tkachenko was driving out of the area Walker was frantically searching around the accreted tree for the package of cash and instructions Tkachenko was supposed to have dropped. At the time Walker was searching, his own delivery—in a large brown grocery bag—had been taken by the FBI from where the instructions had directed him to leave it: behind a utility pole "at a huge tree" at an intersection on Partnership Road.

Minutes after Walker had left his put-down site, FBI agents grabbed the bag and made a quick search. It contained a Diet Coke bottle, a bottle of rubbing alcohol, a box of Q-tips, and a Jergens soap wrapper. The bottles had been washed. The trash, following standard tradecraft, was scrupulously clean; there was nothing that might drip, stain, or smell to attract a curious raccoon or other local animals. Beneath the trash was a package nine inches wide by eleven inches long, and an inch thick, wrapped in a clean white plastic trash bag, sealed with masking tape.

Two agents hid in the woods where the bag was found while other agents rushed the neatly wrapped package to Washington. Twice Walker came back to his drop, obviously trying to puzzle out what had happened: If Tkachenko had found and taken the bag, why had he not left his package?

In Washington, Walker's package was examined at FBI headquarters, not the command center, where Szady awaited orders about what to do with Walker. The package contained a stack of 129 confidential and secret documents from the carrier *Nimitz* and a plastic sandwich bag that enwrapped three letters— two "Dear Johnnie"* and one "Dear Friend." There were also some films and a piece of paper listing *D-Jerry, K-Art, S-Mike, F-Gary,* a note that began, "This delivery consists of material from 'S' and is similar to the previously supplied material."

While the bag was being examined high Justice Department officials conferred with the FBI agents supervising Windflyer. In the U.S.-Soviet espionage war, as in a real war, there are strategic and tactical levels. For Windflyer, John Dion, head of the espionage unit in the Internal Security Division of the Department of Justice, represented the Reagan Administration at the strategic level; the FBI troops, led by Szady at the tactical level, awaited tactical orders.

In a typical dead-drop engagement the strategy would call for apprehending the Soviet pickup officer at the site. Tactically, this had certainly been possible in this case, for the FBI had established extensive, apparently undetected coverage of the site. But the removal of the ready-for-action 7-Up can had sent Tkachenko out of the area. So the get-the-Soviet tactical move had been eliminated by the FBI itself. Because of the FBI's control of the area, it might also have been possible to get the bag back to the site from FBI headquarters, replace it at the site, keep up the stakeout, and watch for developments. This was not done either.

At 11:30 p.m., two and a half hours after Tkachenko had been seen leaving the area, the word came from Dion: Arrest Walker.

Tactical matters were left to the command post. Again there was a delay, inspired probably by a policeman's instinct to make a surprise arrest in the predawn hours when sleep and fatigue are likely to slow down an armed suspect's reactions.

At 12:14 a.m. on Monday, May 20, Walker was tailed to the Ramada Inn in Rockville, Maryland, a few miles from the drop site. Investigators later said that, during the three or so hours

* Later determined to be Whitworth.

that Walker had been lost to FBI surveillance on Sunday, he had registered at the motel under the name John Johnson, giving a false Portsmouth, Virginia, address.

At 3:30 a.m., FBI agent William Wang, claiming to be the motel night clerk, called Walker's room and said that someone had driven into his van, damaging it considerably. Wang asked Walker to come to the front desk and get the other driver's identification. A few minutes later Walker took a step out of Room 763, looked around, and returned to his room.

Down the hall, in the FBI's hastily rented Room 750, it was decided that the arrest of Walker would be made by James Kolouch (one of the agents who had spotted Tkachenko) and Robert W. Hunter of Norfolk, the FBI case agent responsible for coordinating and directing the investigation. Weapons drawn, they took up positions near the bank of elevators. Kolouch, a firearms instructor, was famous for his shooting scores on the FBI firing range.

"We waited what seemed like a long period of time," Hunter later recounted. "It was quite exciting at that point. And a few minutes later, in fact approximately 3:45 a.m., his door opened again, and I heard footsteps, and he quickly came around the corner and punched the elevator with his left hand.

"As he punched the elevator button, Agent Kolouch and I came out of our hiding spot in the hallway, and he heard us as we moved. And he immediately turned . . . a weapon in his hand. So we were standing there, face-to-face, eyeball-to-eyeball, so to speak, with our weapons on each other."

For a moment Hunter thought of pulling the trigger. But "I didn't want to kill him. I wanted to talk to him. I needed to talk to this fellow. That's why I didn't pull the trigger.

"We then said, 'FBI. Drop your gun.' . . . And there was a confrontation that lasted a few seconds. It seemed like a long time, but it was a few seconds, and he did finally drop the weapon. Then we braced him against the wall, and I covered him with my weapon as Agent Kolouch searched him."

When Walker turned and pointed his .38 Special at the agents, a five-by-eight manila envelope slipped from under his arm and fell to the carpeted floor. The envelope contained the maps, photographs, and detailed instructions to the drop site. Walker was read his rights and he signed a document acknowledging this. He was driven to Baltimore, where he was booked. In frisking him at the motel, agents had taken his toupee. When his arrest photo was taken Walker objected because it showed him without his toupee.

Other agents, meanwhile, obtained a warrant to search Room 763. They got the warrant and turned up Walker's private investigator's badge, a compass, a magnifying glass, a leg holster for a .38, and several other items, including the June 1985 issue of *Penthouse.* Another swiftly obtained warrant approved a search of Walker's Norfolk home. Some twenty-five agents divided the house into zones and methodically sifted through what turned out to be incriminating evidence of espionage and an amazingly complete paper trail of Walker's career as a spy.

One of the searchers, an FBI specialist on tradecraft, found classified documents, including a naval warfare publication entitled "Threat Intelligence Summary, Naval Air Forces" and a satellite communications manual. (Whitworth's fingerprints were later lifted from the manual, which had come from his stint at satellite school.) Agents also found the Soviet-built rotor used to read the logic of the KL-47 cryptographic machine.

The paper trail included travel records and planning calendars. The 1985 calendar had a notation for his next face-to-face meeting on September 21. (Instead of Vienna, the meeting would be in Czechoslovakia because Walker had complained about always meeting outdoors in Vienna, especially during the winter.) There were also travel documents, such as a receipt from the Hotel Intercontinental in Vienna in 1978, records of travel to the Philippines in 1978, and to Vienna in 1979, 1980, February 1984, and January 1985.

Two letters from Michael Walker to "Jaws" were also found. In one Michael said he had been named "Sailor of the Month." "If they only knew how much I hate this carrier," he wrote. "I have been taking a few shots here and there. I have a lot of miscellaneous bullshit, I am just a little worried about the quantity. Storing it is becoming a problem. I will look for other methods." In the other letter Michael again referred to storage problems. "At the rate I am going," he wrote, "I will have over a hundred pounds of sovenirs *[sic]*. I have run out of space. . . . Currently, I have two boxes that weigh about fifteen pounds a piece *[sic]*."

In a wicker basket in Walker's living room agents found a gun cane, a sword cane, and a cane that had secret vials in it. Other weapons included two standard shotguns, an automatic rifle, a .357 magnum, and a sawed-off shotgun. Another find was a page out of the December 1982 issue of *Soldier of Fortune* magazine with an advertisement for an espionage course and a special seminar on espionage that was taught by "professionals."

The FBI's richly detailed account of Walker's arrest and house search is in the J. Edgar Hoover tradition of spreading—while tightly controlling—the news of victory. The tradition can be traced all the way back to the manhunt for gangster John Dillinger, who was shot to death by FBI agents as, reaching for his gun, he ran from the Biograph movie theater in Chicago on July 21, 1934.

In 1987 a portrayal of the Dillinger triumph was still being proudly shown on the visitors' tour of the J. Edgar Hoover FBI Building, one of tourist Washington's most popular attractions. What is not remembered are two earlier, bungled attempts to capture Dillinger, including one in which an innocent citizen and an FBI agent were shot to death. The Walker case, in many ways, is the Dillinger case of the 1980s.

The FBI caught Dillinger at the Biograph because of a tip from the keeper of an East Chicago brothel. But Hoover, through his masterly use of publicity, transformed the mundane tip into a legend of dogged FBI scientific sleuthing. Hoover personally helped produce a radio dramatization of the Dillinger manhunt. In the radio version, a Hoover biographer wrote, the gangster is caught "the way he should have been caught: by an inexorable, step-by-step application of FBI science and organization."

Similarly, Hoover manufactured his own World War II spy tale about Dusko Popov, the British double agent code-named "Tricycle." After the war, Hoover, in a *Reader's Digest* article under his name, twisted the facts about Popov without naming him. Hoover wrote of how he had obtained the secret of the microdot through the capture of "a spy" operating in the United States under cover as "a Balkan playboy." In fact, Tricycle was not "captured." He later returned to London and continued to work as a double agent until D day.

Coincidentally, a *Reader's Digest* editor, John D. Barron,

played an important role in the FBI effort to publicize the official story about John Walker. Barron,* a former Navy intelligence officer and an expert on the KGB, testified on his expertise at both of the trials of the FBI's Richard Miller, at the trial of Jerry Whitworth, and at the Marine court martial of Clayton Lonetree, who said he had read Barron's books to learn about the KGB. Barron was so much a part of the prosecution team at the Whitworth trial that Assistant U.S. Attorney William Farmer asked that Barron be allowed to sit with the team during the trial. The judge turned down the request.

FBI officials say that the Department of Justice uses Barron as an expert witness because, as a writer not connected with the bureau, he does not have to worry about whether he will inadvertently divulge a secret while on the stand. "When an agent with clearances testifies," an FBI official told the authors, "he has to be very careful about his words. Under cross-examination he may seem hesitant and uncertain. And he might not look like a good witness to a juror."

As portrayed by what he calls "my associates in Washington," Barron is just a writer who happens to have friends in the bureau and in the CIA. But, testifying under oath in the Whitworth trial, Barron admitted that he did hold a security clearance. He implied that the clearance gives him access to satellite photography. For, while testifying about the selling of a CIA satellite manual to the Soviets, he said that overhead photography is so sensitive "that we can see the color of a man's beard," a detail not generally known—if, in fact, true. Satellite photographs are almost invariably in black and white, and according to a retired CIA officer familiar with satellite imagery, "We'd be lucky to count people, let alone tell whether they had beards."

Barron testified that he did not receive any compensation for his services to the FBI. But he does get a great deal of help that translates into commercial successes for his books and articles.

From such intimate connections, Barron, in his book on the Walker case, *Breaking the Ring,* laid out the official story, which stands as the definitive account of the FBI's capture of Walker

* Author of *KGB, the Secret Work of Soviet Secret Agents* (1974) and *KGB Today, the Hidden Hand* (1983), both were published by Reader's Digest Press.

and the other members of his ring. Like the radio saga about Dillinger, the official Walker story was constructed out of selective facts. Yet, skillful and trusted as he was, even Barron could not turn the FBI's handling of the Walker spy ring into a model operation.

The process can be seen in several espionage cases. The FBI has released numerous details about the spying of James Harper, a case in which the bureau certainly looked good. Similarly, at the trial of NSA spy Ronald Pelton, a great deal of information about tapping and psychological questioning came through the testimony of FBI agents, unaided by Barron. As in the Walker case, the bureau focused its release of information on the *arrest*. In contrast there has never been an officially publicized account of the arrest of FBI betrayer Miller. Much of what did get revealed about him and his Soviet lover came through the efforts of defense attorneys during his two trials.

In the Walker case the weakest links in the chain of events are the activities leading up to and following his arrest. This is obviously the reason why FBI-supplied details accentuate the dramatic, well-choreographed arrest. What the official story does not reveal is:

■ The FBI stumbled over a Navy investigation that centered on Whitworth.

■ Walker apparently had long been under suspicion by the Navy and may have been fed false information to pass to the Soviets.

■ After the FBI knew of Walker's betrayal, he left the country for a scheduled meeting with his KGB handlers.

■ While Walker was overseas the KGB could have warned him that he was under suspicion and could have taken him in from the cold. The KGB decided to drop Walker, dooming him to inevitable arrest.

■ The KGB was more instrumental than the FBI in the ending of Walker's long career.

In the autumn of 1984, from FBI Director William Webster's point of view, the FBI was facing hard times. FBI Counterespionage Agent Richard Miller had been arrested. The cocaine-scam case against John DeLorean had ended in a highly publicized not-guilty verdict. Webster and the FBI needed a triumph to demonstrate to FBI friends and critics in Congress and in the White House that the bureau had lost none of the zing of Hoover's G-men era, whose glory days were still on display in the busy Visitor's Center in the J. Edgar Hoover FBI Building.

Stagecraft has often been an important element of FBI counter-espionage work. When the FBI wants to impress the Soviets and give an example to would-be spies, it sets up a scam, captures the "legal" Soviet officer operating under diplomatic cover, and turns a publicity spotlight on the arrest. The result is that the Soviets learn a lesson and presumably rein in overly zealous intelligence officers. A secondary result is that Congress and the American people see their FBI in action. A well-publicized espionage arrest is good for everybody. And in the fall of 1984 the FBI could certainly use an espionage arrest.

According to the official story, on November 17, 1984, Barbara Walker, who had been divorced from John Walker since 1976 and was living in West Dennis, Massachusetts, called the FBI field office in Boston and told an agent that her ex-husband, a retired Navy warrant officer, was a Soviet spy. A couple of days later—this date is unrecorded in the official story—she called an FBI office in Hyannis Port, a bureaucratic relic of the days when President Kennedy frequently spent time at the family complex there. Twelve days after the first call, Barbara Walker for the first time had a face-to-face meeting with an FBI agent and told her story once more: John Walker, who now lived in Norfolk and had been a cryptographic specialist in the Navy, had been spying for the Soviet for many years. He was probably still spying.

At this point one might expect that the official story would recount how the FBI launched its investigation into what would become one of the most important espionage cases in modern American history. But, curiously, the story concedes that the FBI did nothing. According to the official story, the tip from Barbara Walker was dumped into what was known as a "zero" file. Nor was any immediate action taken as a result of the face-to-face interview.

As the official story takes up the chronology of the case, the next event involves Walker's married daughter, Laura Walker Snyder, who had been approached by her father as a prospective spy. Laura was one of many people who knew that John Walker had been a spy for a long time. The FBI says that Laura called

the Boston field office on January 24, 1985, and inquired about
her mother's repeated and presumably futile attempts to turn in
her former husband as a spy. Once more, according to the official
story, a Walker spy tip was ignored.

Now the official story must be interrupted for three observations:

■   Such studied disregard of espionage tips is totally contrary to
FBI regulations and traditions. Witness, for example, the way the
first anonymous RUS letter was instantly taken to a senior
counter-espionage agent.

■   Walker and Whitworth, in separate instances, were almost
certainly subjects of operations being conducted by the Naval
Investigative Service. This information was given to the authors
by high-level Navy sources.

■   Spies are not always arrested. As welcome as such an arrest
would have been to the FBI in the fall of 1984, Walker was not
arrested and, in fact, during the remainder of 1984 no official
Walker case was even opened.

The apparent apathy of the FBI can be taken as just that. Or
one can call to mind what master spy chief Allen Dulles, Director of Central Intelligence from 1953 to 1962, once wrote:
"Often, even after a spy has been identified, no arrest may take
place because it may be more valuable to watch the spy operate,
to let him lead to other spies and to his employers, than simply to
put him out of business." That philosophy may well have had
relevance in the long, twisting tale of the detection, double cross,
and breaking of the Walker spy ring.

The authors have been cautiously told that by the fall of
1984, Navy investigators had developed a case against Whitworth. That was on one track. On another track, Walker may
also have been under investigation. There are strong indications
that a federal agency was aware of Walker's espionage and was
feeding disinformation to the Soviets through him. The authors
were given this disclosure about Walker soon after the arrest of
the members of the Walker spy ring. The authors were told that
any further information on these events prior to Walker's arrest
would have to wait until his trial.

Walker was never brought to trial, and so the "further information" never came forth. But indications of a long, secret investigation of Walker did come—from a surprising source. Vitaly

Yurchenko, the senior KGB officer who defected to the United States two months after Walker's arrest, had told his CIA debriefers that the KGB did not believe that Walker had been caught as a result of Barbara Walker's tip. The KGB suspected that one of its officers assigned to Walker had been turned by a Western intelligence agency and, while being operated as a double agent, revealed the existence of the Walker ring. (Yurchenko redefected to the Soviet Union in November 1985.)

Back to the official Walker story: In February 1985, as a result of routine supervisory examination of the FBI zero files, the reports about Walker finally surfaced. The FBI counter-espionage apparatus in FBI offices in Washington, Boston, and Norfolk began swinging into action. On March 7 and 8 agents interviewed Laura; on March 19 agents talked to Barbara. On March 25 the FBI convinced Laura to call her father and, with her permission, listened in to the call, during which he asked her about the possibility of her going to work for the CIA. On April 11 the FBI began its court-authorized tapping of Walker's phones. And this led, the following month, to the dramatic arrest of John Walker and the subsequent arrests of Michael and Arthur Walker, and of Jerry Whitworth.

According to the official story there was a delay in the arrest of Whitworth because, for a time, the FBI was trying to find someone named "Wentworth." The FBI had the wrong name, according to the official story, because Barbara and Laura Walker were only able to give the FBI a "phonetic" version of the name of a longtime friend of John Walker who lived in California. Contrary to this official story, Barbara knew Jerry Whitworth quite well and had spent time with him alone, as she would later testify at his trial. And Laura, as she would testify, had known Whitworth well enough to have received a loan from him—and she certainly knew his name, because it appeared on the check.

The search for "Wentworth" is one of many oddities that pop up in the official story. One possible explanation is that by not pressing Laura and Barbara to identify Walker's California friend and by thus dawdling in their arrest of Whitworth, the FBI was giving Whitworth—and perhaps Laura and Barbara—a chance to make moves that would lead authorities to other members of the ring.

Three counter-intelligence officials, all of them familiar with details of the Walker-Whitworth spy ring, have told the authors that they are convinced that not all the members of the ring have been arrested. For an understanding of this belief it is necessary to leave the official story and venture into the John Walker mystery story.

The mystery story began late in 1981, when Jerry Whitworth was transferred from the Naval Telecommunications Center at the Naval Air Station in Alameda, California, for temporary duty at the Naval Communications Station at Stockton. There is reason to believe that Whitworth was sent to Stockton for three months to keep him on the shelf while an investigation established the probability of his espionage and decisions were being made whether to close in on him or leave him in place and feed him disinformation material.

One theory of the probable chain of events is that Whitworth was first suspected of espionage activities by one or more Navy radiomen who wondered about Whitworth's lavish lifestyle and why he so regularly spent his lunch hours "napping" in his $10,000 silver van on the parking lot of the communications station at Alameda. Day after day co-workers observed Whitworth, who usually was carrying his attaché case, entering the van, which was parked about sixty feet from his office. Several of the Navy enlisted men and women who worked with Whitworth remembered the naps in the van with the closed curtains. A chief radioman at Alameda recalled that "quite regularly" Whitworth would head for the van with his attaché case and say, "I'm going to go take a nap. If you need me, I'll be there."

Any suspicions about Whitworth would go through Navy rather than FBI channels. A report from a suspicious sailor would move up the Navy chain of command, which ultimately would lead to the Naval Investigative Service. Because of jurisdictional agreements between the Navy and FBI bureaucracies, the solving of crimes in the Navy—including the crime of espionage—is the task of the Naval Investigative Service, a component of Naval Intelligence. NIS usually handles low-level crimes, such as burglaries on Navy ships or the theft of money from Navy commissary cash registers. NIS is not equipped to find sailors who steal the nation's secret codes. Nor do NIS officials usually find themselves making sensitive counter-espionage decisions—

such as the running of double agents and the handing out of disinformation.

Counter-espionage at that level of sophistication is the responsibility of the Department of Justice, which keeps watch over all counter-espionage investigations through the FBI. But the FBI is not equipped to ferret out spies on the high seas. So there is an unwritten bureaucratic pact that allots the investigation of suspected military spies to each armed service's own investigators. (That is why it was NIS agents, not FBI agents, that investigated charges of espionage by Marine guards assigned to the American Embassy in Moscow.)

Some Navy officials were highly concerned over the Soviets' acquisition of sensitive crypto gear in the *Pueblo* in 1968 and the loss of a considerable amount of equipment in Vietnam in the early 1970s.* Soon after the failure of the Iran rescue mission in 1980, suspicion sharpened that Navy communications were being regularly compromised. A Navy admiral who had specialized communications knowledge told the authors that confirmation came when the National Security Agency informed the Navy that the Soviets were decoding secret and top-secret Navy messages. And trickling into Naval Intelligence from several sources were reports that the Soviets knew too much about U.S. Navy ship movements—especially submarine deployments and fleet exercises.

For a long time intelligence officers had known that servicemen, especially those with knowledge about communications and cryptographic equipment, were aware that the Soviets were trolling for information—and paying well. "Those sailors didn't hear that from some guy with a Russian accent," a naval intelligence analyst said about those rumors. "They heard it from one of their own, someone who could talk their language."

The analyst pointed to what Nevil Shute had written about a group of naval and air officers gathered in a pub during World War II: "When old friends in the service meet for a short drink and a meal, not all of the posters in the world will stop a few

---

* The Navy had a contractor conduct an extensive analysis of the equipment lost in Vietnam under the code name "Cluster Neptune." No copies of the classified report could be located by the Navy in response to requests by the authors.

discreet exchanges on the subject of their work. Leaning upon the bar, they say these things in low tones to each other, so low that nobody can hear except the barmaid at their elbow." Then as now, the conversation is addressed innocently to colleagues in arms who wear the same uniform and same insignia.

NIS investigators would have seen Whitworth as a target for one of those recruiters. Initially an investigation of Whitworth, from the parochial viewpoint of NIS, would have been a Navy matter. Had espionage been suspected in such civilian agencies as the CIA, NSA, or the National Security Council, the full counter-espionage forces of the nation would have been marshaled to track down that most dangerous of spies, the mole. But espionage in the Navy is seen as a Navy problem, far from the civilian agency charged with prosecuting espionage, the Department of Justice, and the Justice branch charged with finding spies, the FBI. Moles on the high seas are a new species, and they are beyond the reach of the FBI.

The authors believe that NIS managed to get Whitworth transferred temporarily to Stockton to make it easier to conduct an investigation at Alameda in his absence. By our theory, around this time a decision was made to keep watch on Whitworth, who was still under Navy jurisdiction, and to pass on suspicions about Walker to the proper civilian authorities, the FBI.

At this point the smoothly running Walker-Whitworth espionage machine begins to break down. During a February 1982 rendezvous in Vienna, Walker's KGB handler found fault with him because of a drop in the quality of the material Walker is supplying. In a while, Walker, showing signs that he desperately needed a new source of secrets, would again try to talk Laura into rejoining the Army and becoming a spy.

Walker had what he later called "minor suspicions" about Whitworth back at the time of his assignment in Stockton, when the cryptographic material dried up. But in October 1982, Walker believed that his luck had changed, for that was when Whitworth, who had been back in Alameda for several months, was flown out to his next assignment, the carrier *Enterprise*. Walker anticipated that Whitworth would be on the carrier for three years and that his cryptographic deliveries would dramatically improve.

On December 5, 1982, Whitworth sent Walker a letter from the *Enterprise* forecasting, as a chief radioman so easily could, the carrier's scheduled movements between January and March 1983. If Whitworth had been under surveillance while on board the *Enterprise,* a record would have been made of the addressees of his letters, which may even have been opened and read by investigators. What did and did not happen when Whitworth was on the carrier is one of the keys to the mystery. There are indications that he was under suspicion and under observation during his tour on the *Enterprise.*

In the spring of 1983, while Chief Radioman Whitworth was aboard, the *Enterprise* also carried the commander of a fleet exercise known as FLTEX 83-1, an extremely important northern Pacific war game involving three carrier battle groups. During FLTEX 83-1, which took the warships relatively near to the Soviet coast, Naval intelligence analysts noticed that Soviet electronic eavesdropping ships were not monitoring the exercise as closely and heavily as they had in the past. That did not make a great deal of sense. A three-carrier exercise is rare, not only because it is so expensive but also because such an exercise plays out tactical plans in the presence of the eyes and ears of the Soviet intelligence ships.

"The most surprising and disappointing aspects of the exercise was a lower expected Soviet reaction," said a report on the exercise. Naval Intelligence developed a theory: The Soviets were getting so much information on the exercise through espionage that they did not need to monitor it closely. Thus the Soviets' own actions helped to indicate the existence of a mole in the Navy. The report does not mention where the mole may have been stationed during FLTEX 83-1.

In June 1983, Walker flew to California to pick up what he expected to be a good crypto delivery from the *Enterprise* after a long dry spell. But Whitworth told Walker that the "cryptographic was somewhat of a disappointment" and "sketchy at best." About all Whitworth could deliver was "a year's worth" of messages that he had photographed with his new Minox. Whitworth also said that he had cached some other messages that he had not yet photographed. Old messages were of far less importance to the Soviets than a steady stream of keylists, as both men

knew. This drop in the quality of Whitworth's delivery is one of
the indications that he was being controlled without his knowledge.

A week after meeting with Whitworth, Walker made a delivery of the film at a standard Washington-area dead drop. Soon
afterward he virtually summoned Whitworth to Norfolk and told
him to bring the *Enterprise* messages that he had not photographed. The carrier was still docked at Alameda. Late in July,
Whitworth flew to Norfolk—after, incredibly, telling a fellow
chief radioman on the carrier where he was going for the weekend. For a Navy chief such a transcontinental weekend round
trip was extraordinary. And it was well remembered.

When Whitworth arrived in Norfolk he did not have the
messages. By way of explanation he told a story of mislaid secrets
mixed with his household goods. He was moving to Davis, California, as part of his looming retirement from the Navy. At this
point Walker had to know that something was wrong, but he did
not know whether Whitworth had merely lost his nerve or had
been turned and was being run, wittingly or unwittingly, as a
double agent.

Sometime in the early 1980s the KGB also began having
doubts about the Walker spy ring, according to Walker himself.
Walker's handlers wondered about Whitworth's transfer to
Stockton, about his loss of access to cryptography, about the
fogged film (from a newly purchased Minox), about the mislaid
stack of messages.

In the labyrinthine world of espionage and counter-espionage, any variation in a pattern inspires suspicion. At meetings
with the Soviets in Vienna in 1983 and 1984, Walker was repeatedly questioned about Whitworth. The KGB had never been enthusiastic about Walker's free-lance recruiting. His handlers had
firmly told him that KGB officers, not their agents, do the
recruiting. Like many moves in the espionage game, recruiting
had its traditions and truths. Soviet practitioners, trained in a
chess-playing culture, believed that variations in any of the basic
moves were dangerously reckless.

The most disturbing variation, for both the KGB and
Walker himself, was Whitworth's abrupt transfer off the *Enterprise* in the late summer of 1983. His scheduled three-year tour of
duty was cut short after less than a year. He abruptly decided not

to reenlist. He also told Walker that his honorable discharge, a routine clerical action, was being held up because of some vague paperwork problem.

"One of the first things the FBI would do when they suspected one of spying," Walker later said, "is they would immediately transfer that person." But, as the "paperwork problem" strongly indicates, any manipulation of Whitworth was more likely the work of the Navy's NIS, not the FBI.

When Whitworth's otherwise predictable and profitable career suddenly ended, Walker was questioned in detail by his KGB handlers. Walker said he relayed the concern of the "buyers" and warned Whitworth that he might be playing a potentially deadly game. "I explained to him," Walker said, "that in the field of espionage one doesn't play games with one's contact. That if one says he's going to be on a ship for three years and he quits after one year, this could be dangerous to one's health. I explained to him that when plans were given to our buyers they had to be adhered to. . . . This would foul up the money flow. It would put us in danger of being assassinated."

At a Norfolk meeting in mid-April, both men made separate decisions. Whitworth would go home to Davis to write his first RUS letter, in which he said, "I've decided to stop supplying material." And Walker would take a terrible risk by attempting to put his sailor-son Michael on active espionage duty.

Walker's decision to substitute Michael for Whitworth was apparently not made known to Barbara Walker, the person who had known longer than anyone else that John Walker had a secret and lucrative life as a spy. Thus begins the final chapter in the mystery story.

Barbara Walker is portrayed in the official story as a wife who, succumbing to the demands of her conscience and propped up by liquor, reluctantly decided to turn in her ex-husband to the FBI. But Barbara Walker herself has said that sometime in 1984, for reasons not patriotic, she walked into the Norfolk office of John Walker's detective agency, threatened to inform on him, and demanded money—or else. Walker turned her down.

"He laughed at me and then he swore and ordered me out of his office," she recalled. "And as I stood at the door, I said, 'You know what this means, don't you? I'm going to turn you in.'"

Although Barbara says she did not know that John had recruited Michael, she did know that John had attempted to recruit their daughter Laura. And she knew that Laura's husband, Philip Mark Snyder, had known about John Walker's espionage at least since 1979.

On July 2, 1982, according to Laura, Philip took their son Christopher away from her and threatened to unmask her father as a spy if she ever tried to get custody of Christopher. Laura told her mother—and the mother told John Walker.

In a fury, he called Laura. "And then he asked me how I would feel if he [Philip] was not around anymore." Laura telephoned her mother on the Fourth of July, 1983, and told her that she was going to try to get Christopher back. The best way for her to do that was to go to the FBI and inform on her father. But, according to the official story, the informing did not take place until Barbara's first drunken call in November 1984.

If, however, the summer of 1983 is looked upon as the time that Walker came under suspicion, the case starts to resemble a classic espionage investigation. In fact, a court document strongly indicates that U.S. counter-espionage forces began watching Walker sometime in August 1983. The affidavit, pertaining to a defense inquiry about wiretapping, was filed in Whitworth pretrial proceedings. It is signed by John J. Dion, the Department of Justice official who late on the night of May 19, 1985, authorized the arrest of John Walker. Dion said in the 1986 affidavit that he had checked wiretaps back to *August 1983,* without explaining the significance of that date.

It was in the summer of 1983 that Whitworth's tour of duty on the *Enterprise* abruptly ended and his "paperwork problem" began. It was in the summer of 1983 that Walker and the KGB became suspicious about Whitworth. There is much more reason to believe those KGB suspicions—that a U.S. agent in the KGB exposed the Whitworth-Walker group to the CIA—than to believe that this long-running spy ring was broken because a drunken ex-wife began making phone calls that the FBI initially ignored and then was slow to follow up.

If a U.S. mole inside the KGB did tip off U.S. intelligence officials about Walker, and if, independently, there was an NIS investigation of Whitworth, the stage was set for a bureaucratic confrontation. U.S. officials are reluctant to discuss how and when U.S. counter-intelligence agents learned of Walker's treason and whether they ran him without his knowledge. But the authors are convinced that Walker and Whitworth were at least under surveillance and most likely being fed disinformation well before Barbara Walker first phoned in her tip.

The FBI admits to having ignored the attempts by Laura and Barbara to turn in John Walker from November 1984 to March 1985. By then there was no longer any chance to continue the disinformation. The FBI had to act on the tip because of the chance that Walker's Soviet case officer would have learned that Walker's ex-wife had gone to the FBI and would have suspected an agent-turning operation was in motion.

By the end of 1984, Barbara was one of many people who knew that John Walker and Jerry Whitworth were spies. The list is amazingly long, as Walker was well aware. He told interrogators that as far back as 1973 he had taken the chance of forging his own security clearance because "I didn't want to be subjected to a background investigation by the FBI, in view of my wife's frequent statements to relatives and friends concerning my espionage."

Even if Walker and Whitworth were not exposed by a KGB mole, many Americans in and out of his family could have accidentally or deliberately informed on Walker. Besides Barbara, Laura, Arthur, Gary, and Michael, there was also Michael's wife, Rachel, who had met Michael Walker through an introduction by John Walker. Walker did not name Rachel as a member of his ring but said he told the Soviets that she "coordinated work" between John Walker and Michael. He said the Soviets were interested in having him recruit Rachel, who had majored in oceanography, because they thought that she might be able to get into a Navy or Pentagon post that would let her get information about the Navy's secret seafloor submarine-detection systems called SOSUS.

Any one of several Navy people were possible informers because they suspected something was amiss with Walker or his friend Whitworth. Other classic potential informers were Walker's many girlfriends. He lavishly spent money on them, took them sailing, gave them expensive gifts, but maintained a relationship best described by the name of his sailboat, *Dirty Old Man*. Some of the girlfriends were young, low-ranking enlisted women in the Navy who would be subject to interrogation during an NIS inquiry into the activities of Walker and Whitworth. Such interrogation would be under the harsh rules of the Code of Military Justice, the set of laws that govern the lives of members of the armed services.

Some of the girlfriends were curious about the source of Walker's money. There was, for example, Myra Jean Barnes, a Navy enlisted dental assistant. She once flew with Walker in his plane to the Bahamas, where he said he had some property. "He was very generous. He seemed to have plenty of money," she remembered. One night, while having drinks with Whitworth, "I mentioned his [Walker's] financial situation to Jerry." Walker, she said, "seemed to be spending money like crazy and doing really well, buying airplanes, and that sort of thing."

She asked Whitworth where their friend Walker got all that money. In her testimony at the Whitworth trial she said Whitworth "told me that Johnny had been selling classified information to an ally. . . ."

Given the long line of potential informers in and out of the Navy, the official story becomes more and more incredible. There is also the matter of a time frame. William M. Baker, an Assistant Director of the FBI, said eleven days after Walker's arrest, "We patiently watched him for six months and waited for him to commit espionage." Using Baker's time frame, that means the FBI started surveillance of Walker in November, when Barbara made her first accusation. The "six months of surveillance" assertion is repeated in at least two sworn court documents prepared in anticipation of a Walker trial. That was the first draft of the official story: Walker's ex-wife betrayed him in November, an exhaustive FBI investigation was immediately launched, and this led to the dramatic arrest of Walker at gunpoint in May.

By July 2 the government had John, Michael, and Arthur Walker, along with Jerry Whitworth, in custody. What had seemed like a near-perfect arrest of a single spy had mushroomed into a complex, confusing assembly of spies and one of the most damaging espionage cases in history. On that day the man at the center of this spy complex told FBI interrogators that he had gotten started in espionage after being recruited by two men, one of them named "Harper," at the Yellow Cab Company in Norfolk. As John Walker told his story, he had gone to the cab company to look for a job. In the course of a conversation with "Harper," Walker said, he was set up in a private intelligence-gathering organization that would provide information to such clients as *Jane's Fighting Ships* and the International Institute for Strategic Studies, a London-based organization that gathers and publishes unclassified information about military and strategic matters.

When the "Yellow Cab" tale did not check out, Walker changed his story, saying that he had begun his spying by walking into the Soviet Embassy in 1968 (and at first giving the fake name of Harper). Walker later explained that he told the Yellow Cab lie because that was to have been his planned trial defense—a claim that he was spying for anonymous "buyers," not the Soviets. Even as early as July, then, Walker was confident that he needed no trial defense because he would never stand trial. He had bargaining chips, the principal one being an understanding that if the Department of Justice treated him right, he would testify as a government witness against his friend and protégé, Jerry Whitworth.

Although the string of espionage arrests bestowed a public triumph upon the FBI, they also presented the FBI with a secret dilemma: Walker, the most notorious American spy since the Rosenbergs, could not be put on trial. For, as Justice officials began constructing the foundation of a trial—the facts that would become the official story—bits of reality kept menacing the earlier scenario of triumph:

■ The Barbara Walker tip story, if revealed in court, would force the admission that the bureau had *ignored* tips on Walker for months. Such disclosures could damage the case because the defense was bound to question the selectivity of prosecution. The defense would undoubtedly ask why Barbara and Laura and the host of others who knew of Walker's espionage were not on trial as co-conspirators. Barbara's participation in two dead drops made her a more likely espionage defendant than Ethel Rosenberg, who was executed for espionage.

■ Walker had in fact *not* been under surveillance for six months. He had gone to Vienna in January 1985 and had a face-to-face meeting with his Soviet handlers during the period the FBI had supposedly "patiently watched him."

■ The Naval Investigative Service apparently had been developing a *Navy* case against Whitworth, meaning that NIS would have to be brought into a Walker trial, diluting the glory of the FBI. Bureaucratic infighting might endanger the legal case against Whitworth and even the one against Walker. Whatever the Navy knew about Whitworth had not been shared with the FBI, as is indicated by the futile search for "Wentworth" and the FBI's failure to identify the author of the "RUS" letters.

◼ In a public trial the bureau would have to explain FBI conjecture about "other members" of the ring beyond Michael and Arthur Walker and Jerry Whitworth. A barrage of such FBI speculation had begun within days after the arrests.

◼ There was embarrassing evidence that during Walker's long career as a spy for the Soviet Union, Walker may have done some other undercover work—*for the FBI*.

Of all the disturbing problems, Walker's January visit to Vienna was the most devastating. How could the bureau have allowed such an important spy to leave the United States and end up in Vienna under the control of the KGB? If the KGB had known of his imminent arrest—as Yurchenko's CIA debriefing indicates—Walker could have been bundled off to Moscow. Or he could have been killed.

(There was a murderous precedent, and every FBI counterespionage agent knew it. Nicholas Shadrin, a young Soviet Navy lieutenant commander, apparently the youngest destroyer commanding officer in the Soviet Navy at the time, had fled to the West with his girlfriend in 1959. After coming to the United States he worked for the Defense Intelligence Agency with a very low-level clearance. In 1966 the FBI began running him as a double agent, supplying him with disinformation that he passed to the Soviets. In 1975, Shadrin reluctantly went to Vienna to meet with his prospective Soviet handlers. Despite promised U.S. protection, he disappeared while in Vienna. Another bit of information dropped by Yurchenko in 1985 was confirmation of Shadrin's death at the hands of his East German kidnappers, who had given him an "accidental" overdose of chloroform.)

Walker returned to Norfolk from Vienna in January 1985, intending to keep his spy business going with Michael—and probably other sailors—as agents in place. But Walker's career was rapidly coming to an end. The instrument may have been what Yurchenko said the KGB suspected: a U.S. mole. Or the

KGB itself may have decided that, because of the suspicious aura around Whitworth, the operation had become so susceptible to penetration and disinformation that it had to be shut down. Or FBI counter-espionage, for reasons still unknown, may have finally been given permission to close in on Walker.

If, as the authors believe, the Navy had suspected that Whitworth was a spy, NIS information about him and Walker should have been passed to the FBI around the fall of 1983, when Whitworth retired from the Navy. But if such information had been passed, it was not acted upon, assuming that the FBI's "Wentworth" episode is true. What that episode indicates is that even at the time of John Walker's arrest, Barbara and Laura Walker were not fully cooperating with the FBI. They may have shielded Whitworth because they were interested only in destroying Walker, not in destroying a spy ring.

There seems little reason to doubt that Barbara Walker called the FBI in the fall of 1984 to turn in her ex-husband. But there is reason to doubt the official story's "zero-file" explanation for the delay in arresting John Walker. The authors believe that the FBI did not move against Walker because some other U.S. government agency already had a claim on him. There are two candidates: the U.S. Navy and the National Security Agency. NSA, knowing that Navy communications had been compromised, may have sanctioned, at a high level in the intelligence community, a *Navy* inquiry. In the intelligence community, NSA carries far more clout than the FBI does.

A Navy investigation of Whitworth, through NIS, would have implicated Walker. If, under NSA direction, the Navy had been feeding disinformation to Whitworth, that operation would have stopped with Whitworth's retirement. But Walker was still recruiting spies. NSA—and possibly the Navy—would be far more interested in continuing the *Navy* code-loss investigation than in building an espionage case. That is the task of the only law-enforcement agency in the U.S. counter-espionage business— the FBI.

Given this scenario, the Barbara Walker tip was a problem rather than a revelation. The FBI, though in desperate need of a triumph, would have been told to stay away from Walker.

The January trip to Vienna drastically changed the scenario. The master spy could have escaped. And another trip to Europe was due. Michael Walker's ship, the *Nimitz*, was scheduled to deploy to the Mediterranean for several months; John Walker would probably meet with his son in Italy, where the KGB had the resources to, in a term of the trade, "exfiltrate" them both. The nightmare of the Walkers suddenly appearing at a Moscow press conference was farfetched but possible. It had happened too often before to Americans and Britons who had betrayed their countries.

There is some evidence that the KGB itself was bracing for a major U.S. counter-espionage move at this time. In April 1985, three months after Walker's last trip to Vienna and a month before his arrest, ex-NSA analyst Ronald Pelton went to Vienna to meet his KGB handlers. Pelton, as he later told the FBI, followed the instructions that had produced successful rendezvous twice before. But this time he was not met. He said he thought that perhaps he had not been recognized because he had recently lost a great deal of weight.

What is much more likely is that Pelton was abandoned because the KGB was getting worried about its Vienna Procedure. If the KGB had suspicions about U.S. penetration of the Walker-Whitworth operation, the arrival of Walker in Vienna in January would have triggered more suspicions. Was U.S. counter-espionage staking out Vienna meetings? Not taking any chances, Pelton's KGB handlers left him hanging. (Yurchenko shortly would give his U.S. debriefers the clues that led to Pelton's arrest in November 1985.)

The answers to why Walker was allowed to go to Vienna may never be definitively known, but it is evident, from facts presented in the official story, that soon after Walker's safe return to the United States, the FBI suddenly discovered the bureau's "zero-file" reports of Barbara Walker and her daughter. The arrest could no longer be delayed.

The arrest of Walker was dramatic and smoothly conducted. But the other spy on the scene, Soviet diplomat Aleksey Tkachenko, was allowed to escape, along with the evidence he presumably carried. Reagan Administration officials may have not wanted the arrest of a Soviet diplomat at that time. There may also have been the possibility that counter-espionage strategists wanted an opportunity to capture Walker so quietly that he could be turned without the knowledge of the Soviets. Whether by plan or bungle, Tkachenko got away from the area, although he had been identified and sighted in the area three times—at 8:20, 8:21, and 9:08 on the evening of May 19, according to FBI records.

Under the U.S.-Soviet espionage ground rules, diplomats in both countries cannot rent automobiles, and so they must drive easily traced, easily followed cars. The ground rules also allow a law-enforcement officer to stop a car with diplomatic license plates, ostensibly to determine whether the car is indeed being driven by a registered member of the diplomatic community. Through this proviso a driver can be "detained," ostensibly to check his identification. This could have been done on the evening of May 19. While Tkachenko was being detained, his car could have been surreptitiously checked. Presumably a large amount of U.S. currency and espionage instructions to Walker would have been found. Tkachenko was not even followed out of the area, let alone stopped.

Within ten minutes after the first spotting of Tkachenko's car, his home address, an apartment in Alexandria, Virginia, was known. His apartment building was not put under surveillance. One government official told the authors that Tkachenko had not previously been identified as a probable KGB officer. Apparently this admission was made to explain the way Tkachenko was handled on May 19.

State Department records show that Tkachenko had been certified as the third secretary at the Soviet Embassy on January 7, 1983. State Department intelligence officials would have routinely passed copies of his diplomatic passport photographs to the FBI, which, just as routinely, would have checked him out as a potential KGB legal. The following month the State Department recognized him as vice-consul in addition to his previous title. As vice-consul, Tkachenko would spend most of his time not at the embassy but at the Soviet Consulate, which is in a residential neighborhood about two miles north of the embassy. The consulate, on California Street off Connecticut Avenue, gets far less surveillance than does the embassy, on Sixteenth Street, the military and naval attachés' office on Belmont Road, or the residence compound on Tunlaw Road.

Soviet counter-surveillance would have established that

Tkachenko was being treated as a "clean" legal and he would be kept in place in that role until his services were required. Although FBI sources insist that Tkachenko had never before been used to serve a drop site, his cool professionalism on the night of May 19 makes him appear to be the skilled local control officer for Walker.

If the FBI had overlooked Tkachenko before May 19, there is no doubt that he became the subject of intense surveillance the day *after* he had appeared to make the pickup and the drop. Agents staked out his apartment and tried to get a chance to examine at least the exterior of his car. But Tkachenko was always accompanied by one or more Soviets, presumably KGB comrades who did not want to give the diplomat the chance to have a moment alone with any American who might want to try to question him about the dead drop—or even attempt to turn him.

Somehow he also managed to clean his car of any Montgomery County soil. When FBI agents were finally able to examine the outside of his car on May 22, they found that the car had been "completely steam-cleaned, the tires, up under the guard walls, the entire under-coating of the vehicle." On the morning of May 23, Tkachenko, his wife, and two children flew from the United States to Moscow. Their departure was so hasty that food was left in the refrigerator of their apartment in suburban Virginia.

The failure to detain Tkachenko would have been another awkward problem for the prosecution to explain at a Walker trial. But instead of a John Walker trial there was the Jerry Whitworth trial, with a kind of John Walker would-be trial inserted inside. David Szady, the headquarters agent in charge of the Walker case, was one of the witnesses called to lay out the facts for the trial-within-a-trial. Szady testified that he had entered the Walker case in March 1985. Under cross-examination, Szady revealed how wide was the spectrum of "official" starting dates for the case.

"The information that started you investigating Mr. Walker, as I understand it, came before March of 1985; isn't that true?" Whitworth defense lawyer Tony Tamburello asked.

"Well, there was—information was received by our Boston office in November, I believe," Szady replied.

"And that came from Mr. Walker's wife, Barbara?"

"Yes."

"And also from his daughter, Laura?"

"The information from Laura came, oh, about a month later. And then actually the total information we obtained from her was during that March time frame."

"So it wasn't until you got the information from Laura that you actually started the investigation in earnest; is that what you're saying?"

"That's correct, once the information was passed on to head-quarters in Norfolk after it had been received in Boston, and *we had other information that confirmed what Barbara was telling us was correct.* Then we began the investigation in earnest." (Emphasis added.)

The John Walker trial-within-a-trial was designed to proudly reveal the core of the case against Walker without having to take the chance of revealing any awkward bits of reality. But the prosecutors of Whitworth would have to anticipate defense challenges of Walker's testimony, and he had a predilection for lying and flunking polygraph tests.

So prosecutors narrowly questioned Walker, trying to confine his testimony to the FBI's official story, which had been thoroughly riveted together by the time of the frequently post-poned 1986 Whitworth trial. The government was curiously protective of Walker during the trial-within-a-trial. Prior to Walker's appearance on the stand, at a courtroom hearing without the jury present, government prosecutors asked the court to prohibit Whitworth's defense attorneys from cross-examination of Walker on the following subjects:

His arrest and conviction for burglary in 1955, when he had just turned eighteen.

Any books, courses on, or methods and techniques of operating clandestinely.

Membership in the John Birch Society, the National Rifle Association, and the Ku Klux Klan.

Any reference to his asking his wife to engage in prostitution to pay off debts.

Any reference to what was called the "exploiting of his brother Arthur."

Any references to Walker's "marital infidelity."

Questions about his alleged suggestion that his daughter get an abortion so she could remain in the military and engage in espionage for him.

Questions about what role Walker played in the firing of Norfolk police officers. (Walker, in his guise as a private investigator, had been involved with many Norfolk police officers. Four left the force in the wake of his arrest. One, a lieutenant, was Walker's contact man for dealing with police officers who provided Walker with records from police computers. Such information could have given Walker leads on sailors who were likely candidates for conversion into Soviet agents.)

James Larson, Whitworth's leading defense attorney, looked at the list and told Judge J. P. Vukasin, Jr., "I am a little hard put to see the basis for the government's objection." The judge also seemed puzzled by some of the requested restrictions.

Larson focused on the KKK issue. "The Ku Klux Klan connection," he said, "develops both from our own investigation, which has been conducted independently, and information that we received from the government in the course of discovery." Larson said Walker had become involved in the KKK through Bill Wilkinson, a Virginia KKK state officer who had served with Walker on the Polaris submarine *Simon Bolivar* around 1966. Wilkinson, according to Larson, was "operating as an agent of the FBI."

Walker's interest in the Klan came at a time when the Navy was concerned about Klan activity in major Navy bases like Norfolk. Confrontations between black and white sailors had been increasing on ship and shore. The worst incidents had come in the fall of 1972, when race riots broke out on the aircraft carrier *Kitty Hawk* and on the *Hassayampa,* a fleet oiler. A month later black sailors staged a sit-down strike on board the carrier *Constellation.* Some Navy intelligence officers wondered if the Klan —and even the KGB—were involved.

Sometime after this wave of racial incidents, according to Larson, an unidentified man contacted Walker, asked him to infiltrate the Klan, and promised him $1,000 for any information he provided. "Now," Larson said, "it would appear from the investigation that we have done and the evidence that is available that the only agency that could have recruited him to engage in this work would have to have been the United States Government, the FBI, or some other investigative wing."

Larson theorized that Walker at some time prior to his arrest had a "special relationship" with the government "as an informant." Assistant Prosecutor Leida Schoggen simply denied that Walker had been an informant, and the issue was left at that. The judge ruled that cross-examination would be allowed on Walker's membership in the Klan and most of the other topics. Walker testified that he was a member of the Klan "for about three months while working undercover." He said he had been "anonymously retained" and "was paid a thousand dollars for the job, which should not have lasted more than four weeks. And I claimed it on my income tax."

Walker would have reported that anonymous $1,000 as income only if he thought—*or knew*—that the U.S. Government had a record of the payment. Walker, as a private investigator, was known to Navy officials in Norfolk long before his arrest. He had been involved in an NIS investigation of a sailor and his firm had conducted background investigations of defense contractor employees. A federal investigator assigned to probe KKK activity in Norfolk could well have turned to Walker for help.

Most of the banned topics on the government's be-nice-to-Walker list had to do with an attempt to give him a good image as a government witness. His testimony was believed to be vital to the conviction of Whitworth, against whom the government had largely a circumstantial case. The FBI went along with the government's decision to make an attractive witness of what an agent privately called "a dirtbag."

The government had to perform the repulsive task of applying cosmetics to Walker's abominable character because an acquittal—or a Miller-style mistrial—for Whitworth was unthinkable. (That horror was enhanced by a depressing coincidence: While Whitworth was being tried in San Francisco the second trial of the FBI's disgraced Miller was going on in Los Angeles.)

The manipulation of reality also included restrictions on FBI speculation about the size of the Walker operation. Walker testified that his KGB case officer had assigned letters to the names Walker had given him: *D* for Whitworth, *S* for Michael

Walker, K for Arthur Walker, and F for his half-brother Gary, a sailor in a Navy helicopter squadron who, according to the FBI, never spied for Walker.

Walker also mentioned an A, but stumbled through an explanation, claiming first that A was another letter for Whitworth and then claiming that "I never did memorize the initials for the players, anyway."

Soon after John Walker's arrest, however, FBI sources had made much of A, saying that the letter represented a spy not yet arrested. The authors have been told that some investigators still believed that one or more spies known to Walker were in place at the time of his arrest. The authors were also told that the FBI, but not the NIS, believed that Michael Walker may have had one or more confederates on the *Nimitz*.

Such speculation would become the subject of defense attorneys' cross-examination in a trial of Walker. But within a month after his arrest the government was contemplating a plea bargain. Using a shorter sentence for Michael as a lever, the Department of Justice offered Walker a life sentence in exchange for a guilty plea from both father and son and a promise to cooperate with intelligence debriefers.

The plea bargain, made public in October 1985, was immediately denounced by Secretary of the Navy John F. Lehman, Jr., who said that the Department of Justice was treating espionage as "just another white-collar crime" and sending "the wrong message to the nation and to the fleet." Lehman insisted that the Navy did not need help from Walker to do a damage assessment.

At the time, Secretary of Defense Caspar W. Weinberger publicly criticized Lehman for his "injudicious and incorrect statement" and moved quickly to stifle any other Pentagon criticism. Weinberger and the plea bargainers from the Department of Justice represented the high-level intelligence community players who wanted to know about Walker's broad effects on national security. The Navy, with Lehman as the point man, wanted to know how Walker had hurt the Navy in the past and whether members of his ring were still spying in Navy ships and stations.

On the national security level the concern was with cryptographic losses and where the Walker ring fit in the worldwide spy war between the United States and the Soviet Union. On the

Navy level the concern was about the effects on such relatively parochial matters as submarine deployments and Soviet knowledge of the tactics of attack submarines and aircraft carrier battle groups.

Navy debriefers were convinced that A and perhaps others existed. "You can expect more arrests," a high-ranking Navy officer told the authors early in 1987. FBI agents denied that more arrests were likely, and none came. The spy named A was officially forgotten.

Navy officials also believe that Walker was involved in one and possibly three Norfolk murders. The FBI shrugged off the murder claims, reflecting the Department of Justice's interest in preserving the cosmetics applied to Walker's character for the Whitworth trial.

One of the murder victims was Carol Ann Molnar, who worked at the Armed Forces Staff College in Norfolk and picked up extra money as a go-go dancer at the Galleon Club in Norfolk. She performed at the club on February 6, 1983, and was not seen alive again. Her body washed ashore on May 1. She had been shot. Carol Molnar worked at the college with Pat Marsee, one of Walker's girlfriends, who accompanied him for at least part of his 1977 Hong Kong-Casablanca spy trip.

The Staff College students are career military officers being prepared for highly responsible staff duties and eventual senior command responsibility. One of Pat Marsee's jobs was to type the classified papers written by the students, all of whom have at least a secret clearance. The Navy and FBI have ignored possible breaches of security or espionage at the Staff College. Like the murders, the Staff College was not considered a worthy subject for investigation.

"We have information that the murder took place, that Miss Molnar was supplying information to Mr. Walker and something went wrong in the espionage scheme and he had to protect himself," defense lawyer Tamburello said in a Whitworth trial court session closed to the jury. A senior Navy intelligence official said much of the same to the authors. But the government convinced the court that there was no need to introduce information about Walker's acquaintance with Carol Molnar, living or dead.

A Navy officer who participated in many of the Walker

debriefings,* linked Walker to the Molnar murder and to the murder of Radioman Pamela Ann Kinbrue. On March 26, 1982, the body of Pamela Kinbrue was found in her car, which had been pushed into the water near Norfolk. Her hands had been tied behind her back and she had been strangled. "We think there is good reason to suspect Walker, that guttersnipe," the officer said. "But the FBI isn't interested." NIS agents believe that either woman could have heard about Walker's espionage and threatened him with exposure. The FBI says Walker has denied any connection with the murder of Pamela Kinbrue or the 1984 shooting death of Garland L. Joyner, Jr., a Portsmouth, Virginia, police detective. That death was later ruled a suicide.

The FBI also seems to have turned away from any investigations into Walker's involvement with Norfolk-area police forces or with Navy facilities in the Norfolk area. Walker frequently called on male and female police officers to help him in his work as a private investigator—his clever cover, which his KGB handlers had enthusiastically supported. Walker also conducted "background investigations" of Navy officers planning post-retirement jobs.

Some of these background investigations—which, on Walker's orders, probed for potentially incriminating information—were done by Laurie Robinson, Walker's business partner at one of his firms, Confidential Reports, Inc., for about three and a half years. FBI sources have repeatedly discounted Walker's private-detective activities as significant to the espionage investigation. There are no indications that the FBI backtracked through his files for possible leads to people who could have been blackmailed into giving up Navy or defense-contractor secrets, people who were candidates for being spy *A*.

Walker's FBI handlers have revealed little about his work as an investigator. One of the few revelations came during the trial of his brother Arthur, who stole and photographed documents from VSE Corporation, a small defense think tank located near Norfolk. Arthur went to work for VSE in 1980. Shortly later, John asked a VSE officer for permission to "sweep" the premises

---

* There were forty-three debriefing sessions of Walker prior to his sentencing. In about twenty-five of those debriefings the Navy and FBI both took part; in the rest there was no Navy presence.

as a test of some electronic equipment he had recently purchased. Permission was granted, and one night, after the offices were closed, Walker entered and ostensibly searched for electronic bugs and telephone taps. Officials have never indicated that they know how many other places he entered, how many bugs he might have found—and, more importantly, could have planted.

Walker has passed some polygraph tests and failed others. There is no way of knowing when he speaks the truth and when he lies. Perhaps the best assessment comes from Robinson. When she testified at the Whitworth trial she did so under court-granted usage immunity, meaning that she could not be prosecuted for anything she said in that courtroom. Before appearing in court she had been told that she was under investigation and might be prosecuted. She had taken a polygraph and the FBI was not satisfied with the results. Federal authorities said that the investigation that involved her centered on the location of the estimated $1 million Walker earned as a spy.

Laurie Robinson testified that she had visited Walker in jail, where, she said, "He told me that part of the plea agreement was that he had to totally cooperate with the government, and what he intended to do was cooperate and then make up stories for them, because only he knew who was involved in the espionage and only he knew the facts of what took place. . . ."

As this is written the question of A and possible successors to Whitworth and Michael Walker remains unanswered. The authors have been told that some investigators believe that at least one Navy communications specialist is still working for the Soviets.

Walker was invaluable to his Soviet spymasters because he could provide information about communications in the Navy, the U.S. armed service that so often carries out vital national security missions. As the nation's only global conventional and nuclear force, the Navy time and again has been used to show the flag and to project force.

By penetrating Navy communications the Soviets were able to eavesdrop on the operational results of high-level decisions. And by having Walker as a spy in place for nearly two decades, the Soviets were able to get valuable lessons about how White

House and Pentagon decision-making processes changed with presidential administrations.

Access to these communications was "the ultimate goal" of Soviet spymasters.

10

"The Ultimate Goal"

"The ultimate goal is to break down the other man's signals security . . . to protect your signals and penetrate the other guy's signals security." The words are those of the late James Jesus Angleton, chief of counter-intelligence for the U.S. Central Intelligence Agency from the 1950s until he left the agency in 1974.

The Soviets have tried hard to penetrate American signals—communications—at all levels of political and military activity since World War II. The chief targets of those penetrations are various military and other government networks. Particular targets have been radiomen in the various services, code clerks at American embassies around the world, the National Security Agency (to learn how well *their*—i.e., Soviet—signals have been penetrated), and even the commercial microwave links that criss-cross the United States. In Washington the Soviet Embassy (four blocks north of the White House) and the residence compound (on the highest point of northwest Washington) bristle with antennas to intercept local communications. Reading through various FBI reports, one gets the impression that even the American spy-catchers are vulnerable to Soviet radio intercepts when they use short-wave radios in the Washington area.

Breaking into an enemy's communications, "reading his mail," has been the goal of spies and intelligence services since the beginnings of recorded history. Many, many battles have been won or lost because one side or the other could read its opponent's intercepted messages. In the twentieth century the extensive use of radio communications—coupled with all of the other modern technologies of war—have made code-breaking at once more difficult and more important. In this century the Russians learned of the importance of signals security through defeat, and the Americans learned through victory.

At the beginning of World War I the Russian armies scored massive victories over their Austrian enemies in heavy fighting in the Tannenberg campaign. However, Russian victory turned to defeat when smaller German forces completely routed the Russian armies because the German commanders were able to intercept Russian radio messages that were being transmitted in the "clear." The Russian officers had a total disregard for communications security while the Germans were keenly aware of the value of radio security and intercept. Even today the U.S. Army uses the Tannenberg campaign in East Prussia as a fundamental example of excellent defensive tactics—which were made possible through German radio intercept of Russian communications.

The Russian Revolution and Civil War, and the later Stalinist purges of military officers, prevented the lessons of signals security from being properly learned. Consequently, in World War II, on the Eastern Front the Germans gained an estimated 70 percent of their most reliable combat intelligence from the intercept of Soviet tactical radio communications.

But in the postwar period those lessons have been learned by the Soviets. Evaluating Soviet military communications, a retired U.S. Army expert on Soviet affairs wrote, "Soviet practices, born of their experiences in two world wars, stress communications security and limit the use of radios." Because "Soviet commanders are very sensitive to communications security," the "primary means of communications is by wire . . . with radio transmissions being permitted only in event of actual enemy contact. . . ." Because of this doctrine, it could be difficult in future ground battles with the Soviets to benefit from code-breaking, as the Allies did when code-breakers solved the Germans' Enigma code system and were able to use decoded messages to anticipate German military actions in World War II.

The United States also has considerable experience in communications intercept or, in the current military jargon, SIGINT

THE EYES OF THE KREMLIN

U.S. Capitol | Navy intelligence complex, Suitland, Md. | FBI | Defense Intelligence Agency, Bolling AFB | White House | National Security Agency, Fort Meade, Md. | State Dept. | Pentagon | CIA

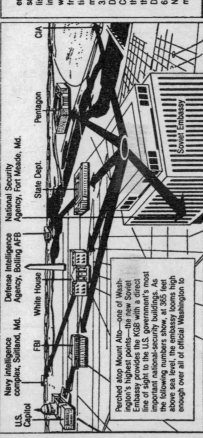

Perched atop Mount Alto—one of Washington's highest points—the new Soviet Embassy provides the KGB with a direct line of sight to the U.S. government's most important national-security buildings. As the following numbers show, at 365 feet above sea level, the embassy looms high enough over all of official Washington to

enable the Soviets to spy with sophisticated photographic and listening devices on the following government buildings, whose approximate distances from the embassy and elevations are: the White House, 2.8 miles, 50 feet; the Pentagon, 3.9 miles, 30 feet; the State Department, 2.7 miles, 30 feet; Congress, 4.3 miles, 70 feet; the CIA, 4.2 miles, 220 feet; the FBI, 3.4 miles, 20 feet; the Defense Intelligence Agency, 6.4 miles, 10 feet; and the Navy Intelligence complex, 9.1 miles, 295 feet

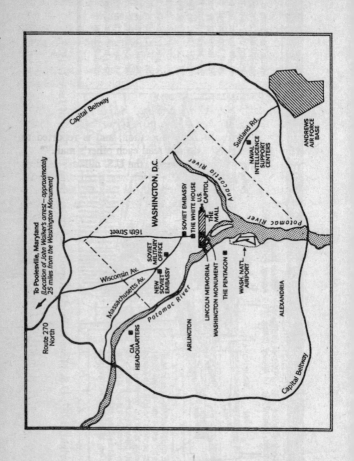

To Poolesville, Maryland
(Location of John Walker's arrest—approximately 25 miles from the Washington Monument)

Route 270 North

Capital Beltway

WASHINGTON, D.C.

16th Street

Wisconsin Av.

Massachusetts Av.

SOVIET EMBASSY

SOVIET MILITARY OFFICE

NEW SOVIET EMBASSY

Potomac River

CIA HEADQUARTERS

ARLINGTON

THE WHITE HOUSE

U.S. CAPITOL

THE MALL

Anacostia River

LINCOLN MEMORIAL

WASHINGTON MONUMENT

THE PENTAGON

WASH. NAT'L AIRPORT

ALEXANDRIA

Potomac River

Suitland Rd.

NAVAL INTELLIGENCE SUPPORT CENTERS

ANDREWS AIR FORCE BASE

Capital Beltway

—signals intelligence. Modern American SIGINT began in 1916, when twenty-seven-year-old Herbert Yardley became chief of the Cryptology Section of the Army. Yardley sought to break into German codes, and in 1919 established the so-called Black Chamber, which was able to decipher Japanese diplomatic codes on the eve of the Washington Naval Conference in 1921. The American negotiators, armed with Yardley's success, were able to push the Japanese delegation as hard as possible to derive the best possible terms for the United States.

Yardley's Black Chamber continued its efforts until 1929, when Henry Stimson was appointed Secretary of State. He immediately closed down the Yardley operation, and is reported to have declared, "Gentlemen do not read each other's mail."*

Between the world wars, however, the U.S. military services pursued code-breaking efforts. The Navy was particularly successful in both analyzing radio traffic of the Japanese and breaking into some of their secondary codes. The U.S. Army was also successful, and cryptologists William F. Friedman and Captain Lawrence F. Stafford succeeded in August 1940 in breaking into the highest Japanese political code, "Code Purple."

Naval Intelligence sought an edge in the code-breaking by a variety of means, including "black-bag" jobs—opening and searching the luggage of Japanese officers and officials in the United States and secretly cracking the safe in the Japanese consul's office in New York. The safe yielded several code books and reports on Japanese espionage in the United States. The Office of Naval Intelligence (ONI) did so well at these black-bag jobs that ONI operatives were used to break into—and trash—the Communist Party of America headquarters in New York ("We even swiped the checkbooks and bankbooks to create even more trouble"). And in 1930 the ONI, as a favor to the Hoover White House, even broke into the Democratic Party's office in New York.

Although wandering somewhat afield in its activities, Naval Intelligence was making progress in breaking Japanese diplomatic and, to a lesser extent, military codes. However, intra-

---

* The quotation may be more mythology than history. Stimson was appointed Secretary of War in 1940 and served throughout the Roosevelt and Truman wartime administrations.

Navy rivalry between the intelligence group at Pearl Harbor and the Navy's intelligence, communications, and war plans groups in Washington reduced the effectiveness of their efforts that *could* have provided adequate warning of the Japanese air attack on Pearl Harbor. Despite the squabbling, the U.S. Navy was able to read the Japanese diplomatic codes on the eve of the attack, and soon after the war began to break into Japanese military codes.

Being able to read Japanese codes helped American military commanders in the Pacific to best employ their limited naval forces. Three of numerous examples demonstrate the implications of the ability to read an enemy's signals.

On January 26, 1942, the U.S. submarine *Gudgeon* was returning to Pearl Harbor after patrolling in Japanese waters, where she had scored no sinkings because of faulty torpedoes. Intercepts of Japanese communications indicated that a submarine would be passing across the *Gudgeon*'s path. Early the next morning, operating submerged, the U.S. submarine detected another undersea craft by sonar.

A periscope check revealed the large submarine *I-73* on the surface. A short time later the *Gudgeon* reached attack position and fired three torpedoes. Moments later the *I-73* blew up, the first Japanese warship to fall victim to an American submarine.

By May of 1942 the Navy was readily able to read Japanese military codes. From their basement offices at Pearl Harbor the code-breakers were able to advise Admiral Chester W. Nimitz, the American Commander in the Pacific, that the Japanese would mount a major assault against Midway atoll to draw out the American fleet for a decisive battle. Forewarned, Nimitz was able to deploy his few, outnumbered warships in a position from which they could surprise the Japanese. In the early June Battle of Midway the Japanese lost four large aircraft carriers with all of their aircraft and most of their pilots; the United States lost one carrier. Midway was the turning point of the war.

At a meeting immediately after the battle, Nimitz welcomed Commander Joseph Rochefort, head of his code-breakers, to a staff meeting with: "This officer deserves a major share of the credit for the victory at Midway," and recommended him for a special award.

Following Midway, the U.S. forces went on a limited offensive in the Pacific. On the morning of April 17, 1943, a U.S. Navy radio intercept station at Dutch Harbor in the Aleutian Islands intercepted a message from the battleship *Yamato,* flagship of the Japanese Fleet. Recognizing the name of the flagship even with the message in code, the Aleutians station flashed the message to Washington. There code-breakers were able to decipher the message, which revealed that the Commander in Chief of the Japanese Fleet, Isoroku Yamamoto, was making an inspection of bases in the southwest Pacific. Details of his schedule were provided.

Armed with this information, U.S. commanders drew up a plan to shoot down the admiral. Just twenty-seven hours after the original U.S. intercept, Army P-38 Lightning fighters found and shot down Yamamoto's aircraft, killing one of the chief Japanese strategists of the Pacific war.

In the European theater the British had made remarkable progress in breaking into the German military codes. The British were helped by a Pole who had worked in the German factory that had produced the Enigma code machines. Still, deriving the keys was a herculean effort, abetted by German mistakes, the capture of codes from German U-boats, and the use of scores of mathematicians. But breaking the codes was vital. For example, in the crucial Battle of the Atlantic against the U-boats in 1942, the Allied losses of merchant ships to submarines grew steadily. In November of that year, 109 merchant ships were sunk—totaling 721,700 tons. The reason for the increased sinkings was the inability of the British to read the latest Enigma key used by the U-boats.

This key was broken on December 13, 1942. The effect was immediate: In December the merchant-ship sinkings fell to forty-four, in January 1943 to only thirty-three. At the same time U-boat sinkings increased. A record nineteen U-boats were sunk in February 1943, fifteen were sunk in both March and April, and then forty-one in May. The U-boats were withdrawn from the major North Atlantic convoy routes.

The distinguished German naval historian Jürgen Rohwer has analyzed the critical convoy battles of this period: "It is clear, therefore, that the cracking of the German code systems was a crucial factor in the convoy battles of April and May [1943] which were seen later to have been the turning point of the U-Boat war." Several factors led to this Allied victory over the

U-boats: increased numbers of long-range patrol aircraft, improved radar, more escort ships, better antisubmarine tactics, and, in some ways most significant, breaking the U-boat Enigma code.

As early as 1941, Admiral Karl Dönitz, head of the U-boat arm (and later of the German Navy), noted how periodically the convoys evaded his U-boat groups: "Coincidence alone it cannot be," stated the U-boat command diary. "[C]oincidence cannot always work on one side and experiences extend over almost nine months. A likely explanation would be that the British from some source or other gain knowledge of our concentrated dispositions and avoid them, thereby running across only [U-]boats proceeding singly."

Dönitz biographer Peter Padfield explained the German's logic in examining this problem:

> The three ways they could get this information were by spies—everything had been done to exclude this possibility—or by deciphering radio messages—the experts in cryptoanalysis at High Command considered this *out of the question*—or by 'a combination of U-boat radio traffic and reports of sightings'. (Emphasis added.)

The German Navy as well as the rest of the German military establishment refused to believe that the Allies could have broken into their cherished Enigma system.

For four decades after World War II the Soviet intelligence services have considered American signals intelligence as "the ultimate goal" of their espionage efforts. For having the keys to American communications means that political and military decisions can be learned, at times as soon as they are known by military commanders or American ambassadors overseas. Of course a Soviet spy or mole in a sensitive position in an American government agency is invaluable. But one or even a few spies can provide access to only a few areas of information. Having the key to communications—when the same types of encryption machines are used worldwide by military and diplomatic activities—can be even more valuable.

The Soviets have been obtaining American cryptographic

material for many years through a parade of Americans who have betrayed the work of the National Security Agency, Army and Navy communications activities, and related efforts. To some degree the Soviets have also obtained information on U.S. systems from spies in allied nations who have had access to American cryptographic equipment. This betrayal probably gave the Soviets occasional keylists for code machines and copies of numerous messages, enabling the Soviets to go back through their records and compare the clear text with the encoded text. The Soviets have also obtained code-machine manuals and documents on code logic and systems.

While this material could enable the Soviets to construct American-type code machines, the actual machines would be invaluable—and they got them. One of the first code machines to be fully compromised was the KL-7. Warrant Officer Joseph Helmich, an Army communications specialist, sold details of that machine to the Soviets in 1963–64. He provided keylists and the supersecret rotors for that device, and possibly for the KW-26 and other equipment. At his 1981 trial the government stated ". . . the residual impact of the compromise continues to the present time because the KL-7 was continuously in use and still is."

Five years after Helmich sold out, with the *Pueblo* capture in January 1968 the Soviets obtained several U.S. code machines, including the widely used KW-7, KWR-37, and KG-14. The KW-7, which also had the designation "Orestes," was the most widely used piece of crypto gear in the U.S. military services, with many in Allied services. The KW-7 used a worldwide keylist to operate, meaning that anyone with a machine and keylist could read military communications (for the period of the list) anywhere in the world.

More machines were lost in 1975 as North Vietnamese troops overran the South, and the U.S.-supplied Saigon forces hastily retreated, leaving their weapons and code machines in their wake. The North Vietnamese and their Soviet allies captured some thirty U.S. code machines; the exact number thirty-two has been mentioned by some sources.

From at least 1968, Chief Warrant Officer John Walker and his comrade in betrayal, Senior Chief Radioman Jerry Whitworth, supplied the Soviets with keylists and innumerable other documents and manuals, permitting them full use of the machines in their possession. Further, the materials and information provided by Walker and Whitworth enabled the Soviets to break into codes used by machines not in their possession.

When the Walker-Whitworth spy ring was revealed in May 1985, opinion varied as to the damage the radiomen had inflicted on the defense establishment. To many U.S. naval officers the implications were beyond their ability to comprehend. Assessing the impact of the Walker-Whitworth betrayal a month after their arrest, Admiral James D. Watkins, the Chief of Naval Operations, declared that the Navy has the problem "bounded and can leave it in the dust behind us. . . . We believe we are on the downside of the problem. . . . We believe we have surrounded it."

Asked specifically about the possible vulnerability of U.S. submarines because of the espionage efforts, Watkins, at a Pentagon press conference, was even more sanguine. He declared that there was no indication that the Soviets had broken the codes that would permit them to detect the U.S. undersea craft "and therefore, we remain convinced that our SSBN [strategic missile submarine] force is still one hundred percent survivable."

But Watkins' key staff officers—more in touch with reality—were much more concerned. Rear Admiral John Butts, Director of Naval Intelligence at the time, in a staff meeting estimated the damage done by Walker-Whitworth: "On a scale of one-to-ten . . . a twelve!" More than a year after the spy ring was broken, a new Chief of Naval Operations, Admiral Carlisle A. H. Trost, said the code material given to the Soviets could have given them the advantage over the United States in a war at sea. Trost's Director of Naval Intelligence, Rear Admiral William O. Studeman, said that "we will likely never know the true extent to which our capabilities have been impaired by the traitorous and infamous acts of Jerry Whitworth."

"Had conflict erupted between the two superpowers," Trost said, the Soviets would have been exploiting information "with the potential to have powerful war-winning implications for the Soviet side." The recovery from the effects of their spying—the "surrounding of the problem" as Watkins put it—will, according to Studeman, "take years and millions of dollars."

* * *

The specifics of how Walker and Whitworth stole America's secrets are frightening because of how simple it was for them—for at least seventeen years. It was so simple that John le Carré would never have woven Whitworth or Walker into one of his spy plots—their operation would have been unbelievable.

In 1968, when he allegedly drove up to Washington to offer his services to the KGB, Walker was a veteran communications specialist who had served in two strategic missile submarines (SSBNs). He was then assigned as a communications watch officer at the headquarters of the Atlantic Fleet submarine force; SubLant, as the command was known, directed the operations of thirty-one Poseidon SSBNs and more than forty nuclear-propelled attack submarines (SSNs). Each SSBN carried sixteen multiple-warhead missiles, forming the most survivable portion of U.S. strategic forces; the SSNs were intended to seek out and destroy Soviet ships and submarines—and to carry out intelligence collection against the Soviets.

At SubLant headquarters, according to Admiral Butts, in the role of watch officer Walker was "running the entire communications center for the submarine force." Also, with his top secret/crypto clearances, he could easily gain access to virtually any equipment manual, communications document, or even operational plan that he asked for. He was able to tell the Soviets about "Flypaper," a highly classified antisubmarine warfare program intended to hunt Soviet undersea craft.

Every month sealed packets with a month's worth of daily keylists for the code machines were given to the communications center. Walker or another custodian for the Classified Materials System (CMS) signed for the packets, broke the seals, and checked the contents.

The watch officer had his own office, and none of the dozen or so enlisted communicators on duty would question his coming or going. On night watch, usually at the beginning of the keylist month, Walker would take the keylists to a Xerox machine in the communications spaces and copy them. Or, if necessary, he would take them into his office and photograph them. Photography was quicker than copying, and avoided the risk of someone coming over to use the machine and seeing him handling the sacrosanct keylists. It would take him twenty to thirty minutes to photograph a month's key material for one system.

Because the keylists were supposed to be destroyed as they were used (although in practice a batch would be destroyed every few days), it was easier to copy the lists in one session, near the beginning of the month. In the year between his call on the embassy and his transfer to radio school in San Diego, Walker provided the Soviets with all of the keylists for the KWR-37 and a great deal of keylists for the KG-13 and the KG-26. All the machines used keys that resembled perforated, IBM punch cards.

With the aid of those keys, the Soviets could, by analyzing submarine message traffic, learn the plans, movements, missions, and positioning strategies of U.S. attack and ballistic missile submarines. The Soviets could essentially read all the war gaming and exercises involving submarines alone or in company with surface ships. In some U.S. exercises submarines and surface ships played Soviet roles. By analyzing those communications, Soviet specialists could determine how Americans *thought* the Soviets would fight a war at sea and estimated the capabilities of Soviet forces.

Walker did not have much to pass along during his two years at the radio school located at San Diego. There Walker used only training keylists for demonstrations in operating the cryptographic equipment. The only material he could sell to the Soviets was "minor message traffic" that he photographed with his Minox camera. However, it was at San Diego that he met Whitworth, one of the instructors who worked for him.

But Walker's next assignment, as CMS custodian on board the *Niagara Falls*, gave him—and hence the Soviets—a bonanza for three years. The *Niagara Falls* was a replenishment ship that periodically would rendezvous with warships to transfer provisions and supplies to them. He had full access to all of the crypto machines on the ship—KW-7, KWR-37, KG-14, KY-8, and KL-47. Following much the same procedure as he had at Norfolk, Walker was able to copy and pass along to the Soviets nearly "one hundred percent" of the keys (and thus access to all messages) handled by those machines.

During that period, from 1970 to 1973, Walker would periodically rendezvous with KGB representatives, usually at six-month intervals, and deliver his packets of film. Thus the Soviets were decoding U.S. communications after the fact *except* that after a certain period they could undoubtedly extrapolate the methodology necessary to break into the communications on a real-time basis. And it was during that period that the United States was withdrawing its forces from South Vietnam and flying intense air strikes against North Vietnam. At this time the United States and Soviet Union had a major naval confrontation in the Middle East during the so-called Yom Kippur War of October 1973. All of these events held great interest for Soviet leaders.

During the Yom Kippur War the Soviets threatened to unilaterally intervene in the Egyptian-Israeli conflict, and U.S. military forces went to Defense Condition (DefCon) III—the highest stage of readiness in peacetime. Although the increase in military readiness was almost immediately reported in the American press, the Soviets may well have had detailed, inside information even as the DefCon III alert was being transmitted to U.S. forces. (Information about U.S. DefCon procedures was one of the high-priority items Walker's KGB handlers requested.)

As the crisis in the Mediterranean intensified, U.S. and Soviet naval forces were reinforced and increased their readiness. Admiral E. R. Zumwalt, the U.S. Chief of Naval Operations at the time, has written, "I doubt that major units of the U.S. Navy were ever in a tenser situation since World War II ended than the Sixth Fleet in the Mediterranean was for the week after the alert was declared."

Again, it was easy for Walker to steal the vital keylists to enable the Soviets to read U.S. communications: "There was no difficulty in [stealing keylists] . . . anyone in the radio room could have gotten the material." If the packets that he wanted were sealed, he would simply break the seal. Reaffixing the seal? "Sometimes as simple as masking . . . or Scotch tape."

From the *Niagara Falls,* Walker went ashore to Norfolk, first to the headquarters of the Atlantic Fleet amphibious force for a few months, and then to the headquarters for the Atlantic Fleet surface forces, where he served until retiring in August 1976. Walker, however, now had a "spy ring"—he had recruited Jerry Whitworth to also steal the "ultimate" secrets: communications.

Whitworth also had full access to the key materials. He served on the remote island of Diego Garcia in the Indian Ocean. There was already increasing U.S. military interest in the region, and the naval communications facility on Diego Garcia was a center for information and intelligence, with Whitworth having full access to the code machines. Prior to being assigned to Diego Garcia he attended a school to learn about new, highly classified satellite communications.

On Diego Garcia he was petty officer in charge of the satellite communications division of the communications station. He managed the technical control facility and was responsible for the custody of classified material, including cryptographic information; the monitoring of fleet broadcasts; and keeping track of ship movements, including Soviet ships. The "monitor rolls," seemingly endless sheets of yellow paper, contained information on all ship movements and operations. Monitor rolls were retained for one month and then destroyed. As long as there was a record of that destruction, the monthly monitor roll could be secreted away somewhere and eventually passed on to the Soviets. There were more than forty-odd code machines on Diego Garcia, and Whitworth had access to all of them.

Whitworth supplied so much cryptographic information to the Soviets that they eventually became discriminating about what they wanted. In particular they wanted the KW-7 keylists; they did not want messages carried on the KW-8 system, encoded voice circuits, or intelligence information, which, apparently, they preferred to get from more sophisticated sources.

After his assignment to Diego Garcia, in mid-1976 Whitworth was assigned to the aircraft carrier *Constellation* in the Pacific. On board the ship he was responsible for the operation and maintenance of crypto and communications equipment. The aircraft carrier is the centerpiece of U.S. naval operations, and usually serves as flagship for a task force or battle group. Thus Whitworth and the Soviets had access to masses of crypto information as well as operational data. He could also pass technical information on equipment in the carrier, including the newly installed satellite communications gear. And the *Constellation* force regularly operated with Allied navies in the Pacific, probably permitting the Soviets to break into their operational concepts and tactics.

Whitworth left the *Constellation* in July 1978 and the following month reported on board the *Niagara Falls,* Walker's old ship, as chief radioman and CMS custodian. The hemorrhage of secrets continued. After only one year aboard ship, Whitworth reported to the telecommunications center at Alameda, California.

This was Whitworth's most lucrative position—from the KGB point of view. At first in his office at the center, and then in a parked van outside, Whitworth photographed keylists and other crypto material. Indeed, several times he was able to provide a complete month's worth of keylists, for which he received a bonus from the Soviet spymasters. Two aircraft carriers were based at Alameda, and the communications center stood radio watch for them while they were in port. A great deal of other classified information passed through the center, which had banks of crypto machines.

For a few months Whitworth was detached to the communications facility at Stockton, California. The crypto material he obtained there is questionable. As we have seen, during that temporary assignment and subsequent duty in the carrier *Enterprise,* he may have been detected, or at least suspected.

In October 1982, with the rank of senior chief radioman, Whitworth went on board the *Enterprise* as communications watch officer. While he had access to secret material, he was not a CMS custodian and could rarely get his hands on keylists. Much of the material he did manage to photograph did not come out.

During FLTEX 83-1, the Navy's first such three-carrier fleet training exercise in the northern Pacific, he was able to garner messages between the U.S. carrier groups and participating Air Force and Canadian units. About forty ships and 250 aircraft were involved in the exercise. Whitworth could have seen virtually all the messages sent and received pertaining to the exercise, including intrusions by carrier-based aircraft into Soviet airspace to test defensive reactions.

The messages that Whitworth did copy were of value to Soviet analysts, who would try to reconstruct the exercise to understand U.S. tactics for war at sea. U.S. Navy intelligence officials estimated that in labor alone that set of messages saved the Soviets at least fifty man-years of analytic labors.

Secrets have relative values. If Whitworth was under surveillance while he was on board the carrier, his controllers would have to let him have something. The exercise communications illustrate the age-old problem of running an unwittingly turned agent: How much is enough? How good must the passed-on secrets have to be?

Whitworth stole about a quarter of the message traffic from the exercise. A Navy specialist on exercises estimated that the exercise generated a stack of messages a foot high, and that Whitworth had stolen three inches' worth, not randomly but selectively. "Basically, what you have here is a cookbook of how we do business," the Navy exercises expert said. "It's a recipe. You know. It's kind of like Coca-Cola. Once you have the recipe, you may do it a little bit different way. But you always come back to the cookbook."

Even without being able to read U.S. radio messages, Soviet communications analysts, working with information from satellite intercepts and signals picked up by eavesdropping ships, can construct a fairly accurate model of U.S. Navy message traffic. "You can find out what stations are communicating with other stations, when, over what frequencies, and how," says George A. Carver, a former deputy director of the CIA and an expert on covert communications.

"You can work out patterns of command subordination, organizational tables, location of units, movements of units, signature characteristics of certain type of messages, such as attack orders, or other kinds of very key things—all without being able to read anything."

With the keylists—"pure platinum to a cryptologist," Carver says—the Soviets got not only a way to read U.S. messages but also a deeper understanding of the architecture of the system. By learning the relationship of varied key materials to different code machines, the Soviets gained knowledge of the patterns of U.S. communications. And, thanks to the steady supply of key materials for at least seventeen years, they could understand, perhaps better than Americans working within the system, the evolution of U.S. cryptographic techniques.

Soviet analysts were like anthropologists able to watch, unobserved, the tribal rites of the U.S. cryptographic community. The loss of keying materials with the arrest of Walker and Whitworth took away day-to-day lore but left the lasting legacy of intimate knowledge. The tribe's privacy has been violated, with enduring, irreversible results.

On October 31, 1983, Whitworth retired from the Navy.

Without Whitworth, Walker's sources were severely limited. And so he turned to his son. Michael Walker stole six classified documents from the Naval Air Station at Oceana, Virginia. In January 1984, Michael Walker, a yeoman, was assigned to the operations division of the aircraft carrier *Nimitz*. He immediately began collecting classified material for his father to pass on to the Soviets. Michael obtained relatively low-grade material—not crypto. Instead of burning documents that he was ordered to destroy, he covertly stuffed them into boxes that he hid near his bunk.

The Walker "spy ring"—in reality just John Walker and Jerry Whitworth—effectively ceased to provide the Soviets with important material in 1983, although they were not arrested until May 1985. But the materials that Walker and Whitworth passed to the Soviets, coupled with the machines they had (actual U.S. equipment and machines constructed from plans and repair manuals), undoubtedly permitted the Soviets to continue to decode U.S. communications after 1985.

Meanwhile, the KGB spymasters were elated to find that another American was willing to betray communications and intelligence secrets. In 1980, Ronald W. Pelton, a fourteen-year veteran of the National Security Agency who had left the organization the year before, walked into the Soviet Embassy just as Walker had done a dozen years before. His offer of providing the Soviets with all of the secrets in his camera-like memory was immediately accepted.

On two trips to Vienna, Pelton spent several days being debriefed by Soviet agents. They were particularly interested in the supersecret Ivy Bells, the interception of Soviet messages sent via undersea cables.

Pelton had an extraordinary memory for detail. He passed no pieces of paper to the Soviets, except perhaps sketches that he made while being interrogated. His visits to Vienna provided the Soviets with invaluable information on how good U.S. signals intelligence was against Soviet activities.

Several other American servicemen attempted to provide the Soviets with communications information. Some even went to Washington and rang the buzzers on the iron gates of the Soviet Embassy and the Soviet Military Office. Even Marines in Moscow and Leningrad were accused of betraying U.S. secrets. The

Marines who were assigned to the American diplomatic posts as
security guards were at first charged with permitting Soviet
agents into sensitive communications spaces. (Although some
charges of espionage by the Marines were dropped, intelligence
officers contend that infiltration by the KGB did take place. Add
to this suspicion the innumerable reports of bugging devices
planted within the embassy and the conclusion is that the Soviets
have had a long and rarely interrupted penetration of U.S. communications. Due to a bungled investigation by the Navy, American officials may never know the full extent of Soviet activity
within the U.S. Embassy and Consulate.)

Beyond "the ultimate goal" of communications and signals
intelligence, the Soviet spymasters instruct their agents and recruiters to seek a broad array of Western technology and information. According to the U.S. Department of Defense, "Each
year Moscow receives thousands of pieces of Western equipment
and many tens of thousands of unclassified, classified, and propri-
etary documents. . . . Virtually every Soviet military research
project—well over 4,000 each year in the late 1970s and over
5,000 in the early 1980s—benefits from these technical documents and hardware." One U.S. intelligence official estimates
that the Soviet Union and its Warsaw Pact allies obtain more
than 70 percent of their high-technology needs from the West,
both legally and illegally.

Nearly all aspects of American political, economic, military,
and technological activity appear to be of interest to the Soviet
spymasters, although major espionage efforts are directed toward
computers and microelectronics. Nearly half of the detected
"trade diversions" to the Soviet Union fall into these categories.
According to the Department of Defense, "The equipment acquired through these efforts is largely responsible for the significant advances the Soviet microelectronics industry has made thus
far, advances that have reduced the overall Western lead in microelectronics from 10 to 12 years in the mid-1970s to four to six
years today."

The computer and microelectronics efforts have led the Soviets to concentrate on the so-called Silicon Valley, just south of
San Francisco. After Washington and New York this is the most
intensive area of Soviet espionage activity in the United States.

The Soviets carry out this activity through legitimate information collection, Soviet agents (legals and illegals), and trying to find Americans who would betray their country.

The Soviet quest for technology has turned Silicon Valley into a spy center as notorious as Vienna. Soviet agents have even attempted to purchase three California banks so the KGB could get a line on which high-tech workers were in need of quick, tax-free spy-for-hire cash. Selling secrets is a new way to make money in Silicon Valley. Agents from China, Japan, France, Israel, and South Korea are also prowling Silicon Valley and other high-tech sites in search of secrets.

In the computer-microchip spy war, acts even more sinister than espionage are chillingly possible. A Soviet agent on board a U.S. Navy warship can do something even worse than steal secrets: He can steal the ship's ability to fight or defend herself. By inserting a "software mole" into the ship's computer system, he can create false orders that will cripple the ship—perhaps long after he has left her. Like an invisible time bomb, the subverted software lies hidden in the computer system, ready to explode in the form of catastrophic commands.

"If an espionage agent should gain access to the classified information stored in a computer system, he could retrieve it for clandestine purposes," two Navy officers warned in 1983. "He also could alter the information stored in the computer so as to significantly change its operation characteristics." At the time of the warning, communications expert Jerry Alfred Whitworth was serving in the nuclear-powered carrier *Enterprise.* At other times in his sailor-spy career he had been commended for going aboard other ships, voluntarily, and examining their communications equipment.

Writing in 1983 in the U.S. Naval Institute *Proceedings,* the authoritative professional journal of the Navy, the officers used three scenarios to illustrate this new form of computer-age sabotage at sea:

■ A reconnaissance plane routinely launched from a U.S. carrier off Lebanon observes the sinking of a warship belonging to a friendly nation. The plane immediately transmits a report through the Worldwide Military Command and Control System (WWMCCS). But only a garbled message reaches Washington.

■ A U.S. Navy task force—a cruiser and three guided-missile

frigates—is steaming off the coast of Oman when one of the frigates makes sonar contact with an unidentified submarine. While the frigate is tracking the submarine, it sinks a tanker near the mouth of the Strait of Hormuz. The officer in tactical command of the task force orders a helicopter-frigate unit to pinpoint the location of the submarine and prepare for an attack. But everything goes haywire. None of the officer's commands get through to the other ships or helicopters. And, with no proof that a submarine was in the area, the United States is blamed for the sinking of the tanker.

■ A ship in a U.S. Navy battle group detects an incoming barrage of enemy cruise missiles. The battle group commander orders his defensive missiles fired. In the air they all self-destruct, leaving the U.S. ship with only second-string defenses that cannot destroy all the enemy missiles.

The hidden actor in the three scenarios was a computer penetrator, a subversive agent who inserted into shipboard computer systems what Navy Lieutenants Peter Grant and Robert Riche, authors of the *Proceedings* article, called "trapdoors" and "Trojan horses." A trapdoor is a small section of a computer program that is swung open by a word or sequence of characters the agent has inserted in the computer software. A Trojan horse, also called a "software mole," is a false command inserted inside a legitimate command.

The reconnaissance plane in the first scenario had a Trojan horse inside its command and control system. When the plane flashed its report its computer software called up a routine "utility program" for setting up the telecommunications link to Washington via the WWMCS. Inside the utility program was a Trojan horse designed by the penetrator's Soviet handlers. The covert subversive program told the legitimate utility program to monitor the message for certain key words—such as *sinking* or *missiles* or the name of a certain country—and, when those words were detected, to garble the message.

The task force lost the submarine because of another Trojan horse, this one cleverly fed information keyed to the Navy's satellite navigation system. This horse told the computer to kill any antisubmarine warfare commands given in a real combat situation that occurred at certain navigational coordinates, in this case a location near the Strait of Hormuz. The horse also knew that

Navy ships do not fire live ammunition in exercises in certain sensitive areas. So the horse would not be activated during an exercise and would remain undetected until the crucial moment when a real incident was taking place in a real trouble spot.

The battle group's missiles destroyed themselves because of a trapdoor built into the ship's radar. The trapdoor was opened by a signal from an enemy plane, which simply transmitted an activating message on a friend-or-foe identification frequency read by the ship's plane-detection radar. The door-unlocking message passed into the computer network and found the door. When it opened out came a planted subversive message that gave false signals to the radar tracking the ship's missiles, blowing them up long before they reached their target.

The vulnerability of warships' computer systems, the authors said, has been known since at least 1975. Around that time the Department of Defense formed "tiger teams" that were told to try to penetrate sensitive defense computers. "Not only were these tiger teams able to break into every one of the computer systems that they had targeted," the authors wrote, "they found that doing so was far simpler than many had expected. Even systems that were advertised as 'secure and unbreakable' by their manufacturers took a relatively short time to penetrate. The tiger teams were able to gain access to desired information and even obtain control over the entire computer system."

Although ideas for protecting the military's computer systems have been developed, many of the ideas have been sidetracked in the rush to modernize computer systems and continually update software. Many of the software-writing private contractors are connected to ARPANET, the Department of Defense Advanced Research Projects Agency's communications network. Someone penetrating that network could insert trapdoors and Trojan horses even before the software is delivered to the Navy. Actual penetration was revealed in 1983 when a student at the University of California at Los Angeles was arrested for breaking into ARPANET, along with more than two hundred computer systems, including that of the Naval Research Laboratory in Washington, D.C.

The lack of adequate computer protection was conceded in the Department of Defense computer security manual that was in use when Whitworth was serving aboard the *Enterprise*. "Operating in a true multi-level security mode," the manual said, "remains a desired operational goal. . . . However . . . this goal cannot generally be obtained with confidence due to the limitations in the currently available hardware/software state-of-the-art."

Admiral Watkins, when Chief of Naval Operations, in a press conference assessing probable losses to the alleged Walker spy ring, hinted concern over computer penetration. "Some technical design communications information has probably been lost . . ." he said. "New designs must now be accelerated and equipment produced more quickly than previously planned." As for the ultimate national security computer network, the WWMCS, there is no reason to believe that it is well protected against Trojan horses and trapdoors. The General Accounting Office reported in 1981 that military users of the system's computer network believed that it was "not considered to be survivable against acts of civil strife, sabotage or war." The House Committee on Government Operations in 1982 called WWMCS "a billion-dollar failure."

The WWMCS, pronounced *Wim-ex* by Pentagon acronym speakers, is supposed to transmit the highest possible level of crisis information to the President and the Secretary of State—and then transmit their orders to military commands. Linked by WWMCS computers are the White House Situation Room, the State Department Operations Center, key intelligence and warning facilities, and military commands throughout the world. A new version of thinking the unthinkable would be the conjuring up of trapdoor and Trojan-horse scenarios in *those* computers.

While such electronic trojan horses are speculative, the day-to-day interception and deciphering of encoded U.S. military and to some degree political communications is probable, even today. Since the late 1940s, beginning with Philby and Maclean, and continuing up through Walker and Whitworth, the Soviets have had access to highly classified U.S. and Allied communications. As noted earlier, with sufficient background, access to communications manuals and equipment (even damaged), the Soviets could break into the U.S. communications on a real-time basis.

Or, if at times they had to wait for the keylists provided by Walker and Whitworth, after-the-event analysis of U.S. communications would still be invaluable. If, for example, the Soviets wanted to know what went on in the Iranian rescue mission, their intelligence collection ships (AGIs) in the Arabian Sea, near the U.S. task force that launched the rescue helicopters, would record all the radio traffic and forward it to Moscow. The Soviets would then wait for the arrival of that specific period's keylists—perhaps many months later—and decode what they had recorded.

Soviet naval analysts would then be able to understand and interpret U.S. naval operations in a crisis and would advise strategists about the best ways to counter U.S. naval action. Political-military analysts would be able to infer information about how U.S. decision-making machinery works. "It's like playing poker and knowing what was in the guy's last hand," a U.S. communications officer said.

Soviet intelligence ships do more than pick up radio transmissions. These AGIs—the Soviets have more than fifty currently in service—and submarines can record all electronic emissions, radar signals, and even ship and submarine acoustic "signatures" as well as radio and microwave-relayed telephone traffic. To a lesser degree satellites and military aircraft flying near the United States can also record such electronic emissions and communications.

There is normally an AGI on station off Bangor, Washington, site of a Trident missile submarine base, and off Holy Loch, Scotland, an advanced base for Poseidon missile submarines. Another operates off the U.S. East Coast, where it can observe the missile submarine operations from Kings Bay, Georgia, and Charleston, South Carolina. That spy ship also travels down to the waters off Florida whenever there is a significant missile test or space launch. Other AGIs trail U.S. and other NATO ships wherever there is a major exercise. (In certain overseas areas, such as the western Pacific and the Mediterranean, Soviet warships complement the AGIs in shadowing Western warships.)

Soviet SIGINT aircraft also complement the AGIs. Among the more interesting aircraft employed in this role is the huge Tupolev Bear-D. Propelled by four turboprop engines, the Bears have regularly flown from bases in the Soviet Arctic around Norway and down, across the Atlantic to Cuba, coming to within a hundred miles of the U.S. East Coast and landing in Cuba. On the flight to Cuba and the return to the Soviet Union, they conduct electronic collection.

The Soviets also have communications intercept stations ashore. These vary from the relatively small installations in their embassies and consulates in Western countries to massive communications intercept facilities along the borders of the Soviet Union and at Lourdes in Cuba and at Camranh Bay, Vietnam. The Cuban facility at Lourdes, only some seventy miles from the U.S. mainland, permits the interception of U.S. domestic telephone calls as well as military communications.

Of course U.S. communications methods and laxness have helped the Soviet SIGINT efforts. The Permanent Select Committee on Intelligence of the House of Representatives has found "appalling those communication security lapses that made the wholesale theft of cryptographic materials . . . possible." And "senior U.S. Government officials are careless about how they use car telephones. Sensitive matters also have been discussed on non-secure communications by senior Administration officials communicating with Air Force One [the President's plane]. . . . The final go-ahead request for Navy aircraft to force down the Egyptian airliner carrying the *Achille Lauro* terrorists was phoned in the open to Air Force One. Ham operators, and presumably interested foreign powers, regularly listen to Air Force One communications."

The primary goal of Soviet intelligence collection efforts is SIGINT. Their next major interest is Western technology, to exploit for their own use and to better understand how to counter Western military systems. The Soviets also observe Western tactics. The watching and analysis of tactics is important because military forces tend to fight in the same manner that they train.

The United States employs sophisticated electronic intercept equipment, with several NATO nations, Japan, and even Communist China providing sites for U.S. intercept stations. Aircraft, warships, and satellites also have a SIGINT capability. But an increasing U.S. reliance on technological spying has overshadowed a crisis: the lack of agents—human intelligence, or HUMINT in military jargon. In the late 1940s the United States lost several agents in Eastern Europe, apparently due to the duplicity of Philby and Maclean. After that, the emphasis shifted to electronics. The United States has still had spies—the most publicized being GRU officer-turned-spy Oleg Penkovskiy in the early 1960s and Polish Colonel Wladyslaw Kuklinski in the early 1980s. But indications are that such coups have been rare.

The Soviets, while using electronic interception to break into U.S. communications, have continued to emphasize the man on the ground—the spy. Americans have been quick to accommodate the Soviets, taking their coin in return for secrets, often ones that electronic spy equipment could not obtain. A tally of the Americans in the NSA, the CIA, the Army, Navy, and industry who have betrayed their nation indicates that the Soviets have been able to complement their electronic intercepts with the keys to understanding them. Commenting on the impact of the betrayal of U.S. communications secrets, Rear Admiral Studeman, the Director of Naval Intelligence, in late 1986 declared that the American spies had "jeopardized the backbone of this country's national defense and countless lives of military personnel," and that "recovery from [Walker's] traitorous activity will take years and many millions of taxpayers' dollars."

At the same time, Admiral Studeman admitted, the Navy has "little confidence that we understand the full extent and scope of the . . . conspiracy and the damage. . . ."

11

"Like One of Us . . ."

In 1975, John F. Lehman, Jr., and James Frederick Sattler were among the several bright young men who circulated in Washington's national security community. Lehman was Deputy Director of the U.S. Arms Control and Disarmament Agency. Sattler was an employee of a reputable foreign-policy research organization. Like Lehman and others at the same mid-level in the community, Sattler was known as a conservative defense intellectual.

Young men of that breed, often brusque and always well educated, had become accomplished authorities on defense issues. Their mission was the transformation of that knowledge into influential contributions at high levels of government. They appeared at the gates of the Pentagon when Secretary of Defense Robert S. McNamara and his aging whiz kids had departed, when defense policies were handed over to the conservatives of the post-Vietnam generation.

"He was like one of us," Lehman said of Sattler, recalling to the authors the early 1970s, when these young conservatives were beginning their careers in government, moving to Pentagon offices from outside positions as consultants on national security matters. Lehman had been president of a Washington management firm that specialized in defense matters. Another executive in the firm was Richard Perle, who also served as specialist on national security and international operations for Senator Henry M. Jackson, one of the most powerful defense advocates on Capitol Hill. Perle would become an Assistant Secretary of Defense, as would another young conservative, James P. Wade, Jr., a technocrat who had served in a nuclear weapons laboratory and the Defense Advanced Research Projects Agency. John Lehman in 1981, at the age of thirty-nine, would become Secretary of the Navy.

Sattler, born in New York City in 1938, had gone to the University of California at Berkeley. He later studied in Germany and Poland. He had taught at the University of Auckland in New Zealand and gone on from there in 1967 to a research fellowship in international relations in West Germany. He became so fluent in German that he was often taken for a native German. He traveled frequently to Europe, teaching, doing research, and attending international conferences. He worked for a time for the Atlantic Institute for Foreign Affairs in Paris.

In Washington, Sattler went to work as a foreign-policy analyst for the Atlantic Council of the United States. The Atlantic Council is one of the citadels of the Washington foreign-policy establishment, focusing its attention on the political and military problems of the North Atlantic Treaty Organization. A privately funded organization, the council long has enjoyed a prestigious membership of retired military and civilian leaders.

In the council professors from the Johns Hopkins University's School of Advanced International Studies find themselves discussing NATO issues with members of the President's National Security Council staff. Members of Congress and their key staffers work on council papers with leading private defense analysts. Together, academic, government, and private-sector authorities examine questions that come before NATO, such as President Carter's decision to defer neutron weapons and the role that NATO navies will play in a conflict with the Warsaw Pact.

Nearly all of the people discussing such matters at Atlantic Council seminars and meetings have high security clearances, and their discreetly advanced ideas often find their way into NATO policy papers and meetings mantled in secrecy. At times Administration officials will use the council sessions as a sounding board for highly sensitive as well as controversial plans and proposals.

James Sattler was part of that world, a political scientist with access to high-level people and ideas, an intellectual who had intimate knowledge of NATO policy but no responsibility for carrying out that policy. (His specialty was East-West trade.) He seemed to like that role—the man on the edge of the policy-making arena, the man who was satisfied with being a witty, well-liked observer of the foreign-policy establishment.

But sometime around 1975, Sattler started looking for another job. His friend John Lehman was deputy director of the arms control agency in the State Department and his friend James Wade was Deputy Assistant Secretary of Defense for Policy Plans. Sattler had tried first for a position under Wade, who, having no job to offer, had passed him along to Lehman. "We all knew each other," Lehman recalled. "We hung around together. We drank beer together. I thought I knew Jim quite well." Lehman was ready to give Sattler a job in the agency, although he was puzzled by Sattler's sudden desire to step from the edge of the foreign-policy establishment to a place inside it.

During the period that Lehman and Sattler were discussing the latter's joining the arms control agency, FBI agents called on Lehman and told him that Sattler was a spy working for East German intelligence, which relayed his information to Moscow. He had also tried to get a job on the staff of the House Committee on Foreign Affairs.

"The agents told me," Lehman remembered, "that his mission was to become more influential in Washington. They asked me to talk to him and see if he would be interested in becoming a double agent." When Sattler arrived for their next meeting Lehman told him what the FBI had said.

"He didn't deny it," Lehman said. "He seemed relieved."

Sattler told Lehman that he had not wanted to try to get a government position. "I told them I was doing pretty well where I was," Lehman quoted him as saying about his controllers. "But they insisted that I would do better as a government official. I was afraid this would happen."

Sattler's assignment was to send back to East Germany and thus to Moscow what one source called "clarifications" of the policy positions of influential people on such subjects as strategic stability and arms control. He was *not* to report on the subjects' vulnerability to blackmail. Nor, until he began making his reluctant job-seeking calls, was he to attempt to get into a policy-making position.

Sattler, like Lehman and Perle, had completed his formal education in Europe. Lehman went to Cambridge, Perle to the London School of Economics and Political Science—and Sattler to East Germany. The path began at college, where Sattler first turned against his native country. Like many young people of those years, he saw himself pitted against the system. And he believed that an individual could make a difference, could even change the world. But, unlike the overwhelming majority of his generation, Sattler decided that the route to changing the system was through a particular kind of espionage.

As he cautiously talked to Lehman about his life, Sattler said that when he had become disillusioned he had gotten interested in Marxism. He left a few blanks in his résumé, skipping the manner in which he was recruited and how he was trained by the East German intelligence service. He said he believed he was on the winning side and regretted only that he had hurt his parents, who lived in New England and knew him only as a self-exile.

"He said, 'I'll have to disappear now,' and he walked out," Lehman said. "I'm told that he went back to East Germany. I heard a rumor a couple of years ago that he had plastic surgery and a new identity and was back here again." Other sources say that he married the daughter of a Latin American military official and emigrated to his bride's country.

Soon after Lehman last saw him, Sattler fled to Mexico, where he unsuccessfully tried to get help from the Soviet Embassy. He then briefly returned to Washington. There the FBI used a little-known federal law to indelibly mark Sattler as a traitor. He was forced to *register as a spy.* On March 23, 1974, he went to the Registration Unit of the Department of Justice's Internal Security Section and filled out Form GA-1, labeled simply "Registration Statement."

On the form he listed all of his visits to foreign countries during the previous twenty years, listed his employer as the Atlantic Council, and checked "Yes" to this question: *Do you have knowledge of the espionage, counter-espionage or sabotage tactics of a foreign government or foreign political party?* He then gave a succinct, and in several respects remarkable, description of his life as a spy:

In 1967, I was recruited by an individual named "Rolf" who identified himself as a member of the "Coordinating Staff of the Countries of the Warsaw Treaty Association." Since then, I have learned that "Rolf" is connected with the section for Strategy and Tactics, Institute for Marxism and Leninism, which is connected with the Central Committee of the SED of the German Democratic Republic (GDR). I drafted and signed a statement indicating my willingness to cooperate with the "Coordinating Staff of the Countries of the Warsaw Treaty Organization" and have received approximately $15,000 for my services. I have also received an "honor decoration" for my services issued to me by the Ministry for State Security of the GDR.*

Since 1967, I have transmitted to my principals in Berlin, GDR, information and documents which I have received from the North Atlantic Treaty Organization and from individuals in institutions and government agencies in the Federal Government of Germany, United States, Great Britain, Canada, and France.

I photographed a portion of this information with a microdisc camera and placed the microdiscs in packages which I mailed to West Germany which I know were subsequently received by my principals in Berlin, GDR. Other documents and information I photographed with a Minox camera and personally carried the film to my principals in Berlin or handed them to a courier. The microdisc camera was given to me by my principal.

Have you received an assignment in the espionage, counterespionage or sabotage tactics of a foreign government or foreign political party? Check (X) Yes ( ) No
Type of instruction received:

Codes and ciphers, microphotography, radio and mail communications, clandestine meetings, concealment devices.

No formal courses; individual instructions by specialists. . . .

---

* Sattler told some friends that he also had been given a commission as a lieutenant colonel.

When he filled out this document Sattler's career as an agent and a potential mole ended. So did his brief stint as a double agent. "Sattler had been turned successfully and was worked as a turned agent," a knowledgeable source told the authors. The source, who knew Sattler quite well, said that U.S. counter-espionage agents turned Sattler long enough to track his communications system, which ran from Washington to Canada to West Germany to East Germany and finally to Moscow. "This—the turning, the registration statement, the vanishing—all happened after Lehman made his cursory attempt at turning him," according to the source.

Sattler told the source and others that he had feared for his life when he was turned by the FBI. He could not hope to return to East Germany because he had become a double traitor. By signing the statement he became useless, and this uselessness to both sides, he believed, saved his life. U.S. counter-espionage officials quickly lost interest in him after they forced him to expose himself as a spy by signing the registration statement.

Lehman talked to the authors in detail about Sattler because he wanted to emphasize that even in an age of mercenary spies there still are those who spy for ideological reasons.

The authors and Lehman were finishing lunch in the "secretary's mess," the Navy's name for his private dining room across the hall from his Pentagon office suite, and Lehman was finishing his account of Sattler. Suddenly his right hand fell, moving in an arc, a fighter pilot's gesture that seemed to symbolize an attack on a target. He said, sharply, "He could have been anything by now. An Assistant Secretary of Defense—or maybe State—by now."

His voice rising, he leaned forward. "I'm convinced there are others like him. Right here in this building. I'm convinced there are moles high in the United States Government." Lehman, with characteristic directness, gave the authors Sattler's name and suggested that we check him out with the FBI.

Earlier in the luncheon conversation Lehman was asked about another spy suspect, Glenn Souther, a Navy petty officer and an expert on satellite photography. "We screwed up on that one," Lehman said, without elaborating. Souther, a former photographer's mate, was a reservist assigned to a naval intelligence

facility in Norfolk. He had disappeared soon after he had been
questioned by FBI agents. Like John Walker, Souther could
probably thank an ex-wife for the visit from the FBI. Ernest
Porter of the FBI public affairs office declined to discuss the case
with the authors. In July 1988, Souther surfaced in Moscow and
the Soviets announced that he had been granted political asylum.

Disappearances of people who hold secrets usually inspire
unpublicized, inconclusive investigations and theories about ideologically inspired espionage. Gary Gnibus, a thirty-one-year-old
weapons engineer, worked on secret projects at the U.S. Army's
Research and Development Center at the Picatinny Arsenal in
New Jersey. After he vanished there was an extensive search for
him for six months, and then an admission of failure by authorities. "Right now," an FBI agent said, "I don't think we have any
real leads, just some ideas. For all we know, he could be dead, in
Russia, or living in Mexico." A second added, "Espionage is one
of several possible scenarios we're looking into."

Another vanished secrets-holder was Air Force Captain William H. Hughes, Jr., a specialist in command, control, and communications systems—a level of military activity well above ordinary communications, where Walker and Whitworth worked.
Hughes was last seen when he was sent from Kirtland Air Force
Base in Albuquerque, New Mexico, to the Netherlands. He was
classified a deserter in 1983. An espionage case was pursued but
not developed.

Many counter-espionage agents believe that spies in the form
of moles frequently try to burrow into the nation's political-military apparatus. Some moles vanish in fear of detection, leaving
behind suspicions and little else. Others are never found. Still
others, like Sattler, do not get the opportunity to burrow.

Sattler was not a very successful spy. "He was a very minor
agent," said someone familiar with the case. "But he had a pattern that could be replicated. And I believe it was." Sattler's
pattern was simple but effective. He showed how a relatively
bright and dedicated ideological agent could talk his way into the
American policy-making establishment.

A startling number of people the authors interviewed for this
book believe, with Lehman, that moles have successfully found
high government posts, trading their allegiance to the United
States for ideological reasons as well as for gold.

Sattler was not caught because the FBI had unearthed him. He, like nearly all spies discovered in recent years, was unmasked because someone informed on him to government authorities. An East German intelligence officer, who has not been named, defected to West Germany and in debriefings named several agents, including Sattler. The chances are great that Sattler, like the several infamous ideological spies who had earlier infiltrated the British intelligence services, would not have been detected by routine counter-espionage techniques. Sattler might well be in a senior position in the Pentagon or State Department today if he had not fallen victim to the habitual defection-redefection twists and turns of East and West intelligence services in divided Germany.

Ideological spies are difficult to detect, and, once detected, difficult to hold and prosecute. The temptation of the arresting country is to use them as pawns in a spy swap because of the Soviets' known loyalty toward captured spies. Soviet intelligence officers may treat a mercenary spy as a mere supplier of valuable goods. But an ideological spy warrants fraternal treatment. In an emergency the Soviets will diligently try to get him or her out of the West and into friendly hands, via a swap or by a disappearing act. The exfiltration of former CIA employee Edward Howard is a recent example of the Moscow Express in action. Howard was whisked to Moscow as smoothly as were his predecessors two decades before, Martin and Mitchell, the National Security Agency defectors, and British traitors Burgess and Maclean, who eluded Her Majesty's Government.

"Ideological affinity is not frequently encountered, although it is a desired inducement," says a U.S. report on Soviet espionage. "Blackmail is a last resort. The most common motivation is financial gain, often combined with conscious or unconscious anger at an employer. . . . Recruitment is more commonly accomplished on the basis of positive inducement than by coercive approaches. . . ."

Money, one such positive inducement, was the most frequent motivation in the many espionage cases that erupted in the 1970s and 1980s. But a few defy a pure monetary explanation. Two spies did claim ideology as their motive to mask their greed and to gain sympathy for their treachery. They were able to attempt this because Jonathan Jay Pollard and Anne Henderson-Pollard were not spying for the Soviet Union. Their client was Israel.

In September 1979 the Navy's Field Operational Intelligence Office* hired Jonathan Jay Pollard, a twenty-six-year-old graduate of Stanford University, as an intelligence research specialist. Jay Pollard, who had also attended the Fletcher School of Law and Diplomacy at Tufts University, was bright and talkative. As an undergraduate he had enjoyed playing hobby-store war games for days at a time. As a Navy researcher he took great delight in browsing through real secrets. Following the standard background investigation, Pollard was given a top-secret clearance plus access to sensitive compartmented information (SCI)—"tickets" that allowed him to be privy to special intelligence sources.

NFOIO had a broad charter to provide the Navy with warnings of foreign naval activity that could threaten the United States or its allies. To keep track of foreign surface ships, submarines, and air forces, the office had access to virtually all of the intelligence-gathering resources of the nation. As Pollard learned about intelligence research he quickly realized that he could wander almost at will through files that he had no legitimate business to see. "He was so conscientious that they let him take anything he wanted," a former colleague would say of him.

Pollard's unit was housed within the Naval Intelligence Support Center (NISC), a massive, almost windowless concrete building in Suitland, Maryland, nine miles southeast of Washington, at the bureaucratic Siberia called simply "the Federal Building Complex." Also at the Suitland federal complex were offices of the Bureau of the Census, Weather Bureau, and the Army's Strategic Communications Command.

Soon after Pollard went to work at NFOIO he made contact with a military attaché at the South African Embassy. As a graduate student, Pollard later said, he had met the attaché and had continued the acquaintance after starting his NISC job. But at one point he reportedly told other Navy officials that he had lived in South Africa, where he fabricated tales of a father who had

---

* NFOIO was pronounced *No-fee-ooh* by acronym speakers. It has since been renamed the Navy Operational Intelligence Center.

been the CIA chief of station. Earlier, while still at Stanford, he had told friends how he had fled Czechoslovakia in 1968 when it was revealed that his father was a CIA operative in Prague. None of this was true.

His fantasies in college also included boasts about connections with the Israeli intelligence service. He once sent himself a telegram addressed to "Colonel" Pollard. Pollard never outgrew lying. He entered false job and education information on his application for government employment. When he was being checked for a security clearance, the Defense Investigation Service background investigation did not pick up the lies.

Through means not publicly revealed, U.S. counter-espionage officials learned of Pollard's contact with the South Africans. The reaction of Pollard's Navy boss was swift. He withdrew the researcher's top-secret and special clearances. Left with a clearance only for secret-level information, Pollard found himself severely restricted in the intelligence business.

If Pollard had handed over secrets to South Africa, they would have rapidly found their way to KGB headquarters in Moscow. Since 1962 a South African naval officer had been working for the KGB. In 1981, when Pollard went to work at NFOIO and approached the South Africans, Dieter Felix Gerhardt, by then a commodore, was serving on the South African planning and operations staff in Pretoria. Privy to all military communications and planning in the country, he certainly would have access to material of the kind that Pollard would supply, and Gerhardt would have passed such prizes on to the KGB spymasters.

The authors have found that at least one other American was providing secrets to the South Africans while Gerhardt was working for the KGB. In September 1981, U.S. Navy Ensign Stephen Baba, assigned to a frigate berthed in San Diego, mailed classified information to the South African Embassy in Washington. The items included a document dealing with electronic warfare and two microfilm code indexes.

The South Africans turned Baba's documents over to U.S. officials. Baba was arrested. In Baba's court martial he said that he wanted money for the documents so that his fiancée in the Philippines could attend college. Baba was sentenced to eight years at hard labor.

Gerhardt was detained in the United States in 1983 by FBI and South African agents. They had been tipped off by Israeli intelligence, the Mossad,* whose own agents in Moscow had observed Gerhardt sitting with his wife, Ruth, in boxes at the Bolshoi Ballet on two of at least five visits to Moscow. Gerhardt was sentenced to life for treason and his Swiss-born wife was sentenced to ten years.

As soon as the Navy officer who had pulled Pollard's clearances was assigned elsewhere, Pollard appealed the downgrading of his clearances. The commanding officer of the NISC, Captain Chauncey Hoffman, sought to have them restored, against the advice of several key NISC department heads. The Director of Naval Intelligence, Rear Admiral Sumner Shapiro, also opposed reinstating the top-secret clearance and special tickets. But Hoffman persisted. As one of his branch chiefs told the authors, "He had to demonstrate that he—not the DNI—was in charge at NISC. We told him that Shapiro might know something that we don't and we shouldn't push. But he was the boss and we prepared the letters he told us to."

Finally, Pollard's higher clearances were restored "in accordance with established procedures." (Hoffman, who had been head of the Naval Intelligence Command—the field activities at Suitland—since July 1980, had also been a supporter of Samuel L. Morison in the face of charges by other NISC employees that the analyst was using classified material in the work he did for *Jane's Fighting Ships.*)

Pollard moved up the bureaucratic ladder to the Naval Investigative Service, and his career improved, just as if nothing had happened. As part of his training he was sent to the prestigious National Defense University in Washington, the most senior of the several schools for military officers and ranking civilians in government service. Pollard flunked one of his courses—on terrorism warning systems—because he failed to turn in a paper he was supposed to have written. The paper was on Israeli intelligence methods.

In June 1984, Pollard went to work for a new, high-priority

---

* *Mossad* is Hebrew for "Institution." Israel's internal security force is Shin Bet, an acronym based on the first two initials of the General Security Service, in Hebrew, *Sherut Bitachon Kalali.*

unit, the Anti-Terrorism Alert Center in the Threat Analysis Division of the Naval Investigative Service. The Chief of Naval Operations had ordered the establishment of the center and had taken a personal interest in it. The center became a hot spot of action and influence in June 1985 after the murder in Beirut of Navy Diver Robert Dean Stethem on hijacked TWA Flight 847. The Navy worked to make the center capable of producing an instantaneous, "specific Navy-Marine look" at threats, with "analyst-to-analyst, real-time" checks of intelligence reports. Given this mandate, the center was able to demand access to information throughout the intelligence community.

Pollard instantly benefited from his presence on the center staff, first as a watch officer and then as a research specialist. In keeping with security theory—but, as will be seen, not with security practice—he was given "compartmentalized" access to such data as satellite photographs and CIA agents' reports. By theory he should have had access only to information pertaining to possible terrorism in the Caribbean and the continental United States. In practice he had access to virtually whatever he said he needed.

Soon Pollard became a dispenser of secrets. He bragged about what he knew to friends and even to casual acquaintances. He took it upon himself to give information, for instance, to an Australian Navy officer with the appropriate name of Peter Mole. Although Mole was authorized to receive certain information on behalf of his government, he was shown far more by Pollard. Mole, for example, got intelligence insights about the breakdown of relations between the United States and New Zealand.

Another recipient of Pollard's one-man intelligence service was Kurt Lohbeck, a supporter of the *mujahedeen* freedom fighters in Afghanistan. Lohbeck, according to a court affidavit, "had access to several key U.S. officials, including [National Security Adviser] Robert McFarlane. . . . On several occasions, Lohbeck showed Mr. Pollard classified documents with security caveats so high that he was unaware they existed."

Pollard advertised to anyone who would listen that he was a staunch advocate of a strong Israel—and that he was a holder of interesting secrets. At least three of his social acquaintances received classified information from him in what authorities believe was an attempt by Pollard to set up a private information service or to use this information to launch a business career after leaving the Navy.

Two of his friends were investment advisers who could make professional use of Pollard's access to analyses of political and economic developments in several countries. Soon after Pollard's arrest, these friends, apparently fearing charges of involvement in espionage, rushed to federal authorities to tell what he had told them. No charges were brought against them, Mole, or Lohbeck.

None of this free-lancing of secrets had anything to do with Pollard's alleged interest in Israel. But in June 1984 he began to focus on the use of his Navy assignment for selling secrets to Israeli officials. Around this time he told his fiancée, Anne Henderson, that a New York friend had informed him that he would soon be "connecting" Pollard to a person for a meeting that would be beneficial to the "existence and survival of Israel." The friend had raised funds for Israel and had helped export high-technology equipment and information to Israel.

Pollard soon went off to New York. He returned to Anne with a story that he had met with a "high-level officer in the Israeli Air Force." "Avi," as Pollard called him, had said that Pollard might do some work for him. "It looks like we might have a relationship going," Pollard told Anne. He also suggested that soon they would be enjoying a better standard of living.

Anne Henderson was used to hearing Jay Pollard speak in this grandiose way. But not so a Washington friend, who was startled one Saturday night that summer when Pollard and Anne appeared unexpectedly at his home and began wildly talking about some mysterious new enterprise. By the reasoning of Pollard, the friend was a likely candidate to become Pollard's assistant in spying for Israel. Pollard believed that the friend's upbringing, as a Jew in a predominantly black Detroit neighborhood, made him sympathetic to "Zionism."

Pollard almost immediately launched into a criticism of his friend's humble life-style. He did not need to live like this when there was money to be made helping Pollard. "We're serious," the friend quoted Pollard as saying. "We're going to do this. Anne's going to go into business for herself."

When the friend asked who she was going to work for, Pollard replied, "The Brothers. This is for the Brothers"—his term for the Israelis. When the subject of money came up Pollard responded, "Oh, this would be roughly two to three thousand dollars [a month]."

The "pitch," as the Pollards later called it, did not work on their friend. On the way back to their Dupont Circle apartment, Anne recalled, she said to Jay, "This was a bad idea. I think you should just forget that you had this conversation." The next morning the friend called Pollard and demanded that they meet right away. The friend said he did not want to have anything to do with any illegal activities and, in fact, should probably report Pollard's thinly veiled offer to federal authorities. Pollard, now frightened, told the friend to say that Pollard "was just telling stories, if anyone ever asked."

Shortly thereafter, Anne, on a business trip in Ohio, got a telephone call from Pollard, who asked her to come home to meet Avi and his wife, Judy. The two couples met over dinner— Jay Pollard, the zealot with a yen for a better life; Anne Henderson, the budding entrepreneur; Judy Sella, the Israeli wife seemingly unaware of all that was going on; and her husband, the dashing Colonel Aviem (Avi) Sella, an Israeli Air Force officer and intelligence operative, in the latter role under cover as a graduate student at New York University. Sella confided to Pollard that he had led the Israeli 1981 air strike on the site where Iraqis were attempting to build nuclear weapons. Sella said he now served as a case officer in an extremely secret Israeli intelligence unit operating in the United States.

Sella and Pollard later met on their own—leaving their wives theoretically ignorant of the espionage being discussed— and Sella got down to business. He asked Pollard for a "sample" of the kind of information he could provide Israel. Sella assured Pollard that he would be paid for his services. The two then worked out a code that Sella would use if he needed to contact Pollard in Washington. Pollard made a list of the pay phones near his apartment. Sella assigned a Hebrew letter to each one. Sella would call Pollard at home and mention a letter. Pollard would then go to the phone indicated by that letter and wait for Sella to call.

A few days later, using this system, Sella arranged a meeting in the public gardens of Dumbarton Oaks, an art gallery and research library in the Georgetown section of Washington. Pollard reportedly got off to a fine start with a surprising first sample: detailed information on the places in Iraq where chemical warfare weapons were manufactured. Later he is believed to have provided similar information about Syrian chemical warfare facilities.

The next Hebrew-letter phone call produced a Pollard-Sella meeting at the Maryland home of an Israeli diplomat. Pollard, who had been told by Sella that Israel had more than enough information on terrorism, brought with him the samples from the first meeting, along with copies of classified radio messages and intelligence summaries. Sella handed them to a man who went upstairs in the home, presumably copied the documents, and returned them to Pollard.

A short time after Sella and his wife again had dinner with Pollard and Anne Henderson, Sella said he was about to return to Israel. The next step for Pollard, Sella said, was a trip to Paris to meet his new handler, "the old man," who would, in intelligence parlance, "task" Pollard and pay him. Pollard was to tell friends and NISC colleagues that the trip was an engagement present from a mythical relative, who would be conjured up whenever Pollard had to explain his newfound wealth.

In November, Pollard and Anne went to Paris for a week. There Sella introduced Pollard to the old man, Joseph (Yossi) Yagur, whose cover position was consul for scientific affairs at the Israeli Consulate in New York. Also at the meeting was Rafael (Rafi) Eitan, a veteran Israeli intelligence official who ran the Israeli Defense Ministry's Liaison Bureau for Scientific Affairs, known as Lekem, a Hebrew acronym. Lekem was the cover for the intelligence unit Pollard had just joined.

While the men conducted business in a Paris safe house, Anne and the wives of Avi and Rafi went shopping and sightseeing. Anne was taken to the jewelry store of Mappin & Webb and told to pick out an engagement ring. She selected a $10,000 diamond and sapphire ring that Sella later purchased and gave to Pollard for presentation to Anne. The Israelis said that as a cover story Anne should tell friends that the engagement ring was a gift from Pollard's "Uncle Joe Fisher."

As Pollard and Anne were about to leave Paris for a trip around Europe, Sella gave Pollard something between $10,000 and $12,000 in cash—Pollard would forget the exact amount—to pay for the trip, a grand tour of the Riviera, Italy, Switzerland,

and Germany. Sella sent off the now officially engaged young couple with the promise of a $1,500 monthly salary for Jay. It was a modern kind of recruitment, in which the fiancée or wife meets the new boss and his wife and is warmly welcomed into the firm.

Back in the United States, Pollard quickly fell into an espionage routine. Under the loose security rules that governed the Naval Intelligence complex at Suitland, Maryland, Pollard could make computerized searches on virtually any subject, regardless of his theoretically "compartmented" clearance or specific "need to know." One of his major sources for the theft of secrets was the Defense Intelligence Agency, a repository of a great deal of military data on Third World nations. By a presidential directive issued in 1984, the DIA was authorized to collect intelligence on terrorism. Using this directive as his entrée, Pollard was able to prowl through DIA's computerized data banks searching for whatever his Israeli handlers wanted.

About three times a week he would gather up the computer printouts, satellite photographs, and secret documents he had been given on his rounds, put them in his briefcase, and walk from his office to a continually manned security checkpoint at the entrance of the Naval Intelligence Support Center, where his office was located. Because he had a specially issued classified courier pass, he could leave NISC headquarters without having his briefcase searched. He would walk to his car in the huge Suitland parking lot and drive to a place where he could not be watched. His favorite spot was a car wash. Sitting in the car while it was going through the suds, scrubber, and rinse, Pollard would transfer the documents from his regular briefcase to a suitcase that he reserved for his espionage deliveries.

Every two weeks or so, on a Friday, Pollard would carry the suitcase into the Washington apartment of Irit Erb, an Israeli Embassy secretary, who would see to it that certain documents were copied. Pollard stole two kinds of documents: those that he had signed out, and was thus accountable for, and those, such as copies of cables, for which there was no accountability. On Sunday he would return to the Erb apartment and collect the accountable documents so he could return them.

On the last Saturday of the month Pollard would meet with Yossi Yagur in another apartment in the same building, which was at 2939 Van Ness Street Northwest, not far from the new, fortresslike Israeli Embassy on International Drive. This apartment was the espionage copy center, the spy chamber. An American lawyer who had dual Israeli citizenship and worked as an adviser to the Israeli Defense Ministry had bought the condominium apartment, for $82,500 in cash, in 1985.

While Yagur went over selected documents with Pollard, other Israelis busily copied or photographed new documents that Pollard had brought. Pollard had been told not to waste his time and talents on terrorism information. Yagur, in his monthly "collection guidance" speech to Pollard, asked for data on certain U.S. weapons systems and, when he got such information, told Pollard about some of the specific ways in which the U.S. secrets had helped Israel. Pollard later said that "a special team of analysts had been established back in Israel just for the purpose of evaluating the operational applicability of all the new information collected."

When Yagur was finished with his evaluation and his "tasking," he paid Pollard his monthly salary of $1,500. In the spring of 1985, Pollard got a raise to $2,500 a month and was invited to take an all-expenses-paid European honeymoon with Anne. Pollard and Anne went to a Washington travel agency and booked a three-week tour with stops in seven European cities. In a flair for the lavish that was reminiscent of Jerry and Brenda Whitworth, Jay and Anne told the travel agent that they wished to be booked only in first-class hotels. They chose Venice as their wedding city. After the wedding they traveled from Venice to Zurich in a $700 private compartment on the Orient Express. From there they went to Israel.

While in Israel, Pollard received more espionage instructions and socialized with Yagur, Sella, and an Israeli known as "Uzi," whom Pollard had previously met in the United States. Pollard also met with Eitan, who was then in a hospital. There were dinner parties and other social evenings, which their wives attended. As a parting gift the Pollards were given more than $10,000 in cash to cover their expenses. Pollard, who was not expected to account for his expenses, would later say he could not remember exactly how much he had been handed. It could have been $14,000.

The Pollards again progressed grandly across Europe for

about two weeks, paying some $4,500 in cash for their stays at luxury hotels and meals at expensive restaurants. A couple of months later, at a meeting with Pollard in Washington, Yagur showed Pollard an Israeli passport with Pollard's photograph and the identity of an Israeli citizen named "Danny Cohen." Yagur gave Pollard a Swiss bank account number and said that $30,000 had already been deposited. A grateful Israel, Yagur said, would add $30,000 to that account every year for the next ten years. After that Pollard would presumably move to Israel as Danny Cohen. The Israeli spy handlers, like the Soviets, knew how to motivate and assure their agents.

Anne, who had worked in the public relations office of the National Rifle Association, now began thinking of a career move. She quit the NRA job and, with the aid of her father, a Washington public relations man, approached the New York public relations firm of CommCore. For some time CommCore had been trying to convince officials in the Chinese Embassy that they needed a course in American public relations techniques. Anne told CommCore that she had the goods that would land the Chinese account. CommCore hired her as a consultant.

Now Jonathan Pollard had a new subject to search out in the secure intelligence-data computers at various Washington intelligence offices. Among the items he brought home were five secret studies on diplomats in the Chinese Embassy and consulates. Anne assiduously took notes on the backgrounds and quirks of the Chinese diplomats and, without the knowledge of CommCore, used U.S. intelligence information to put on a brilliant performance at a briefing at the embassy in September.

Coincidentally, it was in September that Pollard's commanding officer in the Navy first learned that the conscientious researcher on terrorism threats to the United States had been ranging far from his assigned area. The commanding officer was informed that Pollard was conducting computer searches for SCI materials about the Middle East. China, apparently, was not mentioned.

On October 1, Israeli warplanes had bombed, with great precision, the Tunis headquarters of Yasir Arafat, leader of the Palestine Liberation Organization. Pollard knew that the strike had been successful largely because he had given the Israelis important information on the radar installations and air defenses protecting the PLO headquarters. Lurking in his analyst's mind there had to be some fears. There had to be a possibility that U.S. analysis of the raid would reveal that the Israelis had been *too* good. A curious analyst could determine what secret U.S. information about the target area had been checked out—and by whom.

About this time Commander Jerry Agee, Pollard's commanding officer, ordered "especially close scrutiny" of Pollard's work habits and computer runs. He was also watched as he left the office. On October 25, as he started one of his regular Friday delivery days, a co-worker reported having seen him leaving the NISC carrying what appeared to be classified documents.

Now Agee took personal charge of the investigation. Two Fridays later, on November 8, he discovered that Pollard had obtained a printout of SCI information on Middle East subjects. A surreptitious check of Pollard's work space showed that the information was not there. Pollard had taken the sensitive material out of the building. *Where was it? Who had seen it?* Agee, following the double-track procedure that regulations demanded, called both the NIS security office and the FBI.

On Friday, November 15, 1985, Pollard made one of his by-now-routine deliveries to Irit Erb's apartment. On Sunday he appeared for the equally routine pickup of the accountable documents. Irit did not come to the door. Pollard could not get his documents.

On Monday, Pollard, nervous and worried, drove to work. A year before, Samuel L. Morison, another civilian employee at the NISC, had been arrested for stealing classified satellite photographs. Pollard knew more about the case than many other NISC employees because Pollard had taken part in the damage assessment that followed Morison's arrest. The assignment had given Pollard valuable knowledge about NISC security and investigation techniques. And he learned more about the way NISC handled satellite photographs and other classified materials.

Security had tightened at NISC in the year since Morison's arrest. There were more briefcase inspections, more bulletins urging a higher level of security consciousness, and more suggestions that workers keep an eye on each other. In October 1985, Morison had been convicted—not of theft but of espionage. The conviction inspired new gossip about spying at the NISC. Workers joked uneasily about it. Civilians at the Suitland complex spoke suspiciously about the sailor-spies. *How many Walkers have we got here?* And sailors talked to each other about civilians like *that goddamn creep Morison.* There was an uneasiness in the air, perceived by civilian employees and naval personnel at Suitland and by contractors and others who came through the double set of doors that admitted those with proper clearances and business into the Navy's intelligence complex.

Pollard, arrogantly self-confident in both his jobs as analyst and spy, had not realized that the climate of suspicion in the NISC building would affect him. But that Monday morning, when he entered the NISC building, he must have wondered why trusty Irit Erb from the embassy had not made her usual Sunday trip to the apartment, why she had not opened the door to the spy chamber. Whatever his worries, though, Pollard went about his regular duties, both as an analyst of terrorism and a spy for Israel.

That day he made one of his usual searches through SCI material unrelated to his duties and routinely printed out what he wanted. At the end of the day he walked out carrying a package of looted secrets. The package contained sixty classified documents, twenty of them labeled top secret. Pollard flashed his courier's card, passed through the checkpoint, and emerged from the NISC building. He did not notice that several men were following him out to the parking lot.

As he opened the door to his 1980 Mustang, the men crowded around him and identified themselves as FBI and NIS agents. They asked him about the package. Pollard tried to brazen it out, claiming that he was merely carrying the documents to another analyst. Such informal arrangements might bend regulations, but they happened all the time. The agents suggested that they return to the NISC building. Back in his office there, Pollard asked permission to call Anne. He called twice while he was being interviewed, and both times, the agents noted, he asked Anne about taking a cactus from their apartment.

Anne, responding to the code word, grabbed a suitcase full of classified documents, slipped out of the Pollard apartment, and put the suitcase under a staircase. She then went next door and told her friendly neighbor that she and Jay desperately needed help. Anne explained that she had a suitcase full of classified

documents about the Chinese Embassy. She quickly explained
the innocent connection with her public relations free-lancing
and said that Jay would get into unnecessary trouble if security
people found the documents. They had to be destroyed but she
did not dare to carry the suitcase out of the apartment house
herself. She had hastily made a plan: She would go to the plush
Four Seasons Hotel in nearby Georgetown and wait in the lobby
for the friendly neighbor to come to the hotel with the suitcase.
Then Anne would destroy the contents at the hotel.

Anne next called the Holiday Inn in Bethesda, Maryland,
where Avi Sella and his wife were staying. The Sellas and the
Pollards were to have dinner that night at O'Donnell's, a restaurant across from the motel. Anne told Sella that something had
happened and could not be discussed on the phone. She took a
cab from the Four Seasons to O'Donnell's and met alone with
Sella.

She told him all she knew was that "cactus" meant trouble.
Sella went to a phone, called Yagur, gave Yagur's phone number
to Anne, and told her to have Jay call Yagur. He told her to stay
at O'Donnell's until midnight and then go home and await a
phone call. Then Sella gave Anne the cut-out instructions of an
experienced intelligence officer: "You don't know me. You've
never met me. You've never heard my name."

Back at the NISC, Pollard continued to give implausible
explanations for his possession of classified documents. An agent
asked him if he would agree to a search of his apartment. He
declined to allow them to enter it, claiming that they might find
marijuana. Told that the process of obtaining a search warrant
had begun, Pollard stalled for a while and then, believing that
Anne had had time to move the documents, reluctantly gave
permission for a search.

About eleven o'clock Pollard and the agents entered his
apartment. In the Pollards' bedroom, under a pile of Anne's
clothing, the agents found a box containing fifty-seven classified
documents that Anne had missed after the tip-off. Anne returned
home after midnight to find the FBI and NIS agents still searching the apartment and her husband feigning surprise at the discovery of the documents. Soon after she arrived Sella called. Referring to him as "Uncle Joe," Anne said she had unexpected
guests and was unable to talk to him. The agents departed after

warning Pollard that the possession of the material was a security violation. They instructed him to report the next morning to an NIS office, where he would be given a polygraph test.

When the agents finally left early on Tuesday morning, Anne and Jay went to a nearby restaurant where Pollard, following Sella's instructions, called his case officer, Yagur. All Yagur wanted to know was whether Pollard had mentioned Israel in his interviews with the agents. When Pollard said he had not, Yossi Yagur told him to buy time.

On Tuesday, when Pollard reached his office, he began the buying of time. He said that it would not be necessary for him to take the polygraph test because he was willing to admit that he had given five or six classified documents to a friend. After he was advised of his rights, he began talking, and the five or six documents increased to fifty or a hundred—a month, for about a year.

Up to this point NIS agents had been interrogating Pollard. But when he admitted that he had been *paid* for the hundreds of stolen documents, a peculiarity of federal spy-catching arrangements surfaced. When money entered the picture the case shifted from a Navy matter involving misplaced documents to a matter involving espionage. Now a joint NIS-FBI questioning of Pollard began.

Pollard signed an eleven-page statement in which he said he had sold documents to Kurt Lohbeck, a longtime friend. Pollard said he suspected that Lohbeck was somehow using the information to assist a supporter of the freedom fighters in Afghanistan. (The well-connected Lohbeck is himself one of the minor mysteries of the case, for much of what Pollard has had to say about him has been classified and references about him are excised from court papers.)

By rambling on about the documents in detail, Pollard managed to keep the interrogation going through the entire day. On Tuesday night the questioners told him they would take him home and resume the interview the following day. He promised to return to NIS headquarters at Suitland then. His apartment was placed under tight surveillance.

Within their besieged apartment, the couple frantically began tearing up documents and throwing them into the trash. They also tore up a handwritten note that Anne's Israeli hosts in

Paris had written. The note was from Uncle Joe Fisher, who told her he was giving her a ring. What neither Jay nor Anne realized was that the trash would be seized by the surveilling agents. Nor did the Pollards know that their document-filled suitcase had been in federal hands all day. The friendly neighbor to whom Anne had entrusted the suitcase happened to be the daughter of a career Navy officer. On Tuesday morning her husband called NIS and told an agent, "I have some classified information that may be of help to you." NIS and FBI agents soon appeared and took the suitcase away, but it was not opened until Thursday, when authorities obtained a search warrant. (Among many other documents stuffed in the suitcase was a letter from Pollard to Yossi, telling about "cactus," the original South African name for the Crotale anti-aircraft missile that France was developing for South Africa.)

On Wednesday, Pollard went to a pay phone, called the security officer at the Israeli Embassy, identified himself by naming his handlers, and asked for help. He had no way of knowing that he was in the process of being disowned. Avi Sella and Irit Erb were already on their way back to Israel and Yagur would leave on Friday.

After the call Pollard headed off again to the NISC for more questioning and another signed statement. In this one he admitted that he and Anne had traveled in Europe in November 1984 and July 1985 with the money he had received for the documents. His patient questioners were more convinced than ever that he had been spying for a foreign power. Because the psychology of interrogating a spy calls for attempts to bring him around rather than antagonize him, the agents again let him return home. He said he would drive back to the NISC on Thursday after he took Anne to the Washington Hospital Center for an appointment. On Thursday morning Pollard called the Israeli Embassy again and was told by an intelligence officer there, "If you can shake surveillance, you should come in."

When Anne and Jay left the apartment they carried two small bags. Anne also had a bulging purse. The purse and one of the bags were filled with family photos and other keepsakes, including a large bottle of perfume. They also had their birth certificates, marriage license, and the vaccination papers of their cat, Dusty. In one of the bags was Dusty.

Pollard drove Anne to the hospital and waited for her. When they left the hospital, instead of heading home, they took a circuitous route through northwest Washington, heading farther and farther north. Finally, from upper Connecticut Avenue, the Mustang turned onto Van Ness and then into the circular International Drive, location of the Israeli and Jordanian embassies and the Kuwaiti Government office. Waiting on International Drive was a car bearing diplomatic license tags issued to the Israeli Embassy. The Pollard Mustang fell in behind the embassy car, and the motorcade of followed and followers slowly moved along the drive to the Israeli Embassy.

The embassy car and the Pollard Mustang entered the embassy driveway, which leads to an underground garage, through heavy barred gates that slid open to admit the two cars and then shut by remote control. The following FBI agents, respecting diplomatic territory, stayed at a distance and watched as the Pollards got out of their car and began arguing vigorously with several Israelis. Pollard was trying to claim political asylum and the Israelis were not giving any.

After about twenty minutes the two spies gave up trying to come in from the cold, got in their car, and drove back out through the gates, where Pollard was arrested by the swarm of agents gathered on International Drive. (Anne was arrested the next day. Anne's father then assumed care of Dusty.)

Jonathan Pollard proved to be a tougher subject in custody than he had been during the previous days. Although he did withdraw Kurt Lohbeck's name as the recipient of classified documents, Pollard gave little help. Yes, he did give classified information to Israelis, he said. But he was teasing his interrogators, for he went on to say that twice he had served on a U.S. intelligence team that met with Israeli counterparts for an authorized exchange of information. When the agents pressed him for his *unauthorized* disclosures, Pollard declined to name any Israelis.

Revelations about Israeli espionage in the United States set off bitter charges of betrayal. In Washington and Tel Aviv, diplomats worked hard to repair the damage. An Israeli government spokesman immediately branded the espionage a "rogue" operation, "an unauthorized deviation" from Israel's "policy of not conducting any espionage activity whatsoever in the United States, or activities against the United States." Soon after the arrests, however, U.S. government sources told the authors that the espionage was obviously state-sponsored. A senior Israeli officer admitted to them that in view of the amounts of money being paid to the Pollards and the expensive jewelry Anne had received in Paris, "the operation was obviously approved at a relatively high level." And when the name Rafael Eitan leaked out, there could no longer be any doubts.

Eitan, a legendary intelligence officer, had been chief of operations of the Mossad. He also had been an adviser on terrorism to Prime Ministers Menachem Begin and Yitzhak Shamir. Eitan reportedly was the mastermind of the abduction of Nazi war criminal Adolf Eichmann from Argentina to Israel in 1960. Eitan was also said to be the head of the Israeli vengeance squad that tracked down and killed the Palestine Liberation Organization's Black September terrorists who had murdered Israeli athletes at the 1972 Munich Olympics. With that résumé, Eitan could hardly be considered a low-level "rogue" operative.

The shocked reaction of U.S. officials was, for the most part, feigned. Knowledgeable Washington intelligence officials were well aware of previous Israeli intelligence-gathering activities directed against the United States. A 1979 CIA study of Israeli intelligence operations said, for example, that Shin Bet, the Israeli counter-espionage organization, "tried to penetrate the U.S. consulate general in Jerusalem through a clerical employee who was having an affair with a Jerusalem girl. They rigged a fake abortion case against the employee in an unsuccessful attempt to recruit him. Before this attempt at blackmail, they had tried to get the Israeli girl to elicit information from her boyfriend." The report told of several wiretaps and hidden microphones in U.S. offices and residences in Israel, as well as "two or three crude attempts to recruit Marine guards for monetary reward."

In 1965 the Nuclear Materials and Equipment Corporation of Apollo, Pennsylvania, admitted to federal authorities that the company could not account for 381.6 pounds of highly enriched uranium. Experts estimated that at least ten nuclear bombs could be made from the lost uranium. An investigation turned up incriminating evidence tying the company, known as NUMEC, to Israel. One of the Israelis linked to NUMEC was Rafael Eitan.

In March 1978, Stephen D. Bryen, a member of the Senate Foreign Relations Committee staff, met with a group of Israeli officials in the coffee shop of a Washington hotel. Michael Saba, a representative of the National Association of Arab Americans, said that he sat by chance at an adjacent table. Saba later swore in an affidavit that he had overheard Bryen say, "I have the Pentagon document on the bases, which you are welcome to see." The remark, investigators said, referred to a report on bases in Saudi Arabia. Bryen, who denied providing Israelis with classified materials, was, at the time of the Pollard arrests, a Deputy Under Secretary of Defense overseeing the export of defense-related U.S. technology.

As a gesture of good faith in the Pollard case, the Israeli Government turned over to Department of Justice officials, who had gone to Israel, photocopies of 163 U.S. classified documents. Many of them matched those on checkout receipts that Pollard had filled out at various government offices. The Israelis, although thus providing incriminating evidence against Pollard, had made only a token return of the documents he had stolen. Pollard had compromised more than one thousand documents, most of which contained technical information and satellite photographs. Many were hundreds of pages long. More than eight hundred were marked as being top secret.

Some of the most sensitive reports were U.S. estimates of the probability of nuclear weapon development in Iraq and Pakistan. Pollard also supplied, for nearly eighteen months, a steady stream of daily message traffic about U.S. ship positions and operations at U.S. air bases. Assessing the damage, Secretary of Defense Weinberger, who called Pollard's espionage "treason," said, "It is difficult for me . . . to conceive of a greater harm to national security."

Pollard allowed his handlers to study and copy all of his identification credentials, making it possible for other spies to slip in and out of the NISC and other government offices in the Washington area. Pollard may well have not been the only spy on the premises. Israel seemed to have had inside knowledge about the investigation of Pollard before he was first questioned.

Soviet missile systems analyses that Pollard sold to the Israelis revealed how the United States collects tightly held Soviet secrets. Revelations about a technical collection system "is much like the loss of a network of agents," a government damage assessment said. Indeed, such dangerous collection work often is done by U.S. agents whose identity, another report said, "could be inferred by a reasonably competent intelligence analyst."

U.S. intelligence officials had two other worries in the Pollard case: (1) the possibility that the secrets could have been seen by a Soviet mole in Israeli intelligence, and (2) the possibility that the U.S. analysts named as authors on some of the most sensitive reports would become future targets for recruitment or blackmail —by Israelis or by Soviets.

As in many other espionage cases, there was a great deal of publicity at the time of the Pollards' arrest, but no trial. In the past the bureaucratic fighting over prosecution usually pitted a reluctant CIA against eager Justice Department prosecutors. This time the Justice Department fought the State Department, which won by protesting that a trial would exacerbate anti-Israeli feelings. U.S. Attorney Joseph diGenova, who would have prosecuted the Pollards, was afraid of the impact that an "ideological defense" would have on future espionage cases.

Another fear concerned the "false-flag" approach used by KGB officers, who might be able to recruit an American who believed he was spying not for the Soviet Union but for a "friendly" nation. Jerry Whitworth, as diGenova well knew, had wrapped himself in the false flag, claiming that he thought the secrets he stole had been passed to Israel, a claim that he assumed would appeal to a jury. Even though diGenova knew that the Pollards would not face a jury, he asked the court to set an example: "swift, certain and substantial incarceration, without regard to the political beliefs of the parties involved."

The Pollards agreed to a plea bargain in which they cooperated in exchange for consideration. As in the Walker case, the major spy had a relative whose fate could be used to force a bargain. Jonathan Pollard pleaded guilty to espionage, and on March 4, 1987, he was sentenced to life in prison; Anne Henderson-Pollard pleaded guilty to possession of national defense documents and was sentenced to two concurrent terms of five years in prison. She could have received a maximum sentence of ten years and a $10,000 fine.

In the aftermath, Sella was indicted on espionage charges by the United States—and promoted to brigadier general by Israel. Sella, who was given command of one of Israel's most important air bases, later gave up the prized command as part of an Israeli campaign to ameliorate the diplomatic problems between Israel and the United States. Under long-standing U.S.-Israeli legal agreements, the United States could not force the return of Sella for trial.

From the beginning Pollard had insisted that he had not spied for money. "I didn't like the monetary aspect of the relationship, however essential it was," he said in an interview a year after his arrest. "In my mind, assisting the Israelis did not involve or require betraying the United States," he said in a statement filed in U.S. District Court. Pollard also told the court that "anti-Semitism" at NISC had inspired his decision to spy for Israel. Once, he said, when he protested a decision to withhold information on Soviet chemical warfare from the Israelis, Pollard said his superiors had told him that "Jews are overly sensitive about gas because of their experiences during World War II." (Anti-Semitism has been a charge made by several Jewish employees at NISC—and even one non-Jew who had been specifically asked to "spy" on his Jewish senior to ascertain his loyalty after the Pollard case broke. That non-Jew, employed in the administrative side of NISC, resigned from Naval Intelligence rather than put up with such an attitude.)

The government, in a pre-sentence report to the court, scoffed at Pollard's claim that he did it all to provide better antiterrorism information to Israel. Of the thousands of documents that Pollard stole, the government said, "only a minuscule portion" was concerned with terrorism or counter-terrorism. The government, recognizing the way ideology sometimes dilutes the appearance of betrayal, challenged Pollard's contention that money played no part in making him a spy.

The evidence, the government said, "compels the conclusion that defendant had a keen interest in financial gain from the very outset of his relationship with the Israelis. As that relationship ripened, defendant's interest in money, and the life-style which that money made possible, became the force which drove defendant to provide increasingly greater numbers of classified documents despite the growing risk of apprehension."

On November 27, 1985 when the Pollards appeared in court for a routine hearing, two other accused spies were standing before U.S. district judges for similar proceedings. By that spy-filled day, seventeen espionage cases had surfaced in the United States during the Year of the Spy.

The other two spies of November were Ronald Pelton, the former NSA communications specialist, and Larry Wu-Tai Chin, a retired CIA analyst. Like Sattler, Pelton and Chin were caught through informers rather than as a result of counter-espionage efforts. Pelton, betrayed by defector-redefector Vitaly Yurchenko, was of the new spy-for-money breed. Chin, who had been in place for thirty-three years as a spy for the People's Republic of China, was ideological. But he had also collected some tax-free income for his extracurricular duty.

The day after one group of FBI agents arrested the Pollards on International Drive, three other agents called on a retired CIA employee at his office in Alexandria, Virginia, across the Potomac from Washington. The man to whom the agents showed their identification that afternoon was Larry Wu-Tai Chin. He had retired from the CIA in 1981, but he still did contract work for the agency, translating journals and papers picked up through ordinary commercial and academic channels.

The agents told Chin they wanted to interview him. "Why, sure," he genially said. "Come on in."

For a little while the four men sparred, the agents, trained in psychological interrogation, watching their questions glance off the shrugs and bland smiles of Larry Chin. He had been, after all, only a relatively low-level employee for an agency not openly connected with the CIA. He had received a CIA medal for distinguished service. His access to secrets was supposedly as "compartmentalized" as Pollard's and Pelton's.

The agents mentioned that Chin seemed to be rather well off for a man living on a retirement income. He responded by telling them about his shrewd real estate investments and his highly successful system for winning at blackjack.

Chin, who was sixty-three years old when he was interviewed, had worked for the CIA's Foreign Broadcast Information Service (FBIS), which monitors foreign broadcasting and news media. FBIS translators were also called from time to time to translate classified documents. This, for Chin, provided a mole's passageway.

Chin had begun working for Americans in 1948, when China, in the midst of civil war, was an enigma to U.S. policymakers. Chin, known then as Chin Wu-Tai, was one of scores of bright, young, English-speaking Chinese who translated for the scattered American military units ranged across China. "Larry," as the Americans began calling him, worked as a translator in Foochow, Shanghai, and later in Hong Kong.

While Chin was serving as a translator for the U.S. Army Liaison Office in Foochow, a Communist spymaster named Dr. Wang began indoctrinating Chin about the aims of the Chinese Communist Party. When Chin moved to Shanghai to work in the U.S. Consulate there, Dr. Wang again appeared, this time to introduce a Communist on the Shanghai police force who continued Chin's political education.

After Shanghai fell Chin moved with the consulate to Hong Kong, and was by now indispensable. When China entered the Korean War, Chin was often sent to South Korea, where he helped in the interrogation of Chinese prisoners. Around this time Chin first ventured into espionage, U.S. sources say. In Hong Kong he was paid $2,000 by the People's Republic of China Intelligence Service for information on two subjects: the location of Chinese prisoner-of-war camps in South Korea and what questions the Americans and South Koreans were asking the Chinese POWs. The fact that he had two brothers in China may have been used as leverage in his recruitment as an ideological spy.

By 1952, Communist China became a major target of U.S. intelligence. Chinese agents from Taiwan, along with some American agents, were being parachuted onto the mainland, and many of the planes were shot down. But if spies helped raise the toll, Chin was not one of them. Acting under Chinese instructions, he signed up as a translator at the CIA's FBIS monitoring station on Okinawa.

On Okinawa, a small American community concentrated more on listening to China than on doing anything in China. Okinawa was a listening post, and Larry Chin was one of the best listeners. "He was damned good," a former CIA officer remembers. "And he was spying for China almost from the time he started on Okinawa."

Chin's work theoretically kept him away from sensitive matters. As a non-American, Chin was supposed to work only as a monitor, hearing public broadcasts from Chinese mainland cities and then providing transcripts or digests of the broadcasts. He was not cleared for any classified information. But he was so enthusiastic and skilled that he was often called in to handle translations that involved classified matters, such as POW interrogations. The breaching of security compartments would be one of Chin's espionage techniques.

Chin divorced his first wife while on Okinawa. In 1961 he traveled to Hong Kong, where he made contact with his Chinese case officer. He left Okinawa permanently at this time, journeying to the United States. He continued his work at a major Asian monitoring station in Santa Rosa, California. By then he was renowned as a dependable worker—"he could put out twice as much as anyone else," said a CIA officer who knew him. He entered the United States as a foreign national, but he managed to find a sponsor who helped him get American citizenship.

After nine years in California, Chin went to work in Washington for the FBIS, which had just been combined with the Foreign Documents Division at a building in Rosslyn, Virginia, a few miles via the George Washington Parkway from CIA headquarters. FBIS employees, nearly all of whom had foreign backgrounds, had been given routine security checks. That seemed enough, since most of their work involved the reading of open literature and the monitoring of public broadcasting, none of which was classified. And, on the surface, FBIS was not connected with the CIA.

"There was no cover for FBIS," a former CIA officer recalled. "It was in the phone book in England. The cover that the CIA tried to impose was that it was not part of the CIA. We were supposed to never let foreign nationals know that they were working for the CIA. But most of them found out.

"Starting in the late 1960s, and from then on, a lot of compartmentalization broke down. A lot of people were allowed access. At the time of the Falcon and the Snowman, [Admiral Stansfield] Turner tried to cut back on clearances.* I do believe that at that period things got a lot more relaxed.

---

* Turner was Director of Central Intelligence from 1977 to 1981. Falcon and Snowman were the nicknames of Christopher J. Boyce and Andrew D. Lee, who were arrested in 1977 for selling secrets to the Soviets stolen from a CIA contract company.

"Whether actual documents crossed his desk is another matter. By that time, he had high clearances.

"On occasion, a good translator would be borrowed from FBIS when there was need. He might even be given something tightly classified from the operations division." Asked for an example, the former officer cautiously said it was possible that Chin might be asked to read a raw, handwritten report just in from an intelligence or case officer in the field. He also checked and perhaps helped to prepare analyses on Chinese issues sent to the White House.

"He was flamboyant and something of a braggart. He would come back from these 'special assignments' and say he had done 'something interesting.' He was an excellent bridge player and a gambler—he talked constantly about gambling—and had extreme powers of concentration. If anybody could fool a polygraph, he could."

Chin smuggled classified documents out of CIA offices, photographed them, and then returned them, month after month, year after year. Using a pay telephone, he called a number in Toronto and periodically went there to deliver the undeveloped film. He also traveled to Hong Kong, where he had what spies call an "accommodation address" to which he could send postcards setting up meetings, and to Toronto, where he could meet his handlers in diplomatic safety. (Until diplomatic relations were established between the United States and China in 1979, the Chinese Embassy in Toronto was the only safe diplomatic rendezvous for spies in North America.)

In 1970, two years before President Nixon's historic trip to China, Chin claimed that he saw a secret document that hinted at the President's plans to initiate an opening to China. Chin copied the document and got it quickly to Toronto, he later said, because he believed that "if this information was brought to the attention of the highest Chinese leadership, it might break the ice and start the turn from hostility to friendship. I wanted [Premier] Chou En-lai to see it." Chin later bragged that he was not a mere spy but someone whose connections in China made his alleged espionage "comparable to the 'hot line' between Washington and Moscow."

Whatever his peacemaking motives, Chin's Hong Kong bank accounts grew steadily during his career. U.S. authorities estimated that Chinese intelligence officers may have deposited as much as $564,000 in Chin's accounts by the time the FBI agents arrived at his home for their interview. Another estimate put his spy earnings at more than $1 million. He owned more than twenty pieces of property—condominiums, town houses, and apartments in Virginia, Maryland, and Las Vegas—one of his favorite gambling spots.

The agents let Chin talk about the real estate and the blackjack, and then one of them, Mark R. Johnson, said that the government had good reason to believe that Chin had been spying for China.

"How do I know you're not bluffing?" Chin responded.

Johnson replied by talking about a meeting Chin had in Hong Kong on September 17, 1983, with a Chinese intelligence officer named Ou Qiming. Didn't he tell Ou about a CIA employee who would soon be in Hong Kong? And didn't he tell Ou that the employee would be a good candidate for recruitment as a spy? And didn't he give Ou the name of a relative of the man—a relative who was still in China and could be used as a hostage to the espionage?

Chin "was basically stunned," Johnson recalled.

"Only Ou knew," Chin said, and he immediately guessed, with his gambler's instinct, that the deck was loaded. Ou had defected, he told Johnson. Neither then, at the subsequent trial, nor afterward, did the FBI confirm Chin's hunch. Other sources have said that Chin had been turned in by an informer, but not necessarily by Ou.

One of the agents, using a psychological approach similar to the one used in the questioning of Pelton, began telling Chin about two imaginary suspects, one of whom cooperated with agents and one who did not. The agent concluded the tale with a question: "Now, if you were the Department of Justice, which one would you have more sympathy for, the individual who slammed the door in the agent's face or the one who said what had happened and said he was sorry?"

Chin responded carefully, withholding details but generally sketching his long espionage career. He also suggested that he might be valuable as a double agent. He was told that no such deal could be worked until he disclosed everything he knew. Chin was questioned for five hours, including an interruption for food that an agent ordered—takeout from a Chinese restaurant.

When the proper psychological moment came, another agent, Terry Roth, asked Chin if he would sign a written statement.

"That would be evidence coming from the horse's mouth," Chin replied. "And I would be the horse."

What Chin would not learn until his trial was that evidence had been coming from his own mouth. There had been an FBI tap on his phone since May 3, 1982, three months after he had visited Beijing, where he met with Chinese intelligence officials, was honored at a banquet, received a promotion, and got $50,000 in U.S. currency. A month before the wiretap began, $174,000 had been deposited for him in a Hong Kong bank account.

At his trial Chin maintained that his espionage was in reality a personal crusade aimed at improving relations between his native land and the United States. But Johnson, one of his interrogators, said that Chin had boasted that he supplied his spymasters with so much information that it took two Chinese analysts two months to translate and process a shipment. The translations, Chin said, went directly to the highest level of Chinese leadership.

After the jury found Chin guilty of espionage and tax violations, he was put in a county jail in suburban Virginia to await sentence. Facing life, he told reporters that he would serve time with the hope of an eventual spy swap.

He had been in the jail for two weeks when he requested a pair of high-top sneakers. These were given to him. A few days later a jail worker handed him a new plastic liner for a wastepaper basket in a common room. Chin went to his cell. The door snapped locked. A little while later a guard opened the cell to summon Chin to a routine inspection. The spy's body, still warm, was on his cot with the plastic liner knotted at his neck by the long laces of the sneakers. He had said after his trial that he had "nothing to regret" because his espionage actually had been a mission to bring together China and the United States. Life in jail, he said, was "a very small price to pay" for fulfilling his mission.

* * *

When the motive for espionage is love and patriotism rather than money, diplomatic negotiations rather than court trials may settle the case.

Michael Agbotui Soussoudis, thirty-nine-year-old first cousin to Ghana's leader, Flight Lieutenant Jerry Rawlings, was arrested in June 1985 at a Virginia motel where he was planning a lovers' rendezvous with Sharon M. Scrange, a CIA employee. They had met in Accra, the Ghanaian capital, when she was working under embassy cover for the CIA and he was working for his cousin as an intelligence officer. To do his job, Soussoudis became Sharon Scrange's lover.

A Virginia farm girl, Sharon M. Scrange was twenty-eight years old in 1983 when she went to Ghana to work as a CIA operations-support assistant, with top-secret clearance, in Accra, under cover of a clerk at the embassy. On her second day there she met Soussoudis and quickly fell in love with him. For nearly two years she gave Soussoudis what he wanted—secrets and sex.

She later said that she had told her CIA station chief that she was dating Soussoudis. After a while, though, the CIA officer informed her that the ambassador was upset because a Ghanaian official had told him that "a black female in the embassy was having secret meetings with Ghanaians and that she'd better cut it out." She was ordered to "gradually" break off the relationship.

She did not. Nor did she stop copying information from CIA cables in shorthand, neatly transcribing her notes, and passing them to Soussoudis. She hesitated when he asked for the identities of CIA employees and Ghanaians working as agents for the CIA. But, she later told the FBI, Soussoudis, flashing a 9-mm automatic pistol, warned her that "people at the embassy and their families could be hurt" if she did not tell him what he wanted to know. She gave him the names of eleven informants and five CIA employees. U.S. intelligence analysts believe that her information went far beyond her lover. The official U.S. theory is that Kojo Tsikata, the pro-Marxist head of Ghanaian intelligence, passed the secrets to intelligence services in Cuba, Libya, East Germany, and other Soviet bloc countries.

In May 1985, as she was about to leave Ghana for assignment back to CIA headquarters in Virginia, a Ghanaian intelligence officer told her to search CIA files for further information about informers and dissidents in his country. His leader, Rawlings, who had seized power in coups in 1979 and 1981, was worried about being overthrown himself.

Somehow the CIA learned that Ghanaians were pressuring her, and the motel arrests were set up. A hearing on Soussoudis was held before U.S. District Judge Claude M. Hilton, who used the Classified Information Procedures Act to keep his courtroom closed for the hearing to protesting media because classified documents would be revealed. But representatives from the Ghanaian Embassy attended the hearing, thus getting a chance to see secrets that the CIA had gathered about their country.

For everyone but Sharon Scrange, back-room deals were being made by State, Justice, and CIA officials in Washington and Ghana. Soussoudis' court hearing launched complex diplomatic-intelligence bargaining inside the federal spy-catching bureaucracy and between the two countries. Soussoudis pleaded no contest to espionage charges. Judge Hilton sentenced him to twenty years in prison but suspended the sentence on the condition that Soussoudis leave the United States.

In Ghana, four Ghanaians, accused of spying for the CIA, changed their pleas to guilty. As soon as Soussoudis left the United States eight Ghanaians and their families were allowed to leave Ghana and settle in other African countries. No one said what was obvious: They had worked for the CIA. Next, Ghana expelled two reputed CIA officers and two other U.S. Embassy officials and the United States quickly retaliated with the expulsion of four Ghanaians.

Sharon Scrange, sentenced to five years after pleading guilty to the charge of "revealing classified information," later had her term reduced to two years. "Soussoudis, who was basically the culprit in this, wound up getting nothing," the judge said, trying to balance espionage's often strange brand of justice.

Sometimes hate, not love, is the ideological motivation for espionage. A particularly virulent kind of malice seems to have been the inspiration for the treachery of Edward L. Howard, a CIA employee who was groomed for a Moscow post, discovered to be unstable, and then discharged—despite the growing suspicions that he had betrayed the CIA and the nation. Howard's perfidy, however, was a disappointment more than a surprise. He was *known* to be unreliable. His apparently erratic personality helped him get his job.

The CIA has an outdated reputation for recruiting safe and sane, buttoned-down Ivy Leaguers. This may have been true in the early days, when Director Allen Dulles, who had a master's degree from Princeton, found similarly pedigreed men of the Eastern Establishment for the leadership cadre of the agency. But relatively few of the employees who did both the clean and the dirty work were of the elite. An agency that needed linguists and experts in dozens of specialties could not live by Ivy League alone.

Over the years CIA hiring practices had become renowned. Applicants were screened and rescreened in a process that, by some estimates, cast aside as many as 80 percent of those who sought employment. A 1980 study made by the Director of Central Intelligence became a hallmark of personnel security procedures. The study examined 5,204 background investigations conducted by intelligence community agencies. "Adverse information" was disclosed in 1,261 of the cases. As a result of the study, security investigators added a new element: in-depth interviews of the applicants themselves to determine whether they fit the psychological profile of the ideal CIA employee—a bright, trustworthy, and forthright American.

In 1980, the year that the personnel security study was circulating in the intelligence community, Edward Lee Howard, then twenty-eight, applied for work at the CIA. Howard did not fit that profile. But, primarily *for* that reason, he was hired and tapped for an extremely sensitive job: Operating out of the U.S. Embassy in Moscow, he would run Soviet nationals who were spying for the United States.

For purposes known only in the agency, a decision was made to seek out for such jobs people outside the agency's traditional norms. They would be young, aggressive—and fundamentally amoral. They would be people who would *not* be ideological. They would be a match for the KGB opposition in Moscow. They would be hard and cold, though, at least in Howard's case, not so cold that sweat and changes in breathing would not be detected by agency polygraph operators.

"There is a school of thought in the CIA that they need people like that—swashbucklers, adventurers, high rollers—in order to do the spying work," said former Director of Central Intelligence Stansfield Turner. "There's another school, though, that says you want people who have high ethical standards, who make considered judgments on what spying to do and what dirty tricks to do because they realize it's in the best interests of the United States of America. And I think that the issue here is deciding between these two schools and not bringing in the high-roller Howard types."

One side of Howard's complex personality did fit the traditional CIA profile: fluent in German and Spanish; son of a father who made the military a career; a cum laude college graduate; a former Peace Corps volunteer. These were all stellar qualifications. He was also a political conservative.

The other side of his personality was darker. Howard used drugs, had an alcohol problem, and was a petty thief—incredibly, he once had slipped money out of a woman's purse on an airliner in flight. The drug use showed up on his first routine polygraph test; the other aberrations grew out of questions following in later polygraph tests.

Most candidates would have been dropped after the first test. Howard was hired and assigned in the Directorate of Operations, which runs the CIA's routine clandestine services. Not long afterward his wife, Mary, was also hired to work in the same directorate. She did secretarial assignments for the Deputy Director for Operations.

As part of a new personnel policy, Mary Howard was given training as a support worker who would aid her husband and other case officers in the embassy-based CIA operation in Moscow. She might, for example, act as a lookout or counter-surveillance operative while her husband or another case officer served Moscow dead drops. One of the Howards' trainers was Martha Peterson, a CIA officer who had outwitted the KGB until they picked her up in 1977.

Howard, who would have the cover of an embassy budget analyst, was given two lessons that would have disastrous consequences: He was given a great deal of information about CIA operations in Moscow, including the name of at least one Soviet who was spying for the United States. And Howard was trained, by FBI agents, in the art of outwitting surveillants and eluding pursuers.

As Howard's training progressed, his handlers became uneasy about their charge. Given other polygraph tests, he was found to be extremely deceptive. He lied about taking drugs, womanizing, and having marital trouble. The Soviet division of DDO dismissed him, and in 1983 he was discharged from the agency. Howard seethed with bitterness and, in September 1984, told agency employees that he was contemplating espionage. CIA security officials ignored the early-warning signs of betrayal.

With some help from the agency, Howard got a job as an economic analyst for the New Mexico state legislature's Legislative Finance Committee. In 1983 he, Mary, and their newborn son moved into an imitation-adobe house in the El Dorado subdivision south of Santa Fe, and he seemed to settle into life as a state bureaucrat. His dark side, however, flared at least once. On February 6, 1984, he was arrested after a drunken brawl in which he fired a .357 magnum. He was put on probation for five years.

A few months later, on a trip to Europe, Howard met with KGB officers and received money for information he provided. Presumably that information had to do with what he had learned during his tour in the CIA. Another possibility has been raised by Roger Morris, a former foreign service officer who served on the National Security Council: "Obviously, a Soviet spy in Santa Fe routinely would have been after the rich mine of information at the nearby Los Alamos National Laboratory, with its secrets of sophisticated new weaponry and 'Star Wars' technology.

"Not only the Soviets and Eastern Europeans, but presumably 'friendly' nations, too, have agents prowling the U.S. defense establishments that crowd the Rio Grande corridor for ninety miles from Los Alamos south through Albuquerque's Sandia Laboratory, Kirtland Air Force Base, and Manzano nuclear weapon storage complex."

Morris suggested that Howard could have been a KGB support agent or courier for a scientific agent in place in one of those defense establishments. Morris also speculated that Howard's fluency in Spanish and his CIA background would make him a good candidate for reporting on the CIA's Latin American operations that are centered around Santa Fe.

Whatever Howard's activities in New Mexico, intelligence officials are convinced that his self-appointed mission was vengeance against the CIA. Damage assessors had gauged Howard's betrayal not against how much cash he may have received but against contemporaneous disasters in the CIA-Moscow network.

Howard's proposed assignment to Moscow had been well under way in March 1983, when President Reagan and Secretary of State Shultz signed a certificate identifying Howard as a foreign service officer who had been appointed "a Consular Officer and a Secretary." This was the cover that Howard was to use when he went to Moscow. But in June the CIA fired Howard.

At the beginning of summer, Howard went to work in New Mexico. The timetable of his known treachery starts a year later.

September 1984: Howard and his wife go to Austria and he meets with KGB officers. After returning to the United States, Howard tells two CIA employees that he has been thinking about espionage. The CIA reacts by paying for Howard to see a psychiatrist in Santa Fe.

February 1985: Paul M. Stombaugh, a second secretary in the U.S. Embassy in Moscow, is detained; the KGB arrests the Soviet agent he is meeting, A. G. Tolkachev, a Soviet missile and avionics expert. The detention and arrest are not announced.

March 1985: Howard and his wife make a trip to Europe. They tell friends in Santa Fe that they visited Germany.

July 1985: Howard meets with an ex-CIA employee and reveals that he has been a spy for the Soviets. Around this time Howard is believed to have made another trip to Europe to rendezvous with KGB officers.

August 1985: Vitaly Yurchenko, a high-ranking KGB officer who had defected in Rome, is talking to debriefers in a CIA safe house in Virginia. He tells about meeting a walk-in from the National Security Agency in 1980 and gives his interrogators information that leads to the arrest of ex-NSA analyst Ronald Pelton in November 1985. Yurchenko also says that a former CIA employee who had been assigned to Moscow had met with KGB officers in the fall of 1984 and had given up agency secrets about CIA spies in the Soviet Union. The CIA and FBI begin looking for the mole, whose name Yurchenko claimed not to know.

September 1985: The FBI, contacted by the CIA, puts Howard under surveillance and gets authorization for wiretaps. FBI agents confront Howard. He feigns an interest in cooperating when agents approach him on September 20. On September 21— a Saturday, the KGB's favorite espionage day—Howard, with the aid of his wife, eludes FBI agents watching him. (By one account, that night, Howard, in his pajamas, waved good-bye to her as she drove off, heading for Santa Fe. She was followed by an FBI car. Other members of the FBI surveillance team remained behind to watch the house in case Howard left. He did, but they did not know it. He left the house through the back door, sprinted to the cover of a nearby bank, and waited until her car rounded a curve, momentarily out of sight of the FBI car. He darted into the back of the slow-moving car and lay on the floor. Somewhere in Santa Fe, just before the trailing FBI turned a corner, he managed to slip out of the car. He changed clothes in his office and left a resignation letter that enabled Mary to get his state pension contribution.) On September 23 the FBI obtains a warrant for Howard's arrest. By then he is on his way to Moscow, via Texas, Mexico, Vienna, and Helsinki.

September 1985: The Soviet news service, Tass, publishes a long, detailed account of the detention of Stombaugh and arrest of Tolkachev, identified as a worker for "a Moscow research institute." Tass says that the KGB searched Tolkachev's apartment in June and found "codes and ciphers, quick-acting two-way communications radio apparatus" and "miniature cameras of a special design by means of which he photographed secret documents." (U.S. intelligence officials assume that Tolkachev has been executed. They also believe that the Tass story had been designed to throw off suspicion from Howard in case Yurchenko had named him. But the officials could not understand the reason for publishing the story coincidentally with Howard's flight.)

November 1985: During dinner at Au Pied de Cochon, a modest French restaurant in the Georgetown section of Washington, Yurchenko excuses himself, leaves his CIA handler sitting at the table, and walks up Wisconsin Avenue to the Soviet compound on Tunlaw Road. The next day he appears at a news conference in the Soviet Embassy and later on television in Moscow. He claimed that he had been drugged, had not defected, and had escaped as soon as he could. But U.S. intelligence sources insist that he had been a defector and had led them to Pelton and Howard.

March 1986: The Soviets expel Michael Sellers, a second secretary at the U.S. Embassy in Moscow.

May 1986: Eric Sites, of the U.S. Embassy military attaché's office, is arrested on a Moscow street as he is about to have a face-to-face meeting with a Soviet citizen recruited by the CIA. (Sites' wife acted as a lookout, just as Mary Howard had been trained to do.) U.S. intelligence attributes the expelling of Sellers and the arrest of Sites to Howard's betrayal. The United States may never know the full extent of the damage; some agents may have been turned, for example. Former DCI Turner quotes the President's Foreign Intelligence Advisory Board, an independent body reporting directly to the President, as telling the President, "Howard devastated the CIA's human intelligence operations in the Soviet Union."

August 1986: Howard surfaces in Moscow. The Soviet Union announces that it has granted him political asylum for "humane considerations."

September 1986: Howard, appearing on television in Moscow, says, "I love my country. I have never done anything that might harm my country."

The Howard and Yurchenko cases glitter in the hall of mirrors where rival intelligence agencies play their unfathomable games. In one game a spy may fill out an espionage registration form and simply vanish. In another a liar and a drug user can get a sensitive job in the CIA and then vanish into the Soviet Union.

These are the games of intelligence agencies. Another game is played in the nation's defense plants, where those who guard the secrets confront those who work with the secrets, where keeping a secret means keeping a job. Just how seriously the United States Government plays the defense secrets game is a question no one wants to answer.

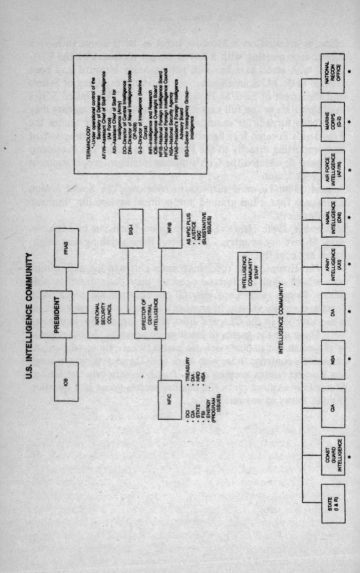

U.S. INTELLIGENCE COMMUNITY

TERMINOLOGY

*—Under operational control of the Secretary of Defense
AF/IN—Assistant Chief of Staff Intelligence (Air Force)
AXI—Assistant Chief of Staff for Intelligence (Army)
DCI—Director of Central Intelligence
DNI—Director of Naval Intelligence (code OP-009)
G-2—Director of Intelligence (Marine Corps)
INR—Intelligence and Research
IOB—Intelligence Oversight Board
NFIB—National Foreign Intelligence Board
NFIC—National Foreign Intelligence Council
NSA—National Security Agency
PFIAB—President's Foreign Intelligence Advisory Board
SIG-I—Senior Interagency Group—Intelligence

PRESIDENT

IOB

PFIAB

NATIONAL SECURITY COUNCIL

SIG-I

DIRECTOR OF CENTRAL INTELLIGENCE

NFIC
- DCI
- CIA
- STATE
- FBI
- ENERGY (PROGRAM ISSUES)
- TREASURY
- DIA
- NRO
- NSA

NFIB
AS NFIC PLUS
- JUSTICE
- NSC (SUBSTANTIVE ISSUES)

INTELLIGENCE COMMUNITY STAFF

INTELLIGENCE COMMUNITY

STATE (I & R)

COAST GUARD INTELLIGENCE

CIA

NSA

DIA

ARMY INTELLIGENCE (AXI)

NAVAL INTELLIGENCE (DNI)

AIR FORCE INTELLIGENCE (AF/IN)

MARINE CORPS (G-2)

NATIONAL RECON OFFICE

12

Stalking, Not Spinning

For five years Panagiotis Takis Veliotis, a big, imperious man who ruled a shipyard as if it were his personal kingdom, supervised the building of nuclear submarines for the U.S. Navy. The yard built attack submarines—intended to seek out and sink Soviet ships and submarines—and large Trident missile submarines, the most survivable part of America's nuclear striking forces. Packed within the hulls of these submarines were the nation's most guarded secrets: the secrets of nuclear propulsion, submarine quieting, code machines, state-of-the-art electronics, the latest antisubmarine torpedoes, and, in the missile submarines, the multiwarhead Trident missiles. A senior official of such a shipyard also learns the performance characteristics of these undersea craft and what problems are being encountered with them.

To work with such secrets requires high security clearances that are granted only after deep background investigations. Veliotis had top-secret Department of Defense clearances and a "Q" access authorization from the Department of Energy, the producer and manager of the nation's nuclear reactors and weapons. Veliotis thus joined the legion of the cleared. The legion consisted of men and women whose lives presumably had been thoroughly scrutinized. The U.S. Government had declared them safe from such weaknesses as debt and personal habits that could subject them to blackmail by foreign spy recruiters.

In 1985, the Year of the Spy, some 4.3 million people held
U.S. security clearances—certificates of approval that allowed the
holders access to classified information. About 1.4 million of the
cleared men and women worked for defense contractors at 14,000
similarly cleared contractor facilities, the offices and factories
that had been checked and approved as working spaces and safe
repositories for secret material.

One of those cleared sites was Veliotis' kingdom—the Electric Boat yard of the General Dynamics Corporation on the eastern shore of the Thames River at Groton, Connecticut. Veliotis
had reached the kingdom by a roundabout route. He had emigrated to Canada from his native Greece in the early 1950s and
soon became a Canadian citizen. He worked as a shipbuilding
executive in Canada until 1972, when he emigrated again, this
time to the United States to work for General Dynamics, the
world's largest defense contractor, as general manager of the
firm's shipyard in Quincy, Massachusetts. The yard's primary
work was the building of civilian ships—liquefied natural gas
tankers that carried supercooled gas.

Previously the Quincy yard had built nuclear-propelled submarines. The Quincy yard still did classified work for the Navy,
including nuclear power-plant designs. Because of this work, the
Quincy yard had been cleared as a top-secret facility; to run the
yard, Veliotis needed that level of clearance. On December 27,
1972, he filled out a Department of Defense personnel security
form. Among other items on the form were questions about Veliotis' place of birth and formal education. He responded that he
had graduated with a degree in physics from Athens University
and had spent three years at the Royal Naval Academy in
Piraeus, earning a degree in engineering.

Veliotis, who claimed to have had a secret clearance while
working in Canada, applied for a reciprocal U.S. secret clearance
based on his Canadian clearance. At the same time he asked for
the type of secret U.S. clearance granted to an immigrant alien.
Neither Veliotis nor three colleagues he brought in from Canada
could qualify, however, for top-secret clearance or for the special
clearance needed to possess NNPI—Naval Nuclear Propulsion
Information, which Admiral Hyman G. Rickover, the czar of the
U.S. nuclear navy, tightly guarded. The security regulations specifically stipulated that immigrant aliens were ineligible for access

to top-secret information, and Rickover had applied that standard to his own cache of secrets.

Pentagon security officials responded to Veliotis' clearance problem with simple expediency: They downgraded the clearance of the yard from top secret to secret, and Veliotis took over. In fact, he ran the yard for *thirteen months* before he received even a secret clearance. One General Dynamics executive was so concerned about potential security breaches that he posted photographs of the Canadians at all entrances to areas containing NNPI and ordered guards to bar entry of all four Canadians. But Veliotis, the guards' imposing, six-foot-five boss, was not the type to stand obediently before a closed door.

General Dynamics had made Veliotis a corporate vice president and upgraded him to executive vice president, making his access to other General Dynamics facilities and programs much easier. At the same time Pentagon officials sped Veliotis to the next stop on his odyssey through U.S. security procedures: a National Agency Check (NAC), which involves a search for information about an applicant through the files of the FBI and other federal agencies. The NAC took less than a month and ended with a "completed favorably" notation, even though investigators could not pin down Veliotis' place and date of birth in Greece or find any U.S. record of any Canadian security clearance issued to him. In January 1974, Veliotis was given a secret clearance by the Defense Industrial Security Clearance Office, which is known in the military-industrial complex by the chipper acronym DISCO.

In the fall of 1977, General Dynamics executives decided to appoint Veliotis general manager of the firm's Electric Boat yard, one of only two U.S. shipyards then building nuclear-propelled submarines. The "EB yard," as it long had been known, was in trouble and so was General Dynamics. Veliotis strode into a yard plagued by astronomical cost overruns on the SSN-688 class attack submarines, shoddy workmanship, and long delays in the building of the new Trident missile submarines, the largest undersea craft yet built in the West—as long as the Washington Monument is tall. EB yard's *only* customer was the U.S. Navy, and within the Navy all relations with the yard were dominated—some would say micro-managed—by Admiral Rickover.

Veliotis started off by demonstrating to all who looked for new leadership at the yard that he was in charge. He immediately fired more than four thousand EB employees. Because General Dynamics believed that only Veliotis, a ruthless, cost-slashing manager, could save the yard, GD executives exerted great pressure on the Pentagon to get his security clearance problem absolutely and finally solved. The Pentagon again accommodated GD by downgrading the yard from top secret to secret. This move may seem simply bureaucratic, but the downgrading set in motion a slackening of security procedures that rippled through the yard, potentially making EB that much more vulnerable to penetration by Soviet espionage.

The Department of Defense *Industrial Security Manual,* the bible of security for the U.S. defense industry, says, for example, that top-secret material can be transmitted only by a "specifically designated escort or courier, the Armed Forces Courier Service, or by an approved crypto system." The U.S. Postal Service or company mails cannot be used, but U.S. registered mails can be used for the lower secret and confidential categories. Similar differentiations govern the handling, storage, and destruction of secret and top-secret material.

Although Veliotis still lacked top-secret clearance, to be ensconced as a fully cleared general manager of EB he needed what the Department of Energy calls Q access clearance, which required a much more intense investigation of his background. The Q investigations produced revelations that should have cost Veliotis the security clearances he already had, along with the Q that he sought:

■ In 1973, when he was in charge of the Quincy yard and had a secret clearance, Veliotis made a trip to the Soviet Union and, contrary to U.S. security regulations, did not report the trip.

■ An FBI check of his murky Greek background disclosed that in June 1954, Veliotis had been convicted in Greece for a money-order fraud and sentenced to forty-five days in jail.

■ Although Veliotis had stated on U.S. security forms that he had emigrated to Canada in 1953 from Greece, the 1954 jail sentence record showed that he could not have emigrated in 1953. Thus the dates and details of his move from Greece to Canada were clouded.

■ Security regulations say that persons requesting even secret clearance must verify date and place of birth, educational achievements, and other recorded milestones of life. U.S. security investigations showed discrepancies in reports of Veliotis' birth-place and birth date, education, and Greek military service. The FBI, for example, had not been able to find any basis for Veliotis' claim that he had been decorated by King Paul and Queen Frederika for his service as an officer in the Royal Hellenic Navy during World War II.

Despite these irregularities in his background, Veliotis got his Q clearance two days before he took over EB. Both Rickover —who at that moment was vigorously supporting him—and senior Department of Energy officials had pushed through the clearance. Veliotis' security problems seemed to be over in 1980 when he, by now a naturalized American citizen, got a top-secret clearance. EB was also upgraded to top secret, as was Quincy.

Veliotis' energetic efforts at the EB yard could not surmount the complexity of the Navy-industrial bureaucracy, Rickover's incessant meddling, and General Dynamics' demands for profits. By 1981, Veliotis had failed and the Navy was urging General Dynamics to remove him. "We insisted that before they got an-other contract they commit to get him out of Electric Boat," Secretary of the Navy Lehman said. "We didn't trust him. . . . We felt he was a poor manager and that he was constantly pick-ing fights with the Navy and the yard."

Meanwhile the government had been quietly investigating Veliotis, not because of his performance at EB and not because of his security problem, but because of financial matters. On Febru-ary 5, 1982, a federal prosecutor notified General Dynamics exec-utives that Veliotis was the target of a federal grand jury investi-gation into alleged kickbacks from a subcontractor. The prosecutor pointedly suggested to a corporation lawyer that he find out where Veliotis was getting all the money to support his lavish living habits—a twenty-room mansion, a condominium in Florida, a yacht.

As a Senate report later stated, a man with a Q clearance who is the subject of a grand jury investigation and is mysteri-ously wealthy "might constitute a security risk; at least DOD [Department of Defense] and Energy Department personnel se-curity experts should have been put on notice that such a poten-tial problem existed." The General Dynamics executives did not inform security officials. In May 1982 they in fact reappointed Veliotis executive vice president. (He was not able to personally accept the reappointment because he was in Greece, allegedly to negotiate a General Dynamics arms sale to the Greek Air Force.)

The day after his reappointment, on May 7, Veliotis called the chairman of General Dynamics to say that he wanted to take an early retirement. On May 10, Veliotis' letter of resignation arrived at corporate headquarters. At the time many Washington observers believed that Veliotis had been let go as part of a "deal," in which the Navy—in the person of the then all-powerful John Lehman—would get rid of Rickover and General Dynamics would get rid of Veliotis. Lehman, at the time, assured the authors that there was no such deal.

Veliotis and a colleague at EB were indicted in 1983 for receiving $2.7 million in kickbacks from a subcontractor who had received a $44 million contract for work on the Quincy-built natural gas ships. Veliotis soon slipped away to Greece, carrying with him years of knowledge about some of America's most secret weapons systems. At this writing he remains a fugitive from American justice.

Senate investigators seeking General Dynamics' original personnel records on Veliotis were told by the firm that his files were inexplicably missing. The FBI refused to give the Senate investigators the bureau's personnel security files on Veliotis. The Senate report concluded with a disregarded recommendation: that the Executive Branch conduct its own investigation of "a potential breach of national security of *serious dimensions.*" (Emphasis added.)

Senator Sam Nunn asked Fred Asselin, the Senate staff investigator who conducted the inquiry into Veliotis, "Are you saying the Executive Branch has not conducted a national security type investigation of Veliotis in spite of all that has happened?"

"That is our understanding, unless they are not telling us," Asselin replied. ". . . It seems to us that they need to find out who the man is. . . ."

"You don't think they have done that?" Nunn persisted. "At least in your conversations with various agencies . . . you have not found a true national security investigation of Veliotis, even to this day?" (The day was April 16, 1985, not quite a month before the arrest of John Walker.)

"We have raised this issue with the Department of Defense and the Department of Energy," Asselin said. "We tried to raise it with the FBI and Department of Justice. In each case, we were met with a lack of enthusiasm for the idea. The principal problem seems to be there is no mechanism whereby they could go forward with such a project."

Later in his colloquy with Asselin, Nunn concentrated on the broad issue of national security rather than the narrower one of industrial security. "You are not saying he breached national security; you are not alleging that," Nunn said. "You are saying nobody really knows at this point; is that right?"

"That is exactly right," Asselin said. ". . . There are many questions raised about the man. . . ."

"Has anyone indicated there has been an extensive check into the trip to the Soviet Union that was not properly reported?"

"There is no evidence. . . . We have yet to find a receptive response that someone should find out who this gentleman is. It may well be everything he put in his forms is accurate. The inconsistencies could be ironed out . . ."

"There are a number of inconsistencies?"

"Yes."

"For which you have no answer?"

"The Government has no answer. . . ."

The disclosures about Veliotis' past were an accidental by-product of a 1985 Senate investigation into "the efficiency and effectiveness of the Government personnel security programs." The investigation focused on the most likely recruits for espionage: immigrant aliens and recently naturalized citizens who apply for security clearances. Investigators discovered that the most fundamental information provided by these high-risk defense-industry workers is often not verified. Veliotis was singled out to show how dangerously inadequate is the system designed to guard the nation's secrets by making sure they are in the hands of trusted secret-keepers.

Another case involved a man much lower on the corporate ladder, William H. Bell, an engineer at Hughes Aircraft Company with a secret-level defense industrial clearance. Bell had gone to work for Hughes in 1952, soon after his graduation from UCLA, and he had never left the firm.

Sometime in 1977, when Bell was fifty-seven years old and recovering from the death of a nineteen-year-old son and a divorce after twenty-nine years of marriage, he struck up a friendship with a neighbor and fellow tennis player. The new friend, Marian Zacharski, had arrived from Poland a year before and had moved into the Cross Creek Apartments in Playa del Rey, California. He was the West Coast branch manager for the Polish American Machinery Company (POLAMCO), a firm incorporated in the United States as the marketing arm for the Polish trade agency Metal Export.

As a salesman for the Polish company, Zacharski sold industrial equipment to the California-based aerospace industry. As a friend of Bell, Zacharski was acting out a relationship that covered a slow, cunning recruitment of Bell as a spy for the Polish Intelligence Service (a member of the same Warsaw Pact spy collective that "Rolf," when he had recruited Sattler, called the "Coordinating Staff of the Countries of the Warsaw Treaty Association"). Zacharski, a superb recruiter, was so ingratiating that Bell told him he resembled Bell's older son, from whom the engineer was estranged.

Tax claims from the Internal Revenue Service, along with other accumulated debt, forced Bell to file for bankruptcy in July 1976. Zacharski sympathized with Bell about his financial problems and paid him about $5,000 for passing along the names of potential customers at Hughes, Lockheed, and Northrop, three of the highest-ranking members of the defense-industry complex, all working on highly classified military projects.

"After almost a year of purely social and recreational contacts," says a U.S. Defense Investigative Service report on Bell, "Zacharski began to ask Bell for unclassified literature from work. Bell at that time was working on radar fire-control for tanks. Zacharski then asked for 'interesting' material and received first Confidential, then Secret documents to look over. Zacharski paid Bell lavishly for his minimal 'consulting' work. And when Zacharski proposed that Bell, for additional thousands of dollars, photograph classified documents and carry them to Europe to meet other Polish representatives, Bell was ready to go along." Soon, he later said, he felt "over his head" and so committed that he could not back out.

Bell had remarried, to a young woman, and was now supporting his wife and her six-year-old son. He was unable to spurn what he knew to be tainted money. "To receive four or five thousand dollars for doing practically nothing," Bell later said, "made me very suspicious." Trained on the job about hostile intelligence recruitment methods, Bell nevertheless ignored his own suspicions. "I needed the money," he simply explained. Later he would go from need to luxury, with the purchase of a Cadillac, a $2,000 necklace for his wife, and a vacation trip to Rio de Janeiro.

Bell stepped over the line to absolute espionage one day when he gave Zacharski a copy of a secret proposal he had written. The document had to do with a type of "quiet radar" Bell had been working on. A tank could aim the radar at an enemy target without alerting the enemy. Knowledge of quiet radar technology would give the Soviets the opportunity to develop detection methods and new tank defensive tactics.

Around this time Bell learned that the Cross Creek Apartments were to be converted into condominiums. Bell did not have enough money to make the down payment needed to buy his own apartment. He turned to Zacharski, who gave him $12,000 in cash. Zacharski also gave Bell a Canon movie camera, which could take frame-by-frame photographs of documents, a tripod, and special film. Zacharski instructed Bell to take documents home from Hughes, photograph them with the camera, and then return them.

Zacharski's next order put Bell in Innsbruck, Austria. He went there in November 1979, with the Canon film in his suitcase. Zacharski had given Bell $2,500 for expenses; Bell, because his wife was an airline flight attendant, made his first spy flight for only $18.

Bell went through a recognition procedure at a restaurant in Innsbruck, made his contact, and then was driven to the outskirts of the city, where a man named Paul showed Bell a photograph of Bell's wife and her son. "He told me that I had a lovely family," Bell later said. "Then he said that our security depended upon each other and that if anybody got out of line that he'd"—meaning Bell or his family—"be taken care of." Paul sweetened what Bell called the "implied threat" with $7,000 in cash.

Back in California, Bell was congratulated by Zacharski, who gave him a list of desired information, *complete with the specific internal Hughes file numbers of the documents*. When the startled Bell asked Zacharski where he got that information, Zacharski "didn't answer me. He just smiled."

Between May 1980 and April 1981, Bell made three more spy trips to Europe, passed more film, and received unknown amounts of cash and gold. His next trip was to be to Mexico City. Bell balked, telling his handlers, "Mexico City is where a spy was caught. I don't recall his name."* Bell never had to go to Mexico City, for his espionage career was about to come to an end.

On June 23, 1981, Bell was told to report to the security office at Hughes. There FBI Agent James Reid introduced himself and, after some preliminary questions, showed Bell a translation of an article that had appeared in a recent issue of a Polish newspaper. The article said that a Pole assigned to the United Nations had defected to the United States. Reid told Bell that the defector "had been providing the FBI with information concerning activities of the Polish Intelligence Service in this country."

"Did he mention me?" Bell blurted. "This is very serious. I would like to talk to an attorney."

Reid told Bell that he could talk with a government attorney or call an attorney of his own.

Bell slumped in his chair and said softly, "I did it. I do not need an attorney."

He made a full confession and signed it. He also agreed to cooperate in an investigation of Zacharski. Five days later, with an FBI listening device strapped under his shirt, Bell met with Zacharski and engaged in an incriminating conversation that led to Zacharski's arrest.

Both men were tried and convicted of espionage. Zacharski was sentenced to life in prison. Bell, in consideration for his help, received a sentence of eight years in prison.

Specialists in industrial security, both at Hughes and in the government, have repeatedly used the Bell case as an example of an espionage disaster waiting to happen. Bell himself once said he had displayed "all the signals, all the classical reasons" for being a spy: financial problems that were quickly followed by unexplained wealth; dissatisfaction with his job; and an open relation-

---

* The name was Andrew Daulton Lee (the Snowman), the partner of Christopher Boyce (the Falcon), the spy from the TRW research firm.

ship with a national of a Communist nation. But no one at Hughes reacted to these signals. And no U.S. spy-catcher detected him. His spying ended in the all too typical way: A defector turned him in.

The easygoing, long-term spying style of James Harper and William Bell shocked security officials, who through the years had largely ignored the defense industry as a potential breeding ground for spies. Bell's espionage inspired an attempt to draw up a behavioral profile of a typical spy. Harper's success triggered an investigation of the Department of Defense's personnel security program. The findings of the investigation became known as "the Harper Report."

Another case that exposed security weaknesses in the defense industry involved Thomas P. Cavanagh, an engineer at the Northrop Corporation. Cavanagh attempted to offer classified documents to a Soviet intelligence officer. Using unexplained methods, the FBI detected the attempt and showed more interest than the Soviets did. An FBI undercover agent, posing as a Soviet, called Cavanagh and set up a meeting.

The meeting was arranged for December 10, 1984, at the Cockatoo Motel, near Los Angeles. Cavanagh, who introduced himself as Mr. Peters, had two items on his mind: "I'm after big money" and he was afraid of being caught.

Cavanagh had first got interested in electronics in the Navy, where, for four years, he had been an interior communications specialist. He had worked at Hughes before going to work for Northrop in 1981. When he went to the meeting that he thought was going to change his life, he was forty years old and separated from his wife. The father of two teenage sons, he made about $40,000 a year, but he was abysmally in debt, with twenty-five credit accounts. His debts, which amounted to more than he made a year, included a $17,000 bill from Club Med. As a senior engineer on what was called a sensitive project in Northrop's advanced systems division, he knew he had something valuable to sell.

Cavanagh, according to the U.S. intelligence analysis of the case, opened his first meeting by saying that he was worried about being caught, "partly because of the recent espionage cases." He mentioned Bell, Boyce, and "the two people in Sunnyvale"—Harper and his wife, Ruby.

"I can't give you the documents and have them back in time," he said, unwittingly speaking to the microphones strapped to the make-believe KGB officers. "They have audits. A guy just came by today and asked me how many secret documents I have."

The FBI agents were startled to learn that, by coincidence, Cavanagh had had a surprise audit of his classified documents on the day he was having his first meeting with the men he thought were KGB secrets buyers.

He also complained about the impossibility of copying documents on Northrop copiers. "You can't run your own copies in the plant," he said. "They got that regulated too." He had brought originals as sample of what he could provide. He had asked the agents to bring a camera and portable copier so that they could copy his wares.

At the next meeting, two days later, he demanded "cash and carry—'cause I'm in debt up to my ears. I'm after big money." He explained that he needed the money fast because he was about to be given a routine security check, and he knew that if he had not paid his debts he would be denied continuance of his clearance. Cavanagh then told what he had to offer: secrets about the highly classified Stealth bomber. He was told that he would be paid $25,000 a month in cash for ten years if he kept supplying a steady stream of Northrop secrets. He agreed. A third meeting was set up.

"Any word on the cash?" Cavanagh asked.

"Oh, we got good surprise for you today," one of the agents replied in his Russian accent.

"Okay. Okay. Am I gonna get it today?"

"*Da. Da.* Yes."

Cavanagh nattered on about the problems he had getting a business loan for his Amway distributorship, about Vietnamese immigrants making so much money, about the bill collectors calling him at work, about his gun collection. He suddenly pulled out a .45-caliber pistol, which he said he was toting because he was nervous. One of the agents asked to look at the gun. Claiming that he was admiring it, he did not give it back.

"Billions of dollars worth of research went into those drawings," Cavanagh said as he handed the documents over to be copied. "Billions!" He was trying to get the price up.

A noise outside the door made him more nervous. One of the agents opened it, looked outside, and said, "It is nothing." A moment later there was a knock. The door opened. "FBI!" shouted the man outside the door. "Freeze! Don't move!"

On March 14, 1985, Cavanagh pleaded guilty to two counts of espionage and was sentenced to two concurrent life terms.

In all three cases—Harper, Bell, and Cavanagh—the FBI trod through the unfamiliar realm of the military-industrial complex. The FBI was comfortable investigating espionage cases in federal agencies, which clearly were within the province of federal counter-espionage. So were the armed services, although often the FBI had to defer to the services' own counter-espionage organizations, which in reality are adjuncts to military units designed to collect intelligence about foreign armed forces. The rules are different inside places like Northrop and Hughes Aircraft, where private enterprise does the hiring and firing, writes the employee handbook, and is responsible for security on a day-to-day basis.

The Pentagon's guardian against espionage on such private grounds is the Defense Industrial Security Program, which is operated by the Defense Investigative Service. The program's major mission, the processing of clearance applications, is handled by the Defense Industrial Security Clearance Office—DISCO, the see-no-evil bureaucracy that cleared Veliotis. The seal of approval for him can be better understood through statistics compiled by Senate investigators who checked on the DISCO investigators: From fiscal year 1980 to fiscal year 1984 DISCO supervised security investigations of 138,252 persons. Only 118 were turned down—*an incredible acceptance rate of 99.91 percent.*

Reacting to the report, Senator Nunn said, "That suggests to me either virtually all of the applicants are of a sterling character, and there is just a remarkable character profile among the people who apply, or that we have a system which is basically ineffective and incapable of weeding out people who should not have security clearance."

The system indeed is ineffective. In the glaring spotlight of the Year of the Spy, the nation's creaking security-clearance machine was shown to be worn out and breaking down. General Richard G. Stilwell, former supervisor of the Department of Defense personnel security program, admitted that he could not sleep comfortably with the knowledge that "personnel security is the most tenuous link in the complex activities designed to protect the national security."

Stilwell, who chaired the committee that produced the Harper Report, said that "the investigative criteria for granting a secret clearance are admittedly and worrisomely very, very minimal—very, very minimal." Once a person is cleared for top secret, the minimal aspects of the system become obvious to employer, employee, and presumably to Soviet intelligence. There is, for example, hardly any enforcement of regulations calling for periodic renewal of clearances. Although reinvestigation is supposedly required every five years on each person with a clearance for top-secret or sensitive compartmented information, Bell's top-secret clearance had not been checked for *twenty-eight years!* And he was not the only neglected secret-holder.

Stilwell's committee estimated that to comply with the five-year reinvestigation regulation, the Defense Investigative Service (DIS) would have to conduct about 115,000 per year; in reality, DIS was conducting only 32,000 a year—and the number was declining. Speaking in 1985, Senator Nunn said, "Given current DIS manpower, it would take the Investigative Service an entire decade to perform the 280,000 clearance reinvestigations required for contractor personnel as of the end of 1984." (The cost of background investigations in 1985 was $400 to $500 each.)

The quality of the investigations was also slipping, primarily because more of them had to be done in less time to relieve the backlog pressure, which Nunn labeled a "nightmare-type operation." It was a very old nightmare. The government's security policies of 1985 were based on an executive order issued by President Eisenhower thirty-two years before. The order, rooted in "loyalty" investigations of the McCarthy era, stated, "The American people must be assured that federal employees are persons of integrity, high moral character, and unswerving loyalty to the U.S." These security requirements, designed to thwart the ideological spies of the 1950s, missed the more likely espionage suspect of the 1980s: the Miller, the Walker, the Pollard, the Pelton, the Bell, the Cavanagh, the Whitworth who peddled secrets for profit.

The most common probe for security risks, the background

investigation, traces to the 1950s, the Eisenhower years, when people tended to stay put, when neighbors were likely providers of information on a person's character, and when local school, police, and employment records were easily found and gladly handed over to government investigators. Times have changed, but the background investigation has not.

"Today's society," says Stilwell, "is very mobile, more people move, both husbands and wives work, and it is difficult to find character references who know the individual being investigated. Because of legislation on privacy and freedom of information, individuals are reluctant to report derogatory information to investigators for fear of reprisal, and employers, schools, and other record repositories will release only limited directory-type information to investigators."

Some states and cities do not cooperate with security investigators for reasons based on recent privacy laws and policies. Many employers—including some of the nation's foremost defense contractors—also bar federal investigators from personnel files or restrict such record searches. One such firm was Bechtel, Inc., the worldwide conglomerate that numbers Secretary of State Shultz and Secretary of Defense Weinberger among its former employees. Bechtel provides DIS investigators records but does not give investigators leads or opportunities to conduct "personal" interviews. Sperry and Texas Instruments have similar policies, as do many other nationally known firms.

Another uncooperative organization is the federal government itself. A contractor may operate under as many as thirty different sets of conflicting security rules. The Department of Defense will accept a Department of Energy Q clearance for conversion to a Department of Defense top secret, but the Department of Energy will not honor a Department of Defense top secret.

The government has two major security investigative agencies: DISCO and the Office of Personnel Management (OPM), the government's leading investigative agency for the federal civilian work force. OPM's principal customer is the Department of Energy, a relatively small agency with an extremely high number of employees requiring clearance (11,841 out of 16,800 in a 1985 count).

The OPM's investigative philosophy drastically differs from that of DISCO's. OPM makes a distinction between suitability for employment (basic fitness for federal employment) and for security clearance (fitness to hold a sensitive position). On the suitability track, OPM background investigators look for lies, such as false educational claims; on the security track, they look basically for the same risks as do DISCO investigators.

The OPM, which usually uses twice as many sources as DISCO, consistently turns down more applicants than does DISCO and often digs up more derogatory information. Routine OPM background checks, for instance, disclosed that the wife of a U.S. nuclear scientist was having an affair with a Soviet agent and that a contractor's employee at the Kennedy Space Center was a convicted murderer who had escaped from a Georgia prison. In contrast with DISCO's acceptance rate of 99.91 percent, OPM reported in 1985 an acceptance rate of 92 to 94 percent. But OPM is so pressed that its self-described "best-product" investigations have been augmented by others of much lower quality. These are conducted by private contractors hired by OPM. The work of one of these firms was so shoddy and suspect that the FBI was called in to investigate the investigators.

One would imagine that only under extraordinary conditions could an émigré from the Soviet Union or an Eastern Bloc country be given a job that involves the handling of information graded secret or higher. Yet more and more émigrés are getting such jobs. The largest employers of Soviet émigrés with security clearances are Hughes Aircraft, Lockheed, TRW, and Grumman, all prime targets for penetration by Soviet intelligence.

A 1985 congressional study of security in the U.S. defense industry showed that 121 Soviet émigrés had top-secret clearances and 1,349 had secret clearances. A mere twenty-three were cleared for the lowest classification level, confidential. Thousands of other applications for clearances for émigrés were in the slow-moving security clearance mill.

FBI sources admit that background security investigations are impossible for émigrés from the Soviet Union or a host of other Eastern Bloc and unfriendly nations, such as Cuba and North Korea. Yet such background checks are demanded by regulations. Ironically, applicants whose backgrounds can be checked may get turned down because of something discovered. But émigrés whose lives cannot be scrutinized get clearances *because* their backgrounds cannot be checked.

In contrast to the 1,493 Soviet émigrés—as well as hundreds from other Communist countries—the Department of Energy considers the problem of unattainable background checks so risky that when Veliotis got his clearance he was one of only *four* cleared foreign nationals out of 201,000 employees, contractors, and other federal workers cleared for access to classified information, special nuclear information, or entry into restricted areas. The Department of Energy ordinarily will not process a request for clearance for a naturalized U.S. citizen unless the applicant, in a written statement to his or her native country, formally renounces previous citizenship.

Similarly, there are many companies like Zacharski's PO-LAMCO—firms operating in the United States that are owned or controlled by Communist or Communist Bloc countries. The Soviets and Eastern Bloc nations operate more than thirty legal, overt trading firms. All of them provide cover for espionage and all of them can legally purchase technology that cannot be exported. The companies do, of course, illegally export the technology. But given the diplomatic and commercial routes available, the companies can easily evade the export ban. The FBI has a list of these firms—but that list is classified! The bureau prefers to dispense the information to contractors on a need-to-know basis.

Bizarre concepts of security can be found throughout the defense industry. The CIA, which reportedly rejects more than half of its applicants, had to rely on Christopher J. Boyce, a wild young man who admitted he could never pass a polygraph test, to guard its supersecret, Rhyolite intelligence satellite program. The Boyce-Lee case dramatically illustrates the differences in the security safeguards of a government agency, where dedicated employees closely protected Rhyolite, and the practices of a major industrial complex where a young drug user who sneered at American ideals—and hated the CIA—was able to hustle a nation's secrets as easily as he could hustle drugs.

If you want to know how to catch a spy, ask a spy who was caught. That was the intent of the Senate Permanent Subcommittee on Investigation in April 1985 when it listened to Boyce, who was brought from an isolation cell in the U.S. maximum security penitentiary in Marion, Illinois, to Room SD-342 of the Dirksen Senate Office Building. In 1977, Boyce, then twenty-four, had been convicted of espionage, along with his boyhood friend, Andrew Daulton Lee. Boyce was sentenced to forty years, Lee to life.

From March 1975 through December 1976, Boyce had removed or photographed classified documents stored in the "black vault" of TRW, a contractor for the CIA in Redondo Beach, California. He then passed the secrets on to Lee, who sold them to KGB officers at the Soviet Embassy in Mexico City. "Obviously," Boyce told the senators, "neither the government's clearance procedures nor the company's security procedures worked very well."

Boyce had gotten his job at TRW through "the FBI branch of the old-boy network." His father, a former FBI agent working as a security officer for a defense firm, set up the job for his son with another former FBI agent who managed security at TRW. Boyce began work as a general clerk in July 1974. By December he had top-secret clearance, access to two special projects, and was cleared to handle National Security Agency keylists for the KW-7 cryptographic machine. He monitored secret communications between the CIA and TRW and had day-to-day knowledge of the CIA-directed intelligence satellite program code-named "Rhyolite."

The Rhyolite satellites were used to monitor radio and long-distance telephone traffic within the Soviet Union. The satellites also picked up the telemetry signals from Soviet missile test flights. The Rhyolite communications intercepts that Boyce so casually stole gave the Soviets immense knowledge about an innovative intelligence-gathering coup. The CIA assumed that Rhyolite was a complete success. Actually, because of Boyce's laid-back treachery, the United States was unwittingly sharing Rhyolite with the Soviet Union.

After his arrest U.S. intelligence backtracked as part of a damage assessment and learned that the Soviets did not begin encrypting their missile telemetry until about six months after the arrest of Boyce and Lee. Analysts theorized that the Soviets preferred to let the CIA detect the telemetry rather than raise suspicions that they possessed the secrets of the Rhyolite satellites.

"While my background investigations were under way," Boyce said, "I heard that friends of my parents had been contacted as references. Speaking as adults, they told the investigators that I was the courteous, bright, responsible son of a good family, exactly as they were expected to say. . . .

"What the investigators never sought was the Chris Boyce who moved in circles beyond the realm of parents, teachers, and other adult-authority figures. To my knowledge, they never interviewed a single friend, a single peer. . . . Had they done so, the investigators would have interviewed a room full of disillusioned longhairs, counter-culture falconers, druggie surfers, wounded paranoid vets, pot-smoking, anti-establishment types, bearded malcontents generally, many of whom were in trouble."

Around the time that Boyce was getting his clearances—primarily by being the son of a former FBI agent and filling out a few forms—his kid sister was being polygraphed so that she could get a job at a 7-Eleven convenience store. Around the time Boyce began stealing secrets the project security manager was concentrating his effort on catching a night janitor in the act of stealing quarters from the office coffee fund. As an example of attitudes toward TRW security, Boyce's immediate superior pasted a chimpanzee's face on his security badge and had a few laughs with his subordinates when he had no trouble getting in and out of M4, the special project building.

Just as Walker and Whitworth elsewhere in the espionage world were photographing keylists for Navy cryptographic gear, Boyce was doing the same with the lists for the CIA KW-7 network. But he sometimes had more trouble than the trained Navy radiomen. Boyce's booty came in a binder lined with sealed plastic envelopes that contained the keylists. He removed the lists from the envelopes, photographed them, then replaced them and resealed the envelope with an iron or a carelessly applied touch of glue. Once, when he had messed up a resealing, a DIS inspector checked the botched code binder but ignored the broken seal.

A TRW spokesman insisted that security procedures were sound when Boyce worked there and that he had exaggerated the drug use, drinking, and horseplay in the black vault. There was, said an executive, only a "limited use of alcohol on the premises." He doubted the chimpanzee security-badge story but admitted that there had been certain discrepancies in the distribution of badges. (Boyce probably made his own TRW top-security badges available to his Soviet spymasters, who would be able to copy and then duplicate them to permit others to enter certain TRW security spaces.)

Every six months, according to the DIS security manual, DISCO must inspect the (supposedly) secure facilities like TRW, Hughes Aircraft, and Systems Control, Inc. (SCI), the place where James Harper and Ruby Schuler conspired to steal documents and sell them to Polish intelligence officers. In fiscal year 1985, DISCO inspectors declared that only *seven* of the nation's nearly 14,000 "cleared facilities" had unsatisfactory security safeguards—a rejection rate even more fantastic than DISCO's employee clearance rate.

By DIS's own figures, 95 percent of facilities inspections are announced at least ten days in advance. Such an inspection at SCI in November 1982 found the "overall security posture to be good." SCI passed another inspection in May 1983. Harper was arrested in October 1983. In December the DIS reinspected SCI and, in one of the most memorable understatements in the annals of recent espionage, reported that security at SCI was not good.

There is another aspect to Boyce's espionage: the potential for KGB-sponsored moles in the United States. During one of his meetings with his KGB handler, the Soviet suggested that Boyce leave TRW and return to college. The Soviets envisioned that a bright young man like Boyce, properly educated and properly guided, could rise to an important position in American society. Others were doing so under the aegis of the KGB—there was James Frederick Sattler, the East Germans' operative who befriended key defense and White House officials, and William Bell Hugle, the wily middleman in the Bell-Hughes Aircraft espionage case, who ran as a Democratic candidate for Congress. (FBI officials will only say of Hugle that he is living outside the United States.)

Are there Soviet moles in U.S. government and key industry positions? "Certainly," responded Secretary of the Navy Lehman. Spy sleuth James Jesus Angleton thought so too. Looking at the broad counter-intelligence picture, former CIA and DIA analyst Raymond Robinson observed, "If we found leaks [in American intelligence] by accident, we must assume a much greater network." Discussing past intelligence operations and the possible impact of leaks or moles on U.S. intelligence, he recalled that during some programs, "We would have a source simply dry up after a few months."

The feeling is similar to that of the late 1940s when American and British agents parachuted into Albania and other Eastern Bloc countries—and then simply disappeared, obviously the victims of KGB actions. It is now known that those intelligence disasters—which helped lead to the U.S. reliance on electronic spies instead of human ones—were caused by British mole Kim Philby.

Robinson's statement about the drying up of sources and the failure of U.S. counter-intelligence to detect Americans who have betrayed their country raises the specter of moles existing in Washington. The probability is high that spies continue to exist in the United States at two levels: At the "working" level—enlisted servicemen and women who have access to technical data, communications, and cryptographic materials—and at the policy level, where such spies as Maclean, Burgess, Philby, and Blunt operated in England.

U.S. counter-espionage has failed for more than two decades. Some observers contend that the failure began when counter-intelligence expert Angleton was fired by DCI William Colby in December 1974. But the earlier spy escapades of too many Americans push the date of the failure of the system to the early 1960s, the time of Sergeant Dunlop, Martin, and Mitchell, who betrayed the secrets of the National Security Agency, and other Americans who merchandised treason.

The most significant fact about modern espionage is simply this: Americans spying for the Soviets are usually caught because of tips from vengeful relatives or by the revelations of defectors from the Soviet Union and Eastern Bloc nations. *The overwhelming majority have not been caught by U.S. counter-intelligence efforts.*

The FBI has failed as a national counter-intelligence agency. So, too, have the other alphabet-soup federal investigative agencies, DIS, DISCO, and OPM, along with its outside helpers. The armed forces and defense industry have also failed to protect their multitude of secrets and failed to detect the spies delivered up by chance and defectors. Further, the military services—and the Department of Defense hierarchy—have made a fetish of selectively releasing information to garner support for programs, regardless of real classifications, while hiding behind the screen of classification those facts that the Pentagon does not wish to see released to the American public.

There are at least five major reasons for this massive and potentially catastrophic failure of U.S. counter-intelligence:

First, the FBI, the nation's principal counter-intelligence agency, is primarily a crook-catching organization. The FBI knows how to catch bank robbers and kidnappers, men and women who commit overt crimes against society, where there is a crime scene to examine and descriptions to send out. Within the FBI few agents have become specialists in counter-intelligence. Typically an agent begins his or her career in a field office like Atlanta, where white-collar crime is the principal problem, and then goes on to other field offices. There may suddenly come a time for counter-espionage work—as there did one fateful day in the Albuquerque field office when Edward Lee Howard had to be put under surveillance. But relatively few field offices have full-time counter-espionage work.

Counter-espionage specialists do serve in the elite Intelligence Division in the FBI's Washington headquarters. Even service there, or on the counter-espionage squad at the Washington field office, does not necessarily lead to a counter-espionage career path.

Counter-intelligence is not the path to advancement in the FBI or any other investigative agency. Clark Magruder, a former deputy head of Naval Intelligence, gave the authors a solid bit of evidence about the scant rewards given to spy-catchers: "The intelligence community awards committee gives most of its awards to intelligence, not counter-intelligence, officers."

Second, the FBI has a very poor image with allied counter-intelligence services, a leftover from J. Edgar Hoover's forty-eight-year reign as director. He disliked double agents and playing out or controlling identified spies. His handling of Britain's most successful double agent, Tricycle, personified that attitude, as did his relationship with William Stephenson (Intrepid), Churchill's intelligence representative in the United States during World War II.

Third, the military services do not have effective counter-intelligence groups. While these units are necessary for certain purposes within the military services, they receive their supervision from chiefs and directors of intelligence who are overwhelmingly concerned with *collecting* intelligence against potential enemies. Counter-intelligence is a sideline activity, and properly so. But when politics or publicity enter the equation, the military's spy-catchers sometimes swing into action, with little success to show for their efforts.

Each service runs its own counter-espionage program, which has scant coordination with other U.S. counter-espionage agencies and little responsibility beyond its own precincts. Army Counterintelligence, asked by Senate investigators for an accounting of its work, responded in 1985 with a turbid answer that ended saying "there are a total of 24 cases where the Army has neutralized espionage activity in the past ten years." Of those neutralized cases, only eight "encompass the following cycles: The investigative phase, the indictment, conviction, and incarceration phase." Translated into standard English and mathematics, that means in an espionage-filled decade Army spy-catchers have successfully brought to justice fewer than one spy a year.

Much of the work of the Naval Investigative Service focuses on theft and fraud at naval clubs and commissaries, drug smuggling, and hunts for homosexuals. In recent years the NIS has also accepted such odd jobs as providing protection to Marine Lieutenant Colonel Oliver L. North when the former National Security Council official received death threats; tracking down reports of waste and fraud aboard an aircraft carrier; and searching for gold missing from a Navy dental unit.

Justice Department officials privately expressed dismay at the NIS venture into counter-espionage when the Marine guard scandal erupted in the U.S. Embassy in Moscow. Inept handling of the interrogation of suspects irreparably harmed potential espionage cases, federal civilian officials said. Lack of evidence, witness retractions, and faulty NIS investigations are cited for the dismissal of most of the charges against the Moscow guards. One defense lawyer, Marine Lieutenant Colonel Michael L. Powell, charged that the NIS had created a "fantasy" case against his client, Corporal Arnold Bracy. The case fell apart as soon as a defense counsel entered the case. The Marines dropped all charges against Bracy.

This is in contrast with the FBI's well-regarded interrogation techniques that, in conjunction with Department of Justice legal and technical expertise, usually produce airtight confessions and prosecutions.

Fourth, the armed services and the Department of Defense continually misuse security classifications.

A landmark Defense Department study in 1985, directed by General Stilwell, stated, ". . . it is clear that the volume of classified documents is enormous. Obviously, the Department [of Defense] needs to protect much of what it is doing with classification controls. Nonetheless, too much information appears to be classified and much at higher levels than is warranted."

During a 1985 Senate hearing, Senator John Glenn asked Stilwell, "How many people do we have cleared secret and up right now—grand total?"

Stilwell said that the Department of Defense had 454,000 military and civilian holders of top secret or higher, two million holders of secret, and 13,000 confidential—"this last is kind of an aberration—"

"Thirteen thousand?" Senator Nunn interrupted.

"It is almost a category that—"

Now Senator Glenn interrupted: "That ranks along with mysterious."

"We still have one category called embarrassing," Senator Nunn added.

Mysterious, embarrassing, or odd—whatever the word applied, it does seem incredible that *secret* gets so large a band of adherents at the Pentagon and *confidential* gets so few. The pyramid of secrecy seems to be upside down.

Recent examples of overclassification abound. The Defense Department refused to make public any photos of the Soviet air-cushion assault craft of the Pomornik class in 1986 because they were being "saved" for a Weinberger report scheduled for publication in early 1987. (NATO allies made photographs available to interested U.S. journalists.) The Pentagon withheld satellite photos of new Soviet fighter aircraft after an Air Force general allowed them to be published as an accompaniment to his congressional testimony. Satellite photos of the Soviets' Nikolayev shipyard were also withheld, even though Morison had given them to a British magazine, which published them.

Senator Sam Nunn tells of attending a classified briefing at which all of the charts used by the briefers were classified secret, including one that simply said, "We must not fail." When Nunn asked why the four words were secret, nobody could give him an answer. So he provided his own: "When you are classifying a whole lot of things, you tend to classify everything. . . . By trying to protect everything, you protect nothing."

Variations of the hide-and-seek-the-secrets game are countless. Presidential directives carefully state that the Defense Department may use only *three* levels of classification: confidential, secret, and top secret. Yet the services continue to manipulate security classifications—literally inventing their own classifications to hide documents that they fear could be embarrassing to them.

For example, after congressional staffer William S. Lind wrote a hard-hitting critique of the Army's unclassified manual *FM 100-5 Operations,* the Army slapped an "unclassified classification" on the document that reads:

DISTRIBUTION RESTRICTION. This publication contains technical or operational information that is for official government use only. Distribution is limited to US government agencies. Requests from outside the US government for release of this publication under the Freedom of Information Act or the Foreign Military Sales Program must be made to Commander, TRADOC, Fort Monroe, VA 23651-5000.

The Army still hands the document out to members of Congress, staffers, and anyone perceived as a potential ally who will help sell Army thinking. To others it is simply "unavailable." The Navy has done the same thing with the *Monthly Progress Report.* This periodical lists the yards in which Navy ships are being built, along with the dates of their past and future keel layings, launchings, and commissioning dates. After severe congressional criticism in the 1970s over delays in ship programs, the issuing Naval Sea Systems Command "restricted" circulation of the document by marking it "For Official Use Only."

The information in the document was readily available through a telephone call to the Pentagon's information offices, a mile from the Naval Sea Systems Command offices. The Pentagon will give the dates and shipyard information, as will press releases issued at the Pentagon for every ship contract award, launching, and commissioning. When journalists appealed the "For Official Use Only" *nonclassification,* the Ships people quickly changed the document's restriction to read as follows to keep it out of circulation:

DISTRIBUTION STATEMENT B
Distribution limited to U.S. Government Agencies only; ADMINISTRATIVE/OPERATIONAL USE; [DATE]. Other requests for this document shall be referred to COMNAVSEA (SEA 907).

The epitome of the secrets game playing came when the Navy refused to release a list of the cryptographic machines that were in the spy ship *Pueblo* that was captured by North Vietnamese forces in January 1968. Copies of such lists exist not only at the Naval Security Command headquarters on Nebraska Avenue in northwest Washington but also in Pyongyang and in Moscow —probably with the machines themselves. Playing such games with security classifications accomplishes little and makes a mockery of the entire system designed to keep the nation's secrets from getting to places like Pyongyang and Moscow.

All too often in recent years, officials in the U.S. intelligence community have perceived both the media and the federal employees who leak information to the media as the enemy. When, for example, Army Lieutenant General William E. Odom, Director of the National Security Agency, talked of espionage in September 1987, he did not mention the KGB or its walk-in spy, former NSA analyst Ronald Pelton. Odom focused his ire on James Bamford, who wrote *The Puzzle Palace,* a critically acclaimed book on NSA. Odom not only suggested that Bamford should have been prosecuted for writing the book; the general also revealed that he had officially referred several unnamed publishers of information to the Justice Department for prosecution. None of the referrals were accepted by the Justice Department. Admiral John M. Poindexter, a chief plotter of "Irangate," had earlier made a similar proposal in his attempts to control the media.

The ultimate in U.S. military security absurdity occurred in 1987, when the U.S. Air Force asked its civilian employees with security clearances to sign an agreement calling on them not to discuss or publish classified information *and information that could be classified in the future.* Thus to the concept of "classified" information was added the bizarre idea of "classifiable" information—ordinary data that someday might undergo a transformation into secret data. The Air Force branded those reluctant to sign the agreement as lacking in "personal commitment to protect classified information."

Procedures were being initiated to punish nonsigners or dismiss them from government service when, under threat of suits filed by the American Federation of Government Employees and a temporary ban against punishing employees who do not sign the form from the Information Security Oversight Office, the Air Force withdrew the requirement for the nondisclosure agreement. However, the future-secret idea developed a life of its own. By the fall of 1987, some 1.7 million civilian and military employees had signed the form.

The effort to protect classified information about possible future secrets—even if the information is not now classified—was ludicrous. Rather than a U.S. government policy, such thoughts were more akin to the commands of Big Brother in George Orwell's *1984* or the mad midnight directives of Joseph Stalin. The desire to withhold virtually all defense and national security information tends to reduce the effectiveness of meaningful U.S. classification policies and hence damages American security in general.

The Pentagon reacts to "unauthorized" disclosure of policy as if it were ambushed. When Bob Woodward's book *Veil* was published, the Chief of Naval Operations ordered all Navy personnel to avoid any "speculation on sensitive operations." The Navy thus chose to stay mum about an issue Woodward raised: the use of Navy submarines in intelligence work. "As in all such matters," the CNO instructions read, "the only acceptable response to questions which may arise from information in the book is 'we do not comment on speculative or hypothetical material.' "

Fifth, a massive and chronic lack of coordination hampers U.S. counter-intelligence activities.

Classic cases are many. For example, more than a year after the FBI placed a tap on Chinese spy Larry Chin's telephone, the

CIA asked him to come back to work full-time as a consultant to the agency. The CIA obviously did not know that a defector from the People's Republic of China had named Chin. Theoretically there is a counter-espionage coordinating group formed to handle exactly this kind of situation. What happens in theory, however, does not always happen in reality, or what sometimes passes for reality in spy-catching.

The most damaging public example of coordination failure came when Edward Howard escaped from FBI surveillance and defected to the Soviet Union. The CIA did not share any information about Howard until it was too late. When he was fired agency security officers did not attempt to get his passport—or, incredibly, the one that he had been issued under a "working name."

"He wiped out the Moscow station," an intelligence official told *The New York Times* in what became a media sideshow over the case, with the CIA leaking information that made the FBI look inept and the FBI doing the same about the CIA. The sideshow finally ended in Moscow, with Soviet media exploiting the defection by putting Howard on a TV talk show.

These failings must be remedied. The existing system cannot hope to stem the flow of classified material, not even the material that *should* be safeguarded. Objective review of the situation calls for the conclusion that a new agency is required to direct U.S. counter-intelligence activities. After discussions with scores of officials involved in counter-intelligence for the Administration and military services, after interviews with several members of Congress, after reading through stack after stack of court records, special reports, congressional testimony, and private correspondence on the subject, the authors believe that the brief for such an agency is clear.

The new activity—for the sake of discussion, call it the National Counter-Intelligence Office—would be placed under the Director of Central Intelligence (DCI). The new Office would be at the level of the National Reconnaissance Office (within the Department of Defense) and the Arms Control and Disarmament Agency (within the State Department). This would *not* place the new Office under the CIA, for the legislation that established the Intelligence Community clearly makes the DCI the overall supervisor of all U.S. intelligence activities, of which the

CIA is only one. Further, there is ample evidence that neither the Congress nor the American people would accept the spy organization also being the spy-catchers.

Such a National Counter-Intelligence Office would support the recommendations of the Commission to Review DOD Security Policies and Practices. The Commission's 1985 report included the proposal to: "Explore with the FBI and Department of Justice the feasibility of DOD counter-intelligence elements playing a wider role in support of FBI responsibilities for monitoring hostile intelligence presence within the United States during periods of unusually heavy activity." But such periods would generally find the Defense establishment preoccupied with military matters. Hence, a separate agency—capitalizing on the counter-intelligence expertise of all federal agencies—should have the lead in counter-espionage.

The new Office must have a deputy director from the military services to head the military division—to provide the much-needed *technical* guidance to the services. Indeed, the counter-intelligence investigations of the military services must be transferred to the direct supervision of the new Office so that all of the nation's counter-espionage activities, civilian and military, will be under one roof.

The National Counter-Intelligence Office would guard the three major sites of espionage penetration: federal agencies such as the FBI and the CIA; the armed services, and, the most neglected place of all, the defense firms that have been especially targeted by Soviet seekers of U.S. high-tech products and inventions. This vulnerable leg of the "security triad" needs more astute direction and protection than what is being provided by DIS, DISCO, OPM, and the private contractors hired to do hasty and often sloppy investigations.

Research into the standards of clearance determinations is particularly needed. Some eye-opening studies, for example, are being conducted at the Navy Postgraduate School in Monterey, California, where researchers examined the records of 27,500 enlisted men and women who were given clearance for sensitive jobs involving nuclear weapons and intelligence work—but had to be discharged for unsuitability early in their training.

Only about 5 percent of military enlistees who receive background checks are turned down, although the percentage of military misfits is much higher. As one of the Monterey researchers tells it, an applicant for military service may have a horrible employment record that marks him or her as a poor risk in the civilian world and still make it, for a brief and perhaps disastrous time, in the world of military secrets.

As an example, the research sketched a picture of a lazy, pot-smoking young man who had been fired from four jobs. "The likelihood is that the fifth employer, if he does any employment checks, will turn him down. But not the Department of Defense. The Department of Defense will accept him and he will be enlisted."

Once in the service, he may well find himself on a track for a sensitive job. Even "if the background investigation is accurate enough to identify these problems, he will probably still be cleared for top secret and for SCI duties," the researcher says.

"I ask you, what kind of a system do we have here where an individual who is unlikely to get good employment outside Defense because of a lousy employment history will still pass muster for our highly sensitive jobs?"

In 1987, two years after the Year of the Spy, an unprecedented event took place in the intelligence community: The head of one key spy agency went to another, taking his hard-won experience with him. The appointment of then FBI Director William H. Webster as Director of Central Intelligence creates an ideal opportunity to make a change in how we look at espionage and the modern merchandising of treason. Here is the chance to withdraw the counter-espionage role from the FBI and establish it under the DCI. This idea has some currency in Washington. When the idea was raised to Senator John Warner, former Secretary of the Navy and currently a senior member of the Senate Armed Services Committee, he responded without hesitation, "To propose this would be a national service." Others on Capitol Hill and elsewhere in Washington agree.

One factor in particular makes Webster attractive to initiate such a counter-espionage office. His predecessor, the late William Casey, carefully obscured the three major roles of the DCI—principal intelligence adviser to the president, head of the intelligence community (as DCI), and head of the Central Intelligence Agency. Casey further blurred the lines—much to the annoyance of members of Congress—by also being a member of President Reagan's cabinet. In contrast, Webster has carefully distinguished his three roles and has declined a chair in the cabinet. This attitude could contribute to Webster's ability to establish a counterespionage office, although some of his former colleagues at the FBI feel that Webster's reluctance to engage in high-level policy decisions weakened his efforts as the nation's chief policeman.

In other ways Webster is the ideal DCI to establish and oversee a new counter-espionage office. He seems to understand the often delicate balance between stern law enforcement and protection of traditional American liberties. "We are different from our competition," Webster said when he was still head of the FBI. "We do not subscribe to the block-control, the block-watch concept. We have something more consistent with our open and democratic society. As our main tactic, therefore, we 'spiderweb' known or suspected intelligence operatives. Spinning our webs with physical and electronic surveillance—all electronic surveillance being court-authorized, by the way—we weave a barrier between hostile agents and our citizens. We hope that the barrier itself will frighten off potential traitors."

Spiderwebs do not stop greedy bears, Russian or otherwise. And people who wait for tips are called waiters, not FBI agents. If Webster wants to improve the nation's spy-catching record, he needs new thinking—and a new organization. Soviet intelligence officers do not steal secrets. American traitors do. They should be the prey, not of spiders but of hunters.

Espionage Cases, 1953–87

The cracking of the "Atomic Spy Ring" of the 1940s and 1950s ended an era. The spy network, which spanned the United States, Great Britain, and Canada, was set up and controlled by the Soviet Union for a single purpose: to steal the secrets of the U.S. atomic bomb. The Soviet spymasters successfully exploited ideological fervor as a motive to inspire people to turn against their countries.

The accused American leaders of that ring, **Julius** and **Ethel Rosenberg**, were tried, sentenced to death for espionage during wartime, and executed on June 19, 1953.

Other members of the ring were:

Harry Gold was a chemist who worked for Soviet intelligence from 1934 to 1945. He received information on the U.S. atomic bomb program from British scientist Klaus Fuchs. Arrested in 1950, he was sentenced to thirty years in prison. He was released on parole in 1965.

David Greenglass was arrested in 1950 after Harry Gold identified him as a source of atomic bomb secrets. Greenglass, Julius Rosenberg's brother-in-law, got fifteen years and was released in 1960.

Morton Sobell, a classmate of Julius Rosenberg, was sentenced to thirty years imprisonment. He became eligible for parole in 1962 and was released in 1969.

The cynical manipulation of the atomic spies would not work again. After the trials and convictions, ideology would rarely be a motive for espionage in the United States. Americans, usually working alone, would spy for cash, not creed.

Spying for money has been going on since the 1960s, but not until the mid-1980s did there seem to be an espionage plague. Seventeen cases became public during 1984 and 1985. The latter year became known as the Year of the Spy.

Espionage comes in many forms. There are spies accused and real, in the armed forces, in federal agencies, in defense plants—the triad of Soviet espionage targets. There are also spies who are not Americans. The list that follows includes all categories.

Many of the cases on the list are discussed in depth in the text. For details, check the index.

SERVICEMEN

Army Sergeant Roy A. Rhodes, spied for the Soviets while he worked at the U.S. Embassy in Moscow in the 1950s. He was sentenced to five years at hard labor.

Air Force Captain George H. French, arrested in 1957 after tossing onto the grounds of the Soviet Embassy a letter offering to sell nuclear bomb secrets. He was sentenced to life imprisonment at a secret court-martial.

C. J. Gessner, U.S. Army intelligence officer, defected in 1962.

Air Force Airman Second Class Robert G. Thompson, a Soviet agent in Berlin from 1957 to 1963. He was arrested in 1965 and sentenced to thirty years. He was released in 1978 in a three-way trade involving an American student held in East Germany and an Israeli held in Mozambique.

Army Sergeant Jack F. Dunlap, assigned to the National Security Agency, committed suicide in 1963. After his death it was discovered that he had been a Soviet spy. The extent of his spying has never been revealed.

Army Sergeant Robert L. Johnson, recruited by the Soviets in Berlin to spy during the 1950s. He later recruited **Army Sergeant James Allen Mintkenbaugh.** They both had long espionage careers. In 1965, Johnson and Mintkenbaugh were sentenced to twenty-five years in prison. Johnson's sentence ended with his murder in prison in 1972.

Air Force Captain Joseph P. Kauffman, passed military secrets to East German intelligence officers. Court-martialed in 1962, he was sentenced to twenty years at hard labor.

Navy Yeoman Nelson C. Drummond, passed classified information to Soviets in London in 1957. Arrested in 1962, he was sentenced to life in prison.

Joseph G. Helmich, Jr., as an Army warrant officer, sold the Soviets cryptographic information in the 1960s. Arrested in 1981, he was sentenced to life imprisonment.

Lieutenant Colonel William H. Whalen, an Army intelligence officer stationed at the Pentagon, he sold secrets to the Soviets. Arrested in 1966, he was sentenced to fifteen years in prison.

Air Force Sergeant Herbert Boeckenhaupt, who worked for the Air Force Headquarters Command in the Pentagon and sold secrets to the Soviets. Arrested in 1967, he was sentenced to thirty years in prison.

Air Force Master Sergeant Walter Perkins, an intelligence specialist at the Air Defense Weapons Center in Tyndall Air Force Base, Florida. Arrested in 1971, he was sentenced to three years.

Air Force Sergeant James D. Wood, of the Air Force Office of Special Investigations. He was arrested in 1973 after FBI agents found hundreds of classified documents in a car he had rented. He had met in Washington with a Soviet diplomat. Wood, who cooperated in the investigation, was given a dishonorable discharge and sentenced to two years in prison.

Marine Corporal Joel Yager, stationed at the Marine Corps Air Station in Iwakuni, Japan, in September 1977. He attempted to sell a secret document and three confidential ones to "a foreign national," who turned out to be employed by the Naval Investigative Service. Yager was not court-martialed.

Yeoman Third Class Eugene L. Madsen, who worked on the strategic warning staff in the Pentagon, was arrested in 1979 for attempting to sell classified information to the Soviets. He was sentenced to eight years.

Air Force Second Lieutenant Christopher M. Cooke, assigned to a nuclear missile silo, walked into the Soviet Embassy in December 1980 and offered information about U.S. intercontinental missiles. Arrested and questioned, Cooke admitted committing espionage. But because of a bungled interrogation, a military court ruled that he could not be court-martialed. He was released from the Air Force.

Michael R. Murphy, a crewman aboard the strategic missile submarine *James Polk,* called the Soviet Mission to the United Nations in June 1981 and offered to make what was later officially described as "a deal that would be beneficial to both the Soviets and himself." Murphy, who had a secret clearance, was honorably discharged from the Navy.

Navy Ensign Stephen A. Baba, who had secret clearance, in 1981 attempted to sell classified documents to South Africa through its embassy in Washington. He was sentenced to eight years at hard labor but the sentence was later reduced to two years.

Corporal Brian E. Slavens, a Marine Corps guard at a Navy undersea weapons installation in Alaska, deserted his post and went to the Soviet Embassy and offered to sell military information for $500 to $1,000. He was given a dishonorable discharge and sentenced to two years of confinement. He served eighteen months.

Private First Class Alan D. Coberly, a Marine deserter, walked into the Soviet Embassy in Manila in 1983. He pleaded guilty to desertion and "other criminal acts." He was sentenced to eighteen months of confinement.

William H. Hughes, Jr., an Air Force captain with knowledge of highly classified communications information, disappeared after being sent to the Netherlands. He was classified as a deserter in 1983.

Lance Corporal Michael R. Moore, a Marine absent without leave from the Naval Air Station at Cubi Point in the Philippines, was apprehended with photographs and other material as he was alleged to be preparing to contact Soviet officials in the Philippines. Investigators said he had "an interest in defecting to the Soviet Union." He was given a convenience-of-the-government discharge.

David A. Hediger, a crewman on a submarine tender, in 1982 called the Soviet Military Office in Washington. There is no public record of any action being taken against him.

Ernest C. Pugh, a sailor stationed at the Defense Language School in Monterey, California, walked into the Soviet Consulate in San Francisco in 1982 and tried to defect. He was given a convenience-of-the-government discharge.

Jeffery L. Pickering, stationed at the Naval Regional Medical Clinic in Seattle, admitted sending a five-page secret document to the Soviet Embassy in Washington. When he was arrested in 1983 he had a plastic addressograph card imprinted with the embassy's address. He was sentenced to five years at hard labor and given a bad-conduct discharge.

Robert W. Ellis, stationed at the Moffett Field Naval Air Station in California, contacted the Soviet Consulate in San Francisco in 1983 and offered to sell documents for $2,000. He was arrested as he attempted to sell the documents to an FBI agent posing as a Soviet intelligence officer. He was given a dishonorable discharge and sentenced to five years at hard labor, but his sentence was reduced to three years.

Hans P. Wold, picked up in 1983 in the Philippines for being AWOL from the aircraft carrier *Ranger,* had photographed top secret compartmented materials and was accused of planning to hand over the secrets to a Soviet contact. He was given a dishonorable discharge and sentenced to four years at hard labor.

Brian P. Horton, a Navy intelligence specialist, was arrested in 1982 for offering to sell classified information to the Soviet Union. Horton made four phone calls to the Soviet Union and wrote one letter offering information on U.S. strategic war plans. He was sentenced to six years in prison.

Marine Corporal Robert E. Cordrey, an instructor at the Nuclear, Biological and Chemical Defense School at Camp Lejeune, North Carolina, was accused of contacting Soviet, Czechoslovak "and other hostile country" representatives, offering information about the subjects he taught. Convicted on eighteen counts of attempting to contact citizens of a Communist country, he was sentenced to twelve years at hard labor and given a dishonorable discharge. But, under a pre-trial plea bargain, his sentence was subsequently reduced to two years. The charges were not contested and the case was kept secret for several months.

Radioman Third Class Michael T. Tobias, who served aboard the tank landing ship *Peoria,* was arrested with three civilians in 1984 for stealing cryptographic key cards and attempting to extort money from the U.S. Government, claiming that an unnamed foreign power had offered $100,000 for the cards. He was convicted of conspiracy and theft of government property. He was sentenced to twenty years in prison.

Bruce L. Kearn, an officer aboard the tank landing ship *Tuscaloosa,* left the ship on an unauthorized leave, taking with him secret documents, including cryptographic material. Arrested in 1984, he was sentenced to four years at hard labor and given a dishonorable discharge. He plea-bargained a one-and-a-half-year sentence.

John Walker, a Navy warrant officer and communications specialist who spied for the Soviets for at least seventeen years, was arrested in 1985; he was sentenced to life imprisonment.

Arthur Walker, John's brother, a former Navy officer, passed secrets to John, who sold them to the Soviets. Arrested in 1985, he was sentenced to life imprisonment.

Michael Walker, John Walker's son, a sailor, stole classified documents and gave them to his father for sale to the Soviets. Arrested in 1985, he was sentenced to twenty-five years.

Jerry Whitworth, John Walker's longtime confederate, as a Navy radioman, passed cryptographic materials to Walker for sale to the Soviets. Arrested in 1985, he was sentenced to 365 years.

Airman First Class Bruce Ott, a clerk at an Air Force base, was arrested in 1986 for attempting to sell classified documents to U.S. agents posing as Soviet spies. He was convicted by a court-martial and sentenced to twenty-five years.

Michael H. Allen, a retired Navy senior chief radioman, was arrested in 1986 for selling classified information to the Philippine military police. He was sentenced to eight years of confinement, fined $10,000, and required to forfeit his retirement pay.

Allen J. Davies, released from the Air Force in 1984 for poor job performance, was accused of seeking revenge by giving the Soviets secrets about reconnaissance programs. He was arrested in 1986 while attempting to pass classified documents to an FBI agent posing as a Soviet contact. Sentence pending.

Glenn Souther, a Navy satellite photography expert, disappeared in 1986 after questioning by the FBI. He surfaced in Moscow in 1988.

Robert D. Haguewood, a third-class Navy petty officer, was convicted in 1986 of selling unclassified documents, which he thought to be government secrets, to an undercover police officer. In a plea bargain, he was sentenced to two years and received a dishonorable discharge.

Marine Sergeant Clayton J. Lonetree, a guard at U.S. embassies in Moscow and Vienna, was arrested in 1987 on suspicion of espionage. He was accused of giving KGB agents top-secret information about embassy layouts and procedures. He was sentenced to thirty years of confinement.

Marine Corporal Arnold Bracy, a guard at the U.S. Embassy in Moscow, was at first implicated with Lonetree. The Marines dismissed charges against Bracy on June 12, 1987.

FEDERAL EMPLOYEES

William H. Martin and **Bernon F. Mitchell,** National Security Agency employees, defected to the Soviet Union in 1960.

Victor N. Hamilton, a National Security Agency employee, defected to the Soviet Union in 1963 and, according to the Soviets, requested political asylum.

John Butenko, a civilian electronics engineer, was convicted in 1964 of conspiring to give information on the Strategic Air Command to the Soviets. He was sentenced to thirty years imprisonment.

Ronald L. Humphrey, foreign service career officer who gave classified documents to **David Truong,** an agent of the Communist government of Vietnam. Both were convicted in 1978. Each man was sentenced to fifteen years in prison.

William Peter Kampiles, a low-level CIA employee, sold the Soviets a technical manual for a U.S. surveillance satellite. Arrested in 1978, he was sentenced to forty years in prison.

Edwin G. Moore II, a disgruntled former employee of the CIA, tried to sell information to the Soviets. Arrested in 1976. Sentenced to fifteen years.

David Henry Barnett, a former CIA intelligence officer, sold the Soviets the names of CIA intelligence officers and operational secrets. Arrested in 1980, he was sentenced to eighteen years in prison.

Sharon M. Scrange, who was recruited to spy for Ghana while working there for the CIA, was sentenced in November

1985 to five years. In May 1986 this was cut to two years, with a recommendation for parole in eighteen months.

Edward L. Howard, a former CIA employee, offered his services to the Soviets and then defected to the Soviet Union just as he was about to be arrested by the FBI. He obtained "political asylum" in the Soviet Union.

Waldo H. Dubberstein, a former CIA and DIA employee, was charged with selling U.S. military secrets to Libya in what was considered an espionage case. In 1983, the day after he was indicted, he was found dead, an apparent suicide.

Dai Kiem Tran, a research physicist at the Naval Research Laboratory in Washington with secret clearance, was identified in 1983 as a Vietnamese intelligence officer. The Navy said he resigned from the laboratory "and took employment with a private company after his security clearance had been turned down."

Larry Wu-Tai Chin, who had spied for China while he worked for the CIA, was convicted of espionage. While awaiting what could have been a life sentence, he was found dead in his cell, apparently a suicide, on February 21, 1986.

Ronald W. Pelton, a former communications specialist at the National Security Agency, sold the Soviets secrets about NSA intercepts of Soviet communications. Arrested in 1985, he was sentenced to life imprisonment.

Richard W. Miller, an FBI agent, was convicted of engaging in espionage with a Soviet émigrée. Arrested in 1984, he was sentenced to life imprisonment.

Jonathan J. Pollard, who worked for the Naval Investigative Service, stole secrets for Israel. He and his wife, **Anne Henderson-Pollard,** were arrested in 1985. He was sentenced to life imprisonment. She was sentenced to five years in prison.

Samuel L. Morison, an analyst at the Naval Intelligence Support Center in Suitland, Maryland, stole classified photographs and sent them to a British publication in 1984. He was convicted of espionage and sentenced to two years in prison.

DEFENSE CONTRACTOR EMPLOYEES

Andrew D. Lee and **Christopher J. Boyce,** who teamed up to sell the Soviets secrets from a CIA contract company, were arrested in 1977. Lee was sentenced to life imprisonment, Boyce to forty years.

William Holden Bell, a Hughes Aircraft employee, sold secrets of several projects to a representative of the Polish Intelligence Service. Arrested 1981, he was sentenced to eight years in prison.

James Durward Harper, Jr., an electronics engineer, sold information on missiles to a representative of the Polish Intelligence Service. Arrested in 1983, he was sentenced to life imprisonment.

Thomas P. Cavanagh, an engineer at the Northrop Corporation, tried to sell secrets about the Stealth bomber to FBI agents posing as Soviets. Arrested in 1984, he was given a life sentence.

Randy Miles Jeffries, a messenger for a company that transcribed congressional hearings, in 1985 gave some classified documents to a Soviet official and later attempted to sell others to an FBI agent posing as a Soviet intelligence officer. Jeffries pleaded guilty to one count of espionage and received a ten-year sentence.

FOREIGN AGENTS

This list does not include all of the "legal" diplomatic spies who were detained and later expelled or expelled without having been detained. From the end of World War II to 1983, the United States expelled as spies more than one hundred Soviets with diplomatic protection. Occasional expulsions continued until 1986, when the United States ordered twenty-five Soviet diplomats at the United Nations to leave the country. This expulsion was followed up by the wholesale dismissal of fifty-five Soviet diplomats stationed at the Soviet Embassy in Washington and at Soviet consulates in San Francisco and New York.

Rudolf Ivanovich Abel, a Soviet "illegal," operated in the United States in the 1950s. Arrested in 1957, he was sentenced to a total of forty-five years on three counts. In February 1962 he was exchanged for Francis Gary Powers, pilot of a U-2 spy plane shot down over the Soviet Union, who had spent eighteen months in a Soviet prison as a spy.

"Rudolph A. Herrmann," a Soviet intelligence officer who operated under that name, illegally entered the United States from Canada in 1968. Detected as a spy by the FBI in 1977, he was run as a double agent until 1980, when he, his wife, and son were granted asylum and resettled in the United States with new identities.

Aleksandr V. Tikhomirov, a United Nations translator, was arrested in Seattle, Washington, in 1970 for "conspiring to obtain material related to the defense of the Northwestern United States" from an Air Force sergeant acting as a double agent. Although Tikhomirov did not have diplomatic immunity, he was allowed to return to the Soviet Union.

Valery Markelov, a Soviet intelligence officer, worked under the cover of a translator at the United Nations. He was arrested in 1972. The espionage indictment was quashed and Markelov was allowed to return to the Soviet Union.

James F. Sattler, an American-born agent for the East German Intelligence Service, was exposed by an East German defector in about 1974, he was briefly turned by the FBI. He disappeared from sight soon after.

Rudolf P. Chernyayev and **Vladik A. Enger,** Soviet employees of the United Nations, were arrested in an FBI scam in 1978. Sentenced to fifty years each, they were traded to the Soviet Union for five Soviet dissidents.

Alexander Kukhar, a second secretary at the Soviet Embassy, was expelled in 1979 at the request of the FBI.

Vladimir V. Popov, a KGB handler of ex-CIA Officer David Barnett, was recalled to Moscow in 1980 after Barnett's arrest.

Lieutenant Colonel Yuriy P. Leonov, a Soviet GRU officer posing as a Soviet air attaché, was detained in 1983 after he accepted some 60 pounds of government documents from a technical editor who was working for the FBI. Leonov was expelled from the United States.

Yuriy Marakhovskiy, a second secretary at the Soviet Embassy, was expelled in 1981 for attempting espionage.

Otto Attila Gilbert, a naturalized U.S. citizen, spied for his native Hungary. Arrested in 1982, he was sentenced to fifteen years.

Vasiliy I. Chitov, a major general and the senior Soviet military attaché in the United States, was expelled in 1982 after being caught in an FBI scam.

Marian Zacharski, an officer of the Polish Intelligence Service, was arrested with **William Bell.** Zacharski was convicted of espionage in 1981 and given a life sentence. In 1985 was swapped, along with three other spies from Eastern bloc countries. [See Zehe.]

Karl F. Koecher, a naturalized U.S. citizen of Czechoslovakian origin, spied for his native country while working for the CIA from 1973 to 1975 and afterward. He and his wife, **Hana Koecher,** were arrested in 1984 as they were about to leave the country. In 1986 they were exchanged for Russian dissident Anatoly Shcharansky.

Svetlana Ogorodnikov, the Soviet émigrée in the Miller case, pleaded guilty to espionage and was sentenced to eighteen years imprisonment.

Nikolay Ogorodnikov, Svetlana's husband and a Soviet émigré, also pleaded guilty to espionage and was sentenced to eight years imprisonment.

Lieutenant Colonel Yevgeny Barmyantsev, an attaché assigned to the Soviet Military Office in Washington, was arrested on April 16, 1983, as he attempted to retrieve what he believed to be secrets dropped by an American working for the FBI. The United States expelled him.

Oleg V. Konstantinov, of the Soviet Mission to the United Nations, was arrested in 1983 after attempting to recruit an American as a spy.

Aleksandr N. Mikheyev, also of the Soviet UN Mission, was expelled in 1983 after trying to get classified information from a congressional aide.

Penyu B. Kostadinov, a commercial counselor at the Bulgarian Commercial Office in New York, was arrested in 1983 after he paid for classified material provided by an American working under FBI control. Kostadinov, who arranged for the exchanging of students between his country and the United States, claimed diplomatic immunity. This was denied. He was swapped in the 1985 deal. [See Zehe.]

Alice Michelson, an East German courier for Soviet intelligence, was apprehended in New York in 1984 as she was boarding a flight bound for Czechoslovakia. She had been given classified material by a U.S. Army sergeant posing as a KGB-recruited spy. Before she was put on trial, she was swapped in the 1985 deal. [See Zehe.]

Alfred Zehe, an East German physicist who lived in Mexico and frequently visited the United States, was arrested in Boston in 1983 after attempting to obtain classified information from a Navy employee voluntarily under the control of the FBI. Sentenced to eight years in prison after pleading guilty to espionage, he was traded back to East Germany in 1985, along with **Michelson, Kostadinov,** and **Zacharski.** In exchange for the four Eastern bloc spies, twenty-five persons held in Eastern Europe were released and turned over to Western officials.

Ernst Forbrich, a West German citizen working in the United States as an automobile mechanic, was arrested in Florida in 1984 after he paid $550 for a classified document obtained from a U.S. undercover agent posing as an Army intelligence officer. Forbrich had begun his spy career in Germany seventeen years before. Authorities said that he had made contact with U.S. soldiers in Germany and then looked them up when they returned to the United States. No official information was disclosed on whatever past success he may have had as a spy. He was sentenced to fifteen years in prison.

Michael A. Soussoudis, Scrange's lover and recruiter, was sentenced in November 1985 to twenty years, which was immediately suspended so that he could be sent back to Ghana in an exchange for eight Ghanaians said to have spied for the CIA.

Colonel Vladimir Makárovich Ismaylov, a Soviet military attaché, arrested June 19, 1986, as he picked up documents deposited in a dead drop by a U.S. Air Force officer working as a double agent for the FBI. He was expelled from the United States in lieu of trial.

Gennadi F. Zakharov, a Soviet scientist employed by the United Nations, was arrested on August 23, 1986. He pleaded no contest in court and was allowed to return to the Soviet Union in a deal that also saw the release of American reporter Nicholas Daniloff, who had been arrested as a spy in Moscow in retaliation for the Zakharov arrest.

OTHER CASES

Philip Agee, a former CIA agent and field officer in Latin America. Although never accused of espionage, he is considered a traitor by his former colleagues. Agee, who wrote **Inside the Company: CIA Diary,** once said that he intends "to expose CIA officers and agents and to take the measures necessary to drive them out of the countries where they are operating." The CIA treats Agee as a defector.

Richard C. Smith, former Army intelligence agent as a soldier and civilian. He was arrested in 1984 for selling information to the Soviets on the U.S. double-agent program Royal Mitre. He was acquitted.

Terms of the Trade

Agent An individual, usually foreign, who acts under the direction of an intelligence agency or security service to obtain, or assist in obtaining, information for intelligence or counter-intelligence purposes, and to perform other intelligence functions.

AGI Western intelligence classification for a naval intelligence collection ship. (AG = miscellaneous auxiliary; I = intelligence collection.)

Background Investigation—(BI) Background investigations are required to provide an individual with a security clearance. It consists of verification of birth, citizenship, education, employment for the past five years, and travel information provided by the individual; a review of all federal agencies for derogatory information (National Agency Check); a credit check; and a scrutiny of appropriate criminal records. (Also see Special Background Investigation and National Agency Check.)

Black Bag Job Slang for surreptitious entry into an office or home to illegally obtain files or other objects.

Case Officer Professional employee of an intelligence organization who is responsible for providing direction to an agent and for recruiting and supervising agents on specific cases.

Central Intelligence Agency—(CIA) The principal U.S. intelligence agency, established in 1947 to collect foreign intelligence and to develop, conduct, or provide support for technical and other programs that collect foreign intelligence. The CIA was the successor to the Office of Strategic Services (OSS) of World War II. The Director of Central Intelligence is head of the CIA.

The headquarters for the CIA is located at Langley, Virginia, a suburb of Washington, D.C.

CI— Counter-intelligence

CIA— Central Intelligence Agency

CIPA— Classified Information Prodecures Act

CMS— Classified Materials Systems

Code Word Word or term assigned to a classified operation or project to help safeguard meaning or intention.

COMINT— Communications Intelligence

COMIREX— Committee on Imagery Requirements and Exploitation

Communications Intelligence—(COMINT) Intelligence information derived from the interception of communications. The term is sometimes used interchangeably with SIGINT (Signals Intelligence).

Communications Security—(COMSEC) The protection of communications from foreign intercept and exploitation. It includes crypto, transmission, and electronic emissions security as well as the physical security of equipment, material, and documents. In the United States the National Security Agency has overall responsibility for COMSEC.

Compartmentation The establishment of separate procedures for handling sensitive intelligence information. Compartmented information is limited to individuals with special security clearances (i.e., code-word clearances).

Compromise The known or suspected exposure of classified personnel, information, or other material to unauthorized persons.

COMSEC— Communications Security

Confidential U.S. security classification for national security information, the unauthorized disclosure of which could be expected to cause *damage* to national security. This is the lowest U.S. security classification. (Also see Secret, Top Secret.)

Control (1) Physical or psychological pressure exerted on an agent or group to ensure that the agent or group responds to the direction from an intelligence agency or service; (2) slang for the head of an intelligence organization or operation.

Counter-espionage Those aspects of counter-intelligence concerned with aggressive operations against another intelligence service to reduce its effectiveness or to detect and neutralize foreign intelligence.

Counter-intelligence—(CI) Intelligence activity intended to detect, counteract, and/or prevent espionage and other foreign clandestine intelligence activities, sabotage, international terrorist activities, or assassinations conducted for or on behalf of foreign powers. Counter-intelligence also refers to the information derived from such activity.

DCI— Director of Central Intelligence

Defense Industrial Security Clearance Office—(DISCO) Department of Defense agency responsible for industrial security clearances for individuals and for facility clearances and security.

Defense Intelligence Agency Department of Defense agency established in 1961 for the coordination of intelligence activities of the military services and to produce military intelligence. DIA also serves as the intelligence agency (i.e., J-2 staff) for the Joint Chiefs of Staff.

Defense Investigative Service Department of Defense agency established in 1972 to conduct security investigations of military personnel, Department of Defense civilian employees, and applicants for employment with civilian firms requiring security clearances.

DIA— Defense Intelligence Agency

Director of Central Intelligence—(DCI) Position established in 1947 to head the Central Intelligence Agency and the Intelligence Community Staff as well as to supervise and implement certain other U.S. intelligence responsibilities.

DIS— Defense Investigative Service

DISCO— Defense Industrial Security Clearance Office

DNI— Director of Naval Intelligence

Electronic Intelligence—(ELINT) Intelligence information derived from the interception, collection, and processing of electromagnetic radiations from sources such as radar. The term ELINT does not include communications intelligence.

ELINT— Electronic Intelligence

FBI— Federal Bureau of Investigation

Federal Bureau of Investigation—(FBI) U.S. agency, under the supervision of the Attorney General, responsible for domestic counter-espionage, counter-intelligence, and surveillance, and foreign intelligence collection within the United States and its territories.

Established in 1908 as the Bureau of Intelligence within the Department of Justice; reorganized as the FBI in 1924 with J. Edgar Hoover named Director with its agents authorized to carry guns. Given national counter-intelligence responsibilities in 1939.

Into the 1960s FBI agents were referred to as "G-men," slang for government men.

GRU—(Glavnoye Razvedyvatelnoye Upravlenie) The Chief Intelligence Directorate of the General Staff, i.e., Soviet military intelligence directorate. It is also referred to as the Fourth Bureau of the Soviet General Staff. Established in 1920 by Leon Trotsky, the GRU is responsible for foreign intelligence collection.

IC— Intelligence Community

Illegal An espionage agent who comes into a country under the guise of a false identity.

Intelligence Community—(IC) Collective term for U.S. intelligence agencies and organizations. The Intelligence Community Staff (ICS), under the Director of Central Intelligence, is the coordinating body for various U.S. intelligence organizations and, supposedly, activities.

KGB—(Komitet Gosudarstvennoy Bezopasnosti) The Committee for State Security has been the Soviet agency responsible for state security since 1954, and additionally for internal security, 1960–66 (a function now carried out by the Minister of Internal Affairs, or MVD). The KGB carries out its security function in part through an extensive and aggressive foreign intelligence collection and special operations effort.

The KGB is the successor to several Soviet intelligence organizations that evolved from the Cheka, established by V. I. Lenin in 1917.

Legal An espionage agent who comes into a country using an official position as his cover (e.g., commercial attaché, clerk).

MI5 British counter-intelligence organization established in the aftermath of the Boer War. Initially formed as MO5 in 1909, it has evolved into MI5 under a director-general, who is responsible to the Home Secretary.

MI6 British Secret Intelligence Service (SIS) established in 1909. Originally the sixth section of British Military Intelligence responsible for overseas espionage. Until 1953 the director-general was a naval or military officer.

NAC— National Agency Check

National Agency Check Part of a background investigation that consists of a review by all federal agencies for derogatory information about an individual.

National Security Agency—(NSA) Department of Defense agency established in 1952 to direct all U.S. cryptographic and signals intercept activities. The military service cryptologic agencies operate under the direction of the NSA. The agency replaced the Armed Forces Security Agency (AFSA). The NSA is located at Fort Meade, Maryland, north of Washington, D.C.

Naval Intelligence Support Center—(NISC) U.S. Navy agency responsible for producing technical intelligence and related research and other support activities. Formed in 1969 by the merger of separate technical and scientific intelligence activities. Located in Suitland, Maryland, a suburb of Washington, D.C.

NIS— Naval Investigative Service

NISC— Naval Intelligence Support Center

NODIS— No Distribution

NSA— National Security Agency

ONI— Office of Naval Intelligence

Q Special clearance for access to nuclear matters; assigned by the Department of Energy (originally by the Atomic Energy Commission).

RD— Restricted Data

Restricted Data—(RD) Classified information related to the design, manufacture, and use of nuclear weapons. Generally used in conjunction with standard security classifications as Secret/RD.

Rezident Soviet term for the senior KGB officer in charge of operations in a specific city or area.

Rules Specific "rules" established for clandestine meetings in high-risk areas, i.e., where those meeting may be vulnerable to hostile counter-intelligence activities. The term is generally prefixed with the location of the meeting, as Moscow Rules.

SBI— Special Background Investigation

SCI— Special Compartmented Information

Secret U.S. security classification for national security information, the unauthorized disclosure of which could be expected to result in *serious damage* to national security, such as a disruption of international relations, or the impairing of the effectiveness of a program, or policy of vital importance. This is the second-highest U.S. security classification. (Also see Top Secret, Confidential.)

SI— Special Intelligence

SIGINT— Signals Intelligence

Signals Intelligence—(SIGINT) General term for the interception, processing, and analysis of information derived from electrical communications and other signals. It is comprised of three elements: Communications Intelligence (COMINT), Electronics Intelligence (ELINT), and Telemetry Intelligence (TELINT).

SMO—(pronounced Shmo) Acronym for Soviet Military Office used by U.S. intelligence community. The office is on Belmont Road near Massachusetts Avenue in northwest Washington.

SMUN—(pronounced Shmoon) Acronym for Soviet Mission to the United Nations used by U.S. intelligence community.

SOD— Special Operations Detachment

Special Background Investigation—(SBI) A review of an individual's background, but with verification of the past fifteen years of employment and travel and a check of the individual's reputation through visits in his neighborhood.

Special Compartmented Information—(SCI) Information that is beyond the classification of secret or top secret, generally given a code word to indicate the specific project or program.

Special Intelligence—(SI) Classification of information relating to sources of intelligence. SI does *not now* signify Signals Intelligence, although that may have been the origin of the term.

Special Operations Detachment—(SOD) Detachment on board ship (e.g., intelligence collection ship *Pueblo*) to conduct special intelligence collection activities. The compartment in which they worked was referred to as the "SOD hut."

TK— Talent Keyhole Code name for satellite photography based on Keyhole (KH) photo-reconnaissance satellites.

TS— Top Secret U.S. security classification for national security information, the unauthorized disclosure of which could be expected to result in *exceptionally grave damage* to national security, such as war or a break in diplomatic relations. This is the highest U.S. security classification. (Also see Secret, Confidential.)

Walk-in Term for a spy who literally walks into an embassy or intelligence activity without prior contact or invitation.

Sources

Much of what we have written is based on our analysis of public records, books and articles, and court documents pertinent to the major espionage events described in this book. Much of what we have written, however, is also based on interviews with individuals involved in espionage and intelligence activities, on examination of private papers and memoranda, and disclosures from other nonpublic sources. In many instances these were provided to us on a strictly not-for-attribution basis. Accordingly, rather than cite specific source notes, we have been forced simply to list some of the people and some of the documents that we have used in the writing of this book.

In support of our judgment that the Walker-Whitworth case was handled in the manner that it was—in an effort to regain credibility by the Federal Bureau of Investigation after several counter-intelligence failings—a detailed list of sources for Chapter 9 is provided in a Special Note at the end of this section.

INTERVIEWS

The authors interviewed several individuals who have been intimately involved with U.S. intelligence and counter-intelligence activities during the past two decades. A number of individuals, however, have asked that they not be publicly acknowledged and their names do not appear here. The authors would like to acknowledge the debt to those individuals as well as to the persons listed below.

David Battis, industrial security expert

Gary Bauer, Domestic Counselor to President Reagan

Neill Brown, Special Agent, Federal Bureau of Investigation

Kathleen A. Buck, former General Counsel of the Air Force and now General Counsel of the Department of Defense

U.S. Senator William S. Cohen

Colonel George Connell, U.S. Marine Corps; Deputy Commander, Naval Investigative Service

John Dion, Chief of the Espionage Prosecutions Unit, Internal Security Section, Department of Justice

Captain C. Dale Everhart, U.S. Navy (Ret.), former Naval Intelligence officer

William (Buck) Farmer, Assistant U.S. Attorney, principal prosecutor at the Jerry Whitworth trial

Owen Frisby, Vice President of the Chase Manhattan Bank, who provided several key introductions for the authors

William W. Geimer, a Washington lawyer who founded the Jamestown Foundation to provide support for defectors from the Soviet Union and Eastern Europe

Joseph W. Harned, Executive Vice President, The Atlantic Council

U.S. District Court Judge Alexander Harvey II

Thomas Henley, former Central Intelligence Agency officer

Vice Admiral Robert Kirksey, U.S. Navy (Ret.), former Director, Navy Command, Control, and Communications

Former Secretary of the Navy John Lehman

Dr. Carolyn Mackenzie, psychiatrist

Clark Magruder, former Deputy Director of Naval Intelligence

Robert F. Muse, attorney for Samuel L. Morison

Ernest Porter, public affairs office, Federal Bureau of Investigation

J. Stephen Ramey, Special Agent, Federal Bureau of Investigation

Raymond Robinson, former analyst with the Central Intelligence Agency and the Defense Intelligence Agency

David Szady, Special Agent, Federal Bureau of Investigation

Captain Vincent Thomas, U.S. Navy (Ret.), former naval public affairs officer involved in a number of intelligence projects, including the *Pueblo* affair

Howard J. Varinsky, a trial behavior consultant who served in that unique role for the defense in the Jerry Whitworth trial

U.S. Senator John Warner

Jerome Zeifman, formerly a counsel for the House Judiciary Committee who served as a post-trial attorney for Ronald L. Humphrey

Also, general discussions about Soviet intelligence with Nicholas Shadrin (Nikolai F. Artamonov) and Milan Vego

One of the authors is in debt to three senior U.S. naval officers who served in key intelligence positions; he was privileged to consult with them. They are: Vice Admiral F. J. (Fritz) Harlfinger, former Director of Navy Command, Control, Communications, and Intelligence; Vice Admiral E. F. (Rex) Rectanus, former Deputy Assistant Secretary of Defense for Intelligence; and Vice Admiral E. A. (Al) Burkhalter, former Director of the Intelligence Community Staff.

We also wish to express our profound appreciation to our patient and indomitable editor, Jane Rosenman.

BOOKS

Intelligence Works

Charles H. Andregg. *Management of Defense Intelligence.* Washington, D.C.: Industrial College of the Armed Forces, 1968.

James Bamford. *The Puzzle Palace.* Boston: Houghton Mifflin Company, 1982. An outstanding analysis of the most-secret U.S. intelligence activity, the National Security Agency.

John Barron. *Breaking the Ring.* Boston: Houghton Mifflin Company, 1987. An attempt to put the Walker-Whitworth spy ring in perspective.

Griffin B. Bell, with Ronald J. Ostrow. *Taking Care of the Law.* New York: Morrow and Company, 1982. The Attorney General's account of catching and prosecuting spies.

Dr. Ray S. Cline. *The CIA Under Reagan, Bush & Casey.* Washington, D.C.: Acropolis Books, 1981. A former Deputy Director of Central Intelligence reviews U.S. intelligence activities from 1941.

William R. Corson, and Robert T. Crowley. *The New KGB.* New York: Morrow, 1985.

Allen W. Dulles. *The Craft of Intelligence.* New York: Harper & Row, 1963.

Stanley L. Falk. *The National Security Structure.* Washington, D.C.: Industrial College of the Armed Forces, 1967.

Captain W. J. Holmes, U.S. Navy (Ret.). *Double-Edged Secrets, U.S. Naval Intelligence Operations in the Pacific during World War II.* Annapolis, Md.: Naval Institute Press, 1979. Description of U.S. code-breaking in the Pacific War and its application.

Henry Hurt. *Shadrin, the Spy Who Never Came Back.* New York: McGraw-Hill Book Company, 1981. Biography of the ex-Soviet officer turned double agent and his death due to the failure of the American intelligence community.

Montgomery H. Hyde. *The Atom Bomb Spies.* New York: Ballantine Books, 1980.

Rhodi Jefferys-Jones. *American Espionage.* New York: The Free Press, 1977.

David Kahn. *The Code Breakers: History of Secret Communications.* New York: Macmillan and Company, 1967.

Robert J. Lamphere, and Tom Shachtman. *The FBI-KGB War: A Special Agent's Story.* New York: Random House, 1986. A leading FBI counter-intelligence expert details spy-hunting in the decade after World War II against the Soviet atomic bomb spies.

Robin Bruce Lockhard. *Reilly: Ace of Spies.* New York: Penguin Books, 1984.

Victor Marchetti, and John D. Marks. *The CIA and the Cult of Intelligence.* New York: Alfred A. Knopf, 1974. Among the first exposés of the CIA, this was the first book the U.S. Government ever took to court to censor.

Bruce Page, David Leitch, and Phillip Knightley. *Philby: The Spy Who Betrayed a Generation.* London: Andre Deutsch Ltd., 1968. A detailed account of the Cambridge three—Burgess, Maclean, and Philby.

Kim Philby. *My Silent War.* New York: Grove, 1968. Philby's own rationalization of his long career of treason.

Chapman Pincher. *Too Secret Too Long.* New York: St. Martin's Press, 1984. View of Soviet espionage penetration of the British intelligence community.

Richard Gid Powers. *Secrecy and Power: The Life of J. Edgar Hoover.* New York: Free Press (Macmillan), 1987.

Thomas Powers. *The Man Who Kept Secrets: Richard Helms and the CIA.* New York: Alfred A. Knopf, 1979. An account of the Central Intelligence Agency under one of its most controversial directors.

Harry Howe Ransom. *Central Intelligence and National Security.* Cambridge, Mass.: Harvard University Press, 1958.

Jeffrey T. Richelson. *The U.S. Intelligence Community.* Cambridge, Mass.: Ballinger Publishing Company, 1985. A description of U.S. intelligence organization and activities.

Andrew Tully. *CIA: The Inside Story.* New York: William Morrow and Company, 1962. An early attempt, by a leading White House journalist, to penetrate the secrecy surrounding the CIA.

Admiral Stansfield Turner, U.S. Navy (Ret.). *Secrecy and Democracy: The CIA in Transition.* Boston: Houghton Mifflin Company, 1985. An account of the Director of Central Intelligence during the Carter Administration, with an interesting perspective on the Kampiles case.

David Wise, and Thomas B. Ross. *The Espionage Establishment.* New York: Random House, 1967. An early effort by two journalists to penetrate the American intelligence community.

Bob Woodward. *Veil: The Secret Wars of the CIA 1981–1987.* New York: Simon & Schuster, 1987.

Peter Wright. *Spycatcher.* New York: Viking Penguin, 1987.

Soviet Espionage

Louise Bernikow. *Abel.* New York: Trident Press, 1970. An intriguing analysis of one of the most significant Soviet agents to penetrate the United States.

John E. Carlson, "The KGB" in James Craft (ed.), *The Soviet Union Today.* Chicago: University of Chicago Press, 1983.

Robert Conquest. *Stalin's Purge of the Thirties.* New York: Macmillan and Company, 1968.

Colonel Oleg Penkovskiy. *The Penkovskiy Papers.* New York: Doubleday & Company, 1965. The purported memoirs of the Soviet GRU official turned-Western spy.

Sidney Reilly. *Britain's Master Spy: His Own Story.* New York: Dorset Press, 1985. A narrative of the birth of the Cheka/KGB by Britain's "ace of spies."

Jeffrey T. Richelson. *Sword and Shield: Soviet Intelligence and Security Apparatus.* Cambridge, Mass.: Ballinger Publishing Company, 1986. A description of Soviet intelligence organization and activities.

Arkady N. Shevchenko. *Breaking With Moscow.* New York: Alfred A. Knopf, 1985. Memoirs of the highest-ranking Soviet official ever to defect to the West. (At the time Shevchenko was Under Secretary General of the United Nations.)

Viktor Suvorov (pseud.). *Inside Soviet Military Intelligence.* New York: Macmillan and Company, 1984. A Soviet defector's attempt to describe the GRU, Soviet military intelligence.

Thaddeus Wittlin. *Commissar: The Life and Death of Lavrenty Pavlovich Beria.* New York: Macmillan and Company, 1972. An account of Stalin's master spy and executioner.

Related Subjects

Commander Lloyd Bucher, U.S. Navy (Ret.), with Mark Rascovich. *Bucher: My Story.* Garden City, New York: Doubleday and Co., 1970. An account of the *Pueblo* affair—and apologia—by the ship's commanding officer.

Jeffrey M. Dorwart. *Conflict of Duty: The U.S. Navy's Intelligence Dilemma, 1919–1945.* Annapolis, Md.: Naval Institute Press, 1983. A history of Naval Intelligence—including its domestic intelligence activities.

————. *The Office of Naval Intelligence: The Birth of America's First Intelligence Agency, 1865–1918.* Annapolis, Md.: Naval Institute Press, 1979. Useful background to contemporary intelligence issues.

Montgomery H. Hyde. *Secret Intelligence Agent.* New York: St. Martin's Press, 1982.

Henry Kissinger. *Years of Upheaval.* Boston: Little, Brown and Company, 1982.

Peter Padfield. *Dönitz, The Last Führer.* New York: Harper & Row, 1984.

Dr. Jürgen Rohwer. *The Critical Convoy Battles of March 1943.* Annapolis, Md.: Naval Institute Press, 1977.

Captain Paul B. Ryan, U.S. Navy (Ret.). *The Iranian Rescue*

Mission: Why It Failed. Annapolis, Md.: Naval Institute Press, 1985.

Rebecca West. *The New Meaning of Treason.* New York: Viking Press, 1964. A classic study of modern British traitors, especially Burgess, Maclean, and Philby.

Rear Admiral Ellis M. Zacharias, U.S. Navy. *Secret Missions.* New York: Paperback Library, 1961.

Adm. Elmo R. Zumwalt, Jr. *On Watch.* New York: Quadrangle, 1976.

GOVERNMENT REPORTS AND PUBLICATIONS

A number of government reports and other documents were made available to the authors through Scott Armstrong and Eric Hoogland of the National Security Archives, Washington, D.C.

Army. FM 100-5 *Operations.* August 20, 1982, and May 5, 1986, editions. There was no restriction on distribution in the first edition cited and considerable restrictions on the second (see Chapter 12).

Canadian Government. *Report of the Royal Commission.* Ottawa: 1946. Account of Soviet atomic espionage against Canada and the United States.

Central Intelligence Agency. "Statement of Central Intelligence Agency Before the U.S. Senate Permanent Subcommittee on Investigations at Hearings on U.S. Government Personnel Security Program," March 1985. Provides details of the Kampiles and Moore cases.

————. *Israel: Foreign Intelligence and Security Services.* Washington, D.C.: 1979.

Department of Defense. *Soviet Acquisition of Militarily Significant Western Technology: An Update.* Washington, D.C.: September 1985.

————. *Soviet Intelligence Operations Against Americans and U.S. Installations Abroad.* Washington, D.C.: July 1968.

————, Commission to Review DOD Security Policies and Practices. *Keeping the Nation's Secrets.* November 18, 1985.

————. Department of Defense Directive 5105.21 "Defense Intelligence Agency." 1961.

————, Defense Investigative Service. *Manual for Personnel Security Investigations.* Washington, D.C.: January 30, 1981.

————, Defense Investigative Service, Industrial Security Institute. Various issues of *Security Awareness Bulletin,* especially:

"The Arthur Walker Story" (August 1986), pp. 1–8 [followed by a "lessons learned" discussion, pp. 9–11]

"Caught Unawares: The Case of William Bell and Marian Zacharski" (June 1983), pp. 2–14.

"The Morison Case" (June 1987), pp. 1–12.

"Partners in Espionage: The case of James Harper and Ruby Louise Schuler (August 1984), pp. 1–8.

"Soviet Industrial Espionage" by Rear Admiral E. A. Burkhalter, U.S. Navy (September 1983), pp. 1–9.

"A Spate of Spies—22 Recent Cases Summarized" (April 1986), pp. 3–17.

"Would-be Spy Meets Phony KGB Agent . . . And Ends Up in Jail, For Real" [Thomas Cavanagh case] (December 1985), pp. 1–6, 9–13.

————, The Joint Chiefs of Staff. JCS Pub. 18 *Operations Security.* Washington, D.C.: December 15, 1982.

————, Office of the Under Secretary of Defense for Policy. *Security Refresher Briefing* (published periodically).

————, Defense Security Institute.

Federal Register. Various issues addressing "United States Foreign Intelligence Activities."

House [of Representatives], Permanent Select Committee on Intelligence. Report 100-5 "United States Counterintelligence and Security Concerns—1986." February 4, 1987.

Navy, Naval Sea Systems Command [and previously Naval Ship Systems Command]. *Monthly Progress Report.* Various editions.

————, Office of Naval Intelligence. *German and Russian Operations, 1940 to 1945.* Washington, D.C.: April 1947. Excerpts from various captured German documents that describe Soviet intelligence operations during World War II.

Public Law 80-253. The National Security Act of 1947, as amended. 50 U.S. Code 402, 403.

Senate, Committee on Armed Services. "Unauthorized Disclosures and Transmittal of Classified Documents." December 19, 1974.

————, Select Committee on Intelligence. Report 94-1161

"Foreign Intelligence Surveillance Act of 1976." August 24, 1976.

————, Select Committee on Intelligence. Hearing 98-519 "National Historical Intelligence Museum." November 3, 1983 [printed 1984].

————, Select Committee on Intelligence. Hearing 99-52. "Soviet Presence in the U.N. Secretariat." May 1985.

————. Report 98-660 "The Foreign Intelligence Surveillance Act of 1978: The First Five Years." October 5, 1984.

————. Report 99-522 "Meeting the Espionage Challenge: A Review of United States Counterintelligence and Security Programs." October 3, 1986.

Lieutenant General L. A. Skantze, U.S. Air Force. Testimony before the House Committee on Armed Services. April 6, 1983. A classic example of "leaking" classified material to a committee to garner funding for a defense project.

TRIAL AND COURT TRANSCRIPTS AND DOCUMENTS

The authors attended part or all of the trials of Morison, Pelton, and Whitworth, as well as the sentencing in U.S. District Court in Baltimore of John Walker and his son, Michael. The authors also reviewed the extensive FBI and court documents related to the cases of Arthur, John, and Michael Walker. Other court documents examined and used included the following:

Affidavit, *United States of America* v. *David Henry Barnett,* October 24, 1980.

Affidavit, *United States of America* v. *Ronald Rewald,* Criminal Docket No. 84-02417, District of Hawaii, 1984.

Affidavit, U.S. District Court San Francisco in the James Harper case filed by Allan M. Power, Special Agent, FBI.

Affidavit, for an arrest warrant and search warrant for Gennadi Fedorovich Zakharov, 1986.

Judgment of the U.S. Court of Appeals for the Fourth Circuit, No. 84-5240, December 4, 1985 (Richard Craig Smith). Motions from Criminal Docket No. 84-92-A, *United States of America* v. *Richard Craig Smith,* Eastern District of Virginia, 1984.

Statement of Facts in support of guilty plea of John A. Walker, Jr., 1985.

Transcript of the trial of Richard W. Miller, 1986.

Transcript of the trial of Samuel Loring Morison, 1985.

Transcript of the trial of Ronald Pelton, 1986.

Transcript of "RUS letters" hearings (Jerry Alfred Whitworth), December 6, 1985.

Transcript of the trial of Jerry Alfred Whitworth, 1986.

MAGAZINE AND NEWSPAPER ARTICLES

The basic public information on recent espionage cases has been derived from the special editions on "Espionage" of the *Current News,* published on a periodic basis by the News Clipping Analysis Service of the Office of the Secretary of the Air Force (SAF/AA), Washington, D.C.

Also helpful have been many of the articles in the *American Intelligence Journal,* published quarterly by the National Military Intelligence Association, and the *Foreign Intelligence Literary Scene,* a bimonthly newsletter of the University Publications of America.

Jack Anderson. "Will the Russians Return the Man She Loves?" *Parade (The Washington Post* supplement), August 28, 1977. The Shadrin dilemma, from his wife's viewpoint.

James Bamford. "The Walker Espionage Case." Naval Institute *Proceedings* (Naval Review), May 1986, pp. 110–19.

———. "USN Spies: Large Leaks, Short Terms." *The Los Angeles Times,* April 19, 1987.

Lieutenant Colonel William P. Baxter, U.S. Army (Ret.). "Soviet Communications: Bare-Bones but Secure." *Army,* August 1982, pp. 30–33.

Howard Blum. "Spy Ring. The Untold Story of the Walker Case." *The New York Times Magazine,* June 29, 1986. The murder suspicions against John Walker.

Brock Bower. "Spying's Dirty Little Secret." *Money,* July 1987, pp. 130–48. Hints on how to recruit and pay a spy.

Rear Admiral E. A. Burkhalter, U.S. Navy. "Soviet Industrial Espionage." *Signal* (Journal of the Armed Forces Communications and Electronics Association), March 1983, pp. 15–18, 20.

William Carley. "Spy Story. How the FBI, Tipped By a Russian, Tracked An Intelligence Leak." *The Wall Street Journal,* March 17, 1987. An account of the tracking down of Ronald Pelton.

Michael Daley. "I Spy." *New York,* April 6, 1987, pp. 34–47. An account of Leakh Boge as an FBI-controlled agent run against Soviet KGB officer Gennadi Zakharov.

Lieutenant Peter Grant, U.S. Navy, and Lieutenant Robert Riche, U.S. Navy. "The Eagle's Own Plume." Naval Institute *Proceedings,* July 1983, pp. 29–34.

Roland S. Inlow. "An Appraisal of the Morison Espionage Trial." *First Principles* (Center for National Security Studies), May 1986, pp. 1–5. Inlow testified for the defense in the Morison trial.

Colonel Peter F. Kalitka, U.S. Army (Ret.). "Knights for Pawns." *American Intelligence Journal,* May 1987, pp. 16–21. A counter-intelligence analysis of the Daniloff-Zakharov case.

Ronald Kessler. "The Spy Game." *Regardie's,* November 1986.

George Lardner, Jr. "Photos Did No Damage, Ex-CIA Official Testifies." *The Washington Post,* October 16, 1985.

David Martin. "How to Keep Soviet Moles Out of Government." *Human Events,* August 20, 1983, pp. 9–14. A noted security expert discusses this aspect of counter-intelligence.

Dan Morain. "Spies Selling New Data–Their Stories to Publishers." *The Los Angeles Times,* July 24, 1986.

Joe Pichirallo. "Israeli Statement on Pollard Spy Case Questioned." *The Washington Post,* June 6, 1986.

Dan Oberdorfer, "The Playboy Sergeant." *The Saturday Evening Post,* March 7, 1964.

Walter Pincus. "Superiors Had Approved Morison's Moonlighting." *The Washington Post,* December 17, 1985.

Ron Rosenbaum. "The Shadow of the Mole." *Harper's,* October 1983, pp. 45–60.

William E. Smith. "Brothers with Blood in Their Eyes." *Time,* March 30, 1987. p. 40. Israeli-American reaction to the Pollard case.

Edgar Ulsamer. "Top Priority for C³I" (Command, Control, Communications, and Intelligence). *Air Force Magazine,* September 1986, pp. 136–46. A discussion of military C³ with comments on vulnerability to Soviet intercept.

"U.S. Intelligence Agencies 'Still Suffering from Scars.'" *U.S. News & World Report,* December 20, 1982, pp. 37–38. An interview with Vice Admiral Bobby Ray Inman, U.S. Navy (Ret.), former Deputy Director of Central Intelligence.

"Vanishing Act by a Popular Spook." *Time,* May 3, 1982, p. 16. Article about the retirement of Admiral Inman.

Lally Weymouth. "Were There Other Pollards?" *The Washington Post,* March 15, 1987. Discussion of why Pollard could not be an Israeli "rogue" operation.

George C. Wilson, and Ruth Marcus. "Navy Says Fleet Code Breached." *The Washington Post,* June 12, 1985.

Scott Winkour. "Requiem for a Traitor." *Houston Chronicle,* July 12, 1987. Detailed report of the espionage case of Thomas Cavanagh.

Bob Woodward, and Michael Dobbs. "CIA Had Secret Agent on Polish General Staff." *The Washington Post,* June 4, 1986.

MISCELLANEOUS SOURCES

James W. Lucas. "Intelligence and National Security, Changing Aspects of the Policy Making Process in the Nixon Administration." July 1973. An unpublished dissertation.

Richard W. Miller, former special agent, FBI, on *60 Minutes,* September 14, 1986.

William Webster, Director, Federal Bureau of Investigation, speech before the Association of Former Intelligence Officers, Fort Myer, Virginia, December 8, 1986.

SPECIAL NOTE

These are the sources for statements made in Chapter 9, "The Spy Who Saved the FBI."

"murky world": The words are those of Tony Tamburello, one of Jerry Whitworth's lawyers, in the address to the jury opening the Whitworth trial, March 24, 1986.

Description of arrest: interviews; affidavits in connection with arrest and FBI applications for search warrants; transcript of testimony by Robert W. Hunter, the official case agent of the Walker case, at the Whitworth trial, April 7, 1986; recounting of the arrest by Michael Schatzow, Assistant U.S. Attorney, at the sentencing; the rearraignment of John and Michael Walker in U.S. District Court, Baltimore, October 28, 1985. On August 12, 1986, the authors were driven by FBI agents over the route that Walker took to the dead drop.

Expert testimony on dead-drop instructions: Gerald Richards, a "questioned document examiner" and expert on espionage tradecraft, testifying at the Whitworth trial, April 16, 1986.

The "Official Story" version of the 7-Up can pickup on Quince Orchard Road: Schatzow. The other version comes from the testimony and cross-examination of FBI Agent David W. Szady at the Whitworth trial, April 7, 1986. (Another FBI source insists that the picking up of the can "was just a goof.")

"completely steam-cleaned": Szady, Whitworth trial, April 7, 1986.

still food in the refrigerator: testimony of Joan Johnson, acting resident manager of the apartment complex where the Tkachenko family lived; Whitworth trial, April 7, 1986.

Hoover and Dillinger: *Secrecy and Power: The Life of J. Edgar Hoover*, by Richard Gid Powers.

Hoover and Tricycle: *Secret Intelligence*, by Montgomery Hyde. The *Reader's Digest* piece by J. Edgar Hoover was published in April 1946 and entitled "The Enemy's Masterpiece of Espionage."

Allen Dulles quote: from Dulles book *The Craft of Intelligence*, Chapter III, "Counterespionage: Spy to Catch a Spy."

Yurchenko's suspicions about Walker tip: Affidavit dated August 26, 1986, and signed by John L. Martin of the U.S. Department of Justice; the affidavit was introduced at the Whitworth trial.

Chief radioman who remembered Whitworth's naps: Frank Olea, testifying at Whitworth trial, April 1, 1986.

Navy intelligence and Soviet monitoring of Fleet Exercise 83-1: Lieutenant Commander James D. Jeeter, on the staff of the Commander in Chief, Pacific, testifying at the Whitworth trial, May 12 and 13, 1986.

Barbara Walker's account of "or else" visit to John Walker's office: Her statements during interview by Barbara Walters, *20/20*, July 17, 1986.

Laura Walker Snyder's recollections: Her testimony at Whitworth trial.

John J. Dion document: Affidavit in the Whitworth pretrial docket. Dion drew up the affidavit, attesting that there had not been any wiretaps on Whitworth, his lawyers, or his wife. The document lists several federal agencies, ranging from the FBI and the Customs Service to the Internal Revenue Service and Central Intelligence Agency, back to August 1, 1983. He gave no reason for selecting that date.

"We patiently watched him for six months": Baker quoted in *The Washington Post,* June 1, 1985.

Walker's "Harper in Norfolk" story: John Walker's testimony at the Whitworth trial, May 5, 1986.

Murder suspicions: Navy sources; Larson during trial; Howard Blum, "Spy Ring. The Untold Story of the Walker Case."

Plea bargains: Confidential sources; statements by Stephen S. Trott, Assistant Attorney General (Criminal Division), on *Meet the Press,* December 1, 1985.

Barron expertise: His testimony, June 11, 1986.

Walker was known in Norfolk: Navy Lieutenant Pennie Cannon Leachman was the prosecutor in a court-martial of Dan Rivas, a Navy enlisted man who worked in the Navy as an air controller and worked after hours as an investigator for Walker. It was Rivas who told NIS agents that he suspected Walker was involved in the Norfolk murders. She testified at the Whitworth trial on June 19, 1986.

Index